Cannabis Use and Dependence
Public Health and Public Policy

The use of cannabis in the late twentieth and this century is an area of medical and moral controversy. Despite its illegality, cannabis is the most widely used drug after alcohol and tobacco among young adults in Australia, the USA and Europe. This book explores the relationship between health policy, public health and the law regarding cannabis use. It assesses the impact of illegality in drug use and relates this to contemporary policy analysis in Australia, the UK, the US and other developed societies. It evaluates current debates about 'safe use' and 'harm minimisation' approaches, as well as examining the experiences of different prevention, treatment and education policies. Written by two leading drug advisers *Cannabis Use and Dependence* makes a valuable addition to this important field of research.

Wayne Hall is Director of the Office of Public Policy and Ethics at the Institute for Molecular Bioscience, University of Queensland, Australia. He has been an adviser to the World Health Organisation and is a current member of their Expert Advisory Panel on Drug Dependence and Alcohol Problems.

Rosalie Liccardo Pacula is an Economist with the RAND Corporation and a Research Fellow with the United States National Bureau of Economic Research. She has published extensively on drug consumption and policy and is a leading adviser in her field.

Cannabis Use and Dependence

Public Health and Public Policy

Wayne Hall
University of Queensland

Rosalie Liccardo Pacula
RAND Corporation, California

CAMBRIDGE
UNIVERSITY PRESS

PUBLISHED BY THE PRESS SYNDICATE OF THE UNIVERSITY OF CAMBRIDGE
The Pitt Building, Trumpington Street, Cambridge, United Kingdom

CAMBRIDGE UNIVERSITY PRESS
The Edinburgh Building, Cambridge CB2 2RU, UK
40 West 20th Street, New York, NY 10011–4211, USA
477 Williamstown Road, Port Melbourne, VIC 3207, Australia
Ruiz de Alarcón 13, 28014 Madrid, Spain
Dock House, The Waterfront, Cape Town 8001, South Africa

http://www.cambridge.org

© Wayne Hall and Rosalie Liccardo Pacula 2003

First published 2003

Printed in China through Bookbuilders

Typeface Adobe Minion 10/12 pt.   System QuarkXPress®   [PK]

A catalogue record for this book is available from the British Library

National Library of Australia Cataloguing in Publication data

Hall, Wayne.
    Cannabis use and dependence: public health and public policy
    ISBN 0521 80024 2.
    1. Cannabis – Health aspects. 2. Cannabis – Government policy.
    3. Cannabis – Law and legislation. I. Pacula, Rosalie Liccardo, 1968– .
    II. Title.
    362.295

ISBN 0 521 80024 2 hardback

To our families:

Pat, Tess and David Hall
and
Joe, Gabriella and Brian Pacula

Contents

List of figures

List of tables

Foreword

Cannabis is the cutting-edge drug for those interested in drug policy reform, the only drug in the Western world for which legal change is a serious possibility. Indeed, changes are already occurring. The German High Court in 1992 declared that a state which allowed alcohol could hardly criminalise the possession of cannabis; the German states have enacted various forms of decriminalisation. Belgium, hardly known as a bastion of drug reform, expanded the frontier of choices by legalising the *use* of the drug in private in March 2003. The Swiss government is in the midst of a long process that may result in full legalisation. The medical marijuana movement in the various American states represents, in part at least, a reaction against the harshness of policy toward recreational use of the drug.

The basis for assessing the desirability of these policy and legal changes is weak. The research base on the health and behavioural effects, let alone the consequences of prohibition is slight. For example, there are no studies of the long-term health effects of cannabis use in the general population, itself a remarkable fact, given the number of health studies that have examined far rarer behaviours. Nor can one more than very roughly assess how much marijuana affects automobile accidents and fatalities.

The stepping stone hypothesis, the belief that marijuana use increases the likelihood that a young person will go on to use of more dangerous drugs, is central to the policy debate. Given the simple facts, that those who use marijuana regularly are much more likely to subsequently use cocaine and heroin, the hawks emphasise this with sincerity and passion. Reformers rest their case on methodologically subtle attacks on the interpretation of these facts and produce models which show that the same patterns of use could be accounted for by factors other than the drug itself. Neither side can be said to have made its case strongly. That does not prevent advocates from expressing great certainty. The reformers' claim that there are no harms is simply wrong. Similarly, the drug warriors' claims as to the severity and breadth of its harms are hugely exaggerated. Indeed, the official US government trumpeting of every finding of adverse effects, often from small-scale and weak studies with conflicting outcomes, would verge on scandal if we were not inured to it.

Wayne Hall and Rosalie Pacula have written the first honest book on cannabis addressing the whole range of issues that need to be considered for a sensible policy discussion. Honesty seems like a modest plaudit for scholars but it is surprisingly rare in the area of drug policy generally. Moreover they bring to the topic established records of research on marijuana policy-related issues. Hall is a psychologist and Pacula an economist, a good combination for this task since it involves both behavioural and policy issues.

Of particular interest is their discussion of the effect of the removal of criminal penalties for possession, the middle ground for which most reform politicians reach. I, like most other scholars, have accepted at face value the research findings of a generation ago that depenalisation of marijuana in twelve American states had no effect on the prevalence of youthful marijuana use. Hall and Pacula report recent analyses that suggest there is less to this finding than meets the eye. States that depenalised did not necessarily create penalty regimes that were in fact much less punitive than those in some of the other states. For example, New York State, which removed criminal penalties for possession, retained them for actual use. Large numbers of New Yorkers pass through the criminal justice system, at least briefly, for use; to the young, depenalisation may seem like a fine point. Laws may simply not be very relevant when arrest is so rare and punishment so slight. The fact that the highest cannabis use rates in Europe are not in the Netherlands, where the drug has been de facto legalised, but in fully criminalised Britain adds to the unease that these kinds of changes are principal drivers.

Hall and Pacula's analysis is, so to speak, sobering. Cannabis is a source of pleasure to many persons but it poses a variety of risks to users and to society. Policy debates give little weight to the pleasures, reflecting the heavy use by the young and consequently concerns about long-term developmental effects. In that sense the discussion is similar to that about the legal drinking age, in which youthful pleasures from drink are also firmly disregarded. The policy argument is centred on whether marijuana prohibition, with its attendant costs and inevitable inequities, produces enough reductions in youthful cannabis use and related harms. There is no alternative to sorting through the mass of evidence. Hall and Pacula have done that and policy-makers and the public will have to decide how to deal honestly with the uncertainties that they produce.

Peter Reuter
School of Public Affairs and Department of Criminology
University of Maryland

Acknowledgements

Wayne Hall

This book has had a ten-year gestation. It began life as a review of the health and psychological effects of cannabis use that I was commissioned to write in May 1992 by the Australian National Task Force on Cannabis (Hall, Solowij and Lemon, 1994). Parts of this review were updated for a 1997 report on the health implications of cannabis by the World Health Organisation and for a series of papers on specific aspects of the health effects of cannabis.

My work on this topic has been funded by the Commonwealth Department of Health and Ageing as part of the core funding of the National Drug and Alcohol Research Centre (between 1992 and 2001), specific grants from the Commonwealth Department of Health (1993 and 2001), and by funding for the Office of Public Policy and Ethics, Institute for Molecular Bioscience, University of Queensland (2002–2003).

Peter Reuter is owed special thanks for encouraging me to write a book that addressed both the health effects of cannabis and the effects of cannabis control policies. He also suggested the collaboration with Rosalie Pacula when my enthusiasm for finishing the book was at its lowest point after taking up my current new appointment at the University of Queensland in September 2001.

I would like to thank the following colleagues at the National Drug and Alcohol Research Centre (NDARC) who contributed to my work on cannabis that is summarised in this book:

Dr Louisa Degenhardt whose doctoral work better informed me about the relationship between mental health and cannabis use, and who provided invaluable assistance by undertaking many research and editorial tasks in preparing this book;

Dr Nadia Solowij who collaborated on the 1994 review of the health effects of cannabis and has kept me up to date with her research on the cognitive effects of chronic cannabis use;

Dr Greg Chesher who provided helpful advice on the scientific literature on cannabis over many years;

Neil Donnelly who collaborated in research on the effects of the South Australian Cannabis Expiation Notice System on rates of cannabis use;

Dr Michael Lynskey who improved my understanding of longitudinal research on adolescent health and the effects of adolescent cannabis use;

Dr Wendy Swift's whose doctoral research improved my knowledge of cannabis dependence;

Dr Alex Wodak who will not agree with everything in this book but who made it a better book by challenging my arguments.

Special thanks are due to Sarah Yeates and Kate Morley from the Office of Public Policy and Ethics for their invaluable help in preparing the manuscript for publication. Without their efforts, under tight deadlines and competing demands, the book would not have been completed.

Finally I would like to thank my wife Pat and children Tess and David for their support throughout the work reported in this book and for allowing me to break a long standing family rule by working on Saturday afternoons in the last two months of work on the book.

Earlier versions of the many chapters have been previously published. Chapter 1 includes material originally prepared for the WHO on assessing the health and psychological effects of cannabis. Chapters 2–12 are extensively updated and revised versions of chapters in Hall, Solowij and Lemon (1994) and Hall, Degenhardt and Lynskey (2001). Chapter 7 on cannabis dependence benefited from the doctoral work of Wendy Swift. Chapter 8 on the cognitive effects of chronic cannabis use is indebted to Nadia Solowij's doctoral work which was published as Solowij (1998). Chapter 11 has been based on work done in collaboration with Michael Lynskey on the educational consequences of adolescent cannabis use. Chapter 13 is based in part upon literature reviewed by Louisa Degenhardt for her doctoral thesis. Chapter 19 develops arguments first expressed in the 1999 Okey Lecture (Hall, 2001).

Rosalie Liccardo Pacula would also like to gratefully acknowledge the contributions of several of her colleagues. In particular, she would like to thank Beau Kilmer, MS, for his excellent research assistance and significant contributions to the sections on marijuana use and crime included in Chapters 14 and 16. The literature review included in these two chapters, in addition to that reflected in Chapter 15, was partially supported by a grant from the National Institute on Drug Abuse to Dr Pacula at RAND.

Chapters 17 and 18, which focus on the legal aspects of prohibited and regulated markets, benefited significantly from discussions and comments with numerous colleagues, including Peter Reuter, Rob MacCoun, Jonathan Caulkins, Jamie Chriqui and Mark Kleiman. The legal framework employed in these two chapters was developed in conjunction with work being conducted by Drs Pacula, Chriqui, MacCoun and Reuter on alternative cannabis depenalisation regimes with funding from the Robert Wood Johnston Foundation.

Finally, Dr Pacula would like to acknowledge the contribution made by her immediate family, particularly her husband Joe, her children Gabriella and Brian, and her sister Kathleen Liccardo, without whose personal sacrifice this project would not have been completed.

Introduction

For over thirty years there has been a recurrent debate in Australia (Senate Standing Committee on Social Welfare, 1977), Canada (Canadian Government Commission of Inquiry, 1970), the United Kingdom (Advisory Committee on Drug Dependence, 1968), and the USA (National Commission on Marihuana and Drug Abuse, 1972) about whether these societies should continue to prohibit the use of cannabis by adults. Cannabis prohibition was introduced in these countries before cannabis use became common among young adults (McAllister and Makkai, 1991; Manderson, 1993) in the late 1930s in the USA and in the early 1960s in countries that signed the UN Single Convention on Narcotic Drugs (1961) which classified cannabis as a narcotic drug with cocaine and heroin (McAllister, 2000).

The debate about the legal status of cannabis in the late 1960s and early 1970s was prompted by the fact that many young people in the US and UK were ignoring the prohibition on cannabis use. The seeming failure of criminal law to deter cannabis use, and the increasing number of young adults who appeared before the courts for using cannabis, prompted calls to repeal or reform cannabis prohibition (e.g. Advisory Committee on Drug Dependence, 1968; Kaplan, 1970; National Commission on Marihuana and Drug Abuse, 1972).

The most popular proposal has been 'decriminalisation': removing criminal penalties for cannabis use while maintaining prohibition. Decriminalisation has been opposed by those who believe that cannabis has serious adverse effects on the health of users and on societies which tolerate its use (e.g. Nahas and Latour, 1992). Proponents of cannabis liberalisation (e.g. Grinspoon and Bakalar, 1993; Zimmer and Morgan, 1997) argue that the major harms arising from cannabis use are consequences of the fact that its use is illegal (such as, fear of arrest, a black-market, and the adverse effects on reputation of a criminal conviction) rather than consequences of its use.

Ideally, societal policies towards cannabis use by young people should be informed by information on: (1) the harm that cannabis causes to the health of those who use it; (2) the harm that cannabis use has on the health of people who do not use cannabis; (3) the extent to which criminal law deters young people from using cannabis; (4) the harms that arise from using the criminal law to deter people from using cannabis; (5) the social costs that would arise from changing laws prohibiting the use of cannabis by young people. Our book attempts to provide the best available information on each of these issues.

We do not attempt to answer a central political question about cannabis policy: How should our societies trade off the social costs of cannabis prohibition and the harms that cannabis causes to young people who use it and others who may be affected by their use? We make clear that such trade-offs are unavoidable, whether they are made implicitly or explicitly. We believe, however, that such trade-offs should be made through the political process in democratic societies. Our aim is to assist the political process by providing a fairer picture of the costs of cannabis use and of the policies that we have adopted towards cannabis. We especially want to move beyond the policy simplification that dominates the cannabis policy debate in many developed countries.

Policy simplifications and their costs

Public debates about socially contentious issues are invariably simplified in the competition for public attention in a crowded media and political marketplace. Proponents of competing cannabis policies have to capture the interest and attention of a busy and often distracted audience; in order to do so they often use highly simplified representations of the debate that meet their audience's need for cognitive economy. The reasons for this have been well stated by Moore and Gerstein (1981):

In a democracy, government policy is inevitably guided by commonly shared simplifications. This is true because political dialogue that authorizes and animates government policy can rarely support ideas that are very complex or entirely novel. There are too many people with diverse perceptions and interests and too little time and inclination to create a shared perception of a complex structure. Consequently, influential policy ideas are typically formulated at a quite general level and borrow heavily from commonly shared understanding and conventional opinions. (p. 6)

The media in many developed societies often represents the cannabis policy debate as if it was a choice between two policy positions: (1) cannabis use is harmless (or at least much less harmful than alcohol), and hence it should be decriminalised (if not legalised); and (2) cannabis use is harmful to health, and therefore its use should continue to be prohibited. The consequence of this simplification is that the societal task of weighing the social costs and benefits of cannabis prohibition and alternative policies has often been reduced to the single question: does cannabis use adversely affect the health of those who use it? This simplification has distorted appraisals of the health risks of cannabis use in a number of ways (Hall, 1997).

First, the public has been presented with highly polarised evaluations of the health effects of cannabis. According to some proponents of decriminalisation, cannabis is 'safer than aspirin' (Ellard, 1992) while their opponents (e.g. Nahas and Latour, 1992) argue that cannabis is a 'deceptively dangerous' drug of high toxicity. The public have been understandably uncertain about what version to believe.

Second, the issues about which disagreement is fiercest distract attention from an assumption implicitly shared by both sides of the debate, namely, that cannabis is a 'special' drug. According to proponents of reform, cannabis differs from other psychoactive drugs in being unusually benign in its effects on the health of the user. To its opponents, cannabis is a 'deceptively dangerous' drug because its lack of acute toxicity disguises the adverse effects that its chronic use has on the personalities of cannabis users and the fabric of society (Walters, 1993). Treating cannabis as a special case has, for these very different reasons, prevented a more rational appraisal of the health effects of cannabis and of public policy towards its use.

Third, the competing appraisals of the hazards of cannabis use have illustrated the phenomenon identified by Room (1984) in debates about alcohol use in colonial societies. Those who disapprove of cannabis use engage in 'problem inflation' in which any evidence that cannabis use is harmful, however suggestive or tentative, is taken at face value and seen to justify a continuation of prohibition. This often elicits a reactive 'problem deflation' among their policy opponents who discount any evidence that some types of cannabis use may be harmful to some users. In behaviour reminiscent of the tobacco industry, they sometimes set such high standards of proof that no harm can conceivably be demonstrated. A fair appraisal of the health effects of cannabis has become a casualty of the debate about its legal status.

Fourth, the controversy about the severity of the health effects of cannabis has been a major obstacle to effective public education about its health risks. Effective education presupposes a consensus upon what the adverse health effects of cannabis are. In the absence of consensus, governments have been reluctant to provide health information on cannabis for want of agreement about the advice to give (Hall and Nelson, 1995). When they have provided health information its accuracy has often been hotly contested by critics of current policy.

Aims of the book

Our aim in writing this book has been to improve the quality of public policy debate on cannabis by ensuring that all relevant issues are addressed. We have been inspired by an influential book on alcohol policy (Edwards et al., 1994) whose approach to alcohol policy we very much admire and would like to emulate. This remains an aspiration in the absence of a tradition of research on patterns of cannabis use and policy that matches the quality of almost a century of scholarly debate about alcohol use and policy. We nonetheless hope that our effort will contribute to the development of an analogous research tradition on cannabis use and public policies towards it.

Our focus is primarily on *recreational* cannabis use in developed countries because it is this type of cannabis use that is most controversial. The debate about the medical uses of cannabis is considered a secondary issue because if recreational cannabis use was legal then anyone who wanted to use it for therapeutic reasons could do so. We also argue that there are ways of allowing the compassionate use of cannabis for medical purposes that do not require substantial changes in current policy towards recreational cannabis use (see Appendix 1).

The evidence we cite is predominantly about recreational cannabis use in developed societies, such as the United States, Europe and Australia This is where debate about cannabis use for recreational purposes has been fiercest; it is also where societal concern about cannabis use has prompted the most research on the harms of cannabis use, and to a much lesser extent, on the effects and costs of existing policy. Similar concerns have begun to emerge about recreational cannabis use in developing societies, including some where cannabis has traditionally been used for religious purposes, such as India. Although patterns of cannabis use have not been well studied in these societies (Hall et al., 1999), recreational cannabis use has appeared among urban youth in India where it has begun to raise similar concerns to those expressed in developed societies (Machado, 1994).

Organisation of the book

The book is organised into eight sections. The first section describes cannabis as a drug and the ways in which it is typically used. Chapter 2 describes what is known about cannabis as a drug: the typical effects sought by users, its psychoactive constituents, the biology of cannabinoids, mechanisms of action, typical doses and methods of use. Chapter 3 reviews data on patterns of recreational cannabis use in developed societies.

The second section of the book (Chapters 4, 5 and 6), reviews evidence on the adverse health effects of cannabis use. These include the acute effects of use (Chapter 4) and the effects of chronic use on cellular, immunological and reproductive functioning (Chapter 5) and cardiovascular, respiratory and gastrointestinal systems (Chapter 6).

The third section of the book (Chapters 7, 8 and 9) examines the psychological effects of chronic cannabis use. These include effects on motivation and the risk of dependence (Chapter 7), effects on cognitive functioning (Chapter 8) and effects on the risk of developing psychosis (Chapter 9).

The fourth section deals with one of the most contentious issues in the debate: the effects of cannabis use on adolescents. Chapter 10 discusses the gateway hypothesis and Chapter 11 discusses the effects of cannabis use on psychosocial outcomes of adolescence.

The fifth section considers the harms and benefits of cannabis use. Chapter 11 summarises the findings of the preceding chapters on the adverse health effects of cannabis and compares these with the health effects of alcohol and tobacco. Chapter 12 considers the possible benefits of cannabis use, something that critics of current policy argue have been ignored in policy debates.

The sixth section considers the cannabis policy debate. Chapter 13 and 14 focus on two central claims of strategic significance to the case for cannabis law reform: whether prohibition has any deterrent effects on cannabis use (Chapter 13) and the economic costs of enforcing the current prohibition on cannabis use and cannabis supply (Chapter 14). Chapter 15 summarises some of the other less tangible costs of cannabis prohibition that have been identified by its critics.

Section seven explores alternative cannabis control policies in some detail. Chapter 16 discusses variations on prohibition that have been proposed and trialled in a number of developed societies. Chapter 17 discusses what is at present only a logical possibility: a legal market in which cannabis could be legally produced, sold and used. We outline the type of heavily regulated legal cannabis market that we believe would be most likely to minimise the harms of increased cannabis use that we argue would be an unavoidable consequence of allowing a legal cannabis market.

The final chapter summarises the arguments that have been developed in the book about the harms of cannabis use and the costs and effectiveness of cannabis prohibition. We end by suggesting some ways to move the cannabis policy debate forward by developing support for incremental policy changes, the costs and effects of which would be systematically evaluated.

Approach to the literature on the health effects of cannabis

Our approach to assessing the health risks of cannabis is to use the same standards that are used to evaluate the health risks of other drugs, ensuring that areas of ignorance are clearly disclosed so that it is easier to identify what we need to know to better inform policy. We also aim to reduce the confusion between questions of fact about health risks and moral issues and vice versa.

Separating the legal and health issues

The quality of both our assessments of the health effects of cannabis and the debate about the legal status of cannabis use would be improved if we clearly separate the two issues. They are understandably connected because the adverse health effects of cannabis use are one of the principal justifications offered for its use being a criminal offence. Consequently, if there were no adverse health effects of cannabis use, a different justification would need to be found for its continued prohibition. One such justification could be that prohibition was justified by societal consensus that it was undesirable for substantial numbers of citizens to spend a large part of their time in an intoxicated state (Kleiman, 1992). Such an argument would be a substantial improvement on moral objections to cannabis use being justified on the grounds of a threat to public health.

The failure to separate the health and legal issues means that the appraisers' views about the legal status of cannabis often prejudice their appraisals of its health effects. As argued above, this has operated in both directions, with opponents of its use inflating its health effects while proponents deflate their estimates, each driven by the implicit assumption that any adverse health effects justify prohibition. A clear distinction between the two issues is one way of ensuring a fairer discussion of both.

Not treating cannabis as a special case

In considering the health effects of cannabis use we have adopted the same approach as has been used to assess the health risks of alcohol and tobacco. This means that we begin with the assumption (derived from pharmacology and toxicology) that cannabis is likely to harm health when used at some dose, at some frequency or duration of use, and by some methods of administration (Fehr and Kalant, 1983). This is true for alcohol, tobacco, opiates, psychostimulants and benzodiazepines. It is also reasonable to assume that because cannabis is an intoxicant like alcohol and is usually smoked like tobacco, it is likely to share at least some of the adverse health effects of these two drugs.

Using a reasonable standard of evidence

If we must prove 'beyond reasonable doubt' that cannabis is a cause of adverse health effects then very few conclusions can be drawn about the adverse health effects of cannabis and very little advice could be given on how to reduce these harms. 'Beyond reasonable doubt' is arguably too high a standard of proof (Fehr and Kalant, 1983). Sensible, if fallible, health advice can be based on conclusions about the most *probable* adverse health effects of cannabis. We have set out the criteria that we have used in making causal inferences about the adverse health effects of cannabis in the introduction to section two. We have generally accepted the consensus of informed scientific opinion as the basis for inferring a *probable* causal connection between cannabis use and a health outcome. Consensus is expressed in authoritative reviews in peer reviewed journals and in consensus conferences of experts (e.g. WHO Program on Substance Abuse, 1997; Institute of Medicine, 1999).

Our approach to the cannabis policy debate

There are a number of technical reasons why the evaluation of competing social policies towards cannabis use cannot be as rigorous as, and is much less likely to achieve consensus than, appraisals of the adverse health effects of cannabis.

First, there is much less empirical evidence on the costs and benefits of different social policies towards cannabis. Much more funding has gone into research on its health effects than to evaluations of law enforcement or drug control policies (Manski et al., 2001).

Second, there are few alternative cannabis policies to evaluate because international agreements on cannabis prohibition have ensured that the policy options available for evaluation typically involve small variations in penalties for cannabis use. Arguments for reform have had to depend upon analogies between the effects of prohibiting cannabis and other drugs (e.g. alcohol prohibition in the USA), other vices (e.g. prostitution and gambling) or limited examples of more adventurous policies in other countries (e.g. the Netherlands) (MacCoun and Reuter, 2001).

Third, as will become apparent, many of the adverse social consequences of cannabis prohibition identified by its critics (e.g. loss of liberty, loss of respect for the rule of law, loss of medical uses of cannabis) are more difficult to measure than diseases and deaths attributed to cannabis use.

Fourth, it is much more difficult to make causal inferences about the effects of social policy on cannabis use and cannabis-related harms than it is to make causal inferences about the health effects of cannabis. There is not the same degree of consensus on standards for evaluating social policies as there is in appraising epidemiological and medical evidence. Policy analysis is typically based upon comparing rates of cannabis use in whole societies or large administrative units (such as States in a Federation). True experiments can rarely be performed (one cannot stratify for history) and there are limited opportunities to use statistical methods to adjust for differences between societies. There are also usually many plausible rival explanations of changes in cannabis use that may occur after a policy change (such as, changes in social attitudes, social and economic conditions, and the measurement of cannabis use and its consequences) (Cook and Campbell, 1979). The task of deciding between competing explanations is made more difficult by the limited data available to distinguish between them. As a consequence of all these factors, the interpretations of the evidence on the effects of different social policies towards cannabis are even more contested than the interpretation of evidence on the adverse health effects of cannabis.

The role of social values

Policy analysis is not and cannot be solely an empirical science. Deciding which policy to adopt involves trade-offs between competing values, such as, public health, individual liberty, public order and so on. Different types of trade-offs are advocated by supporters of competing and incommensurable moral philosophies.

Two types of moral theory are often distinguished: consequentialist and deontological theories (Beauchamp and Childress, 2001; MacCoun and Reuter, 2001). Consequentialist ethical theories judge actions, rules or policies by their consequences. One of the most influential consequentialist theories has been Jeremy Bentham's and John Stuart Mill's utilitarianism according to which the goal of social policy should be to achieve the greatest happiness of the greatest number. A utilitarian evaluation of cannabis policy requires an assessment of the costs and benefits of current and alternative cannabis policies (MacCoun and Reuter, 2001).

Deontological theorists reject the utilitarians' claim that the cannabis policy debate is an exercise in social accounting. Deontological ethical theories assess drug policy by its compliance with categorical moral imperatives, that is, moral principles that admit of no exceptions and that should be obeyed regardless of their consequences (Beauchamp and Childress, 2001). Deontological moral theories have been used to justify both liberal and prohibitionist cannabis policies. On the prohibitionist side of the debate, is 'legal moralism' (MacCoun and Reuter, 2001), the view that cannabis use is wrong in itself, and so should not to be tolerated under any circumstances. Any adverse social consequences of adopting this policy are not regarded as reasons for changing it.

On the other side of the debate are libertarians who argue that individual liberty should never be infringed by the state in order to protect adults from harming themselves. For libertarians, the individual liberty of adults to use any drug that they choose trumps any attempt to justify cannabis prohibition as a way of reducing harms caused by cannabis use. Husak (2002), for example, has argued that the use of all illicit drugs should be decriminalised because it is unjust to impose criminal punishments on individuals for using drugs that harm only themselves.

Consequentialist arguments feature prominently in the cannabis policy debate in many countries, as they do in many other areas of social policy (Goodin, 1995). The costs and benefits of social policies and laws are the coin of social policy debate in pluralist liberal democracies (MacCoun and Reuter, 2001). The policy focus on consequences is in part motivated by the absence of a societal consensus on deontological moral principles (MacCoun and Reuter, 2001). We have adopted a consequentialist approach to the evaluation of cannabis policy in this book. Our aim is to state what is known about the social costs of cannabis use and the social consequences of current and alternative cannabis policy regimes. We aim to present the evidence on the consequences of different policy options, as clearly and fairly as we can and to assess the arguments, as best we can, in the light of the available evidence. Our models have been Kleiman (1992) and MacCoun and Reuter (2001) who provide even-handed analyses of drug policies while avoiding easy and unhelpful equipoise between competing policies.

The criteria that we use in appraising alternative cannabis policy regimes are: their probable effects on patterns of harmful cannabis use; their social costs (criminal justice, victimisation, productivity, dependence, disrespect for law); their health costs (as a component of social costs); and their ability to regulate the quality of the cannabis that is consumed and to maintain its price at a level that minimises harmful patterns of cannabis use. As will be outlined later, our two main criteria for evaluating the strengths and weaknesses of alternative regimes for cannabis are: (1) their likely impact on cannabis use, as reflected in the prevalence of any use, of regular use, and especially of long-term regular use; and (2) their likely impact on social costs, including the costs of the policy and the costs that are averted by the policy.

1

Cannabis the drug and how it is used

2

Cannabis the drug

Cannabis preparations are obtained from the plant *Cannabis sativa* which occurs in male and female forms. The cannabis plant contains more than 66 cannabinoids (ElSohly, 2002), substances that are unique to the plant. The cannabinoid that is responsible for the psychoactive effects sought by cannabis users is Δ^9-tetrahydrocannabinol or THC (Martin and Cone, 1999; Iversen, 2000). It is found in the resin that covers the flowering tops and upper leaves of the female plant (Clarke and Watson, 2002). Most of the other cannabinoids either do not have psychoactive effects or are only weakly active, although they may interact with THC (Martin and Cone, 1999; Iversen, 2000).

The most common cannabis preparations are marijuana, hashish and hash oil. Marijuana is prepared from the dried flowering tops and leaves of the plant. Its THC content depends upon the growing conditions, the genetic characteristics of the plant, and the part of the plant that is used (Clarke and Watson, 2002). The flowering tops have the highest THC concentration with much lower concentrations in the leaves, stems and seeds. Cannabis plants may be grown to maximise their THC production by the 'sinsemilla' method in which only female plants are grown together (Clarke and Watson, 2002).

The concentration of THC in marijuana may range from 0.5% to 5% (ElSohly et al., 2000) while 'sinsemilla' may contain 7% to 14% (ElSohly et al., 2000). The potency of marijuana sold in the USA has probably increased over the past several decades (ElSohly et al., 2000) although it has not increased 30 times as has been claimed in the media (Hall and Swift, 2000). Hashish or hash consists of dried cannabis resin containing 2% to 8% of THC. Hash oil which is obtained by extracting THC from hashish (or marijuana) in oil contains 15% to 20% (Adams and Martin, 1996).

Routes of administration

Cannabis is typically smoked as marijuana in a hand-rolled cigarette or 'joint' which may include tobacco to assist burning. A water pipe or 'bong' is an increasingly popular way of using all cannabis preparations (Hall and Swift, 2000). Hashish may be mixed with tobacco and smoked as a joint or smoked in a pipe, with or without tobacco. Because hash oil is extremely potent a few drops may be applied to a cigarette or a joint, to the mixture in a pipe, or the oil is heated and the vapours inhaled. Whatever preparation is used, smokers typically inhale deeply and hold their breath to ensure maximum absorption of THC by the lungs.

The oral route of administration may also be used. Hashish may be cooked in foods and eaten. In experimental research, THC dissolved in sesame oil is swallowed in gelatine capsules. In India, cannabis may be consumed in the form of 'bhang', a tea brewed from the leaves and stems of the plant.

Cannabis does not lend itself to injection because THC does not dissolve in water (Walsh and Mann, 1999). The injection of crude solutions of cannabis will contain very little THC and may contain undissolved substances that can cause severe pain and inflammation. Iversen (2000) has suggested that the inability to inject cannabis preparations was one of the reasons for the decline in its therapeutic use at the end of the nineteenth century.

Surveys in Australia indicate that all but a handful of cannabis users smoke the drug (Hall and Swift, 2000) because its chemistry and pharmacology make smoking the most efficient way of delivering THC (Martin and Cone, 1999). Given the preponderance of cannabis smoking as the route of administration, the reader should assume that unless otherwise stated smoking is the way in which cannabis is used.

Dosage

A 'typical' cannabis joint consists of between 0.5 and 1.0 g of cannabis and contains between 5 and 50 mg of THC (i.e. between 0.5% and 5% THC). The amount of THC delivered in the smoke varies between 20% and 70% (Martin and Cone, 1999); the rest is burnt or lost in sidestream smoke. The fraction of THC in the joint that reaches the user's bloodstream varies between 5% and 24% (mean 18.6%) (Ohlsson et al., 1980). These variations in THC content of cannabis and cannabis smoke make it difficult to estimate the typical dose of THC that is received when cannabis is smoked.

An occasional user only requires a small amount of smoked cannabis (e.g. 2 to 3 mg of absorbed THC) to experience a brief, pleasurable high but a heavy cannabis smoker may consume five or more joints per day and very heavy users in Jamaica consume up to 420 mg THC in a day (Ghodse, 1986).

Metabolism of cannabinoids

The way that cannabis is used affects the absorption, metabolism and excretion of THC (Brenneisen, 2002). When cannabis is smoked, THC is absorbed within minutes into the bloodstream from the lungs but when it is taken orally THC takes 1 to 3 hours to enter the bloodstream and produce psychoactive effects (Martin and Cone, 1999).

After smoking, THC is metabolised first in the lungs and then in the liver where it is transformed into a number of metabolites (Harvey, 1999). The metabolite 9-carboxy-THC is detectable in blood within minutes of smoking cannabis. It is not psychoactive. Another major metabolite, 11-hydroxy-THC, is marginally more potent than THC and crosses the blood–brain barrier more rapidly. It is found in very low concentrations in the blood after smoking and at higher concentrations after oral use (Hawks, 1982). THC and its metabolites account for most of the psychoactive effects of cannabis (Harvey, 1999).

Peak blood levels of THC occur within 10 minutes of smoking and decline to 5%–10% of their initial level within an hour (Martin and Cone, 1999). This decline reflects the conversion of THC to its metabolites. THC and its metabolites are highly fat soluble and concentrate in lipid-rich tissues (Harvey, 1999). They may remain in the fatty tissues of the body for considerable periods of time, being slowly released into the bloodstream. This slows the elimination of THC from the body (Harvey, 1999).

The time required to clear half of the dose of THC from the body is shorter for daily users (19 to 27 hours) than for inexperienced users (50 to 57 hours) (Agurell et al., 1986). The half-life of THC in chronic users may be 3 to 5 days (Johansson et al., 1988). Because of the slow clearance, THC and its metabolites accumulate in the body with repeated administration. THC is slowly released from fatty tissues into the bloodstream so THC and its metabolites may be detected in blood for several days.

Detection of cannabinoids in body fluids

Plasma levels of THC in cannabis users vary between 0 and 500 ng/ml, depending on the THC content of the cannabis and the time since it was used. Blood levels of THC may decline to 2 ng/ml an hour after smoking a low potency cannabis cigarette but it may take 9 hours to reach this level after smoking high THC cannabis. These levels may persist for several days in chronic users because of the slow release of accumulated THC.

The detection of THC in blood above 10–15 ng/ml generally indicates 'recent' use of cannabis but it is difficult to say how recent. A more precise estimate of the time of consumption is provided by the ratio of THC to 9-carboxy-THC (Heustis et al., 1992). When the levels of 9-carboxy-THC are substantially higher than those of THC this indicates that cannabis was smoked more than half an hour before, if the smoker was a naïve user (Perez-Reyes et al., 1982). Background levels of cannabinoids (particularly 9-carboxy-THC) in regular users make it more difficult to estimate time since last use.

Cannabinoid levels in urine are a weak indicator of recent cannabis use. In general, the more cannabinoid metabolites in urine, the more recent the use (Hawks, 1982). Only minute traces of THC are found in urine because most THC is excreted as metabolites in faeces and urine (Hunt and Jones, 1980). 9-carboxy-THC can be detected in urine within 30 minutes of smoking. This and other metabolites may be detected for several days in first time or occasional cannabis users but regular users may continue to excrete metabolites for weeks (Ellis et al., 1985).

Studies of cannabinoids in saliva have found that THC can be stored for at least 28 days (Johansson et al., 1987). Measurement of cannabinoids in saliva may reduce the time frame for 'recent' use from days and weeks to hours (Hawks, 1982). Salivary THC levels are correlated with subjective intoxication and heart rate (Menkes et al., 1991).

There is no simple relationship between levels of THC (or its metabolites) in blood and psychomotor impairment (Agurell et al., 1986). THC differs from alcohol where psychomotor impairment is correlated with blood alcohol level. This is for two reasons: there is a delay between experiencing the subjective high and THC appearing in the blood; and there are large variations between individuals in the psychoactive effects experienced at the same blood level of THC. A consensus conference of forensic toxicologists concluded that there was insufficient evidence for blood concentrations of THC to provide a legal basis for defining the offence of driving a motor vehicle under the influence of cannabis (National Institute on Drug Abuse, 1985).

Cannabinoid biology

Research during the 1990s has clarified the ways in which cannabinoids act in the human body and brain by identifying 'cannabinoid receptors' sites and the 'endogenous cannabinoids' that act upon them (Institute of Medicine, 1999; Pertwee, 2002). Cannabinoid receptors are the molecular sites in the brain and body at which the active components of cannabis, such as THC, act. These receptors also respond to 'endogenous cannabinoids': substances that naturally occur in the human brain and body that produce similar effects to THC. These endogenous cannabinoids include anandamide (Devane et al., 1992) and 2-arachidonyl-glycerol (2AG) (Pertwee, 2002).

Two types of cannabinoid receptors, CB_1 and CB_2, have so far been identified. Others as yet unidentified may also exist (Wiley and Martin, 2002). The CB_1

receptor is found primarily in the brain. It is responsible for the psychological effects of THC since a drug that blocks the CB_1 receptor also blocks many of the effects of THC in humans (Heustis et al., 2001). The CB_2 receptor is found in the immune system where its role remains unclear. CB_1 and CB_2 receptors belong to a large group of G-protein coupled receptors found in the membranes of nerve cells that are involved in chemical signalling between nerve cells.

Cannabinoid receptors have been found in the nervous system of lower vertebrates, including chickens, turtles and trout (Howlett et al., 1990). This suggests that cannabinoid receptors were present early in evolution, and their conservation suggests that they serve an important biological function in many species, including mammals (Martin and Cone, 1999).

The distribution of CB_1 and CB_2 receptors in the brain, immune and reproductive tissues is consistent with many of their therapeutic and recreational effects (Pertwee, 1999). CB_1 cannabinoid receptors in the brain are most concentrated in brain systems that are involved in controlling mood, motor function, memory formation, food intake, pain modulation, immune, and reproductive functions (Pertwee, 2002).

Cannabis disrupts short-term memory in humans (see Chapter 4). This effect is consistent with an abundance of CB_1 receptors in the hippocampus, the brain region most closely associated with memory (Iversen, 2000). A high density of CB_1 receptors in the basal ganglia and cerebellum is consistent with the fact that cannabinoids interfere with coordinated movement (Martin and Cone, 1999). The fact that the lower brainstem area has few cannabinoid receptors explains why cannabis has no effect on respiratory function in humans and why high doses of THC are rarely lethal (Chesher and Hall, 1999; Iversen, 2000).

Summary

Cannabis is derived from the *cannabis sativa* plant. THC is the constituent of cannabis that produces the psychoactive effects sought by recreational users. Different forms of cannabis (marijuana, heads, hash and hash oil) vary in their potency. Cannabis is predominantly smoked in a joint or in a water pipe because this is the most efficient way to deliver THC quickly to the sites in the brain on which it acts. THC and its metabolites can be detected in blood and urine but there is no simple relationship between these levels in blood or urine and the degree of intoxication or psychomotor impairment. THC acts on brain receptors ('cannabinoid receptors') which are also acted upon by substances that occur naturally in the brain ('endogenous cannabinoids'). Cannabinoid receptors are found in brain regions involved in control of mood, memory, and motor performance, all of which are affected by cannabis.

3

Patterns of use

Measuring cannabis use

Information about cannabis use is collected by surveying representative samples of the general population about their use of the drug. These surveys typically ask whether the person has used cannabis: at any time in their lives (lifetime use), in the past year (past year use), and in the past month (recent use). Given the low rates of weekly and daily cannabis use in most surveys, lifetime use and use in the past year are most often reported.

The validity of self-reported cannabis use is well-supported in carefully designed surveys. O'Malley, Bachman and Johnston (1983), for example, showed that self-reported drug use in three waves of interviews of high school seniors was as reliable as other self-reported behaviour. Although some older adults under-report their drug use during adolescence and early adult life, under-reporting of cannabis use is quite low (Johnston et al., 1994a; Johnston et al., 1994b). Most importantly, whatever biases there may be in self-reported cannabis use are fairly constant over time, meaning that we can be reasonably confident about estimates of *trends* in drug use (Johnston et al., 2001).

Cannabis use in the United States

The best information on cannabis use has been collected in the United States where two major surveys of illicit drug use have been conducted since the early 1970s. The 'Monitoring the Future' project has surveyed nation-wide samples of high school seniors, college students and young adults annually since 1975 (Johnston et al., 1994a; Johnston et al., 1994b). The National Household Survey on Drug Abuse (sponsored by the National Institute on Drug Abuse) has surveyed household samples of person over the age of 12 years throughout the US since 1972.

NIDA Household Survey

NIDA has surveyed approximately 9000 persons aged 12 years and older in randomly selected households throughout the US every two to three years since 1972.

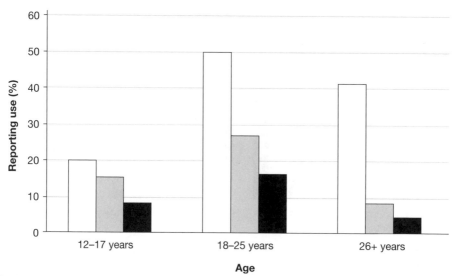

Fig. 3.1   Cannabis use in the USA in 2001 by age. Lifetime usage is shown by the white columns, usage in the past year by the grey columns, and usage in the past month by the black columns.

Since 1991 it has been conducted annually on 30,000 participants (National Institute on Drug Abuse, 1992).

In 2001, 37% of the national sample reported that they had tried cannabis at some time in their life. Only 9.3% reported using cannabis in the past year and 5.4% reported using it in the past month (Substance Abuse and Mental Health Services Administration, 2001). Lifetime use was 20% among those aged 12 to 17 years, 50% among those aged 18 to 25 years, and 37% among those 26 years and older (see Fig. 3.1).

The NIDA Household Survey series from 1974 to 1990 shows that rates of monthly cannabis use among 18 to 25 year olds increased throughout the 1970s and peaked in 1979. They then declined steadily throughout the 1980s to reach their lowest level in 1992 before increasing again in 1992 (see Fig. 3.2).

The Monitoring The Future project

In this series of surveys, the prevalence of cannabis use has been estimated among secondary school students, college students and young adults. Since 1975 approximately 15,000 high school seniors have been surveyed. The samples of college students and young adults who are surveyed each year are a sample of those who were surveyed as high school seniors (about 14%). They have been followed up every two years. Since 1991 national samples of 8th and 10th grade students have also been annually surveyed.

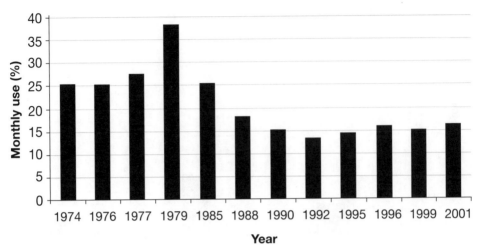

Fig. 3.2   Trends in monthly cannabis use among 18–25-year-olds in the USA.

In the 2001 survey, lifetime cannabis use increased with grade, from 20.4 among grade 8 to 48.9 among grade 12 students (see Fig. 3.3). The same trend was evident in use during the past year and the past month.

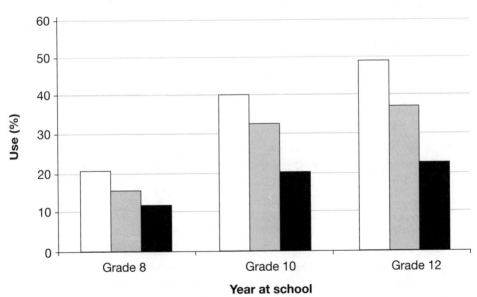

Fig. 3.3   Cannabis use in high school students in the USA in 2001. Lifetime usage is shown by the white columns, usage in the past year is indicated by grey columns, and usage in the past month by the black columns.

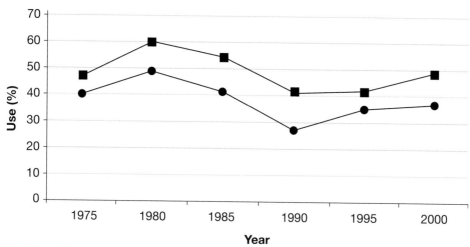

Fig. 3.4 Trends in cannabis use in US grade 12 students 1975–2000. The plot with square points indicate lifetime usage and the line with circular points represents usage in the past year.

The Monitoring the Future surveys have revealed trends in cannabis use among American adolescents since 1975. Among grade 12 students (average age 18 years old) lifetime prevalence peaked at 65% in 1980, then fell by nearly half by the early 1990s. Use in the past year peaked at 51% in 1979 and fell to 22% by 1992. After more than a decade of declining cannabis use among American secondary students, the 1992 and 1993 surveys showed an increase. Cannabis use began to rise sharply among 8, 10 and 12th graders, and to a lesser extent among college students and young adults. The turnaround reflected an increasing initiation rate and a higher rate of continued use (see Fig. 3.4).

The natural history of cannabis use in the United States

Bachman et al. (1997) have used Monitoring the Future data from 14 cohorts of high school seniors and college students who were followed from age 18 to 35 years to assess the effect of major life transitions (such as, entering college or full-time employment, marrying and having children) on the use of cannabis in the past 30 days. They found a steady decline in monthly cannabis use from the early and mid-20s to the early 30s. The pattern was very similar to that for alcohol but quite different to that of tobacco use which was much more persistent.

Major role transitions explained a substantial part of these changes. Those entering college increased their use of cannabis from before college entry but their use only caught up with that of students who did not enter college who used cannabis more often in high school than those who entered college. Bigger declines in use were seen in males and females after marriage and during pregnancy in the case of

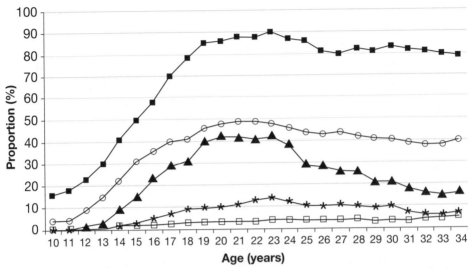

Fig. 3.5   Current monthly use of cannabis, alcohol, cigarettes, other illicit drugs and prescribed psychoactive drugs by age (adapted from Chen & Kandel, 1995). The plot with solid squares indicates alcohol usage, the plot with unfilled circles indicates cigarette usage, the plot with solid trangles indicates cannabis use, the plot with stars indicates usage of other illicit drugs, and the plot with unfilled squares indicates use of prescribed psychoactive drugs.

women. Entering the military had a large impact on cannabis use, probably because of pre-induction and in-service drug testing.

These findings have been confirmed in a more detailed study of a single cohort that was followed from early adolescence into middle adulthood (Chen and Kandel, 1995, 1998). These authors also found that cannabis use began to decline in the early 20s and declined steadily through the 20s and into the 30s. The decline was explained by the increasing responsibilities of marriage, children and employment. Use persisted in those who: did not enter conventional marriage (e.g. remained single or cohabited); did not enter college; and who were unemployed (see Fig. 3.5).

Cannabis use in Canada

A national telephone survey conducted in Canada in 1994 on 12,155 persons aged 15 years and older (Williams et al., 1992) found that 28% of the sample reported using cannabis at some time in their lives. Males were more likely to have used than females in all age groups. Rates of use in the past year declined with age, from a high of 26% among those aged 15 to 17 years to 1% among those aged 55 to 64 years. Rates of discontinuation were substantial.

There have been school surveys conducted in a number of Canadian provinces since the early 1970s. Adlaf and Smart (1991) reviewed findings across six of the ten provinces where surveys had been conducted between the early 1970s and the late 1980s. The most consistent trend was an increase in the prevalence of cannabis use through the 1970s, with a sharp decline through the 1980s, a pattern similar to that in the USA over the same period but at lower rates of use.

Since 1977 Ontario has conducted a series of surveys of students in grades 7, 9, 11 and 13 with sample sizes of between three and five thousand. The rate of cannabis use during the previous 12 months declined from 32% in 1979 to 14% in 1989. Rates of cannabis use were lower in Ontario than in the neighbouring United States. Since the beginning of the 1990s there has been a steady increase in rates of cannabis use in the past year among Ontario high school students, from a low of 11.7% in 1991 to 29.2% in 1999 (Adlaf et al., 2000). More detailed analyses of trends in cannabis use have shown the same pattern of decline throughout the 1980s, followed by an increase in the early 1990s, in Ontario and US students (Ivis and Adlaf, 1999).

Cannabis use in Australia

Cannabis is the most widely used illicit drug in Australia, with 33% of a household sample of adults aged 15 and older reporting that they had used it at some time in their lives in 2001 (Australian Institute of Health and Welfare, 2002). Among 14–19-year-olds the lifetime use of cannabis was 34%, increasing to 59% of 20–29-year-olds before declining with age. Men were more likely to have used cannabis than women in all age groups, with 37% of males versus 29% of females reporting lifetime use in the 2001 survey. As evident in Figure 3.6, cannabis use is strongly related to age, with older adults much less likely to have used cannabis than younger adults (see also Makkai and McAllister, 1998). The low rates of lifetime cannabis use among adults over the age of 40 years reflects the increased initiation of cannabis use among young Australian adults that began in the early 1970s (Makkai and McAllister, 1998).

Most cannabis use was irregular. Three-quarters of women and two-thirds of men who had used cannabis in their lifetime had either not used in the past year or were using less than weekly. The proportion of users who were weekly users was 7% of women and 15% of men. Weekly cannabis use was most common among those aged 20 to 24 years, declining steeply thereafter (Donnelly and Hall, 1994). The percentage of Australians aged between 20 and 29 years who have ever tried cannabis doubled between 1985 and 2001, from 28% to 59% (see Fig. 3.7).

The rate of cannabis use in the past 12 months was 13% in the 2001 NDS Survey. This was a slight decrease on rates of use the 1998 household survey, which found a rate of 18%, but more like those in earlier surveys (Makkai and McAllister,

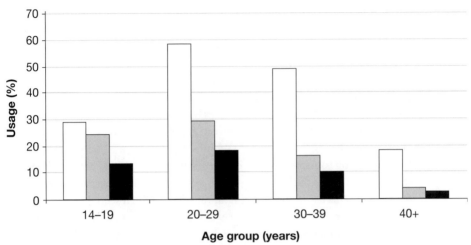

Fig. 3.6   Lifetime and past-year use of cannabis in Australia 2001. White columns indicate lifetime usage, grey columns indicate usage during the previous year, black columns indicate usage in the past month.

1997). Current use of cannabis was more common: among males (16%) than females (10%), and among 14–19-year-olds (25%) and 20–29-year-olds (29%) than among those aged 30 to 39 years (16%) and those over 40 years (4%).

The 1996 Australian School Students Alcohol and Drugs Survey found that 36% of students aged 12–17 had used cannabis (Lynskey and Hall, 1999). Earlier studies of drug use among school aged youth in various Australian states conducted in the early 1990s reported rates of cannabis use between 25%–30% (Donnelly and

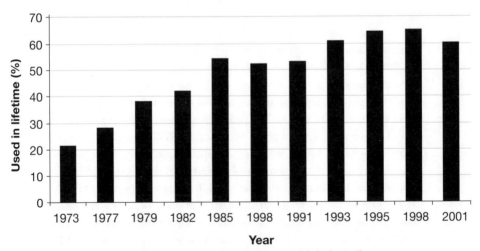

Fig. 3.7   Trends in lifetime cannabis use among 20–29-year-olds in Australia.

Hall, 1994). The 1996 school survey results suggest that there was an increase in the use of cannabis use among youth during the 1990s, a finding that is supported by the NDS household surveys.

Australian cannabis users are most often males, who are under 35 years of age and are more likely to be unemployed than non-users. While persons with higher education levels are more likely to have tried cannabis at some time in their lives, persons with lower levels of education are more likely to be regular users (Makkai and McAllister, 1997). Cannabis in Australia is most typically smoked, and the types of cannabis most commonly used are heads and leaf (Makkai and McAllister, 1997). The preferred mode of administration among younger users is a bong or pipe; older users are more likely to smoke joints (Hall and Swift, 2000).

A major trend in cannabis use among Australian adolescents and young adults has been initiation at a younger age. In the 1998 NDS Survey, one in five cannabis users (21%) born between 1940 and 1949 had initiated cannabis use by age 18, compared to 43% of those born in 1950–59, 66% of those born 1960–69 and 78% of those born in 1970–79 (Degenhardt et al., 2000).

Cannabis use in Europe

Very few European countries have undertaken regular community or high school surveys of drug use. WHO Regional Office for Europe collected data from 21 countries that had surveyed illicit drug use in the general population (Harkin et al., 1997). The few that had trend data on the prevalence of cannabis use (e.g. Denmark, France, Switzerland, and the United Kingdom) all showed that use increased in the early 1990s (Harkin et al., 1997). In all cases, the prevalence of current use was substantially less than lifetime use, indicating that cessation of cannabis use was common. Rates of current use were highest among those aged 15 to 24 years.

The European Monitoring Centre on Drugs and Drug Addiction (EMCDDA) has reported rates of lifetime cannabis use among adults and adolescents in household and school surveys among member states (European Monitoring Centre for Drugs and Drug Addiction, 2002). The median rates of lifetime cannabis use among adults aged between 18 and 64 years was 17%, with a range between 31% in Denmark to 10% in Finland. Rates of lifetime use were higher among younger adults (aged between 15 and 34 years), with a median rate of 23%, and a range between 14% in Sweden and 31% in Denmark. Rates of lifetime use were higher among high school students aged 15–16 years, with a median of 25% and a range between 8% in Sweden and 30% in Spain.

Rates of cannabis use in the past year (which were available in fewer countries) were lower. The median among adults aged 18–64 years was 6% (with a range 1% to 9%). The median among young adults was 10%, with a range between 1% in Sweden and 17% in the United Kingdom (European Monitoring Centre for Drugs and Drug Addiction, 2002).

Smart and Ogborne (2000) have recently summarised survey data on illicit drug use among students in 36 countries during the mid-1990s (circa 1995). Most of these countries were European and developed societies. The highest rates of life-time cannabis use were in Scotland (53%), the United Kingdom (41%) and Wales (33%), followed by the USA (32%), Australia (31%) and the Netherlands (22%).

These data suggest that with the exception of the United Kingdom and Denmark, the rates of cannabis use among young people in Europe are much lower than those in the USA. These rates have increased during the 1990s in those European societies that have undertaken a series of surveys over that time, namely, the Netherlands, Switzerland, and Norway.

Cannabis use in other regions

There are limited survey data on cannabis use in other parts of the world. The results of the few surveys that have been done are often not reported in ways that make it easy to compare findings. Often only rates of lifetime use or use in the past year are reported, and only rarely are data reported on rates of use in different age groups for men and women (Hall et al., 1999). Survey data collected in the early to mid-1990s suggested that rates of cannabis use were generally much lower in Northern Africa, Asia and South America than in the developed countries of Europe, North America and Oceania (see Hall et al., 1999).

More recently, the United Nations Office for Drug Control and Crime Prevention (United Nations Office for Drug Control and Crime Prevention, 2002) has reviewed available data on the use of cannabis in the late 1990s. It estimates that 147 million people (3.5% of the global population over the age of 15 years) used cannabis per year in the period 1998–2000 (United Nations Office for Drug Control and Crime Prevention, 2002). The highest rates of use per capita (see Fig. 3.8) were in Oceania, where 18.8% of adults reported use in the past year, followed by Africa (8.1%), North America (6.6%), Western Europe (6.4%) and South America (4.7%). The proportion of world cannabis consumption accounted for by each region (see Fig. 3.9) reflects the population of each of the regions. This shows that Asia accounts for the largest proportion of world consumption (28%) even though it has one of the lower rates of per capita use, while Oceania with the high-est rate of per capita consumption accounts for only 3% of world consumption.

Factors associated with cannabis use

Age

One of the most consistent findings from survey research is that first use of cannabis typically begins in the teens and the heaviest rates of use occur in the early 20s. Rates of cannabis use remain relatively high during the early 20s but

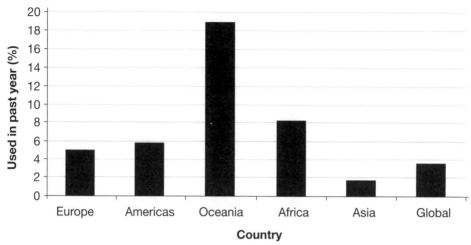

Fig. 3.8   Global cannabis use in the late 1990s (Source: UNODCCP, 2002).

decline thereafter. Chen and Kandel (1995) found that the majority of young adults who experimented with cannabis had done so by age 18 and Bachman et al. (1997) report that rates of use decline steadily from the mid-20s.

Gender

Rates of cannabis use in the lifetime, the past year and the past week are consistently higher among males than females (Adlaf and Smart, 1991; Donnelly and Hall, 1994; Johnston et al., 1994a; Johnston et al., 1994b). Daily use is also much higher among males (Johnston et al., 1994a; Johnston et al., 1994b).

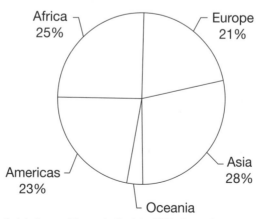

Fig. 3.9   Percentage of global cannabis use in the late 1990s by region

Table 3.1. Prevalence of cannabis use surveys in European countries 1998–2000 (European Monitoring Centre for Drugs and Drug Addiction, 2002)

	Lifetime use (young adults)	12-month use (young adults)	Lifetime use (all adults)	12-month use (all adults)
Belgium	26.1	–	20.8	–
Denmark	44.6	–	31.3	–
Finland	16.6	13.1	9.9	6.2
France	35.7	4.9	22.5	2.2
Germany	30.8	17.0	19.3	8.4
Greece	19.7	13.0	13.1	6.0
Ireland	19.8	17.7	11.4	9.4
Luxembourg	15.8	–	12.9	–
Netherlands	27.3	9.8	19.1	5.5
Norway	20.9	8.1	15.3	4.5
Portugal	26.2	6.2	16.2	3.3
Spain	28.5	12.7	19.8	7.0
Sweden	14.0	1.0	13.0	1.0
United Kingdom	40.4	16.6	27.0	8.6
Median	22.5	10.0	16.5	6.0

Socioeconomic status

The relationship between cannabis use and socioeconomic status (SES) is weak. Among 12th grade students in the United States, there has been no relationship between level of parents' education and cannabis use for the past two decades, except that the lowest parental education group of the five has slightly lower cannabis use than the others (Johnston et al., 1994a; Johnston et al., 1994b). That difference may be more explained in terms of differences in income during adolescence rather than social class differences.

Summary

Patterns of cannabis use have been most extensively studied in the USA, Canada, Australia and Europe. This is probably a biased sample of countries because the surveys were prompted by community concern about cannabis use by young people. Europe generally has lower rates of use than Australia, Canada and the USA, with the highest rates of use in the United Kingdom, Denmark and France. The limited data from developing countries suggest that with isolated exceptions (e.g. Jamaica) rates of cannabis use are much lower in Africa, the Caribbean, Asia and South America than in Europe and English-speaking countries.

Surveys in the USA have found long waves of cannabis use among young people since 1975. Cannabis use increased during the 1970s to peak in 1979 before declining steadily between 1980 and 1991. Use rose sharply in 1992 and increased throughout the 1990s, before levelling off in the late 1990s. There was also a rise in cannabis use during the early 1990s in Australia, Canada, and some European countries.

The 'natural history' of cannabis use in the USA has been for use to begin in the mid- to late teens, reaching its maximum in the early 20s before declining in the mid- to late 20s. Only a minority of young adults use cannabis into their 30s. Marriage and children substantially reduce rates of cannabis use. Cross-sectional survey data in other developed countries produces results that are consistent with this US pattern in that rates of regular cannabis use are low because most young adults discontinue their use.

The health effects of cannabis

The following chapters deal with the adverse health effects of cannabis. We have used the following criteria in making causal inferences about the adverse health effects of cannabis.

Making causal inferences

Standard criteria for making causal inferences (e.g. Hall, 1987) require: that there is an association between cannabis use and an adverse health outcome; that chance is an unlikely explanation of the association; that cannabis use preceded the health outcome; and that plausible alternative explanations of the association can be excluded.

Evidence of association

Evidence of an association between cannabis use and a health outcome is provided by the observation of a relationship between cannabis use and the outcome in a case-control, cross-sectional, cohort, or experimental study. These study designs differ in the ease and expense with which they can be enacted and in the strength of the inference that they warrant.

Excluding chance

Evidence is required that chance is an unlikely explanation of any relationship observed between cannabis use and a health outcome. 'Unlikely to arise by chance' is conventionally taken to mean that it is an event that would occur less than 5% of the time. In the biomedical sciences, the role of chance is evaluated by constructing a 95% confidence interval around the sample value of a measure of association, such as a correlation coefficient, an odds ratio or a relative risk (Altman et al., 2000). A confidence interval provides a range of values of the measure of association that are consistent at the 95% level of confidence with the value observed in the sample. If the confidence interval does not include the value consistent with no relationship, then one is able to infer that there is an association between cannabis use and the adverse health effect.

Ascertaining temporal order

If cannabis use is a cause of an adverse health effect then cannabis use should precede the health effect. Cross-sectional and case-control studies which assess cannabis use and health status at the same time often do not enable us to decide which came first, the cannabis use or the health outcome. The strongest evidence that cannabis use precedes the health effect comes from a cohort study in which the researcher observes that cannabis use precedes the health effect or an experiment in which the experimenter ensures by design that it does so.

Deciding between alternative explanations

The alternative explanation of an association between cannabis use and a health outcome that is often the most difficult to exclude is that the association reflects an unmeasured variable that is the cause of both cannabis use and the health outcome. In cross-sectional surveys of high school-aged adolescents, for example, cannabis users perform more poorly at school than non-cannabis users (Kandel and Logan, 1984). An 'obvious' explanation of this association is that cannabis use is a cause of poor school performance. An equally plausible hypothesis is that lower intellectual ability (or learning difficulties or a poor home environment, etc.) is a cause of both poor school performance and cannabis use (Kandel et al., 1986; Newcomb and Bentler, 1988).

Experiments in which persons are randomly assigned to use cannabis or not provide the 'gold standard' for ruling out common causes. Random assignment to use cannabis or not would ensure that cannabis users and non-users did not differ prior to using cannabis, and hence, any subsequent differences between users and non-users can be attributed to cannabis use rather than to pre-existing differences. This option is often not available because it is impossible for ethical and practical reasons to randomly assign individuals to cannabis use. It would be unethical to force some adolescents to use cannabis, and impracticable to prevent those who were assigned not to use cannabis from doing so.

Experimentation with laboratory animals is the next best option to human experiments on the health effects of cannabis use. In such studies, mice, rats, or monkeys are randomly assigned to receive either high doses of cannabis or placebo. The rates of various health outcomes (e.g. cancers, immunological changes, reproductive effects) are then compared between the experimental and control animals. This strategy has been applied to the study of physical health effects of cannabis use. It has limited application in studying the psychological effects of chronic cannabis use because there are no animal models for mental illness, school performance, and personal adjustment. The usual problems in extrapolating results across species are compounded by the fact that humans and animals use different routes of administration (e.g. oral and parenteral in animals versus smoked in humans), different forms of cannabis (pure THC in many animal studies versus smoked cannabis plant in human use), and very different doses of THC (high doses in animals vs typical long-term low dosing of crude cannabis products smoked by humans).

When a suitable animal model does not exist, and when randomisation of human subjects is impractical or unethical, epidemiological methods are used to rule out common causes in human studies. These involve using statistical methods to estimate the effects that cannabis use has on a health outcome, after adjusting for the effects of any differences between cannabis users and non-users that may affect the outcome (e.g. personal characteristics and life experiences before using cannabis). If the relationship persists after statistical adjustment, then confidence is increased that it is not attributable to the variables for which statistical adjustment has been made. This approach has been used, for example, in longitudinal studies of the effects of adolescent cannabis use on psychosocial outcomes (e.g. Kandel et al., 1986; Fergusson and Horwood, 1997).

An overall appraisal of causal hypotheses

A single research study, no matter how well done, rarely permits us to decide whether cannabis use is a cause of an adverse health outcome. Causal hypotheses are more typically evaluated in the light of a body of research using criteria like those outlined by Hill (1977). These criteria are not sufficient for establishing that an association indicates a causal relationship since it is possible for the criteria to be met and yet to be mistaken in making a causal inference. But generally, the more of the criteria that are met, the more likely it is that the association is a causal one.

Strength of association: the stronger a relationship is the better our ability to predict that cannabis use and a health effect co-occur. Stronger relationships are generally more deserving of trust than weaker ones that are more likely to be artefacts of measurement or sampling.

Consistency: relationships which are consistently observed by different investigators, in different populations, using varied measures and research designs, are more credible than relationships which are not. The persistence of a relationship despite differences in sampling and research methods makes it unlikely that it can be explained by these factors.

Specificity exists when cannabis use is strongly associated with the outcome, and the health outcome is rare in non-cannabis users. It is a desirable but not a necessary condition. If there is specificity we can be more confident that there is a causal relationship but its absence does not exclude the possibility of a complex (e.g. conditional) causal relationship.

Biological gradient refers to a dose–response relationship between frequency and duration of cannabis use and the likelihood of the health outcome. Satisfaction of this criterion is also desirable but not necessary because there may be other patterns of relationship between cannabis use and the outcome, e.g. a threshold effect, an 'all or none', or a curvilinear relationship.

Biological plausibility: If the relationship does not make biological sense, e.g. there is no known mechanism by which it can happen, we have grounds for scepticism. But in the face of compelling evidence of association from well-controlled studies, implausibility is not a compelling reason for rejecting a causal relationship: it may signal that existing theories are wrong, or that we need new theories to explain previously unknown phenomena.

Coherence means that the relationship is consistent with the natural history and biology of the disease. This too is desirable but not necessary: it is desirable if we have independent information that we can trust but its absence is not fatal since the other knowledge with which it is inconsistent may be in error.

Acute health effects

The acute health effects of any drug are easier to appraise than its chronic health effects: the temporal order of drug use and effect is clear; drug use and its effects typically occur closely together in time; and if the effect is not life-threatening or otherwise dangerous, it can be reliably reproduced in a substantial proportion of people by administering the drug under controlled conditions. All these conditions are satisfied for the most common acute psychoactive effects of cannabis. These include the effects that are sought by recreational cannabis users (such as, euphoria and relaxation) as well as the more common dysphoric effects, such as anxiety, panic and depression.

Complications arise in deciding whether to attribute relatively rare acute experiences (such as flashbacks and psychotic symptoms) to cannabis use. In these cases it is often difficult to decide whether these are: rare events that are coincidental with cannabis use; rare consequences of cannabis use that only occur at doses that are much higher than those used recreationally or in vulnerable individuals; the effects of other drugs which may have been taken together with cannabis; are the result of interactions between the cannabis and other drug use, and so on.

Chronic effects

Causal inferences about the long-term effects of chronic cannabis use become more difficult the longer the interval between use and the occurrence of the alleged ill effects. It takes time for adverse effects to develop; it may also take time for a suspicion to be raised about the relationship between cannabis use and the adverse outcome. In the case of tobacco use, for example, it took over three hundred years to discover that it caused premature death from cancer and heart disease, and new health hazards of tobacco smoking continue to be discovered (English et al., 1995). The longer the time interval between cannabis use and the health consequence, the more numerous the alternative explanations of the association that need to be excluded.

In making causal inferences about the chronic health effects of cannabis use there is a tension between the rigour and relevance of the evidence. The most rigorous evidence is provided by laboratory investigations using experimental animals or *in vitro* preparations of animal cells and micro-organisms in which well-controlled drug doses are administered over a substantial period of the organisms' lives and related to precisely measured biological outcomes. The relevance of such laboratory research to human disease, however, is often uncertain.

Epidemiological studies of relationships between cannabis use and human disease are more *relevant* than experimental studies in animals in evaluating health effects in humans. But this relevance comes at the price of reduced rigour in assessing exposure to cannabis and in excluding alternative explanations of associations between cannabis use and health outcomes. There is, consequently, uncertainty about the interpretation of human epidemiological studies that affects interpretations of both relationships between cannabis use and health outcomes ('positive' studies), and studies which fail to observe such relationships ('negative' studies).

A major problem in interpreting positive epidemiological studies is that cannabis use is correlated with other drug use, which is known to adversely affect health (e.g. alcohol and tobacco use). Generally, the heavier the cannabis use, the more likely it is that the person uses other licit (alcohol and tobacco) and illicit drugs (amphetamines, hallucinogens, cocaine, and heroin). This makes it difficult to confidently attribute some of the adverse health effects found in cannabis users to their cannabis use. Statistical control of confounding is the best available approach to deal with this problem.

A different problem arises when interpreting studies that fail to find adverse health effects of chronic cannabis use. In the case of immunological effects, for example, the limited epidemiological evidence suggests that there are no adverse immunological effects of chronic heavy cannabis use in humans (Hall et al., 2001) while the animal evidence suggests that large doses of THC impair cellular and humoral immunity (Klein et al., 2001). The difficulty arises in appraising such negative human evidence: does it mean that THC has few, if any, immunological effects in humans or have the studies lacked the sensitivity to detect any such effects in humans? The answers to this question depend upon the likely magnitude of any such effects, their relationship to cannabis dose, frequency and duration of use, and the ability of studies with small sample sizes to detect them (Hall and Einfeld, 1990).

4

The acute effects of cannabis

Psychological effects

The main reason why most young people use cannabis is to experience mild euphoria, relaxation and perceptual alterations, including time distortion, and the intensification of experiences, such as, eating, watching films, listening to music, and engaging in sex (Tart, 1970; Jaffe, 1985). When used in a social setting, the 'high' may be accompanied by infectious laughter, talkativeness, and increased sociability. The effects of cannabis depend upon the dose received, the mode of administration, the user's prior experience with cannabis, concurrent drug use, and the 'set and setting' – the user's expectations, attitudes towards cannabis, mood state, and the social setting in which it is used (Jaffe, 1985).

Cognitive changes include impaired short-term memory and attention that make it easy for the user to become lost in pleasant reverie and difficult to sustain goal-directed mental activity (Solowij, 1998; Beardsley and Kelly, 1999). Motor skills, reaction time, motor coordination and many forms of skilled psychomotor activity are impaired while the user is intoxicated (Jaffe, 1985; Beardsley and Kelly, 1999).

Some users report unpleasant experiences after using cannabis. These include anxiety, panic, a fear of going mad, and depression (Smith, 1968; Weil, 1970; Thomas, 1993). These are often reported by inexperienced users (Weil, 1970), including patients given oral THC for medical reasons (Institute of Medicine, 1999). More experienced users may report these effects after oral cannabis use because its effects may be more pronounced and of longer duration than they are used to after smoking. These effects can be prevented by preparation of users about the effects they may experience and they can be managed by reassurance and support (Smith, 1968; Weil, 1970). Psychotic symptoms, such as delusions and hallucinations, are very rare experiences that may occur at very high doses of THC, and perhaps in susceptible individuals at lower doses (Smith, 1968; Weil, 1970; Thomas, 1993) (see Chapter 10 below).

Physical effects

The most immediate effect of smoking cannabis is to increase heart rate by 20% to 50%. This occurs between a few minutes and a quarter of an hour after smoking cannabis (Huber et al., 1988; Chesher and Hall, 1999; Jones, 2002). Changes also occur in blood pressure that depend upon posture: blood pressure is increased while the person is sitting, and decreases while they are standing. A user who stands up after lying down may experience postural hypotension and a feeling of 'light-headedness' and faintness (Maykut, 1984). In healthy young users these cardiovascular effects are unlikely to be of any clinical significance (Chesher and Hall, 1999) although they may amplify anxiety if the cannabis-induced palpitations and faintness are misinterpreted as symptoms of serious misadventure.

Toxic dose levels

THC is the component of cannabis that has the highest toxicity in animals via its effects on neural systems. The cause of overdose death in animals is cessation of breathing or the heart stopping, if breathing is assisted (Rosenkrantz, 1983). Because tolerance develops, the toxic dose of THC depends upon the amount by which the dose exceeds the customary dose by a large margin (Compton et al., 1990). Laboratory studies in humans of daily dosing of high levels of THC over weeks have demonstrated tolerance to mood effects, tachycardia, decrease in skin temperature, increased body temperature, and impaired performance on psychomotor tests (Jones et al., 1976).

There are no reported cases of human deaths attributed to cannabis toxicity (Nahas, 1984; Iversen, 2000). With many drugs the toxic dose gets smaller as one moves from mice, rats, monkeys and dogs to humans. With THC, by contrast, humans appear to be much *less* susceptible to the acute toxicity of THC than animals. For example, the dose of THC which kills 50% of animals when administered intravenously is 40 mg/kg in the rat but it is 130 mg/kg in the dog and monkey (Rosenkrantz, 1983). Extrapolation from the animal studies suggests that the lethal human dose of THC is probably of the order of 4000 mg (Gable, 1993), a dose that would be difficult for recreational users to take.

Psychomotor effects

A major societal concern is that cannabis intoxication may impair the psychomotor performance of automobile drivers, increasing accidents among cannabis users who drive a car while intoxicated. Individuals who drive while intoxicated with alcohol are dangerous to others in proportion to their level of alcohol intoxication

(Chesher, 1995). It has been more difficult to decide whether the same is true of cannabis intoxication.

Effects on simulated driving and flying

In simulated driving, subjects use skills that are similar to those involved in driving a car under laboratory conditions designed to emulate the performance of a car. These simulations have two major advantages (Smiley, 1986): cannabis users can be tested after taking large doses of cannabis, and they can be placed in simulated emergency situations to test their level of impairment in ways that would be unethical to do on the road. The difficulty with simulator studies has been in achieving fidelity to on-road driving.

Smiley (1999) who critically reviewed research on the effects of cannabis on simulated driving has argued that the early studies which showed fewer effects than later studies suffered from unrealistic car dynamics. Later studies that used more realistic driving simulators have shown impairments of lane control after cannabis use. Some of the studies have also shown reductions in risk-taking as manifested in slower speeds, and maintenance of a larger distance from the car in front in following tasks (Smiley, 1999).

A number of studies have been done on the effects of cannabis on simulated flying. Janowsky et al. (1976) found increases in errors in keeping the plane at the proper altitude and heading during a simulated flight when pilots had taken cannabis. Yesavage et al. (1985) originally reported that a simulated flying task was impaired up to 24 hours after smoking cannabis but this study did not include a control group. A later study with a control group (Leirer et al., 1989) failed to find impairment more than 4 hours after smoking. A third study (Leirer et al., 1991) also failed to show impairments in performance up to 24 hours after smoking cannabis. Much has been made of the original findings (despite the failure to replicate them) but the effects were very small and of uncertain significance. Jones (1987) has argued that the use of cannabis by pilots 24 hours before flying is more an indicator of poor judgement than a predictor of residual psychomotor impairment.

Effects on driving a car

Studies on the effects of cannabis on driving cars around off-road courses have found that cannabis has modest effects by comparison with alcohol. An early study by Hansteen et al. (1976) showed that a dose of alcohol that produced a BAC of around 0.07 and THC (5.9 mg) produced similar impairment on a traffic-free course. Driving speed decreased after using cannabis but not alcohol. Smiley et al. (1975), using a different type of course, found that time to react to a signal increased after a combination of cannabis and alcohol. Klonoff (1974) studied driving on a closed course, and in city traffic, after a placebo and two doses of smoked cannabis (4.9 and 8.4 mg THC). Driving on the closed course was impaired by both doses. Driving in traffic, however, was not significantly affected. Sutton (1983) also found that cannabis had little effect on actual driving performance.

Peck et al. (1986) recorded performance on a range of driving tasks on a closed circuit on four occasions after the administration of placebo, up to 19 mg of smoked THC, 0.84 g/kg of alcohol, and the combination of both drugs. On most measures, cannabis impaired performance but the effects of cannabis were less than those of alcohol. A series of on-road studies by Robbe and colleagues (Robbe and O'Hanlon, 1993; Robbe, 1994) also found modest impairment of driving after using cannabis on a driving course without traffic, on a highway or in urban traffic. Drivers were aware of their intoxication after using cannabis and slowed down to minimise its impact on their driving (Robbe, 1994).

The effects of cannabis use on on-road driving have been smaller than those of alcohol (Smiley, 1999). Drivers have consistently slowed down after using cannabis (Smiley, 1999) whereas they increased their speed when intoxicated by alcohol. The compensatory behaviour after cannabis use may explain the small effects of cannabis intoxication in on-road studies. For ethical reasons on-road studies have not been able to test the response of cannabis-intoxicated drivers to emergency situations in which there may be less opportunity to compensate for impairment. The few studies which have simulated this situation (e.g. by measuring reaction to other tasks while driving) have shown that cannabis use impairs emergency decision-making (Smiley, 1986, 1999).

A recent study by Ramaekers, Robbe and O'Hanlon (2000) examined the effects on actual driving performance of combined doses of alcohol and cannabis. Their subjects were 8 males and 8 females aged 20 to 28 years who were weekly drinkers and monthly cannabis users. They assessed the effects on driving performance of six combinations of: placebo or alcohol that produced blood alcohol levels around the legal driving limit in Europe (0.04–0.05); and placebo cannabis (from which the THC had been removed) or cannabis that contained two doses of THC (100 μg/kg and 200 μg/kg). The six combinations were given in randomised order under double-blind conditions.

The subjects drove on public roads accompanied by instructors with dual controls to ensure that neither the subjects nor other drivers came to harm. Driving performance was assessed by the driver's capacity to maintain a steady lateral position and to follow a car at a fixed distance when it slowed or accelerated. Driving performance was also rated by the both the subject and the instructor who was blind as to which drugs the subject had received. Neither drug alone had an appreciable effect on lateral position or reaction time when following another car. The combination of alcohol and THC, however, significantly impaired performance and driving performance was rated as poorer by both subjects and the instructor

(Ramaekers et al., 2000). Ramaekers et al. rated the effects of the combined alcohol and THC on road tracking performance as 'severe', with the alcohol and 100 μg/kg dose of THC producing impairment equivalent to a BAC of 0.09 and the 200 μg/kg THC producing impairment equivalent to a BAC of 0.14.

Epidemiological studies of cannabis use and accident risk

Surveys have found that a substantial proportion and often the majority of cannabis users have driven after using cannabis, despite being aware of impairment (Klonoff, 1974; Walsh and Mann, 1999; Adlaf et al., 2003). But epidemiological studies of accident fatalities and injuries have not until recently shown that cannabis users are more likely to be involved in motor vehicle accidents. This differs from alcohol intoxication where case-control studies have shown that persons with blood alcohol levels indicating intoxication are over-represented among accident victims compared to drivers who are not involved in accidents (English et al., 1995). The lack of the evidence in the case of cannabis has reflected major difficulties in obtaining the necessary evidence to assess its role (Chesher, 1995).

There are a substantial number of studies reporting on the frequency with which cannabinoids are found in the blood of drivers in motor vehicle accidents (see McBay, 1986; Chesher, 1995 for reviews). Post-mortem studies of accident fatalities have found that between 4% and 39% of drivers have used cannabis, often in combination with intoxicating doses of alcohol (e.g. Cimbura et al., 1982; Mason and McBay, 1984; Williams et al., 1985). An Australian study of 1045 fatalities (Drummer, 1994, 1998) found cannabinoids in the blood of 11% of drivers, 35% of whom also had intoxicating doses of alcohol. Similar findings have been reported in Californian motorists tested on suspicion of impairment (Zimmerman et al., 1983) and in trauma patients (Soderstrom et al., 1988).

These findings have been difficult to evaluate. First, it is not clear that drivers with cannabinoids are over-represented among accident victims because we do not know how many drivers who have not been involved in accidents have cannabinoids in their blood (Terhune, 1986). Finding a rate of 35% of accident victims with cannabinoids in their blood may seem high but so is the rate of cannabis use among young males, the group who are most likely to be involved in motor vehicle accidents (Soderstrom et al., 1988). A recent survey of self-reported driving within an hour of using cannabis in Ontario, Canada, suggests that cannabis users are over-represented among those killed in motor vehicle crashes in that Canadian province. In this survey 1.9% of drivers reported driving within an hour of using cannabis, much lower than the 13.9% of road fatalities in Ontario in which THC was detected (Walsh and Mann, 1999).

The second difficulty is that the presence of THC or its metabolites in blood does not necessarily mean that a driver was intoxicated by cannabis at the time of an accident (National Institute on Drug Abuse, 1985; see Chapter 2 above). Third, it is also difficult to attribute an accident to cannabis when between one-third and two-thirds of drivers with cannabinoids in their blood also have high blood alcohol levels (McBay, 1986; Chesher, 1995).

'Culpability analysis' has been developed to address these issues (Terhune, 1986). In these analyses, a researcher decides which driver was 'culpable' for an accident using information about the circumstances of the fatal crash that excludes information on their alcohol and drug use. Drivers with no alcohol or other drugs in their blood are used as the control group to see whether the use of cannabis and other drugs increases driver culpability. The problem with these analyses is that the culpability of drug-free drivers is often high, which reduces the ability of the method to detect any increase in culpability among drivers with cannabis and other drugs in their blood.

Most culpability analyses have shown increased culpability among drivers with intoxicating levels of alcohol in their blood (Chesher, 1995). Drivers who have only had cannabis in their blood have been in the minority because most also have intoxicating doses of alcohol (Simpson, 1986; Chesher, 1995). There has been no evidence of an additive effect of alcohol and cannabis in these analyses, despite laboratory studies suggesting that the impairments produced by alcohol and cannabis are additive (Chesher, 1995). These findings have been replicated in two recent Australian studies that used culpability analysis to examine the role of cannabis in fatal (Drew et al., 1972) and non-fatal motor accidents (Longo et al., 2000). There was a strong relationship between alcohol level and culpability in each study but neither study found any relationship between THC and culpability.

Bates and Blakely (1999) have reported a meta-analysis of culpability analyses of the contribution of cannabis and alcohol to motor vehicle accidents. They estimate from three studies of fatal accidents that cannabis alone significantly reduced culpability for an accident by comparison with drug-free drivers (OR = 0.59). The combination of alcohol and cannabis increased culpability but they were unable to decide whether cannabis increased culpability over that of alcohol alone because the culpability rate among drivers with alcohol only in their blood was so high.

A number of other epidemiological studies have found an association between cannabis use and accidents (Andreasson and Allebeck, 1990; Polen et al., 1993). Andreasson and Allebeck who studied mortality over 15 years among 50,465 Swedish military conscripts found that men who had smoked cannabis 50 or more times by age 18 had a higher risk of premature death (RR = 4.6). Motor vehicle accidents accounted for 26% of these deaths. The increased risk was no longer significant after statistical adjustment for antisocial behaviour and alcohol and other drug use in adolescence (Andreasson and Allebeck, 1990).

Polen et al. (1993) compared health service use by 450 people who did not use cannabis and 450 persons who smoked cannabis daily. They were selected from people who were screened by Kaiser Permanente Medical Centers between July 1979 and December 1985. Cannabis-only smokers had an increased use of medical care for accidental injury during two years of follow-up. Sidney et al. (1997a) reported deaths rates after 10 years among 65,171 members of the Kaiser Permanente Medical Care Program aged between 15 and 49. The sample comprised 38% who had never used cannabis, 20% who had used less than 6 times, 20% who were former users, and 22% who were current users. Regular cannabis users had an increased rate of death (RR = 1.33) but this was explained by AIDS-related deaths in men, probably because cannabis use was correlated with male homosexual behaviour in this cohort.

Gerberich et al. (2003) analysed the relationship between self-reported cannabis use and hospitalisation for accidental injury in the same cohort of 64,657 HMO members. They found that current cannabis users had higher rates of all-cause injury, self-inflicted injury, motor vehicle accidents and assaults than former cannabis users or non-users, in both men and women. These relationships persisted for all-cause injury after controlling for other variables including alcohol and tobacco use among both men (RR = 1.28) and women (RR = 1.37). The relationships for motor vehicle accidents (RR = 1.96) and assault (RR = 1.90) persisted after statistical adjustment among men but not among women, reflecting much lower rates of both cannabis use and accidents in women than men in the cohort.

Mura et al. (2003) have recently reported the first case-control study of the relationship between THC and its metabolites in the serum of 900 persons hospitalised for injuries sustained in motor vehicle accidents and 900 controls of the same age and sex admitted to the same hospitals for reasons other than trauma. The study participants were admitted to six French hospitals in Grenoble, Le Havre, Limoges, Lyon, Poitiers and Strasbourg between June 2000 and September 2001. Drivers were deemed to be positive for recent cannabis use if the THC blood concentration was greater than 1 ng/ml at the time of testing (an average of 1.8 hours after admission). The proportion found with THC by this definition was higher in cases (10%) than controls (5%) (OR = 2.5). The highest proportion of cases with THC was found among those under the age of 27 years. They did not statistically adjust for blood alcohol level in these analyses but did report that in 60% of their cases THC was found alone. THC was associated with alcohol in 32% of cases.

Epidemiological data on self-reported accidents

There is evidence from surveys that suggests that cannabis use may increase the risk of accidents. Two surveys of self-reported accidents among adolescent drug users found a relationship between self-reported cannabis use and involvement in accidents. Cannabis smokers were approximately twice as likely to report being involved in accidents than non-marijuana smokers (Smart and Fejer, 1976; Hingson et al., 1982b).

A recent study from the Christchurch Child Development Study (Fergusson and Horwood, 2001) has examined the relationship between self-reported cannabis use and motor vehicle accidents in a large birth cohort while controlling for other characteristics of cannabis users that predicted an increased risk of accident. Fergusson and Horwood found that those who had used cannabis 50 or more times in a year between the ages of 18 and 21 years had a rate of accidents that was 1.6 times higher than those who had not used cannabis. This was only true for 'active' accidents, those in which the individual was independently judged (on the basis of a narrative description of the accident) to have some responsibility for the accident. It was not true of accidents that were caused by the actions of another driver or an animal. However, the relationship disappeared when Fergusson and Horwood statistically controlled for the fact that heavier cannabis users were more likely to drink and drive. They concluded that 'much of the elevated traffic accident risk amongst cannabis users is likely to be more due to the characteristics of those who use cannabis than to the effects of cannabis use on driver performance' (p. 710).

Summary

The most common adverse acute effects of cannabis use are anxiety and distressing experiences that occur in a substantial minority of cannabis users. No fatal overdoses have been reported in the medical literature and are unlikely to occur. Cannabis adversely affects the performance of a number of psychomotor tasks in ways that are related to dose and task difficulty. Cannabis has smaller effects than alcohol on psychomotor performance in driving simulator tasks probably because cannabis users are more aware of their impairment and engage in less risky behaviour than persons intoxicated by alcohol. It has been difficult until recently for technical and ethical reasons to determine whether the impairment produced by cannabis increases the risk of motor vehicle accidents among users. There is now reasonable evidence from a large longitudinal study and a case-control study of cannabinoids in the blood of hospitalised motor vehicle accident victims that driving after using cannabis doubles the risk of motor vehicle accidents. Cannabis use is especially likely to increase the risk of an accident when it is used with alcohol.

5

The cellular, immunological and reproductive effects of chronic cannabis use

This chapter reviews the evidence on the effects of chronic cannabis use on three aspects of users' health. It begins with a review of the effects of cannabis use on cellular function. This focuses on the capacity of cannabis to produce mutations in body and germ cells that may produce cancers. The second section reviews evidence on the effects of chronic cannabis use on the immune system. The third section considers the possible effects of chronic cannabis use on users' reproductive systems. This is an important issue because cannabis is most heavily used by young adults during their early reproductive years and a substantial minority of women use cannabis during their pregnancies.

Mutagenicity and carcinogenicity

If THC or other cannabinoids produce mutations in the genetic material of a user's somatic or body cells (such as those of the lung) then chronic cannabis use could be a cause of cancer. If it produces changes in the genetic material of germ cells (the sperm and ova), then genetic mutations could be transmitted to the children of cannabis users. Studies of animal cells suggest that THC can produce changes in cellular processes in the test tube, including cell metabolism, DNA synthesis, and cell division (Nahas, 1984). The effect of these changes, however, seems to be to stop cell division rather than to produce cellular changes that lead to cancer (MacPhee, 1999).

There is no evidence that THC and other cannabinoids are mutagenic in microbial assays, such as the Ames test (MacPhee, 1999). There is contradictory evidence on whether THC can produce breaks in chromosomes (Marselos and Karamanakos, 1999). MacPhee (1999) has argued that even if the cannabinoids do produce chromosomal abnormalities these are more likely to lead to death of the affected cell than to its malignant transformation. A recent study of carcinogenicity in rats and mice found no evidence that THC was carcinogenic (Chan et al., 1996).

There is more consistent evidence that cannabis *smoke*, like the smoke produced by burning tobacco, is mutagenic *in vitro*, and hence, is a potential carcinogen (Leuchtenberger, 1983; Marselos and Karamanakos, 1999). Cannabis smoke causes chromosomal aberrations, it is mutagenic in the Ames test, and it produces cancers in the mouse skin test assay of carcinogenicity (MacPhee, 1999). The laboratory evidence on the mutagenicity and carcinogenicity of cannabis smoke is consistent with evidence that it contains many of the same carcinogens as cigarette smoke (Leuchtenberger, 1983).

Because it is cannabis smoke rather than pure cannabinoids that may be carcinogenic (Bloch, 1983) cannabis smoking is most likely to cause cancers in the body sites that receive the heaviest term exposure to cannabis smoke, namely, the upper aerodigestive tract (mouth, tongue, oesophagus) and lung (MacPhee, 1999).

Cancers of the aerodigestive tract

As already noted, there are good reasons for suspecting that cannabis may cause lung cancer and cancers of the aerodigestive tract (the oropharynx, nasal and sinus epithelium, and the larynx). One is the similarity between the carcinogens found in cannabis and tobacco smoke which is an accepted cause of cancers in these organs (Doll and Peto, 1980; International Agency on Cancer, 1990). The major difference between tobacco and cannabis smoke is the presence of cannabinoids in cannabis smoke and nicotine in tobacco. There are also some differences in the amount of various carcinogens among their individual constituents, with cannabis smoke typically containing higher levels than tobacco smoke (Leuchtenberger, 1983).

Second, Fligiel et al. (1988) reported that the same histopathological changes that are believed to be precursors of lung carcinoma can be observed in the lungs of chronic cannabis smokers. These results confirmed the earlier finding of Tennant (1980; 1983) who performed bronchoscopies on 30 US servicemen stationed in Europe who had smoked large quantities of hashish and experienced symptoms of bronchitis. Recently, Barsky et al. (1998) have reported mutagenic changes in lung tissue of cannabis smokers of the same type found in tobacco smokers.

Third, these studies have recently been supported by case reports of cancers of the upper aerodigestive tract in young adults who have been chronic cannabis smokers. Donald (1991) reported 13 cases of advanced head and neck cancer occurring in young adults under 40 years of age. Eleven of the 13 had been daily cannabis smokers. At least five also smoked tobacco, and at least three were heavy alcohol consumers, both known risk factors for cancers of the upper aerodigestive tract (Vokes et al., 1993; English et al., 1995). Similar findings have been reported by Taylor (1988) in a retrospective series of 10 upper respiratory tract cancers occurring in adults under the age of 40 years over a four-year period. Caplan and Brigham reported two cases of squamous cell carcinoma of the tongue in men aged 37 and 52 years (Caplan and Brigham, 1990). Since 1986 there have been a total of 74 such cases reported in the medical literature (Zhang et al., 1999).

Case reports provide limited support for the hypothesis that cannabis use is a cause of upper respiratory tract cancers. There are no controls and cannabis exposure has not been assessed in a standardised way in ignorance of the case or control status. These are all standard design features to minimise bias in case-control studies of cancer.

Two epidemiological studies have recently been reported on the association between cannabis smoking and cancers. Sidney et al. (1997b) reported a study of cancer incidence in an 8.6-year follow-up of a cohort of 64,855 members of the Kaiser Permanente Medical Care Program (KPMCP) who answered questions about cannabis use in a multiphasic screening study between 1979 and 1985. Their age at entry was 33 years and they were followed until death, diagnosis of cancer or HIV/AIDS, exit from the KPMCP or 31 December 1993 (a mean of 8.6 years). Data was collected from a cancer registry and California mortality data collection. The prevalence of cannabis use was: 38% never users, 20% experimenters (used less than 6 times), 20% past users, and 22% current users.

There was no overall excess of cancer incidence among those in the cohort who had ever used cannabis or who were current users compared to non-users. Tobacco smokers had a higher risk of tobacco-related cancers (regardless of cannabis use) but cannabis smokers did not. Males who had ever smoked cannabis had a higher risk of prostate cancer (RR = 3.1) and so did males who were current cannabis smokers (RR = 4.7). There was a borderline association between cannabis use and cervical cancer among women (RR = 1.4) (Sidney et al., 1997b).

Zhang et al. (1999) recently compared rates of cannabis use among 173 cases of primary squamous cell carcinoma of the head and neck and 176 controls. The cases were seen at the Memorial-Sloan Kettering Hospital in 1992–1994 and the controls were age- and sex-matched cancer-free blood donors at the same hospital. Cases were more likely to have used cannabis than controls (14% and 10% respectively). The odds ratio was 2.6 after adjustment for cigarette smoking, alcohol use and a number of other known risk factors. There was also a dose–response relationship between frequency and duration of cannabis use and the relationship was stronger among adults under the age of 55 years (OR 3.1). The authors considered and rejected the possibility that selection bias may have over-estimated the strength of the association by showing that cases reported a prevalence of cannabis use that did not differ from that in the population.

The positive result of the Zhang et al. study is more convincing than the negative result of Sidney et al. on cancers of the aerodigestive tract for two reasons. First, the Sidney et al. cohort was too young (average age of 43 at follow-up) to see many excess cases of cancer attributable to cannabis smoking. Second, although it did find an increased cancer incidence among tobacco smokers the chances of finding cancers attributable to cannabis smoking were reduced by the low rates of heavy cannabis use. Only 22% of the sample reported regular cannabis use at intake and this meant having used cannabis six or more times. We know that many if not most of these users would have discontinued their cannabis use between recruitment and follow-up (Bachman et al., 1997). Subsequent follow-ups of this cohort and larger and well designed case-control studies will provide better evidence on the relationship between cannabis smoking and cancer risk.

Childhood cancers

Three case-control studies have suggested that cannabis use during pregnancy is associated with an increased risk of cancer in children born to these mothers. This association was first reported in a case-control study of acute nonlymphoblastic leukemia (ANLL), a rare form of childhood cancer. The study was not designed to test hypotheses about a relationship between cannabis use and ANLL. Instead, it was designed to examine the association between this childhood cancer and maternal and paternal exposures to petrochemicals, pesticides and radiation. Maternal drug use, including marijuana use, before and during pregnancy, was assessed as possible covariates to be statistically controlled in any relationships between ANLL and other exposures.

Unexpectedly, the mothers of children with ANLL were 11 times more likely to have used cannabis before and during their pregnancy than were the mothers of controls. The relationship persisted after statistical adjustment for other risk factors. Comparisons of cases whose mothers did and did not use cannabis during their pregnancies showed that cases with cannabis exposure were younger, and had a higher frequency of specific ANLL cell types than did the cases without such exposure. Reporting bias on the part of the mothers of cases is an alternative explanation of the finding because reports of cannabis use were obtained after the diagnosis of ANLL. If the mothers of affected children were more likely to seek an explanation in their behaviour during their pregnancies they may have made them more likely to report cannabis use than mothers of controls. The rates of cannabis use among controls were much lower than the rates in case-control studies of other childhood cancers but even when the rate of cannabis use was adjusted upwards the odds ratio was still greater than 3 and statistically significant. Nonetheless, since this was an unexpected finding which emerged from a large number of exploratory analyses conducted in a single study it needs to be replicated.

There are two other case-control studies that report an increased risk of rhabdomyosarcoma (Grufferman et al., 1993) and astrocytomas (Kuijten et al., 1992) in children born to women who reported using cannabis during their pregnancies. Neither of these studies was a planned investigation of the association between these childhood cancers and maternal cannabis use. In each case, cannabis use was one of a large number of possible confounding variables that were measured for purposes of statistical control. Their replication is a research priority.

There is no suggestion that the incidence of any of these cancers has increased over the period 1979–1995 that could be accounted for by maternal cannabis use during pregnancy (Hall and MacPhee, 2002). The incidence of ANLL, for example, has not increased during this period (Smith et al., 2000). It has remained steady. The same has been true for soft-tissue sarcomas (which include rhabdomyo-sarcomas) (Gurney et al., 2000b). The incidence of CNS malignancies (about 52% of which are astrocytomas) did increase between 1979 and 1995 (Gurney et al., 2000a) but this is unlikely to reflect maternal cannabis use. Incidence was steady between 1979 and 1985 when it abruptly increased and remained more or less steady thereafter (Gurney et al., 2000a). Since 1985 was the year in which magnetic resonance imaging became widely available in the USA the increase is most likely to be the result of improved diagnosis rather than an increase in incidence (Gurney et al., 2000a).

Immunological effects

The possibility that cannabis reduces immune system function is important for several reasons. First, CB_2 cannabinoid receptors are present in the immune system, indicating that THC and other cannabinoids may act on the immune system (Roth et al., 2002). Second, tobacco smoking suppresses immunity so it is a reasonable hypothesis that cannabis smoke may also do so (Nahas, 1984). Third, a reduction in immunity caused by cannabis use could have public health significance because large numbers of young adults use the drug (Munson and Fehr, 1983). Fourth, if cannabinoids have immunosuppressive effects then this may limit their therapeutic use in patients with impaired immune systems.

There have been a number of difficulties in deciding whether cannabis impairs the functioning of the immune system. First, in the majority of studies to date animal and human cell cultures have been exposed to cannabis smoke or cannabinoids, and the effects of cannabis and cannabinoids on immune system function have been assessed in whole animals. Second, there have been very few epidemiological studies of immune system functioning and disease susceptibility in chronic cannabis users to assess how serious these immunological risks may be in human cannabis users (Cabral and Pettit, 1998; Klein et al., 2001; Roth et al., 2002).

Effects of cannabinoids on humoral immunity

The effect of cannabinoids on humoral immunity has been assessed *in vitro* by measuring their effect on the number and functioning of animal and human

B-cell response to sheep red blood cells. Cannabinoids do not consistently alter humoral immunity assessed in this way (Munson and Fehr, 1983).

B-cell function has also been assessed *in vitro* by measuring the proliferation of B-cells in response to chemicals which stimulate these cells to divide, and by assessing antibody production in B-cells that have been exposed to cannabinoids. While cannabinoids consistently impair B-cell responses in mice, no such effects have been consistently observed in humans, and the positive studies have produced results that are within the normal range (Munson and Fehr, 1983).

Antibody formation to THC has been demonstrated in animals. There are also clinical reports in humans that cannabinoids can exacerbate existing allergies, and there are several reports of allergy to cannabinoids in humans (Klein et al., 2001). Hollister (1992), however, has questioned the clinical significance of this evidence, arguing that: 'it is far more likely that allergic reactions, which have been extremely rare following the use of marijuana, are due to contaminants (e.g. bacteria, fungi, molds, parasites, worms, chemical)' (p. 163).

Effects of cannabinoids on cell-mediated immunity

Researchers have examined the effects of cannabinoids on both the numbers and functioning of T-cells and macrophages. The results have been inconsistent with some studies showing reductions (Nahas, 1984) while others have not (Dax et al., 1989). There is also mixed evidence on the effect of cannabinoids on T-cell functioning as assessed by response to chemicals which stimulate these cells to divide. *In vitro* exposure of T-cells to cannabinoids has also produced mixed results while animal studies have showed a decreased T-cell response (Munson and Fehr, 1983).

Hollister (1992) has concluded that the effects of cannabinoids on cell-mediated immunity 'usually involved doses and concentrations that are orders of magnitude greater than those obtained when marijuana is used by human subjects' (p. 161). Klein (1999), who reviewed the literature published during the 1990s, agreed, concluding that while almost 'every function examined, from antibody production to phagocytosis, is affected in some way by the drug, especially when *in vitro* models are employed ... for the most part, relatively high drug concentrations are required' (p. 363), the immune effects are not related to the doses that cause psychoactive effects in human users, and the effects are reversible.

Effects of cannabinoids on host resistance

A number of studies in rodents (mice and guinea pigs) have suggested that high doses (200 mg/kg) of cannabinoids decrease resistance to infection, e.g. with *Lysteria monocytogenes* (Morahan et al., 1979), and *herpes simplex type 2* virus (Morahan et al., 1979; Mishkin and Cabral, 1985; Cabral et al., 1986; Cabral and Pettit, 1998).

A consistent finding in humans has been that exposure to cannabis *smoke* adversely affects alveolar macrophages, cells in the respiratory system that are the body's first line of defence against many micro-organisms that enter the body via the lungs (Leuchtenberger, 1983). Early studies of these cells obtained from cannabis smokers have demonstrated abnormalities (Tennant, 1980). Studies exposing alveolar macrophages to cannabis smoke in the test tube have demonstrated that their ability to inactivate *Staphylococcus aureus* (Leuchtenberger, 1983; Munson and Fehr, 1983) and the fungus *Candida albicans* (Sherman et al., 1991) has been impaired. However, it is the noncannabinoid components of cannabis smoke that produce the effect (Leuchtenberger, 1983; Klein et al., 1998). The doses required to produce these effects have often been very high, raising doubts about whether these findings can be applied to human users (Klein et al., 2001).

The possibility of tolerance developing to the immunological effects of cannabinoids also creates uncertainty about the human implication of animal and *in vitro* studies. If immunological tolerance develops with chronic use, then the small effects projected from the animal studies would be substantially reduced in humans. Given that tolerance develops to other cannabinoid effects it would not be surprising that this was also true of their immunological effects.

The clinical significance of these immunological impairments in chronic cannabis users is uncertain because there have been too few human studies. Three field studies of chronic cannabis users in Costa Rica (Carter, 1980), Greece (Stefanis et al., 1977), and Jamaica (Rubin and Comitas, 1975), failed to find any evidence of increased susceptibility to infectious diseases. But these negative findings were based on less than 100 users which is too few to detect a small increase in the incidence of common infectious and bacterial diseases. Large-scale epidemiological studies are needed to exclude the latter possibility.

One epidemiological study has been reported by Polen et al. (1993) who compared health service utilisation in nonsmokers and daily cannabis smokers who were enrolled in a health maintenance organisation. They found increased presentations for respiratory conditions among cannabis-only smokers but its significance remains uncertain because infectious and non-infectious conditions were not distinguished. Further studies like this are needed to enable a more informed decision to be made about the risk that chronic heavy cannabis smoking poses to the immune system.

Klein (1999) concluded that the public health significance of cannabinoid immunomodulation was 'still unclear' because there were too few experimental or epidemiological studies of the effects of cannabis exposure on host resistance to bacteria, viruses and tumours and the studies that have been done have used high doses of cannabinoid that have limited applicability to human cannabis use.

Effects of cannabis on immunity in immunocompromised persons

Studies of the effects of cannabinoids on patients with immune systems compromised by AIDS may provide one way of detecting any immunological effects of cannabinoids. AIDS patients and advocacy groups have proposed that cannabinoids should be used to improve appetite and well-being in AIDS patients (see Chapter 13). Monitoring the impact of cananbis use on immune functioning in such patients provides one way of assessing the immunological effects of cannabinoids. If there were no effects in patients with compromised immune systems it would be reasonable to infer that there was little risk of immunological effects in healthy users.

Several epidemiological studies have examined the effects of self-reported cannabis use on progression to AIDS among HIV-positive homosexual men. Kaslow et al. (1989) reported a prospective study of progression to AIDS among 4954 HIV-positive homosexual and bisexual men. Cannabis use did not predict increased progression to AIDS and it was not related to changes in immunological functioning. There was also no relationship between marijuana use and progression to AIDS in HIV-seropositive men in the San Francisco Men's Health Study (N = 451) over 6 years (DiFranco et al., 1996).

There was an increased risk of progression to AIDS among cannabis users in the Sydney AIDS Project (Tindall et al., 1988). In this study 386 homosexual men were followed for over 12 months to see what predicted progression to AIDS. The Institute of Medicine (1999) has described this finding as 'less reliable' than those of Kaslow et al. and DiFranco et al. because the study had a short follow-up period and the way that AIDS was defined probably meant that many of their 'HIV positive cases' already had AIDS.

A study of mortality among a cohort of HMO patients (Sidney et al., 1997a) did find an association between cannabis use and death from AIDS. This finding, however, has been attributed to confounding of cannabis use and sexual preference (which was not assessed in the study). Unmarried men had much higher rates of marijuana use than married men so the authors argued that cannabis use was a marker for high-risk sexual behaviour rather than an independent risk factor.

Reproductive effects of cannabis

Cannabis is widely used by adolescents and young adults during the peak age for reproduction. Animal studies in the mid-1970s raised concerns about the possibility that cannabis use during the period of sexual maturation might adversely affect reproductive outcomes. These studies indicated that large doses of THC reduced the secretion of gonadal hormones in both sexes (Brown and Dobs, 2002) and adversely affected foetal development when cannabis extract or THC was administered during pregnancy (Bloch, 1983; Nahas, 1984). These concerns seemed confirmed by case reports of breast development (gynaecomastia) in young men aged 23 to 26 years of age, all of whom had a history of heavy cannabis use (Harmon and Aliapoulios, 1972) and by a report that males who were chronic cannabis users had lower plasma testosterone, a lower sperm count and motility, and abnormalities in sperm (Kolodny et al., 1974). These reports raised concerns that fertility would be impaired in men, and unfavourable pregnancy outcomes would occur in women who used cannabis, such as: foetal loss, low birth weight, and an increased risk of birth defects and perinatal death.

Effects on the male reproductive system

In animals, marijuana, crude marijuana extracts, THC and some purified cannabinoids depress the male reproductive endocrine system (Bloch, 1983; Brown and Dobs, 2002) If used chronically, cannabis reduces plasma testosterone levels, retards sperm maturation, reduces the sperm count and sperm motility, and increases the rate of abnormal sperm (Bloch, 1983; Murphy, 1999). Although the mechanisms for these effects are unclear they probably occur directly from the action of THC on the testis, and indirectly via its effects on the hypothalamic secretion of the hormones that stimulate the testis to produce testosterone (Brown and Dobs, 2002).

. Studies on the effects of cannabis on human male reproductive function have produced mixed results (Brown and Dobs, 2002). An early study by Kolodny et al. (1974) which reported reduced testosterone, sperm production, and sperm motility and increased abnormalities in sperm was not replicated in later studies (Brown and Dobs, 2002). This included a larger, well-controlled study of chronic heavy users which failed to find any difference in plasma testosterone at study entry, or after three weeks of heavy daily cannabis use (Mendelson et al., 1974). Other studies have produced both positive and negative evidence of an effect of cannabinoids on testosterone for reasons that are not well understood (Brown and Dobs, 2002). If there are effects of cannabis on male reproductive functioning, their clinical significance in humans is uncertain because testosterone levels have generally remained within the normal range even in the studies which have found effects (Hollister, 1986).

The hypothesised relationship between cannabis use and gynaecomastia also seems unlikely (Brown and Dobs, 2002). The reductions in testosterone in the positive studies were too small to produce gynaecomastia among heavy male cannabis smokers (Harmon and Aliapoulios, 1972). A small case-control study failed to find any relationship between cannabis use and gynaecomastia in 11 cases and controls (Cates and Pope, 1977). Studies in humans and animals have not shown any increase in secretion of the hormone prolactin, the most likely mechanism to produce such effects. As Mendelson et al. (1984) have argued, if chronic cannabis use caused gynaecomastia, one would expect to have seen many more cases in the clinical literature as a result of the widespread use of cannabis by young males during the past few decades.

Effects on the female reproductive system

The experimental animal studies suggest that cannabis and THC interferes with the hypothalamic–pituitary–gonadal axis in female rats (Bloch, 1983; Brown and Dobs, 2002). Chronic cannabis exposure also delays oestrus and ovulation (Murphy, 1999).

There have been very few human studies of the effects of cannabis on the female reproductive system because of fears that cannabis use may produce birth defects in women of childbearing age who would be the subjects in such experiments (Rosenkrantz, 1985). Two studies have been reported with conflicting results. In an unpublished study Bauman (1980 cited by Nahas, 1984) compared the menstrual cycles of 26 cannabis smokers with those of 17 controls and found a higher rate of anovulatory cycles among the cannabis users. Mendelson and Mello (1984) observed hormonal levels in a group of female cannabis users (all of whom had undergone a tubal ligation) under controlled laboratory conditions. They failed to find any evidence that chronic cannabis use affected sex hormones or the duration of the cycle.

Foetal development and birth defects

THC crosses the placenta in animals (Bloch, 1983) and humans (Blackard and Tennes, 1984) so it is possible that cannabis use during pregnancy may cause birth defects if THC, and other cannabinoids, interfere with the normal development of the foetus, i.e. are teratogenic. The animal evidence indicates that in high doses cannabis can produce resorption, growth retardation, and malformations in mice, rats, rabbits, and hamsters (Bloch, 1983). Resorption and growth retardation have been more consistently reported than birth malformations (Abel, 1985) and the doses that produce malformations have been very high (Abel, 1985). Birth malformations have been observed more often after the administration of crude marijuana extract rather than THC, suggesting that other cannabinoids may produce any teratogenic effects. Bloch (1983) concluded that THC was unlikely to be teratogenic in humans because 'the few reports of teratogenicity in rodents and rabbits indicate that cannabinoids are, at most, weakly teratogenic in these species' (p. 416).

Human studies

Epidemiological studies of the effects of cannabis use on human development have produced mixed results for a number of reasons. First, adverse reproductive outcomes and heavy cannabis use during pregnancy are relatively rare. Hence, unless cannabis use produces a large increase in the risk of abnormalities, very large sample sizes will be required to detect adverse effects of cannabis use on foetal development (Fried and Smith, 2001). Many of the studies that have been conducted have been too small to detect effects of this size (e.g. Fried, 1980; Greenland et al., 1982).

Second, there are difficulties in identifying cannabis users among pregnant women. The stigma of admitting to using drugs during pregnancy may encourage under-reporting, This is compounded by women forgetting about their drug use during early pregnancy when asked about drug use late in pregnancy or after the birth (Day et al., 1985). If a substantial proportion of cannabis users are misclassified as non-users, any relationship between cannabis use and adverse outcomes will be attenuated (Zuckerman, 1985).

Third, even with large sample sizes, there are difficulties in interpreting associations found between adverse pregnancy outcomes and cannabis use. This is because cannabis users are more likely to have adverse pregnancy outcomes for other reasons e.g. they are more likely to use tobacco, alcohol and other illicit drugs during their pregnancy (Eyler and Behnke, 1999), are less likely to seek antenatal care, and have poorer nutrition than women who do not use cannabis (Fried, 1980; Tennes et al., 1985). These differences make it difficult to attribute any relationship between reproductive outcomes and cannabis use to cannabis use *per se*. Sophisticated forms of statistical methods are needed to separate the effects of cannabis from these confounding risks.

Despite these difficulties, it has been generally (but not always) reported that cannabis use in pregnancy is associated with reduced birth weight (Gibson et al., 1983; Hatch and Bracken, 1986; Zuckerman et al., 1989; Fergusson et al., 2002). This relationship has been found in the best controlled studies, and it has persisted after statistically controlling for potential confounding variables (e.g. Hatch and Bracken, 1986; Zuckerman et al., 1989; Fergusson et al., 2002). A recent meta-analysis of these studies (English et al., 1997) has found that regular cannabis smoking during pregnancy produces a small decrease in birthweight. The effect is smaller than that caused by tobacco smoking during pregnancy, a finding confirmed in one of the largest of these studies of 12,000 British women (Fergusson et al., 2002).

There has been no consistent relationship between cannabis use and birth abnormalities. There was an early report that children born to women who had smoked cannabis during pregnancy (who had *not* used alcohol) had features similar to the foetal alcohol syndrome (e.g. Milman, 1982, p. 42). Epidemiological studies since then, however, have not generally found an increase in congenital abnormalities among children born to women who used cannabis during pregnancy (Hingson et al., 1982a; Gibson et al., 1983; Tennes et al., 1985; Zuckerman et al., 1989). One study reported a five-fold increased risk of children with foetal alcohol-like features being born to women who reported using cannabis (Hingson et al., 1982a). The significance of this finding is uncertain because there was *no* relationship between self-reported alcohol use and 'foetal alcohol syndrome' features. An additional study reported a small increase in the rate of birth abnormalities among children born to women who reported using cannabis but this result was no longer statistically significant after adjustment for confounders (Linn et al., 1983).

Zuckerman et al. report the most convincing failure to find an increased risk of birth defects among women who used cannabis during pregnancy. They studied a large sample of women among whom there was a substantial rate of cannabis use that was verified by urinalysis. There was a low rate of birth abnormalities among the cannabis users, and no suggestion of an increase by comparison with the controls.

Post-natal development

Cannabis use during pregnancy could possibly affect the post-natal development of the child by exposing the developing embryo's brain to cannabinoids *in utero*. A small number of animal studies have provided suggestive evidence of such effects. The most extensive research evidence in humans comes from the Ontario Prospective Prenatal Study which studied developmental and behavioural abnormalities in children born to women who reported using cannabis during pregnancy (Fried, 1980, 1985, 1991, 1996; Hutchings and Fried, 1999; Fried and Watkinson, 2000; Fried and Smith, 2001).

In this study, mothers were asked about their drug use during pregnancy and their children were measured on the Brazelton scales after birth. They were neurologically assessed at one month, and assessed again by standardised scales of ability at six and twelve months. The results indicated that there was some developmental delay shortly after birth in the infants' visual system, and there was also an increased rate of tremors and startle among the children of cannabis users (Fried and Smith, 2001). The behavioural effects discernible after birth had faded by one month, and no effects were detectable in performance on standardised ability tests at six and twelve months.

Effects attributed to cannabis use were subsequently reported at 36 and 48 months (Fried and Watkinson, 1990) but these were not detectable at 60 and 72 months (Fried et al., 1992). These results are suggestive of a subtle developmental impairment occurring among children who had experienced a shorter gestation and prematurity (Fried and Smith, 2001). There is a possibility that the tests used in later follow-ups are insufficiently sensitive to the subtle effects of prenatal cannabis exposure, although they did detect the effects of maternal tobacco smoking during pregnancy on behavioural development at 60 and 72 months (Fried and Watkinson, 1990; Fried et al., 1992). The cohort has now been followed up to age 9 to 12 years. No differences were found between children who were and were not exposed to cannabis during pregnancy on full scale IQ score but there were differences in measures of perceptual organisation and higher cognitive processes (Fried and Smith, 2001).

Attempts to replicate the OPPS findings have been mixed. Tennes et al. (1985) studied the relationship between cannabis use during pregnancy and postnatal development in 756 women, a third of whom reported using cannabis during pregnancy. The children were assessed shortly after birth using the same measurement instruments as Fried (1980), and a subset were assessed at one year of age. There was no evidence of impaired development of the visual system, and no increased risk of tremor or startle among the children of users. There was also no evidence of any differences at one year.

Day et al. (1994) have followed up children at age 3 born to 655 teenage women in Pittsburgh between 1990 and 1995. The women were questioned about their substance use throughout their pregnancy. Day et al. found a relationship between the mothers' cannabis use during pregnancy and the children's performances on memory and verbal scales of the Stanford–Binet Intelligence Scale at age 3. Further follow-ups of these children have been reported at age 6 and 10 (Goldschmidt et al., 2000; Cornelius et al., 2002). At age 6 prenatal cannabis use was associated with reduced height, after controlling for alcohol and tobacco use and other predictors of impaired growth (Cornelius et al., 2002). By age 10, antenatal cannabis use was associated with increased delinquency and problem behaviour, as rated by both the mother and a teacher. This seemed to be mediated by the effects of maternal cannabis use on inattentiveness in the child (Goldschmidt et al., 2000).

Summary

There is reasonable evidence that *cannabis smoke* contains many of the same mutagenic and carcinogenic substances as tobacco smoke. THC does not appear to be mutagenic or carcinogenic. The major forms of cancer that may be caused by cannabis smoking are cancers of the aerodigestive and respiratory tracts. There are case histories of upper respiratory tract cancers in cannabis smokers that are supported by one case-control study but not by a large prospective cohort study. Case-control studies have found associations between maternal cannabis smoking and three childhood cancers but these findings have not been supported by any changes in the incidence of these cancers over the period 1979–1995.

There is animal evidence that THC can impair the cell-mediated and humoral immune systems and decrease resistance to infection. The relevance of these findings to human health is uncertain because the doses that produce these effects in animals are very high, and tolerance may develop to these effects in human users.

There is mixed evidence on the effects of cannabis on the human immune system. The small number of studies that have produced adverse effects have not been replicated and the reported changes have been small and within the normal range. The clinical and biological significance of the small effects in chronic cannabis users remains to be determined by well-designed epidemiological studies.

Any immunological effects of cannabis may be most easily detected in users who are immunocompromised. Two of three prospective studies of HIV-positive homosexual men indicated that continued cannabis use did *not* find any increased progression to AIDS. A recent epidemiological study that compared health service utilisation by nonsmokers and daily cannabis-only smokers provided suggestive evidence of increased medical care for respiratory conditions among cannabis smokers.

High doses of THC disrupt the male and female reproductive systems in animals. It is uncertain whether these effects also occur in humans because high doses of THC were used in animal studies. Studies in human males have produced inconsistent results and there have been no well-designed studies in human females. If cannabinoids have such effects in humans, their clinical significance in normal healthy young adults remains unclear.

Cannabis use during pregnancy is unlikely to be a major cause of birth defects but it is associated with a lower birthweight. There is suggestive evidence that infants exposed to cannabis in utero may experience behavioural and developmental effects during the first few months after birth. Some studies have reported subtle cognitive and developmental differences in early childhood in children who have been exposed to cannabis antenatally. Two recent follow-up studies have produced evidence of impaired physical growth at age 6 and a higher rate of problem behaviour, as described by mothers and teachers, at age 10.

6

The cardiovascular, respiratory and gastrointestinal effects of chronic cannabis use

Cardiovascular effects of cannabis

The most consistent effect of cannabis in humans and animals is an increase in heart rate (Perez-Reyes, 1990). This effect parallels the experienced 'high' and is related to the dose of THC (Perez-Reyes, 1990; Chesher and Hall, 1999). The hearts of healthy young adults will only be mildly stressed by the acute cardiovascular effects of cannabis (Tennant, 1983).

An increased heart rate is most pronounced in occasional cannabis users because the increased heart rate decreases with regular cannabis use as users become tolerant to the effects of THC (Chesher and Hall, 1999; Sidney, 2002). Tolerance to these cardiovascular effects develops within 24 hours in laboratory studies and, in some cases, even large amounts of cannabis had little effect on heart rate (Benowitz and Jones, 1975). Tolerance to these effects has also been observed in chronic heavy cannabis users in Costa Rica (Carter, 1980), Greece (Stefanis et al., 1977), and Jamaica (Rubin and Comitas, 1975).

There are a number of concerns about the effects of cannabis use on patients with ischaemic heart disease, hypertension, and cerebrovascular disease (Jones, 2002; Sidney, 2002). These include the possibilities that cannabis use may cause cardiac arrhythmias, chest pain, and myocardial infarction (or heart attack) that may not be noticed because the analgesic effects of THC may mask chest pain and delay treatment-seeking. Cannabis smoking also increases the level of carboxy-haemoglobin in the blood, decreasing the amount of oxygen reaching the heart, increasing its work and, perhaps, increasing atheroma formation. Patients with cerebrovascular disease could have strokes induced by changes in blood pressure and patients with hypertension could experience exacerbations of their disease for the same reason (Chesher and Hall, 1999).

A number of laboratory studies have found adverse effects of smoking cannabis cigarettes on patients with occlusive heart disease. Aronow and Cassidy (1974) compared the effect of smoking a cannabis and a placebo cigarette on heart rate and the time required to induce chest pain in an exercise tolerance test. Heart rate increased by 43%, and the time taken to produce chest pain halved after smoking a cannabis cigarette. Aronow and Cassidy (1975) compared the effects of smoking a single cannabis cigarette and a high nicotine cigarette in 10 men with occlusive heart disease, all of whom were cigarette smokers. Smoking cannabis produced a 42% increase in heart rate, compared with a 21% increase after smoking the tobacco cigarette. Exercise tolerance time was halved after smoking a cannabis cigarette by comparison with a tobacco cigarette. These findings have been confirmed by Gottschalk et al. (1977).

It is unlikely that healthy young adults who smoke cannabis intermittently will develop clinically detectable heart disease as a result of their cannabis smoking because most will discontinue their use by their late 20s (Bachman et al., 1997). There are case reports of cardiovascular deaths occurring in young adults after smoking cannabis (e.g. Bachs and Morland, 2001) although many of these show signs of undiagnosed coronary artery disease at post-mortem (Bachs and Morland, 2001).

Adverse cardiovascular events are more likely to occur among middle-aged cannabis users who initiated use in the late 1960s and early 1970s who are now at increased risk for heart disease (Institute of Medicine, 1999; Sidney, 2002). Mittleman et al. (2001) reported a case-crossover study of the role of cannabis smoking in an acute myocardial infarction (heart attack). They asked 3882 patients who had had a myocardial infarction in the previous 4 days about their use of cannabis in the hour before it occurred, and compared this with their typical frequency of use. Cannabis was smoked by only 3.5% of patients, 12.5% of those under the age of 44 years, in the previous year. Nonetheless, the risk of a myocardial infarction increased 4.8 times in the hour after smoking cannabis. The risk dropped rapidly after the first hour, as one would expect given the time course of the effects of THC and carbon monoxide on heart function. The effect of smoking cannabis was smaller than using cocaine in earlier studies (a 24-fold increase). Mittleman et al. estimated that a 44-year-old adult who used cannabis daily would increase their annual risk of an acute cardiovascular event from 1.5% to 3%. They concluded that although cannabis smoking was 'a rare trigger of acute myocardial infarction' it 'may pose a health risks to patients with coronary heart disease and perhaps to individuals with multiple coronary risk factors' (p. 2808).

Effects on the respiratory system

Regular cannabis smoking is likely to adversely affect the respiratory system for a number of reasons (Tashkin, 1999). Cannabis smoke is similar to tobacco smoke, and contains a higher proportion of particulate matter and some carcinogens (e.g. benzpyrene) than tobacco smoke (Van Hoozen and Cross, 1997; Tashkin, 1999). The inhalation of cannabis smoke deposits potentially carcinogenic substances on lung surfaces. Cigarette smoking is a cause of respiratory diseases, such as bronchitis, emphysema, and cancers of the lung, oral cavity, trachea, and oesophagus (English et al., 1995). Although tobacco smokers smoke many more cigarettes than cannabis smokers, cannabis smoke is typically inhaled more deeply, and users hold their breath longer, thereby depositing more particulate matter in the lung (Tashkin, 1999).

Chronic bronchitis and obstructive pulmonary disease

A series of studies conducted by Tashkin and his colleagues since the mid-1970s provides convincing evidence that chronic cannabis use impairs lung function and causes symptoms of respiratory disease (see Tashkin, 2002 for a summary). One of their early studies evaluated the effects of heavy daily cannabis smoking on respiratory function. The subjects were young male cannabis smokers who were studied in a closed hospital ward where they were given free access to as much cannabis as they wanted for between 47 and 59 days. Lung function tests showed a significant decrease in the function of large and medium-sized airways over the study and the degree of impairment was related to the number of cannabis cigarettes that had been smoked.

Tashkin and his colleagues (1987) subsequently recruited four groups of patients for a longitudinal study. These were: marijuana-only smokers (MS, n = 144), marijuana and tobacco smokers (MTS, n = 135), tobacco-only smokers (TS, n = 70), and non-smoking controls (NS, n = 97). At baseline Tashkin et al. (1987) found higher rates of bronchitis symptoms (cough, bronchitic sputum production, wheeze and shortness of breath) in all types of smokers (MS, MTS, TS) than in non-smoking controls. Cannabis and tobacco smokers did not differ in the rates of these symptoms. Lung function tests showed poorer functioning and greater abnormalities in small airways among tobacco smokers whereas cannabis smokers had poorer large airways function than non-cannabis smokers.

Follow-up studies of this cohort have provided more detail on the different effects of cannabis and tobacco smoking on lung function (Tashkin et al., 1990). The first follow-up study two to three years after the baseline study retested almost half of these subjects, most of whom were in the same smoking categories as at baseline. At both baseline and follow-up, cough, sputum, and wheeze were more common in smokers than among nonsmokers. There was no significant change in the respiratory status of any of the smoking groups over time when those individuals who ceased smoking were excluded. The same was found when the subjects were followed up 3 to 4 years after first assessment. In addition, the group that smoked both marijuana and tobacco showed both types of damage found in those who only smoked cannabis or tobacco.

Tashkin and his colleagues (Gong et al., 1987; Fligiel et al., 1988) studied the histopathology of the lungs in a sample of their cohort. Fligiel et al. (1988) compared the bronchial abnormalities in 30 males who were heavy cannabis only smokers with those of 17 cannabis and tobacco smokers, 15 tobacco-only smokers and 11 non-smoking controls. All subjects who smoked showed more severe abnormalities than nonsmokers. Many of these were more common in cannabis smokers, and they were most marked in men who smoked both cannabis and tobacco. These abnormalities occurred at a younger age in cannabis than tobacco smokers, despite the fact that cannabis smokers smoked a quarter the number of joints compared to the number of cigarettes smoked by tobacco smokers.

Laboratory studies (Tashkin, 1988; Wu et al., 1988) suggest a number of reasons why cannabis smoking may be more toxic to the respiratory system than tobacco smoking. Cannabis smokers inhale 40% to 54% more smoke than tobacco smokers, inhale more deeply, taking in more particulate matter per puff, and hold their breath four to five times longer than tobacco smokers. As a result, cannabis smokers retain more particulate matter, and absorb three times more carbon monoxide, than tobacco smokers (Wu et al., 1988).

Bloom et al. (1987) examined the relationship between smoking 'non-tobacco' cigarettes and respiratory symptoms and function in the general population. A sample of 990 individuals aged under 40 years were studied in a prospective community study of obstructive airways disease. Fourteen per cent reported that they had smoked a 'non-tobacco' cigarette (the same as the rate of cannabis smoking in general population surveys). Nine per cent were current and 5% were ex-smokers of 'non-tobacco' cigarettes. On average non-tobacco cigarettes were smoked 7 times per week for 9 years. Non-tobacco smokers were more likely to have smoked tobacco and they inhaled more deeply than tobacco smokers.

Non-tobacco smokers reported more cough, phlegm, and wheeze, regardless of whether they smoked tobacco or not. They also had poorer respiratory function. Those who had never smoked had the best functioning, followed in order of decreasing function by current cigarette smokers, current non-tobacco smokers, and current smokers of tobacco and non-tobacco cigarettes. Non-tobacco smoking alone had a bigger effect on respiratory function than tobacco smoking alone, and the effects of both types of smoking on respiratory function was additive.

Sherril et al. (1991) reported on respiratory symptoms and respiratory function in follow-ups of this sample. Non-tobacco use declined over time, as did the quantity smoked per week. At each follow-up non-tobacco smokers were twice as likely to report chronic cough, chronic phlegm and wheeze as non-smokers. The increased rate was not explained by tobacco use. The rate of symptoms increased with the number of non-tobacco cigarettes smoked per week and with the length of time that non-tobacco cigarettes had been smoked. Non-tobacco smokers also showed impairment on all measures of respiratory function.

Taylor et al. (2000) studied symptoms of respiratory disease and respiratory function in 1037 New Zealand adults who were followed from birth until age 21. They compared symptoms of respiratory disease and respiratory function in those who were: cannabis dependent, cigarette smokers and non-smokers of tobacco and cannabis. Tobacco smokers had a higher rate of chronic bronchitis, wheeze and cough than non-tobacco smokers and the rate of these symptoms increased with the number of cigarettes smoked per day. Cannabis dependent subjects had higher rates of wheezing, shortness of breath, chest tightness and morning sputum production than non-smokers, after taking account of tobacco use. Among cannabis dependent subjects the effects of cannabis use were similar to those of smoking 1–10 tobacco cigarettes per day. A higher proportion of cannabis dependent subjects had impaired respiratory function and the adverse effects of tobacco and cannabis smoking on respiratory function were additive.

Taylor et al. (2002) have reported a subsequent follow-up of this cohort to age 26 in which more detailed analyses were undertaken on the cumulative effects of cannabis on respiratory function (objectively assessed by forced expiratory volume and vital capacity). The study assessed cannabis use at ages 18, 21 and 26 years and also carefully controlled for the effects of cigarette smoking which was assessed at the same ages. They found that the heaviest cannabis users (900 or more occasions of use by age 26 years) had 2.6% to 7% reductions in lung function (as assessed by the ratio of forced expiratory volume to vital capacity). After controlling for tobacco smoking the relationship was of marginal statistical and clinical significance. The authors argued that given the short time frame of the follow-up, 'the trend suggests that continued cannabis smoking has the potential to result in clinically important impairment of lung function' (p. 1055).

Respiratory cancers

As discussed in detail in Chapter 5, there is good evidence that cannabis *smoke* is mutagenic and carcinogenic and hence a potential cause of cancer in the aerodigestive and respiratory tracts that are regularly exposed to such smoke (Van Hoozen and Cross, 1997; Tashkin, 1999). There are case reports of aerodigestive tract cancers among relatively young adults who have been daily cannabis users. A case-control study has found an association between cannabis smoking and head and neck cancer (Zhang et al., 1999) but the only prospective cohort study to date did not find an increased incidence of head and neck or respiratory cancers (Sidney et al., 1997b). The relative youth of the participants and the low prevalence of regular cannabis use in this study reduced its ability to detect an increase in respiratory cancers. Further cohort, and additional case-control studies are needed to clarify the seriousness of this risk (see Chapter 5 for a more detailed discussion).

Effects on the gastrointestinal system

Experimental studies in animals have not reported any evidence that THC causes liver damage (Sprauge et al., 1973; Ham and DeJon, 1975) and there is no human evidence that the chronic use of cannabis disturbs liver function (Chesher and Hall, 1999). Animal studies have suggested that cannabinoids reduce intestinal motility, increasing the passage time for food (Masur et al., 1971; Drew et al., 1972).

Anecdotally cannabis increases appetite ('the munchies' or 'hash hungries') (Siler et al., 1933; Snyder, 1970; Tart, 1970). THC in the form of dronabinol (Marinol) has been shown to produce weight gain when used to treat nausea and vomiting caused by cancer chemotherapy. A similar weight gain was reported when used in patients with HIV infection (Plasse et al., 1991). There are now objective data to support the anecdotal reports for the 'hash hungries', and there are indications that it has potential therapeutic uses as an appetite stimulant (see Chapter 13).

Summary

Smoking cannabis increases heart rate and affects blood pressure but there is no evidence that these adversely affect the normal cardiovascular system. These effects may be less benign in patients with hypertension, cerebrovascular disease and coronary atherosclerosis because THC increases the work of the heart. There is now evidence that cannabis can precipitate a myocardial infarction in persons at high risk of cardiovascular disease. Persons with coronary artery disease or cerebrovascular disease would be advised not to smoke cannabis.

Cannabis smoking causes chronic bronchitis, impairs functioning of the large airways and produces pathological changes in lung tissues that may be precursors of lung cancer. Case studies and a case-control study suggest that cannabis may cause cancers of the aerodigestive tract. Additional studies of the role of cannabis in these cancers is a high research priority.

There is little or no human or animal evidence that cannabinoids affect liver function. The most dependable gastrointestinal effect of cannabis is in reducing nausea and stimulating appetite.

3

The psychological effects of chronic cannabis use

This section reviews evidence on three adverse psychological effects that have been attributed to chronic cannabis use. These are: the effects of regular cannabis use on motivation; the effects of chronic regular use on cognitive functioning; and the contribution that cannabis use might make to the onset and exacerbation of psychotic disorders, including schizophrenia.

A number of common issues emerge in considering these three types of effect. First, all three concerns have been prompted by case histories of individuals whose motivation or cognitive performance had been adversely affected, or who exhibited psychotic symptoms after using cannabis. Second, as we will point out, case histories have a limited capacity to inform us about whether cannabis use plays a causal role in these disorders. In each case, a plausible alternative explanation that has to be excluded is that the relationship arises because people who are most likely to use cannabis are at higher risk of impaired motivation, a preoccupation with cannabis use, cognitive impairment and psychosis, *before* they used cannabis. The causal criteria outlined in the introduction to Section 2 are critical in sorting out cause and effect. Third, the question of whether cannabis does play a causal role in each of these disorders is important because all of the disorders can have serious adverse consequences for the persons affected and their families.

7

Cannabis dependence

Motivational effects

Chronic daily cannabis users in Egypt and the Caribbean have been reported to showed impaired motivation (Brill and Nahas, 1984). Some young cannabis users in the USA in the early 1970s who were described as apathetic, withdrawn, lethargic and unmotivated (McGlothlin and West, 1968) were said to suffer from an 'amotivational syndrome' (McGlothlin and West, 1968). The difficulty with these case reports was in disentangling the effects of chronic cannabis use from poverty, poor education and pre-existing psychiatric disorders (Edwards and Gross, 1976).

The effects of cannabis use on motivation were assessed in a number of field studies of chronic cannabis users in Costa Rica (Carter, 1980), Jamaica (Rubin and Comitas, 1975) and the USA (Halikas et al., 1982). Rubin and Comitas (1975), for example, found that Jamaican farmers who regularly smoked cannabis laboured more intensely but less efficiently after using cannabis. A study in Costa Rica, comparing cannabis smokers and non-users, produced mixed results (Carter, 1980). Non-users were more likely to be in full-time employment and to be stably employed but users who had steady jobs or were self-employed smoked more cannabis than those who were not.

A follow-up study of long-term cannabis users in the USA suggests that the amotivational syndrome is rare among long-term users. Halikas et al. (1982) assessed symptoms of the amotivational syndrome in 100 regular cannabis users six to eight years after they were first interviewed. Only three individuals reported amotivational symptoms in the absence of depression and they did not differ from the other cannabis users in their patterns of use.

Laboratory studies of long-term heavy cannabis use have also failed to clearly show that cannabis impairs motivation (Edwards and Gross, 1976). Early studies conducted by the LaGuardia Commission (see Mendelson et al., 1974) reported deterioration in behaviour among prisoners given daily doses of cannabis over a period of weeks but these reports were uncontrolled. A controlled study using standardised measures of performance failed to observe any effects of cannabis use (Mendelson et al., 1974).

The amotivational syndrome remains contentious because of differences of opinion about the value of clinical observations and controlled studies. Those who accept the existence of the syndrome appeal to the small number of cases fitting the description of an 'amotivational syndrome' (Cohen, 1986). Sceptics are more impressed by the unsupportive field and laboratory studies. A more productive approach may be to regard the 'amotivational syndrome' as comprising symptoms of chronic cannabis intoxication that occur in individuals who are dependent on cannabis. This assimilates the phenomena included under the amotivational syndrome within a category that is applied to other psychoactive drugs; it also obviates any need to invent a new psychiatric syndrome (Edwards and Gross, 1976).

Cannabis dependence

For much of the 1960s and 1970s cannabis was not regarded as a drug of dependence because it did not seem to produce tolerance or a withdrawal syndrome like that seen in alcohol and opioid dependence. Views began to change in the early 1980s when a broader conception of drug dependence was adopted in part as a result of Edwards and Gross's (1976) redefinition of the alcohol dependence syndrome which was subsequently extended to all forms of drug dependence (Edwards et al., 1981). This new conception reduced the importance of tolerance and withdrawal and increased that attached to compulsion to use, a narrowing of the drug-using repertoire, rapid reinstatement of dependence after abstinence, and the high salience of drug use in the user's life. It is reflected in the Fourth Revised Edition of the Diagnostic and Statistical Manual (DSM-III-R and DSM-IV) of the American Psychiatric Association (American Psychiatric Association, 1994).

Drug dependence in DSM-IV

Substance dependence comprises 'a cluster of cognitive, behavioral and physiologic symptoms indicating that the individual continues use of the substance despite significant substance-related problems' (p. 176) (American Psychiatric Association, 1994). A diagnosis of substance dependence is made if *three* or more of the following criteria occur at any time in the same 12-month period:

1 tolerance, as defined by either of the following:
  a need for markedly increased amounts of the substance to achieve intoxication or desired effect
  b markedly diminished effect with continued use of the same amount of the substance
2 withdrawal, as manifested by either of the following:
  a the characteristic withdrawal syndrome for the substance
  b the same (or closely related) substance is taken to relieve or avoid withdrawal symptoms

3 the substance is often taken in larger amounts or over a longer period than was intended;

4 there is a persistent desire or unsuccessful efforts to cut down or control substance use;

5 a great deal of time is spent in activities necessary to obtain the substance (e.g., visiting multiple doctors, driving long distances), use the substance (e.g. chain smoking), or recover from its effects;

6 important social, occupational, or recreational activities are given up or reduced because of substance use;

7 the substance use is continued despite knowledge of having a persistent or recurrent physical or psychological problem that is likely to have been caused or exacerbated by the substance (American Psychiatric Association, 1994).

Cannabis tolerance and withdrawal

Tolerance to many of the behavioural and physiological effects of THC has been demonstrated in animals (Compton et al., 1990; Adams and Martin, 1996; Maldonado, 2002). Research has shown that the cannabinoid antagonist SR 141716A (which immediately reverses the effects of THC) produces a withdrawal syndrome in rats, mice and dogs that have been maintained on THC (Aceto et al., 1996; Cook et al., 1998). The antagonist produces a more compressed and accentuated withdrawal syndrome than the milder, more prolonged symptoms that occur in human users (Maldonado, 2002). The relatively long half-life and complex metabolism of cannabis may also result in a less intense withdrawal syndrome than drugs such as opiates (Childers and Breivogel, 1998). The mechanisms for tolerance and withdrawal are unknown but they probably involve changes in cannabinoid receptor function (Adams and Martin, 1996; Childers and Breivogel, 1998; Maldonado, 2002).

Cannabis withdrawal symptoms have also been reported in human laboratory studies (Compton et al., 1990). Jones and Benowitz (1976), for example, studied the effects of 210 mg dose of oral THC per day given in a fixed dosing schedule to healthy male volunteers with extensive histories of cannabis use. Over the 30-day study, the positive effects of intoxication declined and there was a recovery in social, cognitive and psychomotor performance which was initially impaired by this dose of THC.

Jones and Benowitz (1976) abruptly withdrew regular cannabis smokers after approximately two weeks on high doses of oral THC. Within six hours, they complained of 'inner unrest' and after 12 hours they reported 'increased activity, irritability, insomnia, and restlessness' that were also observed by staff. The intensity of abstinence symptoms was correlated with THC dose and frequency of use, and these symptoms were reduced by using cannabis (Jones et al., 1981). Recent laboratory studies by Haney et al. (1999a; 1999b) have observed withdrawal symptoms at much lower doses of THC given orally and by smoking. The most common symptoms reported were anxiety, depression and irritability.

Studies in clinical and non-clinical samples of long-term cannabis users have reported withdrawal symptoms, such as anxiety, insomnia, appetite disturbance and depression (Stephens et al., 1994; Wiesbeck et al., 1996; Swift et al., 1998a; Copeland et al., 2001a). Critics have pointed out that these have been uncontrolled studies that relied upon retrospective self-reports of symptoms measured in unstandardised ways (Smith, 2002).

A number of recent controlled studies have provided clearer evidence for a human cannabis withdrawal syndrome. Kouri and Pope (2000) reported a controlled prospective study of withdrawal symptoms among chronic cannabis users who were assessed daily for 28 days while in a hospital ward. Their ratings of mood, anxiety, depression, irritability were compared to those of a control group of abstinent former heavy cannabis users and non-users. Over the 28 days the chronic cannabis users showed decreases in mood and appetite and increases in irritability, anxiety, physical tension, and physical symptoms. Scores on the Hamilton Depression and Anxiety scales also increased. These symptoms appeared within 24 hours and were most pronounced during the first 10 days although the increased irritability and tension persisted throughout the 28 days.

Budney et al. (2001) reported a controlled study of withdrawal symptoms in 12 long-term daily cannabis users who were not seeking help to stop their use. The subjects who were recruited through newspaper advertisements had their mood and behaviour monitored daily for 16 days during which they: (1) smoked cannabis as usual (days 1–5); (2) abstained from cannabis (verified by urinalysis) for 3 days (days 6–8); (3) returned to cannabis smoking for 5 days (days 9–13) and abstained again for 3 days (days 14–16). The following symptoms increased in severity during the abstinence period and disappeared with the resumption of cannabis use: aggression, anger, craving for cannabis, decreased appetite, irritability and sleep difficulty. Three of these changes were also found during the second cycle of abstinence and resumption of use: craving for cannabis; decreased appetite and sleep difficulty. These self-reported changes were corroborated by the ratings of irritability and restlessness by an independent observer during the first cycle of abstinence and resumption of use.

Epidemiological studies of cannabis dependence

The Epidemiological Catchment Area (ECA) study provided data on the rates of cannabis abuse and dependence in the US population in the early 1980s (Robins and Reiger, 1991). It found that 4.4% of the US population met DSM-III criteria for cannabis abuse or dependence at some time in their lives. A third of these (38%)

reported problems with cannabis use in the last year. Men had a higher risk of cannabis dependence than women, with the highest rate among 18- to 29-year-olds. (Anthony and Helzer, 1991). Surveys using similar methods to the ECA have produced similar estimates of the rate of cannabis dependence in Canada and New Zealand (Wells et al., 1992; Hwu and Compton, 1994; Russell et al., 1994).

The National Comorbidity Survey (NCS) conducted in the USA between 1990 and 1992 (Anthony et al., 1994) reported that 4.2% of adults met DSM-III-R criteria for cannabis dependence at some time in their lives. The Australian National Survey of Mental Health and Wellbeing (Hall et al., 1999) found that 1.7% of Australian adults met ICD-10 criteria for a diagnosis of cannabis dependence, and 0.1% met criteria for harmful use in the previous year. One in four (23%) of those who had used cannabis more than five times in the last year met criteria for cannabis dependence or harmful use. Withdrawal symptoms and a persistent desire or attempts to control use were among the most commonly reported dependence symptoms (Swift et al., 2001).

Studies of long-term cannabis users

Australian surveys of long-term cannabis users have found that a substantial proportion are cannabis dependent. Among 243 rural cannabis users, who had used cannabis several times a week for 19 years, 57% qualified for lifetime DSM-III-R and ICD-10 cannabis dependence diagnoses (Swift et al., 1998b). The most common dependence symptoms reported were frequent intoxication during daily activities (73%) and a strong urge to use cannabis (75%). Few reported withdrawal symptoms (5%) or using cannabis to relieve withdrawal symptoms (20%) in large part because few were ever abstinent but half (54%) reported tolerance. Only 26% believed they had a problem with cannabis and only 9% had sought help to stop.

Among 200 young Sydney adults who had used cannabis at least weekly for 11 years, 92% met criteria for a DSM-III-R lifetime diagnosis of dependence and 40% were classified as severely dependent (Swift et al., 1998a). Tolerance and withdrawal were reported by 78% and 76% respectively but use to relieve withdrawal symptoms was reported by only 39%. Most met criteria for cannabis dependence in the past year according to DSM-III-R (77%) and ICD-10 (72%) criteria. A follow-up of these users found that cannabis use and dependence symptoms were stable over a year (Swift et al., 2000). The majority (81%) of the sample still met criteria for cannabis dependence during the last year.

The risk of cannabis dependence

Kandel and Davis (1992) estimated that one in three near-daily cannabis users met DSM-III criteria for dependence. The risk of dependence among less frequent users of cannabis is probably lower than this (Hall et al., 1994). In the ECA study 17% of those who used cannabis more than five times met DSM-III criteria for dependence at some time in their lives (Anthony and Helzer, 1991). Anthony et al. (1994) estimated (using the National Comorbidity Study data) that 9% of lifetime cannabis users met DSM-III-R criteria for dependence at some time in their lives. This compared to 32% of nicotine, 23% of heroin, 17% of cocaine, 15% of alcohol and 11% of stimulant users.

We suggest the following rules of thumb for the risks of cannabis dependence. For those who have ever used cannabis, the risk is of the order of one in ten. Among those who use the drug more than a few times the risk of dependence is between one in five and one in three. For daily users the risk is more like one in two. All else being equal, the more often cannabis is used, and the longer it is used, the higher the risk of becoming dependent on it.

The following factors predict a higher risk of regular involvement with cannabis: poor academic achievement, deviant behaviour in childhood and adolescence, nonconformity and rebelliousness, personal distress and maladjustment, poor parental relationships, earlier use, and a parental history of drug and alcohol problems (Shedler and Block, 1990; Brook et al., 1992; Kandel and Davies, 1992; Newcomb, 1992).

The consequences of cannabis dependence

The large discrepancy between the estimates of cannabis dependence in the community and the small number of cannabis users who seek treatment suggests that many cases remit without treatment, as is also true for alcohol and nicotine dependence (Helzer et al., 1991). Kandel and Davies (1992), for example, found that by age 28 to 29, less than 15% of daily cannabis users were still using daily. As outlined in Chapter 2, Bachman et al. (1997) found that most regular cannabis users discontinue their use during the mid to late twenties. These statistics suggest that cannabis dependence is a disorder with a high rate of remission in the absence of treatment.

Research among cannabis users who fail to quit unassisted and who seek help suggest that dependence can be troubling for some heavy users (Budney and Moore, 2002; Stephens et al., 2002). These users report cognitive and motivational impairments which may interfere with work performance, lowered self-esteem and depression, and complaints by spouses and partners about their frequent intoxication (Budney and Moore, 2002). There is no doubt that some dependent adult cannabis users report impaired performance and a reduced quality of everyday life (Copeland et al., 2001a); the same is true for some cannabis dependent adolescents (Crowley et al., 1998). The levels of impairment associated with cannabis dependence are similar to those found in other forms of drug dependence (Budney and Moore, 2002; Dennis et al., 2002).

Dependent cannabis users seek professional help in Australia, the United States and Europe. The National Census of Clients of Australian Treatment Service Agencies (Webster et al., 1992; Torres et al., 1995) found that the proportion of cases in which cannabis was the *main* drug problem increased from 4% in 1990 to 7% in 1995 and 11% in 2000 (Copeland and Conroy, 2001). Between 1994 and 1998 cannabis was the primary drug of abuse for between 11% and 26% of clients of treatment agencies in the United States (United States Office of National Drug Control Policy, 1998). It was a primary or a secondary drug problem for 35% of persons seeking treatment in the USA in 1998, and the most common drug problem among adolescents who sought treatment in that year (Dennis et al., 2002). Cannabis was the primary drug problem for between 2% and 16% of clients attending treatment agencies in the European Union in 1998 (European Monitoring Centre for Drugs and Drug Addiction, 1998).

Stephens and colleagues (1993) described the symptoms reported by 382 users who sought help to cease cannabis use. These included: an inability to stop using (93%), feeling bad about using cannabis (87%), procrastinating (86%), loss of self-confidence (76%), memory loss (67%) and withdrawal symptoms (51%). Similar symptoms have been reported by users in recent US studies (Stephens et al., 1994; Budney et al., 1998; Stephens et al., 2002) and in an Australian study of problem cannabis users (Copeland et al., 2001a). In the Australian study withdrawal symptoms were reported by 96% of 229 long-term cannabis users seeking help to stop using.

Recent studies of adolescents seeking substance abuse treatment indicate that cannabis dependence symptoms, including withdrawal symptoms are common among adolescent users (Crowley et al., 1998; Tims et al., 2002). Crowley et al. (1998), for example, reported on the prevalence of cannabis dependence among 165 male and 64 female adolescents aged 13 to 19 years who were referred to a specialist substance abuse treatment service by juvenile justice or social service agencies. They found that 80% of males and 60% of females met criteria for cannabis dependence. Two-thirds of those who were cannabis dependent reported symptoms of withdrawal and a quarter reported using to relieve withdrawal symptoms. Rates of progression from first use to dependence were also high in this population: with 83% of those reporting use at least six times developing dependence on the drug.

The treatment of cannabis dependence

Although many users may succeed in quitting without professional help some users who are unable to stop on their own will need assistance to do so. Until recently there has been a paucity of research to assist in deciding what type of treatment to provide to dependent cannabis users who seek help.

Stephens et al. (1994) reported a randomised controlled trial of behavioural treatment for cannabis dependence. Some 291 subjects were randomly assigned to one of three treatments: (1) a 14-session group-based relapse prevention intervention (RPSG); (2) an individualised advice (IAI) two-session intervention using principles of motivational interviewing adapted from Miller's Drinker's Checkup; and (3) a delayed treatment condition (DTC) in which participants did not receive any treatment for four months.

At the four-month follow-up all three groups had reduced their cannabis use but two treatment groups (which did not differ from each other) showed the largest reduction. In the treatment groups 37% were abstinent compared with 9% in the delayed treatment group. The amount of cannabis use also declined to 30% of baseline in the treatment groups and to 70% of baseline in the delayed treatment group. Abstinence rates declined over time but the two treatments did not differ at 7 months (32% and 36%), 13 (26% and 28%) and 16 months (29% and 28%) after treatment. Twenty-two per cent of participants were abstinent throughout the 16-month follow-up and their abstinence was corroborated by partners and family members.

Budney, Higgins, Radinovich and Novy (2000) reported a controlled comparison of three treatments for 60 cannabis dependent patients. The three treatments were: motivational enhancement to quit (M), motivational enhancement plus behavioural coping skills (MBT), and MBT plus voucher-based incentives to remain abstinent (MBTV). In the latter, vouchers for retail items were exchanged for urine samples that were negative for cannabinoids. The MBTV group had a longer period of continuous abstinence (4.8 weeks) than the other two groups which did not differ from each other (2.3 and 1.6 weeks). By the end of the 14-week study fewer than 10% of the participants remained abstinent.

Copeland, Swift, Roffman and Stephens (2001) randomly assigned 229 cannabis-dependent adults to three treatments: a 6-session cognitive behavioural intervention; a single-session cognitive behavioural treatment and a delayed treatment control group who were offered treatment four months after the other two groups. Only 6.5% of all subjects (n = 11) were continuously abstinent for the 8-month follow-up period. All were in the two treatment groups. There were also larger reductions in cannabis use and cannabis-related problems in the two treatment groups.

In all of these studies rates of abstinence at the end of treatment have been modest (20%–40%) and rates of subsequent relapse have been substantial so that rates of enduring abstinence have been very modest (Budney and Moore, 2002). Nonetheless, treatment does substantially reduce cannabis use and problems. These outcomes are not very different from those observed in the treatment for alcohol and other forms of drug dependence (Budney and Moore, 2002). Much more research is needed before sensible advice can be given about the best ways to achieve abstinence from cannabis. In the absence of such evidence, treatment providers should avoid replicating experience in the treatment of alcohol dependence where inpatient treatment has been widely adopted in the absence of any evidence that it is more effective than outpatient forms of treatment (Miller and Hester, 1986; Heather and Tebbutt, 1989).

Summary

Some heavy users report impaired motivation but there is no compelling evidence that chronic cannabis use produces a unique amotivational syndrome. The motivational effects of chronic cannabis use are more appropriately regarded as a symptom of cannabis dependence (as defined in DSM-IV). Chronic cannabis use produces tolerance, some users report withdrawal symptoms on cessation of use, and there is clinical and epidemiological evidence that heavy cannabis users experience problems controlling their cannabis use, and continue to use despite experiencing adverse consequences of use. Cannabis dependence is the most common form of drug dependence after alcohol and tobacco in the USA and Australia, reflecting the high rates of cannabis use among adolescents and young adults in these societies. The risk of developing the syndrome is of the order of one in ten among those who ever use the drug; between one in five and one in three among those who use cannabis more than a few times; and around one in two among those who become daily users. Dependent cannabis users who seek help to stop using report that it produces substantial impairments in daily living. Cannabis dependence responds to the same type of treatments used to treat alcohol dependence, producing similarly modest rates of sustained abstinence.

8

The effects of cannabis use on cognitive functioning

Cannabis acutely impairs cognitive performance so it is possible that chronic use may cause longer-lasting cognitive impairment. This possibility seemed to be supported by clinical observations in the USA during the early 1970s (e.g. Kolansky and Moore, 1971) that young adults who had used cannabis weekly or more often had poor attention span, poor concentration, and confusion (Kolansky and Moore, 1971). More recently, long-term cannabis users seeking help to stop using cannabis report impaired memory and thinking (Stephens et al., 2000). The difficulty with these reports has been in ruling out the possibilities that these cognitive impairments preceded cannabis use or that they were due to other drug use.

Cross-cultural studies

One research strategy in searching for any cognitive effect of cannabis has been to assess the cognitive performance of heavy cannabis users in cultures with a tradition of such use. An early report by Soueif (1971) illustrates the problems with this strategy. Soueif studied Egyptian male prisoners of whom 850 were hashish smokers and 839 controls. The hashish users performed more poorly than the controls on 10 out of 16 measures of cognitive performance (Soueif, 1971) but the two groups differed in other ways that may have affected cognitive performance, namely, the hashish users were less well-educated and more likely to use opiates and alcohol than the controls (Carlin, 1986).

In the late 1960s three cross-cultural studies were conducted in Jamaica (Rubin and Comitas, 1975), Greece (Kokkevi and Dornbush, 1977) and Costa Rica (Satz et al., 1976) to assess the effects of chronic cannabis use on cognitive functioning. It was assumed that any cognitive effects of chronic daily cannabis use would be apparent in users with a long history of heavy cannabis use, a pattern that was common in these cultures.

These cross-cultural studies users provide equivocal evidence of subtle cognitive impairment among long-term cannabis users. Some studies failed to find any differences (e.g. Rubin and Comitas, 1975) and the others found modest cognitive impairment in persons with a long history of heavy cannabis use (Page et al., 1988). The negative results cannot be attributed to short duration or low intensity of cannabis use because these subjects had used between 17 and 23 years, and the amount of THC consumed per day ranged from 20–90 mg in the Jamaican study to 120–200 mg in the Greek sample. The positive studies are weakened by the fact that cannabis users had higher rates of polydrug use, poor nutrition, poor medical care, and illiteracy that may have biased studies towards finding poorer performance among cannabis users. Many of these studies also failed to ensure that subjects were not intoxicated when they were tested.

Laboratory studies of daily cannabis dosing

A different strategy for investigating the cognitive effects of chronic cannabis use is to study the cognitive performance of persons who use cannabis daily over periods of weeks. These studies have controlled the quantity, frequency, and duration of cannabis use, as well as nutrition and other drug use, by observing subjects in a hospital ward while they use cannabis. All such studies have used pre- and post-drug observation periods. The sample sizes in these studies have been small and cannabis has been used for between 21 and 64 days.

Dornbush et al. (1972) administered cannabis containing 14 mg THC to 5 regular cannabis users for 21 days. They were tested before and 60 minutes after using cannabis on short-term memory and digit symbol substitution. Performance on the short-term memory test decreased on the first day of drug administration but gradually improved until by the last day of the study it had returned to baseline. Performance on the digit symbol substitution test was unaffected by cannabis but improved with time as a result of practice. Mendelson, Rossi and Meyer (1974) studied the effects of 21 days of cannabis use on 20 healthy, young male subjects who smoked as much cannabis as they wanted to. Short-term memory was impaired whilst intoxicated but there was no impairment of performance after cannabis smoking. Three other studies have also failed to detect cognitive effects (Cohen, 1976; Frank et al., 1976; Harshman et al., 1976).

Controlled studies of chronic cannabis users

Research studies in the late 1980s and in the 1990s improved upon the earlier studies of chronic cannabis users by using control groups, verifying abstinence from cannabis before testing, and measuring the quantity, frequency and duration of cannabis use. More effort was also made to relate specific cognitive processes to quantity, frequency and duration of cannabis use. These studies have more consistently found small cognitive impairments in chronic cannabis users.

A study by Block et al. (1990) addressed a major concern with earlier studies by ensuring that cannabis users and controls did not differ in cognitive ability *before* they started using cannabis. Block et al. (1990) matched users and non-users on the Iowa Tests of Basic Skills which was administered in the fourth grade of high school well before cannabis use began. Block and colleagues compared 144 cannabis users, 64 of whom were light users (less than 4 times per week for 5.5 years) and 80 heavy users (5 or more times per week for 6.0 years) with 72 age-matched controls. Twenty-four hours of abstinence was required before testing. Heavy cannabis users performed more poorly on tests of verbal expression and mathematical skills on the 12th grade version of the Iowa test than did light users or controls.

Fried et al. (2002) recently examined the impact of cannabis use on IQ in 70 children who were followed up in the Ottawa Prenatal Prospective Study until age 17–20 years. These children had had their IQ assessed before adolescence on the Wechsler Intelligence Scale for Children and their IQ was assessed at age 17–20 years using the Wechsler Adult Intelligence Scale (WAIS). Cannabis use was assessed at the second assessment by self-report and urinalysis at age 17–20 years. The impact of cannabis use on IQ was assessed by the change in IQ between the two assessments. The heavier the cannabis use at age 17–20 the more likely the young person was to show a *decline* in IQ. When users were classified into groups defined by frequency of cannabis use (non-use, light, heavy and former users), the groups did not differ in IQ before cannabis use but the IQ of the heavy using group was 4 points less than that of controls. Fried et al. pointed out that this effect was similar in magnitude to that of maternal alcohol or cocaine use during pregnancy and larger than the effects of low-level exposure to environmental lead on IQ.

Solowij et al. (Solowij et al., 1991, 1995) studied the effects of long-term cannabis use on specific types of information processing, testing Miller and Branconnier's (1983) conjecture that cannabis users are unable to exclude irrelevant stimuli when attending to a task. Solowij et al. assessed attentional processes in long-term cannabis users using performance and brain event-related potential (ERP) measures of underlying cognitive processes. They measured the amplitude and latency of ERP components that had been shown to reflect stages of information processing.

Solowij et al. (1991) studied 9 cannabis users aged 19–40 who had used cannabis 5 days per week for 11 years. They were matched on age, sex, years of education and alcohol consumption with 9 controls who had either never used or used it fewer than 15 times in their lives. Subjects were excluded if they had a history of head injury, neurological or psychiatric illness, had used other drugs, or had high levels of alcohol consumption. The groups did not differ in premorbid IQ estimated by the NART score. Cannabis users were asked to abstain from cannabis and alcohol for 24 hours before testing and two urine samples were analysed to ensure that they did so.

Subjects performed an auditory selective attention task in which random sequences of tones varying in location, pitch and duration were presented through headphones while brain electrical activity (EEG) was recorded. They were asked to attend to a particular pitch presented in a particular ear, and to respond to long duration tones by pressing a button. Cannabis users performed significantly more poorly than controls, making more errors and showing a longer reaction time. They were also less able than controls to filter out irrelevant information, suggesting that their ability to efficiently process information was impaired.

In a second study Solowij et al. (1995) assessed relationships between degree of impairment and the frequency and duration of cannabis use. Thirty-two cannabis users were divided into four groups (N = 8) defined by frequency (light: 2 or fewer times per week vs more than 3 times per week) and duration (short: 4 or fewer years of use vs long: 5 or more years of cannabis use). Subjects were matched to a group of non-user controls (N = 16). The cannabis users performed worse than the controls and the greatest impairment was in the heavy-user group. Different cognitive processes seemed to be affected by frequency and duration of cannabis use. The long-duration user group found it harder to ignore irrelevant stimuli than the short-duration users and controls who did not differ. There were no differences between groups defined on frequency of use. The impairment in the ability to filter out irrelevant information increased with the number of years of use but it was not related to frequency of use. By contrast, speed of information processing was related to frequency of cannabis use but not to duration of use.

Solowij (1995) assessed whether these ERP changes in long-term cannabis users persisted after extended abstinence from cannabis. She studied 32 former users who had used cannabis for 9 years and had been abstinent for 2 years. She found partial recovery of functioning: the speed of information processing was not reduced in the ex-users but their ability to ignore irrelevant stimuli remained impaired. The degree of impairment increased with the length of cannabis use and was unrelated to the length of abstinence.

Leavitt and colleagues assessed cognitive functioning (Leavitt et al., 1992; Leavitt et al., 1993) in subjects screened for current or past psychiatric and medical disorders and CNS injury. They compared daily cannabis users who had at least 3 years of use with a group who had used for 6–14 years, a group who had used on a daily basis for 15 years or more, and a non-user control group. There were 15 subjects per group. They found a dose-response relationship between test performance and intensity of cannabis use. Controls performed best, followed by daily cannabis users, with the poorest performance in the very long-term using group (Leavitt et al., 1992; Leavitt et al., 1993).

Pope and Yurgelun-Todd (1996) compared the cognitive performance of heavy and light cannabis-using college students. The heavy users (n = 65) had used for at least 2 years, and on 28 of the past 30 days which was confirmed by cannabinoids in their urine. The light users (n = 64) who had used no more than 3 days in the past month had no cannabinoids in their urine. The authors argued that their infrequent users would 'differ less from heavy users on some possible confounding variables than would control subjects who had never used cannabis at all, while still differing sharply from heavy users on ... extent of recent cannabis use' (p. 521) (Pope and Yurgelun-Todd, 1996).

Subjects were admitted overnight to a hospital ward to ensure that they were abstinent from cannabis for at least 19 hours before being tested. The two groups did not differ on any social or demographic variables, except that heavy users came from more affluent families, and scored more poorly on Verbal IQ and self-reported Scholastic Aptitude Tests. These differences were statistically adjusted for when comparing the two groups on the neuropsychological tests. The groups did not differ on tests of digit span, auditory sequential processing, the Stroop Test or the Wechsler Memory Scale. They differed on tests that assessed attention (the Wisconsin Test, the Benton VFT, and the CLVT). These differences persisted when adjusted for differences in verbal IQ, self-reported SAT score and other drug use.

Pope et al. (2001) compared the cognitive performance of 63 current daily cannabis users who had used 5000 times in their lives with 45 former heavy users with a similar lifetime exposure who had not smoked more than 12 times in the past 3 months and 72 controls who had not smoked cannabis more than 50 times in their lives. Subjects underwent a 28-day washout from cannabis use monitored by urinalysis during which they were assessed on a neuropsychologial test battery on days 0, 1, 7 and 28. Heavy current users scored more poorly than control subjects on tests of verbal learning on days 0, 1 and 7 but these differences disappeared by day 28. The deficit was correlated with urinary levels of cannabinoids at baseline but uncorrelated with duration of lifetime use. They interpreted the results as evidence that long-term cannabis use produced residual effects on cognitive functioning.

Solowij et al. (2002) compared the cognitive functioning in 102 long-term near-daily cannabis users who sought treatment for cannabis dependence with that of 33 non-user controls. The users were subdivided into 51 long-term users (mean of 23.9 years of daily use) and 51 shorter-term daily users (mean of 10.2 years use). Users were abstinent for 17 hours prior to being assessed on 9 neuropsychological tests that were selected to detect the impaired cognitive functioning reported in previous studies. Long-term users performed more poorly than short-term users on tests of memory and attention, with long-term users showing impaired learning and retrieval. The longer they had used cannabis the poorer the performance on these tests. This suggested that it was duration of use rather than frequency of use that was associated with poorer cognitive performance.

Bolla et al. (2002) have reported findings that conflict with those of both Pope et al. (2001) and Solowij et al. (2002). They evaluated the cognitive performance of 22 heavy cannabis users who were 22 years of age and had used 48.5 joints per week for 4.8 years. They divided them into three groups that differed in frequency of use: 7 light users who used 10.5 joints per week; 8 medium users who had used 42.1 joints per week; and 7 heavy users who had used 93.9 joints per week. Cognitive performance was assessed after 28 days of abstinence (ensured by urinalysis) to control for residual effects of cannabis use. Bolla et al. found a dose–response relationship between frequency of cannabis use and cognitive performance, despite the facts that so few young users were studied and they had used for a relatively short period of time. They did *not* find a relationship between cognitive functioning and duration of cannabis use.

Epidemiological evidence

Lyketsos et al. (1999) reported a prospective epidemiological study of the effect of cannabis use on cognitive functioning. They followed 1318 adults for 11.5 years after they were first assessed on the Mini Mental State Exam (MMSE) to assess cognitive decline over that time. They also inquired about cannabis, alcohol and tobacco use. Lyketsos et al. found that the mean MMSE score declined by 1.2 points over 11.5 years, with the largest decline among older participants. There was, however, no relationship between cannabis use and decline in MMSE score. This persisted when adjustments were made for age, sex, education, minority status and use of alcohol and tobacco (Lyketsos et al., 1999). This study shows that cannabis use does not produce *gross* impairment of cognitive function but for a number of reasons it does not exclude the possibility that cannabis use causes more subtle cognitive impairment. First, only 57% of those initially interviewed were followed up and those lost to follow-up had poorer MMSE scores at first assessment. Second, the MMSE is a screening test for gross cognitive impairment. It is not sensitive to small changes in cognitive functioning (Bowie et al., 1999). Third, cannabis use was assessed only once on study entry and more than two weeks of daily use qualified as 'heavy cannabis use'. Since cannabis use declines steeply with age (Bachman et al., 1997) few people in this sample would have been daily cannabis users for any length of time.

Studies of neurotoxicity

Human studies of brain anatomy have generally failed to find gross 'brain damage' in chronic cannabis users (Wert and Raulin, 1986; Solowij, 1998; Solowij, 1999).

The human studies of cognitive functioning suggest that cannabis may produce more subtle changes in brain function that existing methods of brain imaging are unlikely to detect (Solowij, 1998; Solowij, 1999). Wert and Raulin (1986) proposed that 'there are no gross structural or neurological deficits in marijuana-using subjects, although subtle neurological features may be present'. The type of deficit that they thought more likely to occur 'would be a subtle, functional deficit which could be assessed more easily with either psychological or neuropsychological assessment techniques' (p. 624).

A number of studies have demonstrated altered brain function and metabolism in humans following acute and chronic use of cannabis using cerebral blood flow (CBF), positron emission tomography (PET), and electroencephalographic (EEG) techniques. In the most recent carefully controlled study, Block and colleagues (2000b) found that after more than 26 hours of supervised abstinence frequent cannabis users (17 times per week for 4 years) showed substantially lower resting levels of brain blood flow (up to 18%) than controls in a large region of posterior cerebellum and in prefrontal cortex. The most recent study using sophisticated measurement techniques showed that frequent but short-term cannabis use does not produce structural brain abnormalities, or global or regional changes in brain tissue volume or composition when assessed by magnetic resonance imaging (MRI) (Block et al., 2000a).

Summary

Cannabis use does not produce *gross* cognitive impairment like that seen in heavy consumers of alcohol (Pope and Yurgelun-Todd, 1996; Solowij, 1998). There is growing evidence, however, that long-term daily cannabis use produces more subtle impairments in memory and attention (Solowij, 1998; Solowij, 1999). Expert opinion is divided on the significance of these differences in cognitive performance. Some sceptics still argue that we cannot exclude the possibility that these differences indicate pre-existing differences in cognitive ability, differences in other drug use, or a failure to ensure abstinence from cannabis (e.g. Gonzales et al., 2002). Increasingly more commentators believe that there are real, if small, differences in cognitive functioning between long-term cannabis users and controls (e.g. Pope et al., 1995; Block, 1996; Pope and Yurgelun-Todd, 1996; Solowij, 1998). They argue that recent better-controlled studies make the sceptics' explanations implausible.

There are still uncertainties about the interpretation of these differences. The conflicting evidence on whether these impairments are related to duration or frequency of use (Solowij, 1998; Pope et al., 2001; Pope, 2002) underlies a disagreement about whether these differences reflect the residual effects of heavy cannabis use (e.g. Pope et al., 1995; Pope and Yurgelun-Todd, 1996; Pope, 2002) or the cumulative effects of chronic cannabis use on cannabinoid receptors in the CNS (Solowij, 1998). It is also unclear whether these subtle impairments will affect cognitive performance in everyday life (e.g. Gonzales et al., 2002; Pope, 2002) and whether there will be complete recovery of cognitive function after sustained abstinence from cannabis.

9

Cannabis use and psychotic disorders

There are a number of good reasons why it is a plausible hypothesis that cannabis use may be a cause of psychotic disorders, severe mental illnesses in which hallucinations, delusions and impaired reality testing are predominant features. First, THC is a psychoactive substance which produces some symptoms found in psychotic disorders: euphoria, distorted time perception, cognitive and memory impairments (Thornicroft, 1990). Second, in laboratory studies high doses of THC have produced psychotic symptoms in normal volunteers, including visual and auditory hallucinations, delusional ideas, thought disorder, and symptoms of hypomania (Georgotas and Zeidenberg, 1979). Third, clinical observers in countries which have a long history of chronic cannabis use, such as India, Egypt, and the Caribbean, have described 'cannabis psychoses' (Brill and Nahas, 1984; Ghodse, 1986).

It is useful to distinguish three types of hypotheses about relationships between cannabis use and psychosis (Hall, 1998). The strongest hypothesis is that heavy cannabis use causes a unique 'cannabis psychosis'. This hypothesis assumes (1) that the psychosis would not occur in the absence of cannabis use, and (2) that the causal role of cannabis can be inferred from the type of psychotic symptoms and the observations that psychotic symptoms are preceded by heavy cannabis use and remit with abstinence.

A second hypothesis is that cannabis use may precipitate an episode of schizophrenia. This hypothesis assumes that cannabis use is one factor among many others (including genetic predisposition and other unknown causes) that act together to cause schizophrenia. It does not assume that a causal role for cannabis can be inferred from the symptoms of the disorder, or that the disorder will necessarily remit when cannabis use ceases.

Third, if cannabis use can precipitate schizophrenia, it is also probable that it can exacerbate its symptoms. However, cannabis use may exacerbate symptoms of schizophrenia (even if it is not a precipitant of the disorder) by reducing compliance with treatment, or interfering with the effects of the neuroleptic drugs that are used to treat it.

Making causal inferences

In order to infer that cannabis use is a cause of psychosis in any of these ways we need evidence: that there is an association between cannabis use and psychosis; that chance is an unlikely explanation of the association; that cannabis use preceded the psychosis; and that plausible alternative explanations of the association can be excluded (Hall, 1987).

Evidence that cannabis use and psychosis are associated and that chance is an unlikely explanation of the association are readily available. There are a now a number of prospective studies showing that cannabis use precedes psychosis. The difficult task is excluding the hypothesis that the relationship between cannabis use and psychosis is due to other factors (e.g. other drug use, or a genetic predisposition to develop schizophrenia and use cannabis).

Since ethical considerations limit experimental human studies and there are no suitable animal models, epidemiological methods must be used to rule out common causal hypotheses. These estimate the relationship between cannabis use and the risk of developing a psychosis after adjusting for variables that may affect the risk (e.g. personal characteristics prior to using cannabis, family history of psychotic illness, and other drug use). If the relationship persists after statistical adjustment, then we can be confident that it is not due to the variables for which statistical adjustment has been made.

'A cannabis psychosis'

There are case reports of 'cannabis psychoses' (Bernhardson and Gunne, 1972; Chopra and Smith, 1974; Solomons et al., 1990; Wylie et al., 1995) that describe individuals who develop psychotic disorders after using cannabis. Chopra and Smith (1974) reported one of the largest, a series of 200 patients who were admitted to a psychiatric hospital in Calcutta between 1963 and 1968 with psychotic symptoms that followed the use of cannabis. The most common symptoms 'were sudden onset of confusion, generally associated with delusions, hallucinations (usually visual) and emotional lability ... amnesia, disorientation, depersonalisation and paranoid symptoms' (p. 24). Most psychoses were preceded by using large amounts of cannabis and those who used the most potent cannabis developed psychoses after the shortest periods of use.

The findings of Chopra and Smith have been supported by case series which suggest that large doses of potent cannabis products can produce a 'toxic' psychotic disorder with 'organic' features of amnesia and confusion. These disorders have been reported in the Caribbean (Harding and Knight, 1973), New Zealand (Eva, 1992), Scotland (Wylie et al., 1995), South Africa (Solomons et al., 1990), Sweden (Bernhardson and Gunne, 1972), and the United Kingdom (Carney et al., 1984).

These disorders have been attributed to cannabis use for combinations of the following reasons: the onset of the disorders followed the use of large quantities of cannabis; the affected individuals were confused, disorientated and amnesic; some had no personal or family history of psychosis; their symptoms remitted within days to weeks of enforced abstinence from cannabis use; recovery was complete, with the person having no residual psychotic symptoms like those seen in schizophrenia; and if the disorder recurred, it was only after the individual resumed cannabis use (Hall, 1998).

Some commentators (Thornicroft, 1990; Gruber and Pope, 1994) have criticised the poor information on cannabis use and its relationship to the onset of psychosis, the person's premorbid adjustment and their family history of psychosis. They also emphasise the varied clinical picture of 'cannabis psychoses' as reported by different observers.

Controlled studies

A number of controlled studies have been conducted over the past 20 years (Thacore and Shukla, 1976; Rottanburg et al., 1982; Imade and Ebie, 1991; McGuire et al., 1994; McGuire et al., 1995; Nunez and Gurpegui, 2002). Studies have either compared persons with 'cannabis psychoses' with persons who have schizophrenia, or compared psychoses occurring in persons who have and have not used cannabis prior to presenting for treatment. Their results have been mixed, in part because of the small sample sizes and variations in research methods (Hall, 1998).

Psychotic symptoms and cannabis use in community samples

Several studies have examined the relationship between cannabis use and psychotic symptoms in the general population. Tien and Anthony (1990) used data from the Epidemiologic Catchment Area study to examine correlates of reporting one or more 'psychotic experiences' (four types of hallucinations and seven types of delusional belief). They compared 477 cases who reported one or more of these symptoms in a one-year follow-up with 1818 controls who did not. Cases and controls were matched for age and social and demographic characteristics. Daily cannabis use was found to double the risk of reporting psychotic symptoms (after statistical adjustment for alcohol use and psychiatric diagnoses at baseline).

Thomas (1996) reported the prevalence of psychotic symptoms among cannabis users in a random sample of people drawn from the electoral roll of a large city in the North Island of New Zealand. One in seven (14%) cannabis users reported 'strange, unpleasant experiences such as hearing voices or becoming convinced that someone is trying to harm you or that you are being persecuted' after using cannabis.

The National Survey of Mental Health and Wellbeing (NSMHWB) conducted in Australia in 1997 included a screening questionnaire for psychotic symptoms (Hall et al., 1998). Among those under 50 years of age who screened positive for a psychotic disorder, 7.8% (n = 27) met ICD-10 criteria for cannabis dependence in the past 12 months. This was 17.2% of all persons diagnosed with cannabis dependence. A diagnosis of cannabis dependence increased the chances of reporting psychotic symptoms 1.71 times, after adjusting for age, affective and anxiety disorders, smoking status and alcohol dependence (Degenhardt and Hall, 2001).

Cannabis use and schizophrenia

Clinical studies

In case-control studies (Schneier and Siris, 1987; Smith and Hucker, 1994), patients with schizophrenia are more likely to use cannabis than other psychiatric patients or normal controls (Warner et al., 1994). The prevalence of use in schizophrenic patients has varied between studies but it is generally higher than rates in the general population (Warner et al., 1994). These variations are probably due to differences in the sampling of patients, with younger cases reporting higher rates than older persons with chronic disorders. Generally, cannabis is the most commonly used drug after alcohol and tobacco, and it is often used with alcohol (Mueser et al., 1992; Hambrecht and Hafner, 1996).

The controlled clinical studies provide conflicting evidence on the correlates of substance abuse in schizophrenia apart from finding that young males are over-represented among cannabis users (Hall, 1998), as they are in the general community (Donnelly and Hall, 1994). In some studies, cannabis users have had an earlier onset of psychotic symptoms, a better premorbid adjustment, more episodes of illness, and more hallucinations (Dixon et al., 1990; Arndt et al., 1992; Hambrecht and Hafner, 1996). Other controlled studies have failed to replicate some of these findings (Zisook et al., 1992; Cuffel et al., 1993; Kovasznay et al., 1993).

A recent clinical study has adopted a novel approach to studying the relationship between cannabis use and psychosis (Phillips et al., 2002). In this study, 100 young people (49% male with an average age of 19.3 years) were identified as being at 'ultra high' risk of psychosis on the basis of one or more of the following: schizophrenia in a first degree relative; the presence of attenuated psychotic symptoms; or a brief limited psychosis. Cannabis was the most commonly used drug in the 12 months preceding assessment (35%), with 18% meeting criteria for cannabis dependence in the previous year. Cannabis use, however, did not predict an increased risk of developing an acute psychosis during the follow-up period, regardless of whether cannabis use was defined as any use, frequent use or dependent use in the past year.

Population studies

Community surveys of psychiatric disorders, such as the ECA, have reported higher rates of substance-use disorders among persons with schizophrenia (Anthony and Helzer, 1991). Nearly half of the patients identified as schizophrenic in the ECA study had a diagnosis of substance abuse or dependence (34% for an alcohol disorder and 28% for another drug disorder) (Regier et al., 1990). These rates were higher than the rates in the general population, namely, 14% for alcohol disorders (Helzer et al., 1991) and 6% for drug abuse (Anthony and Helzer, 1991). The most common patterns of substance use among 231 cases of schizophrenia in the ECA study were: alcohol (37%) and cannabis (23%), followed by stimulants and hallucinogens (13%), narcotics (10%) and sedatives (8%). The most common combination of drugs was alcohol and cannabis use (31%) (Cuffel et al., 1993). These findings were replicated in Edmonton, Alberta (Bland et al., 1987).

In the Australian NSMHWB, 11.5% of those who reported that they had been diagnosed with schizophrenia, met ICD-10 criteria for a cannabis-use disorder in the past 12 months and 21.2% met criteria for an alcohol-use disorder. After adjusting for confounding variables, those who met criteria for cannabis dependence were 2.9 times more likely to report that they had been diagnosed with schizophrenia than those who did not.

Explanations of the association

One explanation of the association is that cannabis use precipitates schizophrenia in vulnerable persons. This is consistent with the earlier age of onset of psychosis among cannabis users (with their drug use typically preceding symptoms), and the fact that cannabis users have better premorbid adjustment, fewer negative symptoms, and better treatment outcome (Allebeck, 1991).

Another possibility is that the association between cannabis use and an early onset and good prognosis are spurious. Arndt et al. (1992) argue that schizophrenics with a better premorbid personality are more likely to be offered cannabis by peers than persons with schizophrenia who are socially withdrawn. There is also evidence (Bromet et al., 1995) that persons with acute onset psychoses usually have a better premorbid adjustment and a better prognosis. They also have greater opportunities to use cannabis and other illicit drugs than withdrawn persons whose illness has an insidious onset.

A third possibility is that cannabis use is a consequence (rather than a cause) of schizophrenia. For example, cannabis and other drugs may be used to medicate the unpleasant symptoms of schizophrenia, such as depression, anxiety, lethargy, and anhedonia, or the unpleasant side effects of the neuroleptic drugs that are often used to treat the disorder (Dixon et al., 1990).

Precipitation of schizophrenia

The most convincing evidence that cannabis use may precipitate schizophrenia comes from a 15-year prospective study of cannabis use and schizophrenia in 50,465 Swedish conscripts (Andreasson et al., 1987). This study investigated the relationship between self-reported cannabis use at age 18 and the risk of being diagnosed with schizophrenia in the Swedish psychiatric case register during the next 15 years.

Andreasson et al. found that those who had tried cannabis by age 18 were 2.4 times more likely to receive a diagnosis of schizophrenia than those who had not. The risk of a diagnosis of schizophrenia was related to cannabis use in a dose–response way to the number of times cannabis had been used by age 18. Compared to those who had not used cannabis, the risk of developing schizophrenia was 1.3 times higher for those who had used cannabis 1 to 10 times, 3 times higher for those who had used cannabis between 1 and 50 times, and 6 times higher for those who had used cannabis more than 50 times.

These risks were substantially reduced after statistical adjustment for variables that were related to the risk of developing schizophrenia. These included having a psychiatric diagnosis at age 18, and having parents who had divorced (as an indicator of parental psychiatric disorder). Nevertheless, these relationships remained statistically significant after adjustment. Compared to those who had never used cannabis, those who had used cannabis 1 to 10 times were 1.5 times more likely, and those who had used 10 or more times, were 2.3 times more likely to receive a diagnosis of schizophrenia. Andreasson et al. (1987) argued that this means that cannabis use precipitates schizophrenia in vulnerable individuals.

Other authors have offered a number of alternative explanations of the Swedish finding. First, there was a large temporal gap between self-reported cannabis use at age 18 and the development of schizophrenia over the next 15 years or so (Negrete, 1989). Because the diagnosis of schizophrenia was based upon a case register there was no data on how many individuals used cannabis up until the time that their schizophrenia was diagnosed. Andreasson et al. argued that cannabis use persisted because cannabis use at age 18 was also strongly related to the risk of attracting a diagnosis of drug abuse.

A second possibility is that schizophrenia was misdiagnosed. On this hypothesis, the higher rate of 'schizophrenia' among heavy cannabis users reflected cannabis-induced psychoses which were mistakenly diagnosed as schizophrenia (Negrete, 1989). Andreasson et al. (1989) examined 21 cases of schizophrenia among conscripts in the case register (8 of whom had used cannabis and 13 of whom had not). They found that 80% of these cases met the DSM-III requirement that the symptoms had been present for at least six months, thereby excluding the diagnoses of transient drug-induced psychotic symptoms.

A third hypothesis is that the relationship between cannabis use and schizophrenia was due to the use of amphetamine. Persons who use cannabis in adolescence are at higher risk of later using amphetamines (Kandel and Faust, 1975) which can produce an acute paranoid psychosis (Bell, 1973). Amphetamines were the major illicit drugs of abuse in Sweden during the study period (Inghe, 1969). The evidence that psychotic symptoms persisted beyond 6 months (Andreasson et al., 1989) also makes this an unlikely hypothesis.

A fourth hypothesis is that cannabis use at age 18 was a symptom of emerging schizophrenia. Andreasson et al. (1989) rejected this hypothesis, noting that the cannabis users who developed schizophrenia had better premorbid personalities, a more abrupt onset, and more positive symptoms than the non-users who developed schizophrenia. Moreover, there was still a dose–response relationship between cannabis use and schizophrenia among those who had no history of psychiatric disorder. The persuasiveness of this evidence depends upon how confident we can be that a *failure* to identify a psychiatric disorder at conscription meant that no disorder was present.

A fifth hypothesis depends upon the validity of the self-reported cannabis use at conscription. Andreasson et al. (1987) acknowledged that cannabis use was probably under-reported because this information was not collected anonymously. They argued, however, that this would under-estimate the relationship between cannabis use and schizophrenia. This is true if the schizophrenic and non-schizophrenics conscripts were equally likely to under-report. If, for example, pre-schizophrenic subjects were more candid about their drug use, then the apparent relationship between cannabis use and schizophrenia could be due to response bias (Negrete, 1989). This seems unlikely in view of the strong dose–response relationship between the frequency of cannabis use by age 18, and the large unadjusted relative risk of schizophrenia among heavy users.

A number of longitudinal studies have since been reported that address many of the criticisms of the Andreasson et al. study. Zammit et al. (2002) reported a follow-up of the Swedish cohort study, reporting on risk over a 27-year follow-up that covers most of the risk period for the onset of psychotic disorders in a cohort that was first studied when 18–20 years old. This study improved on the earlier study in a number of ways. The psychiatric register provided more complete coverage of all cases diagnosed with schizophrenia; there was better statistical control of a larger number of potential confounding variables, including other drug use, IQ, known risk factors for schizophrenia and social integration; the study distinguished between cases that occurred in the first 5 years of the study period and those that occurred more than 5 years afterwards in order to look at the possible role of a prodrome; and the study undertook separate analyses in those who only reported using cannabis at the initial assessment.

Zammit et al. found, as did Andreasson et al., that cannabis use at baseline predicted an increased risk of schizophrenia during the follow-up period. They also found a dose–response relationship between frequency of cannabis use at baseline and risk of schizophrenia during the follow-up. They demonstrated that the relationship between cannabis use and schizophrenia persisted when they statistically controlled for the effects of other drug use and other potential confounding factors, including a history of psychiatric symptoms at baseline. They estimated that 13% of cases of schizophrenia could be averted if all cannabis use were prevented (i.e. the attributable risk of cannabis to schizophrenia was 13%). The same relationships were observed in the subset of the sample who only reported cannabis use at baseline and among cases diagnosed in the first 5 years after assessment and for the 22 years afterwards. The relationship was a little stronger in cases observed in the first 5 years, probably reflecting the decline in cannabis use that occurs with age.

Zammit et al.'s findings have been supported by a study conducted by Van Os and colleagues (2002). This was a three-year longitudinal study of the relationship between self-reported cannabis use and psychosis in a community sample of 4848 people in the Netherlands. Subjects were assessed at baseline on cannabis and other drug use. Psychotic symptoms were assessed using a computerised diagnostic interview. A diagnosis of psychosis·was validated in positive cases by a diagnostic telephone interview with a psychiatrist or psychologist. A consensus clinical judgement was made on the basis of the interview material as to whether individuals had a psychotic disorder for which they were in need of psychiatric care.

Van Os et al. substantially replicated the findings of the Swedish cohort and extended them in a number of important ways. First, cannabis use at baseline predicted an increased risk of psychotic symptoms during the follow-up period in individuals who had not reported psychiatric symptoms at baseline. Second, there was a dose–response relationship between frequency of cannabis use at baseline and risk of psychotic symptoms during the follow-up period. Third, the relationship between cannabis use and psychotic symptoms persisted when they statistically controlled for the effects of other drug use. Fourth, the relationship between cannabis use and psychotic symptoms was stronger for cases with more severe psychotic symptoms that were adjudged to need psychiatric care. Van Os et al. estimated the attributable risk of cannabis to psychosis was 13% for psychotic symptoms and 50% for cases with psychotic disorders adjudged to need psychiatric treatment. Fifth, those who reported any psychotic symptoms at baseline were more likely to develop schizophrenia if they used cannabis than were individuals who were not so vulnerable. They estimated that cannabis use accounted for 80% of the increased risk of developing a psychotic disorder that warranted treatment among vulnerable individuals.

Arseneault et al. (2002) reported a prospective study of the relationship between adolescent cannabis use and psychosis in young adults in a New Zealand birth cohort (N = 759) whose members had been assessed intensively on risk factors for psychotic symptoms and disorders since birth. Psychotic disorders were conservatively assessed according to DSM-IV diagnostic criteria, with corroborative reports from family members or friends on social adjustment. They assessed psychotic symptoms at age 11 *before* onset of cannabis use and distinguished between early and late onset of cannabis use. They also examined the specificity of the association between cannabis use and psychosis by conducting analyses of the effects of: (1) other drug use on psychotic symptoms and disorders; and (2) cannabis use on depressive disorders.

Arseneault et al. found a relationship between cannabis use by age 15 and an increased risk of psychotic symptoms by age 26. Controlling for other drug use did not affect the relationship. The relationship was no longer statistically significant after adjustment for reporting psychotic symptoms at age 11, which probably reflected the small number of psychotic disorders observed in the sample. The small number of cases also limited the ability of the study to examine predictors of psychotic disorders at age 26. The measurement of cannabis and other drug use was crude (viz, none, once, 2 times, and 3 or more times) although this was more likely to work against finding relationships. An interesting result was the specificity of the effects of cannabis on psychotic symptoms: there was no relationship between other drug use and psychotic disorders and no relationship between cannabis use and depression. There was also an interaction between psychosis risk and age of onset of cannabis use, with earlier onset being more strongly related to psychosis. There was also the suggestion of an interaction between cannabis use and vulnerability, with a higher risk of psychosis among cannabis users who reported psychotic symptoms at age 11.

Fergusson, Horwood and Swain-Campbell (2003) have reported a longitudinal study of the relationship between cannabis dependence at age 18 and the number of psychotic symptoms reported at age 21 in the Christchurch birth cohort in New Zealand. They assessed cannabis dependence using DSM-IV criteria and psychotic symptoms were assessed by 10 items from the SCL-90. Because this was a birth cohort that had been assessed throughout childhood and adolescence Fergusson et al. were able to adjust for a large number of potential confounding variables, including self-reported psychotic symptoms at the previous assessment, other drug use and other psychiatric disorders. They found that cannabis dependence at age 18 predicted an increased risk of psychotic symptoms at age 21 years (RR of 2.3). This association was smaller but still significant after adjustment for potential confounders (RR of 1.8).

The longitudinal studies find consistent associations between cannabis use in adolescence and the occurrence of psychotic symptoms in early adult life but all share a weakness: there is uncertainty about the temporal relationship between cannabis use and the timing of the onset of psychotic symptoms. Subjects in these studies have usually been assessed once a year or less often and asked to report retrospectively on their cannabis use during the preceding number of years, often as crudely as the number of times that cannabis was used or the number of times it was used per week or month.

A recent French study provides greater detail on the temporal relationship between cannabis use and psychotic symptoms using an experience sampling method (Verdoux et al., 2002). These investigators asked 79 college students to report on their drug use and experience of psychotic symptoms at randomly selected time points, several times each day over 7 consecutive days. The ratings were prompted by randomly programmed signals sent to a portable electronic device that the students carried. The students were a stratified sample from a larger group so that high cannabis users (N = 41) and students identified as vulnerable to psychosis (N = 16) were over-represented in the sample. Vulnerability to psychosis was indicated by reporting one or more psychotic symptoms in the past month during a personal interview.

Verdoux et al. found a positive association between self-reported cannabis use and unusual perceptions and a negative association between cannabis use and hostility. That is, in time periods when cannabis was used, users reported more unusual perceptions and less hostility. These relationships depended upon vulnerability to psychosis: in vulnerable individuals cannabis use was more strongly associated with strange impressions and unusual perceptions and its use did not decrease feelings of hostility in the way that it did in individuals who lacked this vulnerability. They also found a relationship between self-reported use of psychostimulant drugs and unusual perceptions and thought influence but these relationships were independent of those between cannabis use and psychotic experiences. There was no temporal relationship between reporting unusual experiences and cannabis use, as would be expected if some form of self-medication were involved.

Exacerbation of schizophrenia

Clinical reports suggest that schizophrenic patients who continue to use cannabis have more psychotic symptoms (Weil, 1970), respond poorly to neuroleptic drugs (Bowers et al., 1990), and have a worse clinical course than those patients who do not (Turner and Tsuang, 1990). These reports have been supported by controlled studies.

Negrete et al. (1986) conducted a retrospective study of the relationship between self-reported cannabis use and symptoms using used clinical records in 137 schizophrenic patients who had a disorder for at least six months. They compared the rates of hallucinations, delusions and hospitalisations among cannabis users with those among patients who had previously used cannabis, and those who had never used cannabis. There were higher rates of hallucinations and delusions, and more hospitalisations among current cannabis users and these relationships persisted after statistical adjustment for age and sex differences between the groups.

Cleghorn et al. (1991) compared the symptom profiles of schizophrenic patients with histories of substance abuse, among whom cannabis was the most heavily used drug. Drug abusers had a higher prevalence of hallucinations, delusions and positive symptoms than those who did not abuse drugs.

Jablensky et al. (1992) reported a two-year follow-up of 1202 first episode schizophrenic patients in a ten-country WHO Collaborative study. They found that the use of 'street drugs', including cannabis and cocaine, during the follow-up period predicted more psychotic symptoms and hospitalization. Martinez-Arevalo et al. (1994) also reported that continued use of cannabis during a one-year follow-up of 62 DSM-diagnosed schizophrenic patients predicted a higher rate of relapse and poorer compliance with anti-psychotic drug treatment.

Linszen et al. (1994) reported a prospective study of 93 psychotic patients whose symptoms were assessed monthly over a year. Twenty-four of their patients were cannabis users (11 were less than daily users and 13 were daily cannabis users). Despite the small samples, they found that the cannabis users relapsed to psychotic symptoms sooner, and had more frequent relapses in the year of follow-up, than the patients who had not used cannabis. There was also a dose response relationship: daily users relapsed earlier, and more often, than the less-than-daily users who, in turn, relapsed sooner, and more often, than the patients who did not use cannabis. These relationships persisted after statistical adjustment for premorbid adjustment, and alcohol and other drug use during the follow-up period.

The major cause of uncertainty about this relationship is the contribution of confounding factors, such as differences between patients who do and do not use cannabis in premorbid personality, family history, and other characteristics. This is unlikely in the WHO schizophrenia study (Jablensky et al., 1992) and the Linszen et al. study (1994), both of which used statistical methods to adjust for many of these confounders. The other difficulty is separating the contributions that cannabis and alcohol make to the exacerbation of schizophrenic symptoms. The concurrent use of alcohol is common, and the heavier the cannabis use, the more likely they are to use psychostimulants and hallucinogens (Mueser et al., 1992). Only the Linszen et al. study statistically adjusted for the effects of concurrent alcohol and drug use and found that the relationship persisted. Our confidence that the effect is attributable to cannabis would be increased by replications of the Linszen et al. finding.

Intervention studies

If we could reduce cannabis use among patients with schizophrenia who use cannabis, then we could discover whether their disorders improved and their risk of relapse was reduced. The major difficulty with this strategy is that it presupposes that we can successfully treat substance use disorders in persons with schizophrenia. Dependence on alcohol and other drugs is difficult to treat (Heather and Tebbutt, 1989), and many persons with schizophrenia have characteristics that predict a poor outcome, namely, they lack social support, may be cognitively impaired, unemployed, and do not comply with treatment (Mueser et al., 1992; Kavanagh, 1995).

There are very few controlled outcome studies of substance abuse treatment in schizophrenia (Lehman et al., 1993). Few of these have produced large enough benefits of treatment, or treated a large enough number of patients, to provide an adequate chance of detecting any positive impacts of abstinence on the course of disorders. The few that have been large enough (Jerrell and Ridgely, 1995) have not reported results separately by diagnosis.

Self-medication

The self-medication hypothesis is superficially plausible but the evidence in its favour is not very compelling (Blanchard et al., 2000). The reasons that most persons with schizophrenia give for using alcohol, cannabis and other illicit drugs are similar to those given by persons who do not have schizophrenia, namely, to relieve boredom, to provide stimulation, to feel good and to socialise with peers (e.g. Noordsy et al., 1991; Mueser et al., 1992). The drugs that are most often used by patients with schizophrenia are also those that are used by their peers, namely, tobacco, alcohol, and cannabis.

In favour of the self-medication hypothesis, is the evidence that some schizophrenic patients report using cannabis because its euphoric effects relieve negative symptoms and depression (e.g. Schneier and Siris, 1987; Dixon et al., 1990; Peralta and Cuesta, 1992). Dixon et al. (1990), for example, surveyed 83 patients with schizophrenia who reported that cannabis reduced anxiety and depression, and increased a sense of calm but at the cost of increased suspiciousness.

Hamera et al. (1995) examined correlations over 84 consecutive days between self-reported psychotic symptoms, licit and illicit drug use, and medication compliance in 17 persons with schizophrenia. They only found relationships between nicotine and prodromal psychotic symptoms and between caffeine use and symptoms of anxiety and depression but no relationships were found between psychotic symptoms and alcohol or cannabis use. Their negative results have recently been supported by Verdoux et al. (2003) who found that cannabis use predicted psychotic symptoms in the following few hours but not vice versa.

Summary

The hypothesis that there is a 'cannabis psychosis' is still contentious. In its favour are case series and the small number of controlled studies. Critics of the hypothesis emphasise the fallibility of clinical judgements about aetiology, the poorly specified criteria used in diagnosing these psychoses, the dearth of controlled studies, and the striking variations in the clinical features of 'cannabis psychoses' (Poole and Brabbins, 1996). It is a plausible hypothesis that high doses of cannabis can produce psychotic *symptoms* but the evidence for specific 'cannabis psychoses' is less compelling because the clinical symptoms reported by different observers have been so mixed.

There is now epidemiological evidence that cannabis use exacerbates the symptoms of schizophrenia. This is supported by the findings of a number of retrospective and prospective studies that have controlled for confounding variables. It is also biologically plausible. Psychotic disorders involve disturbances in the dopamine neurotransmitter systems since drugs that increase the release of dopamine produce psychotic symptoms when given in large doses, and neuroleptic drugs that reduce psychotic symptoms also reduce dopamine levels (Stahl and Muntner, 1996; Moore et al., 1999). Cannabinoids, such as THC, increase dopamine release in the nucleus acumbens (Tanda et al., 1997).

The evidence from prospective epidemiological studies indicates that it is likely that cannabis use precipitates schizophrenia in persons who are vulnerable because of a personal or family history of schizophrenia. This hypothesis is consistent with the stress–diathesis model of schizophrenia (Gottesman, 1991; Bromet et al., 1995) in which the likelihood of developing schizophrenia is the product of stress acting upon a genetic 'diathesis' to develop schizophrenia. There is also evidence that a genetic vulnerability to psychosis increases the risk that cannabis users will develop psychosis (McGuire et al., 1995; Arseneault et al., 2002; Verdoux et al., 2002).

The most contentious issue is whether cannabis use can cause schizophrenia that would not have occurred in its absence. The estimated attributable risk in early studies was 7% (Andreasson et al., 1989) but higher estimates (13%) have been produced in more recent studies and one study has estimated that cannabis use is a contributory cause of 50% of cases in need of treatment (Van Os et al., 2002). The puzzle is that the *treated* incidence of schizophrenia, and particularly early onset, acute cases, has not obviously increased during the 1970s and 1980s (Der et al., 1990) when there have been substantial increases in cannabis use among young adults in Australia and North America (Donnelly and Hall, 1994). Although there are complications in interpreting such trends (Kendell et al., 1993), a large reduction in treated incidence has been observed in a number of countries which have a high prevalence of cannabis use and in which the reduction is unlikely to be a diagnostic artefact (Joyce, 1987). Debate has not been about any increase in incidence but about whether incidence has declined or remained stationary (Jablensky, 1999).

Effects on adolescent development

For understandable reasons, community concern about the effects of cannabis use on adolescents has played a central role in debates about cannabis policy. One concern that has dominated the debate is whether adolescents who use cannabis are more likely, *as a result* of using cannabis, to use other more dangerous illicit drugs, such as cocaine and heroin (Goode, 1974; DuPont, 1984; Kleiman, 1992). This has been described as the 'gateway hypothesis'.

A second set of concerns has been about the effects that adolescent cannabis use may have on psychosocial outcomes, such as, educational achievement, employment, involvement in crime, and mental health. A reasonable concern is that regular cannabis intoxication may interfere with the adolescent's transition from childhood to adulthood by impairing school performance, and adversely affecting interpersonal relationships and important life choices, such as whom and when to marry, and what occupation to pursue (Polich et al., 1984; Baumrind and Moselle, 1985).

Because of concern about the adverse effects of adolescent cannabis use in the USA in the late 1970s the US government funded a number of prospective studies of the antecedents and consequences of adolescent drug use (Kaplan et al., 1984; Kandel, 1988; Newcomb and Bentler, 1988). These, and subsequent studies in the USA and other countries, have begun to distinguish the effects of users' pre-existing personal characteristics and the effects of their cannabis and other drug use on their risks of using other illicit drugs, their school performance, and their psychosocial adjustment more generally. The most important of these studies are reviewed in the following two chapters.

10

Is cannabis a gateway drug?

Cross-sectional surveys of adolescent drug use in the United States and elsewhere have consistently shown three types of association between cannabis use and the use of other illicit drugs, such as heroin and cocaine (Morral et al., 2002).

First, American adolescents during the 1970s and 1980s showed a typical sequence of involvement with licit and illicit drugs in which almost all who tried cocaine and heroin had first used alcohol, tobacco and cannabis (Kandel, 1975; Kandel, 2002). The sole exception to this generalisation has been found in samples of inner city youth for whom a wide range of illicit drugs are more readily available (Golub and Johnson, 2002).

Second, during the same period there was a strong relationship between *regular* cannabis use and the later use of heroin and cocaine. Kandel (1984), for example, found that only 7% of American youth who had never used cannabis reported using another illicit drug. This figure was 33% among those who had used cannabis, and 84% among current daily cannabis users. The same relationships have been observed in surveys of drug use in Australia (Donnelly and Hall, 1994).

Third, the earlier the age at which any drug was first used, the more likely the user was to use the next drug in the sequence (Kandel, 1978; Donovan and Jessor, 1983; Kandel, 1984, 1988; Kandel, 2002). So those who begin to use alcohol and tobacco at an early age were the most likely to use cannabis; early cannabis users, in turn, were more likely to use hallucinogens and 'pills' (amphetamines and tranquillisers); and early users of 'pills' were, in turn, the ones most likely to use cocaine and heroin.

The relationships between cannabis and heroin use found in the cross-sectional studies have also been reported in longitudinal studies of drug use. In one of the first such studies (Robins et al., 1970) followed-up 222 African-American adolescents identified from school records until age 33 and interviewed them about their drug use in adolescence and young adulthood. They found that young men who had used cannabis before the age of 20 were more likely to use heroin than those who had not. These results have been confirmed in longitudinal studies by Kandel and her colleagues (Kandel et al., 1986; Kandel and Yamaguchi, 2002) in which drug use has been assessed in adolescents who have been followed into early adulthood (Kaplan et al., 1984; Yamaguchi and Kandel, 1984a, 1984b).

These patterns of drug involvement have not been confined to the USA. In New Zealand, for example, studies of drug use in two birth cohorts (McGee and Feehan, 1993; Fergusson and Horwood, 1997, 1999, 2000) have found the same sequence of involvement with drugs and the same predictors of progression. In New Zealand cocaine and heroin are much less readily available than in the USA or Australia (Fergusson and Horwood, 2000).

These patterns of drug involvement – the typical sequencing and the increased risk of progression among early initiators and regular users – are among the most robust findings in drug use epidemiology. How they are to be explained is one of the most contested issues in epidemiology and drug policy. For the sake of simplicity, we distinguish three types of explanation of the association between cannabis and other illicit drug use. The first hypothesis is that there is no causal relationship; that the association between cannabis and other drug use is explained by common factors that cause both early cannabis use and subsequent use of other illicit drugs. The second and third hypotheses assume different causal relationships between cannabis use and the use of other illicit drugs. One hypothesis is that the pharmacological effects of cannabis increase an adolescent's propensity to use other illicit drugs. The other sociological hypothesis is that the relationship between cannabis and other illicit drug use arises because cannabis and other illicit drugs are supplied by the same blackmarket with the consequence that cannabis users have more opportunities to try other illicit drugs.

Each of these competing hypotheses is evaluated in the light of the available evidence during the remainder of this chapter. As we will argue, there is no single piece of evidence that is decisive in choosing between the hypotheses so we must look for convergent support for one of the hypotheses from the findings of studies that use multiple methods of independent imperfection.

Is the relationship between cannabis and other drug use due to common factors?

The common cause hypothesis appeals to characteristics of the individuals who use cannabis that also make them more likely to use other drugs. The explanation might be in terms of individual propensities to engage in socially deviant conduct, such as drug use, criminal acts and precocious sexual activity. These propensities could be of environmental origin or they may be due to a shared genetic vulnerability to develop different types of drug dependence.

Selective recruitment

One plausible alternative explanation of the association between daily cannabis use and the use of other drugs is 'selective recruitment'. On this hypothesis, there is selective recruitment to cannabis use of socially deviant young people who have a predilection to use intoxicating drugs like alcohol, cannabis, cocaine and heroin (Fergusson and Horwood, 2000). The sequence of drug involvement, on this hypothesis, simply reflects the differing availability and societal disapproval of different types of drug use (Donovan and Jessor, 1983). Alcohol and tobacco use precede cannabis use because alcohol and tobacco are more readily available to adolescents and their use by adults is more socially approved than that of cannabis. Cannabis use precedes heroin use for the same reasons. On this hypothesis, cannabis use does not cause the use of other illicit drugs. Rather, cannabis and heroin use would be common consequences of pre-existing propensities to use all of these drugs (Kaplan et al., 1984; Newcomb and Bentler, 1988).

The selective recruitment hypothesis is supported by the substantial correlations between nonconforming adolescent behaviours, such as, high school drop out, early premarital sexual experience and pregnancy, delinquency, and early alcohol and illicit drug use (Jessor and Jessor, 1977; Osgood et al., 1988). All of these are correlated with nonconformist and rebellious attitudes and with antisocial conduct in late childhood (Shedler and Block, 1990) and early adolescence (Jessor and Jessor, 1977; Newcomb and Bentler, 1988). Regular cannabis users are more likely than their peers: to have a history of such antisocial behaviour (Brook et al., 1992; McGee and Feehan, 1993); to be nonconformist and alienated (Jessor and Jessor, 1978; Shedler and Block, 1990; Brook et al., 1992); to perform poorly at school (Bailey et al., 1992; Hawkins et al., 1992; Kandel and Davies, 1992); and to use drugs to deal with personal distress (Shedler and Block, 1990; Kaplan and Johnson, 1992). The more of these risk factors that adolescents have, the more likely they are to use cannabis and other drugs (Scheier and Newcomb, 1991; Brook et al., 1992; Newcomb, 1992).

The selective recruitment hypothesis has been tested in longitudinal studies by assessing whether cannabis use predicts the use of heroin and cocaine after statistically controlling for differences between cannabis users and non-users in personal characteristics (Fergusson and Horwood, 2000). Yamaguchi (1984b), for example, found that the relationship between cannabis use and 'harder' illicit drug use persisted after statistically controlling for pre-existing adolescent behaviours and attitudes, interpersonal factors, and the age of initiation into drug use. They interpreted this as evidence that the relationship between cannabis use and the use of other illicit drugs was causal. The same finding has emerged in several other studies (Robins et al., 1970; O'Donnell and Clayton, 1982; Kandel et al., 1986).

Fergusson and colleagues (1997, 2000, 2002b) have reported a prospective study of 990 New Zealand children who were followed from birth to age 21 years and regularly assessed on a rich set of potentially confounding psychosocial variables that were statistically controlled for. These variables included: family background (socioeconomic status, parental conflict and divorce, childhood sexual abuse, parental punishment and parental attachment); parental adjustment (parental alcohol and drug problems, criminality and illicit drug use); individual characteristics of the young person (gender, intelligence, novelty seeking); early adolescent development (cigarette smoking, frequency of alcohol use, juvenile offending, school drop out, conduct problems and attitudes towards drug use); peer affiliations (peer use and problems with alcohol and other drug use); and personal history of risk-taking.

Fergusson and Horwood (1997) found a strong dose–response relationship between the frequency of cannabis use by age 16 (no use, use less than 10 times and use more than 10 times) and development of a substance use problem with cannabis, alcohol or other substances by age 18. There was also a strong association between the social background of the adolescents and their likelihood of having used cannabis by age 16. Early cannabis users came from lower socioeconomic status families with a history of parental conflict, parental criminality, alcohol and drug use, and low parental attachment. They also had a history of conduct problems, low self-esteem and high novelty seeking, and were likely to affiliate with delinquent peers. Adjustment for these family and personal factors substantially reduced but did not eliminate the relationships between early cannabis use and the use of other illicit drugs.

Fergusson and Horwood (2000) reported similar analyses in a subsequent follow-up of the birth cohort. They found that 69% of their sample reported using cannabis by age 21 and just over a quarter had used other illicit drugs, although only 4% had used cocaine or opiates. They found a strong dose–response relationship between the number of times that cannabis had been used at any age and the later risk of using another illicit drug. Those who had used cannabis once or twice were 3.5 times more likely to have used other illicit drugs: the risks were 12.0 times higher for those who had used 3 to 11 times, 41.3 for those who had used 12 to 49 times and 142.8 for those who had used 50 times or more.

The strength of the relationship between frequency of cannabis use and the use of other illicit drugs was reduced when confounding factors were statistically controlled for. Nonetheless, the relationships showed the same dose–response relationship, namely, 2.8 for those who had used once or twice, 7.7 for those who had used 3 to 11 times, 21.3 for those who had used 12 to 49 times and 59.2 for those who had used 50 times or more. These findings suggest that the selective recruitment hypothesis is unlikely to wholly explain the association between cannabis use and other illicit drug use.

Fergusson, Horwood and Swain-Campbell (2002a) have replicated these results in further analyses of the cohort at age 21. They used fixed effects regression methods to control for the effects of unobserved individual differences in propensity to use other drugs between early and late cannabis users. They also found a dose–response relationship between cannabis use and the risk of using other illicit drugs. The only variation was that the relationship varied with age of first cannabis use: the earlier that cannabis was first used, the higher was the risk of using other illicit drugs.

A recent study has provided renewed support for the common cause hypothesis. Morral et al. (2002) reported a simulation study that modelled a common cause model of the association between cannabis use and the use of other illicit drugs. They asked whether a simple common cause model would reproduce the three types of relationship that are usually interpreted as supporting the gateway hypothesis, namely, cannabis users' higher risk of trying harder drugs; the sequence of initiation in which cannabis use precedes the use of other illicit drugs; and a dose-response relationship between frequency of cannabis use and the use of other illicit drugs.

The common factor model that Morral et al. tested only assumed that individuals differ in their propensity to use a variety of drugs. They made no assumptions about the nature of this propensity, allowing that it may reflect combinations of personal characteristics, peer group drug use and the availability of drugs in individuals' neighbourhoods. The model only assumed that the propensity to use drugs was correlated with the opportunity to use them and with the age of first use of cannabis and other illicit drugs. Most importantly, their model assumed that there was *no* correlation between (1) the opportunities to use and age of first use of cannabis and (2) the opportunities to use and age of first use of other illicit drugs. Morral et al.'s common cause model reproduced all three 'gateway' patterns. Cannabis users were more likely to use harder drugs; cannabis use preceded the use of other illicit drugs, and there was a dose–response relationship between the frequency of cannabis use and the use of other illicit drugs.

Morral et al.'s study also raised questions about the effectiveness of testing the common factor model by seeing if relationships between cannabis use and other drugs persist after controlling for various indicators of the propensity to use cannabis and other drugs (e.g. Fergusson and Horwood, 2000). They presented evidence that this research strategy was only successful if the indicators were perfectly correlated with the propensity to use cannabis and other drugs. When the indicator measures were less than perfectly reliable spuriously high estimates of the residual association between cannabis use and the use of other illicit drugs remained after statistically controlling for the indicators.

A shared genetic vulnerability to drug dependence

Behavioural genetic studies of drug use suggest that genetic vulnerability to drug dependence may be a common explanation of the association between cannabis and other illicit drug use. Studies of identical and non-identical twins indicate that there is a genetic vulnerability to developing dependence on alcohol (Heath, 1995), cannabis (Kendler and Prescott, 1998) and tobacco (Han et al., 1999). A substantial part of the genetic vulnerability to developing dependence on these three drugs is shared, as are the family and environmental factors that influence alcohol and cannabis dependence (True et al., 1999). The genetic contribution to dependence on 'harder' drugs is less certain because rates of use in these twin studies have typically been too low to provide powerful tests of this hypothesis.

Lynskey et al. (2003) have recently used twin data to test the hypothesis that the association between cannabis use and the use of other illicit drugs can be explained by shared genes and environment. They examined the relationship between cannabis and other illicit drug use in 311 monozygotic (136) and dizygotic (175) Australian twin pairs in which one twin had and the other twin had not used cannabis before the age of 17 years. This study provided a strong test of a common cause, whether this is due to shared genes, shared environment or some combination of the two. If the association was attributable to a shared environment then discordant twins should not differ in the use of other illicit drugs. Similarly, if the association was attributable to shared genetic vulnerability to drug dependence then there should be no difference in the use of other illicit drugs between monozygotic twins who did and did not use cannabis before age 17.

Lynskey et al. found that the twin who had used cannabis before age 17 was more likely to have used sedatives, hallucinogens, stimulants and opioids than their co-twin who had not. Twins who had used cannabis were also more likely to report symptoms of abuse or dependence on cannabis and other illicit drugs than their twin who did not. These relationships persisted after controlling for other factors that predict an increased risk of developing drug abuse or dependence. They also persisted when the analysis was confined to twin pairs in which both had used cannabis at some time in their lives.

The findings of Lynksey et al. when taken together with those of Fergusson and Horwood (2000) suggest that shared genetic and/or shared environment explain a substantial part of the association between cannabis use and other illicit drug use. The size of the association in the study of twins after statistical adjustment was substantially smaller (RR ~ 2–4) than that reported in the study of Fergusson and Horwood (2000) (RR ~ 59). The Morral et al. study raises the question: Is the residual association between cannabis use and other illicit drug use in the twin study the result of measurement error or does it mean that cannabis use makes a small, direct causal contribution to the risk of using other illicit drugs, after taking account of common causes? We will return to this question after reviewing the evidence for two competing causal explanations of the association between cannabis and other illicit drug use.

Competing causal explanations of the association

If we assume that the association between cannabis and heroin use is not explained by pre-existing differences between cannabis users and non-users, then how does cannabis use 'cause' other illicit drug use?

Pharmacological hypotheses

The hypothesis that the pharmacological effects of cannabis use predisposes regular cannabis users to use other illicit drugs (Nahas, 1990; Walters, 1993) hypothesises that cannabis use produces changes in the CNS that sensitise cannabis users to the euphoric effects of other drugs. Nahas (1990) hypothesised that 'the biochemical changes induced by marijuana in the brain result in a drug-seeking, drug-taking behaviour, which in many instances will lead the user to experiment with other pleasurable substances' (p. xxiii).

Animal studies provide a rigorous way of testing the plausibility of pharmacological hypotheses by controlling exposure to cannabis and other drugs and other confounding factors. As their critics note, however, this greater rigour is purchased at the cost of their uncertain relevance to human cannabis users. It has been difficult, for example, to train rats to self-administer cannabinoids because they find their effects aversive (McGregor et al., 1996) and the doses of cannabinoids used in animal studies are much higher than those used by human cannabis users who smoke (rather than injecting it as in animal studies).

Some animal studies (e.g. Tanda et al., 1997) have been misinterpreted as evidence for a pharmacological explanation of the association between regular cannabis use and other drug use (Wickelgren, 1997). These studies indicate that common neural pathways underlie the rewarding effects of cannabis, cocaine, heroin and nicotine (MacCoun, 1998). All of these drugs act on the dopaminergic neurotransmitter systems that are involved in the 'reward centres' in the midbrain, the nucleus accumbens. This does not necessarily mean that THC 'primes' on the use of other illicit drugs (Zimmer and Morgan, 1997) but it increases the plausibility of such a hypothesis by suggesting a mechanism to explain how it could occur.

Two recent animal studies have directly examined the plausibility of a pharmacological explanation of the gateway phenomena (Cadoni et al., 2001; Lamarque et al., 2001). These studied cross-sensitivity between cannabinoids and opioids and stimulant drugs in rats. They provided some evidence for cross-sensitivity between cannabinoids and opioids, although this was qualified in one study because it was only observed in a strain of rats that were highly responsive to drug effects (Lamarque et al., 2001). A number of features of these studies raise questions about their relevance to gateway patterns of adolescent drug use. First, these effects were produced by injecting high doses of cannabinoids whereas most adolescents only smoke cannabis intermittently. Only a small minority of adolescents who use cannabis very heavily would expose themselves to these levels of cannabis use (Lynskey, 2002). Second, the cross-sensitisation between cannabinoids and opioids was symmetrical: that is, animals who were administered opioids were cross-sensitive to cannabinoids and vice versa (Cadoni et al., 2001). This suggests that if opioids were more readily available than cannabis, then opioids would be a gateway to cannabis use.

One of the most popular policy implications drawn from the gateway phenomena has been that our drug prevention policies should attempt to delay adolescent alcohol, tobacco and cannabis use with the aim of reducing rates of subsequent illicit drug use (e.g. Polich et al., 1984). If this hypothesis is correct then programs that delay alcohol, tobacco and cannabis use should also reduce the rates of other illicit drug use. Most prevention studies have evaluated programs that aim to prevent tobacco use and to delay alcohol use, the most widely used drugs in adolescence. These studies have provided some evidence that preventing or delaying tobacco and alcohol use can reduce subsequent rates of cannabis use (Botvin et al., 2002).

For several reasons no studies to date have demonstrated that delaying cannabis use can prevent the later use of other illicit drugs. First, many preventive programs that address illicit drug use have not been evaluated and among those programs that have it has proven difficult to demonstrate that prevention programs have an effect on the use of less commonly used illicit drugs (Gerstein and Green, 1993; Manski et al., 2001). Second, if the gateway hypothesis is correct, even the most effective prevention programs would produce very modest reductions in the use of other illicit drugs. This is because of their modest impacts on 'gateway drug' use and the rarity of 'harder' illicit drug use in representative samples of youth (Caulkins et al., 1999). Third, very large sample sizes are required to detect any effect that delaying cannabis use may have on the rates of use of other illicit drugs. Given these difficulties, it is perhaps unsurprising that very few studies have examined the effects of delaying 'gateway drug use' on later illicit drug use.

Economic studies

Economic analyses of the contemporaneous relationship between the demands for different drugs can provide support for a pharmacological explanation of the gateway pattern. These studies examine the impact of policy changes and price movements on rates of gateway drug use, such as the effects of alcohol taxes and law changes on rates of cannabis use, and changes in criminal penalties for cannabis use on cannabis and other illicit drug use. These studies show significant cross-price effects between substances (see Kenkel et al., 2001 for a review). The only reason why the price of one substance, say cannabis, should influence the consumption of another substance, is if the demands are interrelated.

DeSimone (1988) evaluated the temporal relationship between cannabis and other illicit drug use using data from the 1988 NLS. DeSimone (1988) estimated the current demand for cocaine as a function of past cannabis use (as reported in the 1984 survey) and other correlates of cocaine demand in a sample of individuals who had not previously used cocaine. This model suggested that prior use of cannabis increased the probability of using cocaine by more than 29%, even after controlling for unobserved individual characteristics. This provides evidence that the observed sequence of use was not due to a spurious correlation. The model could not distinguish the causal mechanism through which demand for the two drugs was related. It could be explained either in terms of pharmacological reinforcing effects of drug use or by differences in the marginal cost of using the two drugs that changes over time (Pacula, 1997; Kenkel et al., 2001).

Social environmental hypotheses: the role of exposure opportunities

Pharmacological explanations of the relationship between cannabis use and the use of heroin have difficulty explaining a number of facts about drug use. First, very few cannabis users become regular users of other illicit drugs; cannabis experimentation and abandonment is more the norm (Chen and Kandel, 1995). Second, those heavy cannabis users who use other illicit drugs often continue to use cannabis. As Donovan and Jessor (1983) have noted: '... "harder" drugs do not serve as substitutes for "softer" drugs. Rather, a deepening of regular substance use appears to go along with a widening of experience in the drug domain' (pp. 548–49).

Third, the pattern of progression in drug use among American adolescents in the 1970s was conditioned by drug availability (Kandel, 1978). Among cohorts of heroin users in the 1950s and 1960s, prior involvement with cannabis was confined to geographic areas of the US in which it was readily available (Goode, 1974). Research on African-American adolescents found that in these communities cocaine and heroin often preceded the use of the less readily available hallucinogens and 'pills' (Kandel, 1978). Similarly, American soldiers in Vietnam were also more likely to use heroin before they used alcohol because heroin was cheaper and more freely available in that setting than alcohol (Robins, 1993).

The historical and geographical variations in illicit drug use sequences suggest a sociological explanation of the higher rates of progression to heroin use among heavy cannabis users. One hypothesis is that regular cannabis users are more likely to use other illicit drugs because they have more opportunities to use other drugs than peers who do not use cannabis. Regular cannabis use, on this hypothesis, increases involvement in a drug-using subculture which, in turn, exposes cannabis users to opportunities to use other illicit drugs. Their drug-using peers might also be expected to approve of other illicit drug use (Cohen, 1972; Goode, 1974).

There have been few direct comparisons of 'exposure opportunities' between cannabis users and non-users. Fergusson and Horwood's (2000) analysis of the

Christchurch Child Development Study provided a limited assessment of the contribution made by affiliation with drug-using peers to the relationship between cannabis and other illicit drug use. They assessed the effects of self-reported peer use of alcohol, cannabis and other illicit drugs on the relationship between cannabis and other illicit drugs. The inclusion of peer drug use reduced but did not eliminate the relationship between cannabis and other illicit drug use.

Wagner and Anthony (2002) examined the effects of exposure opportunities to cannabis and other drugs on cannabis and other illicit drug use among young adults (aged 12 to 25 years) in the pooled 1991–1994 US National Household Surveys of Drug Abuse. They assessed exposure opportunities by the age at which a respondent first reported an opportunity to use tobacco or alcohol, cannabis and cocaine. Wagner and Anthony found that young people who had used alcohol or tobacco were three times more likely to report an opportunity to use cannabis (75% vs 25%) and they had these opportunities at an earlier age than those who had not used alcohol or tobacco. Alcohol and tobacco users were also much more likely to use cannabis when the opportunity arose than young people who had not used alcohol or tobacco (85% vs < 25%). And they did so sooner than peers who had not (50% of alcohol and tobacco users had used cannabis within 1 year of first offer whereas fewer than 20% of non-alcohol and non-tobacco-users had used within 5 years of first offer). These relationships did not change when young people who had used within a year of first opportunity to do so were excluded from the analysis (to reduce the possibility that the relationship was due to active cannabis seeking by some young people).

Wagner and Anthony also found that opportunities to use cocaine were strongly related to cannabis, alcohol and tobacco use. Only 13% of young people who had not used alcohol, tobacco or cannabis reported an opportunity to use cocaine. This compared with 26% of alcohol and tobacco users, 51% of cannabis only users, and 75% of those who had used alcohol, tobacco and cannabis. Those who had used cannabis were 15 times more likely to accept an offer to use cocaine than those who had not. These relationships did not change when young people who used cocaine within a year of their first opportunity to use were excluded from the analysis. This provides the most direct evidence to date that drug use influences the opportunity to use and the likelihood of accepting the opportunity presumably provided within one's peer group.

Conclusions

Among American adolescents in the 1970s the use of alcohol and tobacco typically preceded use of cannabis which in turn preceded the use of hallucinogens and 'pills', and heroin and cocaine. Generally, the earlier the age of first use, and the more often any drug in the sequence was used, the greater the chance that the young person would use the next drug in sequence. The significance of the role of cannabis in this sequence of drug use remains controversial.

A simulation study suggests that the phenomena that are usually interpreted in terms of a gateway effect for cannabis can be explained by the common characteristics of those who use these drugs. Other well-controlled longitudinal studies suggest that the association between cannabis use and the use of other illicit drugs is not *wholly* explained by common causes. Selective recruitment to cannabis use and shared genetic and environmental factors explain a fair part of the relationship but a discordant twin study suggests that genetics and shared environment do not wholly explain the relationship. This leaves open the possibility that cannabis use makes some direct, albeit small, causal contribution to the risk of using other illicit drugs. If this is true it is unclear what type of causal relationship this might it be.

The hypothesis that cannabis use has a direct pharmacological effect on the use of later drugs in the sequence is most appealing to many parents but the evidence is not compelling. Animal studies show cross-sensitivity between cannabinoids and opioids but at higher levels of dose than would be received by the majority of young cannabis users. And the cross-sensitivity is symmetrical, meaning that it is not a specific effect of cannabis so much as an effect of using substances that act on key neural reward structures. Intervention studies provide a potentially promising way of evaluating the gateway hypothesis but these have not so far produced clear-cut data because of the modest effects that they have on cannabis use.

Any causal relationship between cannabis and other illicit drug use is more likely to be sociological than pharmacological. The association probably reflects a combination of: (1) the selective recruitment to heavy cannabis use of persons with pre-existing personality and attitudinal traits (that may be at least partially genetic) that predispose to the use of intoxicants; (2) cannabis users affiliating with drug-using peers who provide more opportunities to use other illicit drugs at an earlier age; (3) supported by socialisation into an illicit drug subculture which has favourable attitudes towards the use of other illicit drugs.

11

Adolescent psychosocial outcomes

Adolescent cannabis use and educational performance

A major parental concern about adolescent cannabis use is that it will impair educational performance and increase the risk that a student will discontinue their education. This is a plausible outcome because cannabis use impairs memory and attention and so could interfere with learning (Baumrind and Moselle, 1985). Regular cannabis use could produce poorer school performance in high school and increase the chance that a student would drop out of school. If the adolescent's school performance was marginal to begin with, then cannabis use could increase the risk of high-school failure. Because of the importance of education in occupational choice, any effects of adolescent cannabis use on education could ramify throughout the individual's adult life.

Cross-sectional surveys have found associations between cannabis use and poor educational attainment among school children and youth. Resnick et al. (1997), for example, reported lower grade-point averages among cannabis users in a US national sample of 12,118 adolescents. An Australian study of 199 high school students aged 13–16 years found that young people who were heavy cannabis users had a more negative attitude toward school and a poorer record of school attendance than those who were not (Jones and Heaven, 1998). Lifrak et al. reported a negative correlation between cannabis use and scholastic competence for boys (but not for girls) in a sample of 271 seventh- and eighth-grade students (Lifrak et al., 1997). Novins & Mitchell (1998) also reported a significant association between poor school performance and cannabis use for males (but not for females) in a sample of 1464 American Indian adolescents. This association persisted after adjustment for antisocial behaviours, peer affiliations and other substance use.

A number of studies have also shown that cannabis use is higher among young people who either no longer attend school or who had high rates of school absenteeism. For example, Lynskey et al. (1999) found that young people in the Australian School Students' Alcohol and Drugs Survey who reported being away from school the day before the survey had higher rates of cannabis use than students who attended school on that day. Similarly, Fergusson, Lynskey and Horwood (1995) found that truancy was more common among cannabis users in 1000 New Zealand children studied from birth to the age of 16 years. They found that 75.8% of those who reported frequent truancy had used cannabis compared with only 8.7% of those who did not. Finally, Swaim et al. (1997) reported that lifetime rates of cannabis use were almost twice as high among school dropouts as among those who were still at school.

Explaining the relationship between cannabis use and educational outcomes

Four types of explanation need to be considered: (1) cannabis use is one of the causes of poor educational performance; (2) poor performance is one of the causes of cannabis use; (3) cannabis use and poor educational performance are part of a syndrome of problem behaviour in adolescence; and (4) cannabis use and poor educational performance are not directly related but share common causes.

The first explanation of the association has been supported by Kandel, Davies, Karus and Yamaguchi (1986) who argue that early cannabis use encourages continued use of cannabis and the use of other illicit drugs, leading to anti-conventional behaviours such as early school-leaving.

The second alternative is that heavy cannabis use is a *consequence* of poor educational attainment. This is supported by the finding that poor educational performance is a risk factor for cannabis use (Kelly and Balch, 1971; Jessor, 1976; Hundleby and Mercer, 1987; Duncan et al., 1998). Hawkins et al. (1992), who reviewed this evidence, concluded that poor educational performance and low commitment to school are risk factors that *precede* cannabis use. This hypothesis and the first hypothesis that cannabis use is a cause of poor school performance are not mutually exclusive. Both causal processes could be at work (Krohn et al., 1997): poor school performance may increase the risks of using cannabis, which in turn worsens school performance.

A third alternative explanation is that cannabis use and poor educational attainment are reflections of a common syndrome of problem behaviour. According to Jessor and Jessor (1977), a wide range of problem behaviours occurring in adolescence are manifestations of a common syndrome of problem behaviours. This syndrome, Donovan and Jessor (1985) suggested, reflects unconventionality which increases risks of norm-violating and problem behaviour.

The final possibility is that the observed associations between early cannabis use and poor educational outcomes are not causal but are instead the result of common factors that increase the risk of both early cannabis use and poor educational performance. This hypothesis is supported by the fact that the risk factors and life pathways for early cannabis use overlap considerably with those for poor educational performance. These include: community norms and attitudes towards the use of drugs; social disadvantage and family dysfunction; personality and individual propensities to violate norms; and affiliation with delinquent and drug-using peers (see Kandel, 1980; Newcomb and Bentler, 1989; Hawkins et al., 1992).

Longitudinal studies of cannabis use and educational outcomes

These explanations can only be distinguished in prospective studies in which young people are assessed over time on cannabis use, educational attainment and other potentially confounding factors, such as family and social circumstances, personality characteristics and delinquency (Rutter, 1988). Such studies enable researchers to specify whether cannabis use or poor educational performance comes first. They also permit researchers to examine causal pathways between cannabis use and educational outcomes by statistically adjusting for confounding variables. They provide answers to the question: Do young people who use cannabis have poorer educational outcomes than those who do not, when we allow for the fact that cannabis users are more likely to have a history of poor school performance and other characteristics before they used cannabis?

A number of recent prospective studies have examined the associations between cannabis use and educational attainment. Newcomb and Bentler (1988) followed 654 high school students over 8 years to examine the effects of early drug use on educational attainment at ages 19 to 24 years. They examined the extent to which cannabis, alcohol and drug use were associated with poor school performance in young adulthood, after taking account of the effects of confounding factors. Their analyses indicated that early substance use (which included cannabis use) predicted abandonment of a college education.

Similar results were obtained by Fergusson, Lynskey and Horwood (1996) who examined the relationship between cannabis use before the age of 15 years and early school-leaving at age 16. Their sample consisted of nearly 1000 young people who had been followed from birth to age 16 years and were assessed on cannabis use at age 15 and on a wide range of other health and psychological outcomes at age 16. The 10% of the sample who had used cannabis by the age of 15 had elevated risks of school problems at age 16 and 22.5% had left school before age 16 (the minimum school-leaving age in New Zealand) compared with only 3.5% of those who had not used cannabis. The frequency of truancy between 15 and 16 years was also higher among those who had used cannabis before the age of 15 years (31.5%) than those who had not (4.7%).

Fergusson and colleagues also found that young people who used cannabis before age 15 differed from those who had not *before* using cannabis. They showed early delinquency, poorer mental health and educational achievement, affiliations with delinquent or substance-using peers, and more family dysfunction. The relationship between early cannabis use and early school-leaving persisted after statistical adjustment for these differences. After allowing for the effects of the pre-existing differences, young people who used cannabis before the age of 15 years were 3.1 times more likely to leave school before age 16 than peers who had not used cannabis. In a later follow-up of the same birth cohort, Fergusson and Horwood (1997) reported that cannabis use before the age of 16 years was associated with an increased risk of leaving school without formal qualifications. This relationship also persisted after control for a wide range of potentially confounding covariates.

Duncan et al. (1998) examined patterns and correlates of drug use over time in 664 adolescents who were assessed at three time points. Academic failure predicted higher levels of drug use (including cannabis use) at first assessment. Declining academic performance during the study was also associated with increasing drug use. They suggested that much of the effect of cannabis use on academic performance was the result of affiliations with delinquent and drug-using peers.

Ellickson et al. assessed cannabis use and a range of other factors in seventh-graders who were followed-up for 5 years (Ellickson et al., 1998). Cannabis use predicted early school-leaving among Latino students, after controlling for demographic variables, family structure, academic orientation and early deviance. Young Latinos who were heavy cannabis users were much more likely to leave school before graduating. After controlling for these confounding factors, cannabis use did not predict leaving school early for Asians, Blacks or Whites.

Krohn, Lizotte and Perez (1997) reported that the use of alcohol and other drugs during adolescence increased the risks of leaving school early. In a sample of 775 high-risk adolescents studied from age 13 to 20 years early use of alcohol, cannabis and other illicit drugs predicted early school-leaving for males but not for females.

Tanner, Davies and O'Grady (1999) examine the influence of drug use (assessed between 14 and 17 years) on social outcomes assessed between 25 and 30 years used in the US National Longitudinal Study of Youth. The outcomes included educational and employment outcomes. After controlling for socio-demographic background, cognitive skill and educational expectations, early drug use predicted early school drop out, failure to graduate from high school and failure to obtain a college degree in males and females. In males, early drug use was also related to lower occupational status and unemployment.

Similar findings have been reported by Brook, Balka and Whiteman (1999) in a sample of 1182 Puerto Rican and African-American students who were followed for 5 years. Young people who reported using cannabis once a month or more at age 14 were more likely to leave high school before completing 12th grade, even after controlling for factors assessed at age 14. Additionally, young people who used cannabis at least monthly at age 14 years were more likely to report delinquency, other drug-related problems, sexual risk-taking and to have more friends who exhibited deviant behaviour.

In summary, longitudinal research studies that have examined the effect of cannabis use on a variety of measures of educational performance have generally shown that early cannabis use predicts early school-leaving in particular. The hypothesis that cannabis use is a cause of poor educational performance has been supported by the fact that the relationship persists after statistically controlling for differences between cannabis users and non-users. In these studies early cannabis use also predicts an increased risk of engaging in early sexual activity (Rosenbaum and Kandel, 1990), unplanned parenthood during adolescence (Mensch and Kandel, 1992; Krohn et al., 1997), unemployment (Fergusson and Horwood, 1997), and leaving the family home early (Krohn et al., 1997).

Explaining the association between cannabis use and early school-leaving

There are a number of hypotheses that may explain why cannabis use increases the risk of early school-leaving and poor school performance. The first possibility – that heavy cannabis use produces an 'amotivational' syndrome – was suggested in the late 1960s and early 1970s (Smith, 1968). The evidence reviewed in Chapter 7 suggests that this is not a useful explanation; it is more parsimonious to regard impaired motivation as a symptom of cannabis dependence.

A second explanation is that chronic cannabis use causes cognitive impairment, which in turn increases the likelihood of leaving school early. The evidence reviewed in Chapter 8 suggests that regular cannabis use did not produce marked cognitive impairment in adults who had used for 10 or more years (Solowij, 1998). Solowij (1998) has argued that daily cannabis use over 3 or more years produces more subtle impairment in selective attention, the ability to ignore irrelevant sensory information (Solowij, 1998). Solowij noted that it was difficult to predict how these subtle impairments would affect adolescent functioning in school (Solowij, 1998). The adults in the studies reviewed by Solowij, for example, used cannabis daily for an average of 10 years. By contrast, in the study reported by Fergusson and Horwood (1997) the 'heavy' cannabis use group included those who had smoked cannabis on at least 10 occasions. There is no evidence in the scientific literature on adults that such low levels of use are associated with any lasting cognitive impairment.

A third explanation is simpler. This is that cognitive impairment in cannabis-using adolescents is the result of the *acute* effects of cannabis intoxication rather than the cognitive effects of long-term use. If a young person is intoxicated by cannabis every day their school performance would suffer, especially if it was poor to begin with (Lynskey and Hall, 2000).

A fourth hypothesis is that early cannabis use leads to the precocious adoption of adult roles, including leaving school early to join the workforce (Newcomb and Bentler, 1988). There is support for this hypothesis in that in addition to leaving school early adolescent cannabis-users are more likely to marry early and experience a teenage pregnancy and childbirth.

A fifth hypothesis is that much of the influence of early cannabis use on later development can be attributed to the social setting in which adolescents regularly use cannabis, namely within a group of delinquent and substance-using peers (Fergusson and Horwood, 1997). According to this hypothesis, the important causal factor is that cannabis use occurs in a peer group that rejects conventional values, such as high educational achievement and social conformity, and which instead encourages nonconformist behaviour and a premature transition to adulthood.

These hypotheses are not mutually exclusive. It is probable that the impaired educational performance of adolescent cannabis-users is attributable to a combination of acute cognitive impairment, affiliation with peers who reject school and a desire to make an early transition to adulthood (Lynskey and Hall, 2000).

Other effects of adolescent cannabis use

Occupational performance

Among those young adult cannabis users who enter the workforce the continued use of cannabis and other illicit drugs in young adulthood could impair job performance for the same reasons that it impairs school performance, namely, the effects of chronic intoxication. There is some suggestive support for this expectation in that cannabis-users have higher rates of unemployment than non-users (Robins et al., 1970; Kandel, 1984) but this comparison is confounded by the different educational qualifications of the two groups.

Longitudinal studies have suggested that there is a relationship between adolescent marijuana use and job instability among young adults which is not explained by differences in education and other characteristics which precede cannabis use (e.g. Kandel et al., 1986). Newcombe and Bentler (1988) examined the relationships between adolescent drug use and income, job instability, job satisfaction, and use of public assistance in young adults, while controlling for differences between users and non-users in social conformity, academic potential and income in adolescence. They found that adolescent drug users had a larger number of job changes than non-drug users. Newcombe and Bentler conjectured that this reflected either impaired work performance, or a failure to develop conscientiousness, thoroughness, and reliability.

Fergusson and Horwood (Fergusson and Horwood) included unemployment for 3 months or more as one of their early outcomes in the follow-up of their birth cohort at age 18 years. There was a dose–response relationship between frequency of cannabis use at age 16 and unemployment. The rate of unemployment among those who had never used cannabis was 9.5% compared to 18.9% and 37.5% among those who had used 1–9 times and 10 or more times respectively. After statistical adjustment for peer affiliations, the relationship was no longer statistically significant (12.2%, 13.4% and 14.6% respectively).

Schwenk (1998) reviewed evidence on the relationship between cannabis use and job performance in adults in laboratory studies, surveys, observational studies, anthropological studies and studies of drug testing. He concluded that although there were associations between cannabis use and poor job performance in laboratory studies and some surveys the effects of cannabis use were small and the results were more consistent with the hypothesis of 'spurious correlation' between the characteristics of cannabis users and poor job performance than between cannabis use and poor job performance.

Interpersonal relationships

Cross-sectional studies of drug use in young adults have shown that heavy cannabis use predicts a lower chance of marriage, an increased rate of cohabiting, an increased risk of divorce or terminated de facto relationships, and a higher rate of unplanned parenthood and pregnancy termination (Robins et al., 1970; Kandel, 1984). Kandel (1984) also found that heavy cannabis users were more likely to have a social network in which friends and the spouse or partner were also cannabis users. These findings have been confirmed in analyses of the longitudinal data from this cohort of young adults (Kandel et al., 1986).

Newcombe and Bentler (1988) found that drug use in adolescence predicted an increased rate of early family formation in late adolescence and of divorce in early adulthood. They suggested that early drug involvement leads to early marriage and unplanned parenthood which result in divorce. Newcombe and Bentler interpreted this finding in terms of their theory of 'precocious development' in which adolescent cannabis users bypass the typical maturational sequence of school, work and marriage in order to prematurely adopt adult roles without the necessary growth and development to ensure their success in these roles.

Mental health

A number of studies have found an association between cannabis use and poor mental health. Kandel's (1984) cross-sectional study found that level of cannabis use was associated with lower satisfaction with life and greater risk of having consulted a mental health professional or having been hospitalised for a psychiatric disorder (Kandel, 1984). Longitudinal analyses of this same cohort found weaker associations between adolescent drug use and adult mental health; the strongest relationship was between cigarette smoking in adolescence and symptoms of depression in adulthood (Kandel et al., 1986).

Newcombe and Bentler (1988) found strong relationships between adolescent drug use and emotional distress, psychoticism and lack of a purpose in life. Emotional distress in adolescence predicted emotional distress in young adulthood but there were no relationships between adolescent drug use and emotional distress, depression and lack of a purpose in life in young adulthood.

Fergusson and Horwood (1997) found a dose–response relationship between frequency of cannabis use by age 16 and a DSM-IV anxiety and depressive disorder, and a suicide attempt. These relationships were no longer statistically significant after adjusting for confounding factors. In a later report, Fergusson, Horwood and Swain-Campbell (2002b) found a dose-response relationship between cannabis use and suicidal behaviour that did not disappear after controlling for confounding variables. The relationship was also stronger for those who initiated cannabis use at an earlier age.

Brook, Cohen and Brook (1998) reported a longitudinal study of the relationship between alcohol, tobacco and cannabis use and mental health among 975 adolescents followed from age 13.7 years until 22.1 years in New York state. Early cannabis use predicted antisocial behaviour after controlling for earlier antisocial behaviour but it did not predict an increased risk of anxiety and affective disorders. The strongest relationships between adolescent drug use and adult mental disorders were between cigarette smoking, illicit drug use (other than cannabis) and depression.

McGee, Williams, Poulton and Moffit (2000) reported a longitudinal study of the relationships between cannabis use and mental health in a New Zealand birth cohort. They found that rates of cannabis use were higher among young people with mental disorders at 15, 18 and 21 years. Cannabis use at age 15 did not predict mental health problems at age 18 but having mental health problems at age 15 (alcohol dependence and conduct disorder) predicted cannabis use at age 18. Cannabis use at age 18 also predicted alcohol dependence and conduct disorders at age 21. McGee et al. argued that the lack of a relationship between cannabis use and anxiety and affective disorders suggests that cannabis use was not a form of self-medication in anxious and depressed individuals.

A number of studies have found associations between adolescent cannabis use and depression. A survey of a representative sample of Australians aged 13–17 years found that those who had used cannabis were three times more likely than those who had never used cannabis to meet criteria for depression (Rey et al., 2002). Fergusson and colleagues (1997) examined the association between cannabis use and major depression in their birth cohort study in Christchurch, New Zealand. They found that 36% of adolescents who had used cannabis 10 or more times by the age of 15–16 years met criteria for a mood disorder at that age compared with 11% of those who had never used cannabis and 18% of those who had used cannabis 1–9 times.

Similarly, the Zurich cohort study of young people followed from 20 to 30 years of age found that by age 30 years, those who had ever met criteria for depression were 2.3 times more likely to report weekly cannabis use (Angst, 1996). A study by

Patton and colleagues (2002) of a cohort of young adults (aged 20–21 years) in Victoria found that 68% of females who reported daily cannabis use in the past year were depressed – an odds ratio of 8.6 compared to non-users. Two other US longitudinal studies have reported conflicting results. Brook and colleagues (1998) found no relationship between the involvement with cannabis use and DSM-III-R depressive disorders over 10 years of follow-up. A study of students aged 12–14 years found that those reporting lifetime cannabis use had higher depression scores, and 42% met criteria for DSM-IV major depression at some point in their lives (Kelder et al., 2001).

Suicide

A small number of studies have examined the relationship between cannabis use and suicide among adolescents (see Hillman et al., 2000 for a review). Several of these have found an association but it remains unclear whether it is explained by other factors. An analysis of cross-sectional data from the US National Comorbidity Survey found an association between self-reported suicide attempts and the dependence on a number of drugs, including alcohol, sedatives, stimulants, cannabis, and inhalants (Borges et al., 2000). The risk for cannabis dependence was still significant after adjusting for socio-demographic factors and other psychiatric disorders, such as depression and alcohol dependence (an odds ratio of 2.4).

Beautrais, Joyce and Mulder (1999) reported a case-control study of the role of drug use in serious suicide attempts that resulted in hospitalisation. They compared rates of cannabis use among 302 consecutive hospital cases treated for serious suicide attempts with that in a random sample of 1028 people in the community. They found that 16% of the suicide-attempters had a cannabis-use disorder (cannabis abuse or dependence) compared with 2% of the controls. Controlling for social disadvantage and having a diagnosis of depression or alcohol dependence substantially reduced the association but did not eliminate the association (reducing the odds ratio from 10 to 2).

The evidence from a small number of prospective studies is more mixed. Fergusson and Horwood (1997) also found a dose–response relationship between frequency of cannabis use by age 16 and the likelihood of reporting a suicide attempt, but the association did not remain after controlling for confounding factors. Patton et al. (1997) reported a longitudinal study on suicide attempts and self-harm in a cohort of 2066 Victorian secondary school students followed from age 15 and 16 to age 21. They found that cannabis was associated with self-harmful behaviour among females but not males, after controlling for depression and alcohol use.

Andreasson and Allebeck (1990) reported an association between cannabis use and suicide deaths in their follow-up of 50,465 conscripts. They found that the risk of suicide was four times higher among heavy cannabis users. A more detailed analysis of predictors of suicide in this cohort reported by Allebeck and Allgulander

(1990) found that inpatient psychiatric hospitalisation by age 18 was the strongest predictor of suicide risk (OR = 11.3). Use of 'narcotics' (which includes cannabis) did not predict suicide independently of a psychiatric diagnosis (OR =1.3) but a diagnosis of alcohol dependence (OR = 4.3) and drug dependence (OR = 3.6) did.

Delinquency and crime

Cross-sectional studies of adults indicate that there is a relationship between cannabis use and a history of lifetime delinquency (e.g. Robins et al., 1970; Kandel and Logan, 1984), having been convicted of an offence, and having had a motor vehicle accident while intoxicated (Kandel and Logan, 1984). Surveys of drug use in young people in the juvenile justice system find high rates of regular cannabis use (Salmelainen, 1995; Trimboli and Coumarelos, 1998) and a relationship between level of involvement with cannabis and frequency of property offences.

Longitudinal studies reveal an interesting pattern of relationships between cannabis use and crime. Johnston et al. (1978) analysed the relationship between drug use and delinquency across two waves of interviews of adolescent males. Their cross-sectional data showed a strong relationship between delinquency and involvement with illicit drugs. However, analyses of changes in drug use and crime over time indicated drug users differed from non-drug users in their rate of delinquent acts *before* their drug use. The onset of illicit drug use (including cannabis) had little effect on delinquent acts, except among those who used heroin, whose rates of delinquency increased.

Newcomb and Bentler (1988) reported a positive relationship between drug use and criminal involvement in adolescence but mixed results on the relationship between adolescent drug use and criminal activity in adulthood. Adolescent drug use predicted *drug* crime in young adulthood but not after controlling for other variables.

Fergusson and Horwood (1997) assessed four types of delinquency in their analysis of the consequences of adolescent cannabis use. These were: three or more violent offences, three or more property offences, arrested by police, and convicted of an offence. There was a dose–response relationship between each of these and frequency of cannabis use by age 16 that persisted after adjustment for differences between adolescents who did and did not use cannabis by age 16. It also persisted after adjustment for drug use and criminal behaviour among peers, indicating that it was not explained by affiliating with delinquent peers. The same pattern of results was reported in a later follow-up of this cohort at age 21, with the additional finding that the relationship was strongest among those who initiated cannabis use at an early age (Fergusson et al., 2002a).

Brook et al.'s (1999) longitudinal study of 627 African-American and 555 Puerto Rican youth in New York City assessed self-reported violence towards others. They found that early cannabis use predicted a doubling of the risk of self-reported violence towards others, after adjusting for other covariates (but not for a history of delinquency and violence prior to using cannabis).

Arseneault et al. (2000) reported a longitudinal study of mental disorders and violence in a cohort of 961 New Zealand youth followed from birth to age 21. Violence was assessed using self-report and police records of convictions. They found that 7.6% of the sample reported that they had engaged in violence in the past year and 4% had been convicted of violent offences. There were strong associations between self-reported and officially recorded violence and alcohol dependence, cannabis dependence and schizophrenia. Controlling for a history of conduct disorder in childhood substantially reduced the association between cannabis dependence and violence. The authors argued that the residual relationship reflected the involvement of cannabis-dependent and conduct-disordered adolescents in drug markets where violence was used to resolve disputes.

Summary

Young people who use cannabis are at increased risk of adverse psychosocial outcomes including impaired educational achievement, poor mental health, criminal behaviour, and reduced life opportunities. Longitudinal studies suggest that these associations are partly explained by the fact that young people who use cannabis in early adolescence are those who were at greatest risk of using other drugs, engaging in delinquency, experiencing poor mental health, attempting suicide, and doing poorly at school *before they began to use cannabis*.

Not all of the relationships between cannabis use and these poorer social outcomes can be explained this way. Early cannabis use appears to impair the school performance of adolescents whose performance was poor before they began to use cannabis. It also predicts involvement in criminal behaviour after controlling for a history of conduct disorder, perhaps by exacerbating pre-existing antisocial behaviour and encouraging affiliation with delinquent peers. It possibly increases the risk of suicide but this remains to be clarified by better-designed studies.

Plausible mechanisms that may explain these associations have been suggested by Fergusson and Horwood (1997), namely, that adolescents who are socially disadvantaged and have conduct problems as children are more likely to become early cannabis users. Early cannabis use also increases the chances of an unconventional lifestyle as a result of affiliating with delinquent and substance-using peers, and disengaging from conventional social roles such as completing education and obtaining a job. The acute effects of cannabis intoxication may also play a role by encouraging impulsive behaviour and impairing cognitive performance in the minority of students who are daily cannabis users.

5

Harms and benefits of cannabis use

The first chapter in this section (Chapter 12) summarises the results of the analysis of the health effects of cannabis that have been presented in the preceding chapters. It also compares the health and psychological effects of cannabis with those of alcohol and tobacco. Our purpose in making these comparisons is to minimise the double standards that have sometimes been used in appraising the health effects of cannabis.

Our comparison of health effects is not intended to be an implicit argument for cannabis legalisation, as some critics have claimed any such comparison is (e.g. Ghodse, 1996). Proponents of cannabis law reform have used as one of their arguments the assertion that cannabis use produces fewer adverse health effects than alcohol and tobacco (e.g. Zimmer and Morgan, 1997). Statements of fact do not have straightforward implications for policy, as Hume observed over 200 years ago. There is a compelling argument to be made in the opposite direction, namely, given the adverse public health impact of alcohol and tobacco use in Western societies, we should be very cautious about encouraging the widespread use of a recreational drug that may combine some of the adverse health effects of alcohol with those of tobacco smoking (e.g. Drummond, 2002).

The benefits of cannabis use – the subject of Chapter 13 – are more controversial still. Proponents of current policy are reluctant to discuss the possibility that cannabis use may have any benefits. Proponents of reform have, with few exceptions, also been softly spoken on the benefits of recreational cannabis use apart from the potential use of cannabis and cannabinoids to treat symptoms of chronic illnesses that are unresponsive to current medical treatment. We briefly discuss the empirical evidence on the therapeutic uses of cannabis. We discuss the policy debate about 'medical marijuana' in an appendix because, as we argue in more detail there, the 'medical marijuana' debate is a marginal issue in the larger policy debate about the legal status of recreational cannabis use. As this chapter makes clear, there has been very little research on the benefits of recreational cannabis use. We have included a chapter on the topic because we believe that the benefits of recreational use should be explicitly discussed when debating societal policies towards cannabis use.

12

Comparing the health effects of cannabis with alcohol and tobacco

This chapter compares the most probable adverse health effects of cannabis use with those of alcohol and tobacco, two commonly used psychoactive substances in Western societies that produce similar effects (alcohol) and share a common route of administration (smoking) with cannabis.

Anyone attempting to make such comparisons confronts a number of difficulties. The first are difficulties in making causal inferences about relationships between cannabis use and the adverse health outcomes (see the introduction to Section 2). The second difficulty is the dearth of information on the size of many of the risks that cannabis use poses for users. Both reflect the lack of epidemiological research on the health effects of cannabis by comparison with the research on the health risks of alcohol and tobacco use.

Our approach

We approach these issues as follows. First, we identify the most probable causal relationships between cannabis use and specific health effects using standard criteria for assessing evidence for causal relationships. Second, in so far as it is possible, we have quantified the severity of personal and public health risk for each adverse health effect that can be attributed to cannabis. We have estimated approximate relative risk, and the prevalence of the relevant pattern of use. Third, we have compared these approximate estimates with best estimates of the mortality and morbidity burden of alcohol and tobacco. This has been done initially by indicating the specific adverse health effects that cannabis may share with alcohol and nicotine. This is followed by a discussion of the probable quantitative risks of cannabis by comparison with those of alcohol and nicotine. The results of recent studies of the burden of disease are also discussed.

In making these comparisons, we acknowledge two limitations. First, we have relied on epidemiological evidence on the health consequences of cannabis use that is largely based on studies conducted in the English-speaking countries, and most particularly the United States. Second, the comparisons of health effects are also largely confined to effects on the health of users. Apart from motor vehicle accidents there has been very little research on the effects that cannabis use may have on the health of persons who do not use cannabis. Such indirect health effects have not been well-studied for alcohol and tobacco with the exceptions of motor vehicle accidents and violence in the case of alcohol, and environmental tobacco smoke and deaths caused by fires in the case of tobacco. These effects deserve more attention than they have received, but in the absence of research we have not included them in our comparison.

The probable adverse health effects of cannabis

Acute effects

The major acute psychological and health effects of cannabis intoxication are:
- anxiety, dysphoria, panic and paranoia, especially in naive users;
- impairment of attention and memory while intoxicated;
- psychomotor impairment, and probably an increased risk of accidental injury or death if an intoxicated person drives a motor vehicle or operates machinery;
- an increased risk of psychotic symptoms among those who are vulnerable because of a personal or family history of psychosis;
- an increased risk of low birthweight babies if used during pregnancy.

Chronic effects

The major health and psychological effects of chronic cannabis use, especially daily use over many years, remain uncertain but the major *probable* adverse effects appear to be:
- respiratory diseases caused by smoking as the method of administration, such as chronic bronchitis and impaired respiratory function;
- development of a cannabis-dependence syndrome, characterised by an inability to abstain from or to control cannabis use;
- an increased risk of developing cancers of the aerodigestive tract, i.e. oral cavity, pharynx, and oesophagus.
- subtle impairment of attention and memory, which persists while the user remains chronically intoxicated, and may or may not be reversible after prolonged abstinence from cannabis.
- a decline in occupational performance marked by under-achievement in adults in occupations requiring high-level cognitive skills, and impaired educational attainment in adolescents.

High-risk groups

A number of groups are at increased risk of experiencing some of these adverse effects.

- Adolescents with a history of poor school performance whose educational achievement may be reduced by the cognitive impairments produced by chronic intoxication with cannabis;
- Adolescents who initiate cannabis use in the early teens are at higher risk of becoming dependent on cannabis and of using other illicit drugs;
- Pregnant women who continue to smoke cannabis are probably more likely to give birth to low birthweight babies, and perhaps to shorten their period of gestation;
- Persons with a number of pre-existing diseases who smoke cannabis are probably at an increased risk of precipitating or exacerbating symptoms of their diseases. These include:
  - individuals with cardiovascular diseases, such as coronary artery disease, cerebrovascular disease and hypertension;
  - individuals with respiratory diseases, such as asthma, bronchitis, and emphysema;
  - individuals with schizophrenia who are at increased risk of precipitating relapses to the disorder and exacerbating its symptoms;
  - individuals who are or have been dependent upon alcohol and other drugs are probably at an increased risk of developing dependence on cannabis.

Two special concerns

Two issues that require brief discussion are the health implications of: the long-term storage of THC in body tissue; and any increases in the average THC content of cannabis that may have occurred in recent decades in developed societies.

Storage of THC

Repeated use of cannabis at frequent intervals can lead to the accumulation of THC in fatty tissues in the human body where it may be stored for considerable periods of time (see Chapter 2). The storage of cannabinoids *would* be serious cause for concern if THC were a highly toxic substance which remained physiologically active while stored in body fat. However, THC is not a highly toxic substance and it is not active while stored because its receptors are not present in body fat (Iversen, 2000). One concern about THC storage has been that the release of stored cannabinoids into blood could produce symptoms of cannabis intoxication, as in 'flashback experiences' (e.g. Negrete, 1988; Thomas, 1993). Such experiences have been rarely reported by cannabis users (e.g. Edwards, 1983), and their significance is uncertain because those who report these experiences have often used other hallucinogenic drugs.

Increases in the potency of cannabis

Cohen (1986) claimed that research undertaken in the 1970s and early 1980s underestimated the adverse health effects of cannabis because it was based upon the use of less potent cannabis (0.5% to 1.0% THC) than was used in the USA in the late 1980s (3.5% THC in 1985–86). This claim has been repeated in the scientific media (e.g. Ashton, 2001; Drummond, 2002) and in Australia claims have been made that there has been a 'thirty-fold' increase in the THC content of cannabis (Hall and Swift, 2000).

The USA is the only country that has analysed the THC content of cannabis products over the past few decades. This shows an increase from the early 1970s to the mid-1980s but critics have argued that samples studied in the 1970s were unrepresentative of cannabis at that time. They cite data from cannabis tested in the same period by independent laboratories which shows much higher THC levels. More recent US data have shown that the THC content of seizures increased from 3.3% in 1980 to 4.4% in 1998 (ElSohly and Ross, 1999; ElSohly et al., 2000).

A more important factor in determining exposure to THC may have been changes in patterns of cannabis use between 1970 and 2000. Survey data in Australia (Degenhardt et al., 2000b) and the USA (Johnson and Gerstein, 1998) indicates that young people initiate cannabis use at an earlier age than was the case in the 1980s. Earlier initiation of use increases the risks of cannabis dependence and the adverse health effects of use (see Chapter 10). Regular cannabis use also makes users tolerant to the effects of THC, encouraging the use of more potent cannabis preparations (Hall and Swift, 2000). Over the past two decades a large-scale illicit cannabis industry has developed in many countries that aims to meet the demand for cannabis from daily users who prefer more potent forms of cannabis (Hall and Swift, 2000). These changes in patterns of use – earlier initiation of use and more regular use of more potent cannabis products – have probably increased the amount of THC consumed by regular cannabis users (Hall and Swift, 2000).

It is difficult to estimate the health effects of any increase in the amount of THC consumed because these may depend upon the type of health effect and the user's experience with cannabis. The use of more potent forms of cannabis will probably increase the adverse psychological effects of cannabis use among naive cannabis users. This may discourage further experimentation. Increased THC exposure among regular cannabis users may increase the risk of accidents among those who drive while intoxicated, especially among those who also use alcohol. It may also increase the risk of dependence. Respiratory risks may be marginally decreased if cannabis smokers titrate their doses of THC, about which uncertainty remains.

A comparison of the health effects of alcohol, cannabis and nicotine

Acute effects
Alcohol

Some of the acute adverse effects of cannabis use are similar to those of alcohol. First, both drugs produce psychomotor and cognitive impairment. In the case of alcohol, the impairment increases risks of fatal and nonfatal accidents (Institute of Medicine, 1987; English et al., 1995). It has been until recently less certain whether cannabis intoxication on its own increases motor vehicle accident risk but this is now looking likely. The combined adverse effects on driving of using alcohol and cannabis also appear to be additive.

Alcohol and cannabis intoxication differ in their relationship to intentional injury. Alcohol intoxication is strongly associated with aggressive and violent behaviour at the population level (Room, 1983; Lenke, 1990; Cook and Moore, 1993). There is also increasing evidence that alcohol may play a role in suicide (Edwards et al., 1994). There is very little evidence of a causal relationship between cannabis use and violence in developed societies and the evidence on the relationship of cannabis to suicide risk is unclear.

Second, there is good evidence that substantial doses of alcohol taken during pregnancy can produce a foetal alcohol syndrome (English et al., 1995). There is reasonable evidence that cannabis use during pregnancy reduces birthweight but no evidence that it causes birth defects.

Third, alcohol use has one acute health risk that is not shared with cannabis. In large doses alcohol causes death by asphyxiation, alcohol poisoning, cardiomyopathy and cardiac infarct. By contrast, there have been no human overdose fatalities caused by cannabis.

Tobacco

Cannabis and tobacco share two major acute health risks: the irritant effects of smoke upon the respiratory system and the stimulating effects of THC and nicotine on the cardiovascular system. Both can adversely affect persons with cardiovascular and respiratory diseases. In each case, the respiratory effects primarily arise from the fact that the drug is smoked. The cardiovascular effects represent a combination of the adverse effects of smoking and the specific effects of nicotine and THC on the cardiovascular system.

Chronic effects
Alcohol

There are a number of risks of chronic use that alcohol and cannabis may share. First, heavy use of both drugs can produce a dependence syndrome. Withdrawal symptoms are milder in dependent cannabis users who abruptly stop using cannabis; the abrupt cessation of alcohol use in severely dependent drinkers produces a withdrawal syndrome that can be fatal in a small proportion of cases, if not properly treated (Hall and Zador, 1997).

Second, there is reasonable evidence that chronic heavy alcohol use can produce psychotic symptoms and psychoses in some individuals, either during acute intoxication or the process of withdrawal (Edwards et al., 1997). There is good evidence from prospective studies that regular cannabis use may produce psychotic symptoms and precipitate schizophrenia in individuals with a personal or a family history of psychiatric disorder. Regular cannabis use also appears to worsen the course of schizophrenia.

Third, chronic heavy alcohol use can indirectly cause brain injury – the Wernicke-Korsakov syndrome – with symptoms of severe memory defect and an impaired ability to plan and organise (Edwards et al., 1997). Chronic cannabis use does not produce cognitive impairment of comparable severity but there is evidence that it subtly impairs cognitive functioning in ways that may or may not be reversed after abstinence.

Fourth, chronic heavy alcohol use impairs occupational performance in alcohol-dependent adults (Edwards et al., 1997). There is some evidence that chronic heavy cannabis use produces similar, albeit less marked, impairments in the occupational and educational performance of adolescents and adults.

Fifth, chronic, heavy alcohol use increases the risk of premature mortality from accidents, suicide and violence (Edwards et al., 1994; English et al., 1995). There is as yet no comparable evidence that chronic cannabis use increases mortality from these causes.

Sixth, alcohol use is a contributory cause of cancer in various tissues and organs of the digestive system and breast (English et al., 1995). There is increasing evidence that chronic cannabis smoking may cause cancers in the aerodigestive tract.

Seventh, heavy alcohol use is a major cause of liver cirrhosis, gastritis, high blood pressure, stroke, cardiac arrhythmias, cardiomyopathy, pancreatitis, and polyneuropathy (Edwards et al., 1997). On the other hand, alcohol use is associated with a reduction in the risk of heart disease (Edwards et al., 1994). There is no equivalent evidence of adverse or protective mortality effects for cannabis.

Tobacco

Chronic cannabis and tobacco smoking cause chronic respiratory diseases, such as chronic bronchitis (English et al., 1995). They probably also share an increased risk of cancers of the aerodigestive tract (i.e. the mouth, tongue, throat, oesophagus, lungs). The increased risk of cancer in the aerodigestive tract is a consequence of the shared route of administration by smoking. Like tobacco smoking, chronic cannabis smoking probably also increases rates of respiratory infection and adversely affects the function of the heart.

Tobacco smoking is associated with a wide variety of other chronic health conditions with which cannabis smoking has not so far been implicated. These include cancer of the cervix, stomach, bladder and kidney, coronary heart disease, peripheral vascular disease, and stroke, as well as cataracts and osteoporosis (English et al., 1995).

Comparing the magnitude of risks

Many of the quantitative risks of cannabis use can only be guessed at in the absence of studies of the dose–response relationship between cannabis use and adverse health effects. The following 'guesstimates' for the most probable adverse health effects of cannabis are based on data where possible but when in doubt we have made the worst-case assumption that the relative risks of cannabis use are comparable to those of alcohol or tobacco.

Motor vehicle accidents

If driving while intoxicated with cannabis produced a comparable increase in the risk of accidents to that produced by driving while intoxicated with a blood alcohol level of 0.05% to 0.10%, then the RR of an accident while intoxicated by cannabis would be 2 to 4. A recent meta-analysis suggests that this may be too high for drivers who have only used cannabis; it may be more applicable to those who have used cannabis and alcohol (Bates and Blakely, 1999).

The strong association between cannabis and alcohol use makes it difficult to assess the public health impact of cannabis use on motor vehicle accidents. The epidemiological studies indicate that, in its own right, cannabis makes, at most, a very small contribution to motor vehicle accidents. Its impact on road safety may be to amplify the adverse effects of alcohol in the majority of cannabis users who drive after using both alcohol and cannabis.

Respiratory diseases and cancers

If we assume that a daily cannabis user who smokes 5 or more joints per day faces a comparable risk of respiratory disease to that of a 20 a day tobacco smoker, then the RR of developing chronic bronchitis would be 6 or greater for those who had ever smoked cannabis, and substantially higher among those who had been daily cannabis smokers over many years (English et al., 1995). It would be higher still in cannabis smokers who also smoked tobacco. The risks of respiratory infection may be doubled in regular cannabis smokers.

If we make the same worst case assumptions about daily cannabis smoking then the RR of developing cancers of the respiratory tract would be: 5 for oropharyngeal cancer, 4 for oesophageal cancer, and 7 for lung cancer (English et al., 1995). These risks would be substantially higher among cannabis smokers who also smoked tobacco.

Respiratory diseases such as bronchitis are likely to have greater public health significance than respiratory cancers. Respiratory cancers develop after much longer exposure to cigarette smoke (15 to 20 years) than chronic bronchitis and there are very few users who smoke cannabis for more than 5 years (Bachman et al., 1997).

On current patterns of use in developed societies, cannabis smoking will make a small contribution to respiratory cancers because only a minority of cannabis users become daily users, and a much smaller proportion of them smoke cannabis beyond their middle twenties (Bachman et al., 1997). Among this minority, concurrent cannabis and tobacco use may exacerbate each other's adverse effects on respiratory function and infections.

Low birthweight babies

Making a worst-case assumption, a woman who smokes cannabis during pregnancy may double her chance of giving birth to a low birthweight baby (English et al., 1995). The public health significance of cannabis smoking during pregnancy will be much lower than that of tobacco smoking because the prevalence of cannabis smoking during pregnancy is so much lower than that of tobacco smoking. The risk of a low birthweight baby will be higher among women who also smoke tobacco.

Schizophrenia

The adjusted estimated RR from the study by Andreasson et al. (1987) was that an adolescent who had smoked cannabis 50 or more times by age 18 had a 2 to 3 times higher risk of developing schizophrenia than an adolescent who had not been a cannabis smoker. Similar estimates of relative risk have been produced in more recent prospective studies.

If we assume that the relationship between cannabis use and schizophrenia is causal, cannabis use would account for around 13% of new cases of schizophrenia. There is one estimate that it may account for 50% of more chronic cases. It has been difficult to detect any increase in the incidence of schizophrenia caused by increased rates of cannabis use among adolescents and young adults (Der et al., 1990).

Dependence

Estimates from US data in the late 1970s and early 1980s suggest that 10% of those who have ever used cannabis become dependent on it (see (Hall et al., 1994). The comparable risks were high among those who have ever used tobacco (32%), opiates (23%) and alcohol (15%) (Anthony et al., 1994).

Cannabis dependence is the most common adverse health effect of cannabis. On the ECA and NCS estimates, 4% of the adult US population met diagnostic criteria for cannabis abuse or dependence during their lifetime. The consequences of cannabis dependence are probably less severe than those of alcohol and there seems to be a high rate of remission of symptoms in the absence of treatment but a rising number of individuals is seeking help to stop using cannabis.

Overall public health significance

A number of attempts have been made to make quantitative comparisons of the effects of alcohol, tobacco and illicit drugs on mortality, morbidity and societal costs in Australia. These estimates cover a period when rates of cannabis use in Australia were among the highest in the developed world (see Chapter 3).

Holman et al. (1988) estimated that in 1986 there were 23,639 deaths attributable to drug use in Australia. 17,800 deaths were attributed to tobacco, 5360 to alcohol and 479 to illicit drugs. Some 289 (60%) of the illicit drug deaths were attributed to illicit opiate use. None were attributed to cannabis. There was the same rank order in person-life years lost (92,023 for tobacco, 66,034 for alcohol and 16,438 for illicit drugs) and bed days (1,014,336 for tobacco, 1,009,591 for alcohol and 57,361 for illicit drugs). No morbidity was attributed to cannabis use because the authors argued that 'apart from dependence, abuse and withdrawal', no other adverse health effect of cannabis was 'sufficiently substantiated or quantified' (p. 377).

English et al. (1995) updated the Holman et al. estimates using Australian mortality data for 1992. They included estimates of the protective effects of moderate alcohol consumption on deaths from cardiovascular disease. The protective effect of alcohol reduced the number of deaths attributed to it from 5,360 in 1986 to 3,660 in 1992. Tobacco and illicit drugs were responsible for 18,290 and 488 deaths respectively. Opiates were responsible for 92% of the illicit drug deaths. No deaths were attributed to cannabis, which accounted for 1% of bed days attributed to illicit drug use (for the treatment of cannabis dependence and abuse).

Ridolfo and Stevenson (2001) updated the English et al. estimates for Australia in 1998. They used a different method to estimate the protective effect of alcohol on cardiovascular deaths. Alcohol now produced a *net reduction* of 2371 deaths because moderate alcohol use averted more deaths than immoderate use caused. The number of deaths attributed to tobacco increased from 18,290 to 19,019 and the number attributed to illicit drugs increased from 488 to 1023 because of a large increase in opiate overdose deaths.

Collins and Lapsley (1991) estimated the economic costs of drug abuse in Australia in 1988 using Holman et al.'s findings. The total economic cost was

$14.4 billion, $6.8 billion of which was attributed to tobacco, $6.0 billion to alcohol and $1.4 billion to illicit drugs. (Collins and Lapsley, 1996) updated this analysis in the light of English et al.'s (1995) study. Total costs increased to $18.9 billion, with tobacco accounting for 67% ($12.4 billion), alcohol for 23% ($4.5 billion) and illicit drugs 9% ($1.7 billion), with most of this due to illicit opiate use.

Similar results were obtained by Xie, Rehm, Single and Robson (1996) in their estimate of the health costs of alcohol, tobacco and cannabis use in the Canadian province of Ontario in 1992. The direct health care costs attributable to alcohol were C$442 million, while tobacco was responsible for C$1,073 million, and *all* illicit drugs for C$39 million (Xie et al., 1996). Cannabis contributed $8 million to costs.

Burden of disease estimates

The Global Burden of Disease Study (Murray and Lopez, 1997) estimated the public health impact of alcohol, tobacco and illicit drugs by adding life years lost (LYL) to weighted years lived with disability to estimate the total Disability-Adjusted Life-Years (DALYs) attributed to each type of drug use. According to their estimates, 3.5% of the global DALYs could be attributed to alcohol, 2.6% to tobacco, and 0.6% to illicit drugs (Murray and Lopez, 1997). Heroin use made the largest contribution to the burden of illicit drug use. The authors caution that 'because of the great difficulty in reliably estimating prevalence of illicit drug use, and of reliably quantifying its health effects, the estimates for this risk factor may well be too low' (p. 310). Ezzati et al. (2002) updated Murray and Lopez's estimates of alcohol, tobacco and illicit drug use as contributors to global disease burden. They did not include cannabis in their estimates of deaths and disability attributable to illicit drugs because of the absence of epidemiological data that would permit estimates to be made.

The Australian Burden of Disease and Injury study (Mathers et al., 1999) adapted the approach of Murray and Lopez to estimate the contribution that alcohol, tobacco and illicit drugs made to the burden of disease and injury in Australia. The study findings differed from those of the GBD study because the Australian study estimated the disease burden averted by moderate alcohol use. Tobacco accounted for 9.7% of the total burden of disease in Australia, followed by alcohol with 2.2% and illicit drugs with 1.8%. Among illicit drugs, the majority of the burden was due to illicit opioid use (1.2% of total burden). There were no deaths attributed to cannabis use and cannabis dependence and abuse accounted for 0.2% of DALYs (Mathers et al., 1999).

These studies of mortality and morbidity, economic costs and disease burden attributable to alcohol, tobacco and illicit drugs differ in their rankings of the contributions made by alcohol and tobacco depending upon whether they include a mortality benefit from moderate alcohol or not. There is little doubt, however, that on current patterns of use and given the comparative state of knowledge about their health effects: (1) alcohol and tobacco are much more damaging to public health in developed societies than illicit drugs; and (2) cannabis use makes no known contribution to mortality and a minuscule contribution to disability.

Predicting the effects of changes in the prevalence of cannabis use

Estimates of the public health impact of cannabis use under a policy of prohibition do not provide an answer to the policy question: what impact would cannabis have on public health if it were legal to use it and it was as widely used as alcohol and tobacco?

It would be unwise to predict the public health consequences of increased cannabis use by multiplying the harms cannabis causes under current policy by the number of additional users that would be estimated under a more liberal legal regime. This calculation assumes that the risks of cannabis use would not change if cannabis were more freely available. This is unlikely to be true for two reasons. First, the type of person who uses cannabis when its use is legal and it is widely available may differ from the type of person who uses it when it is illegal and its use is socially disapproved. Second, patterns of cannabis use could also change in different ways for different users, decreasing some risks in some user populations and increasing risks in others. The net effects on cannabis-related harm of changes in who uses cannabis and how they use it are difficult to predict.

There are different patterns of alcohol consumption and alcohol-related problems in 'dry' and 'wet' cultures (Room, 2001). If cannabis use were legal, it may be easier to educate adults to reduce some of its health risks, for example, by swallowing rather than smoking cannabis and not driving after using cannabis. On the other hand, experience with alcohol and tobacco suggests that increasing adults' access to drugs will also increase use by adolescents who engage in riskier patterns of drug use than older adults.

It is difficult to predict the net effect on public health of increasing cannabis use among adolescents and harm-reduction efforts among adult users. All that can be said with confidence is that if the rate of cannabis use were to approach that of cigarette smoking and alcohol use, its adverse impact on public health would probably increase. It is impossible to say by how much it would increase.

Summary

Cannabis when used daily over years or decades can harm the health of users. Uncertainty remains about: (1) which of these effects can be wholly attributed to cannabis use; and (2) the relationships between patterns of cannabis use (frequency and duration) and these health effects. The most probable adverse effects of chronic heavy cannabis use over years are in order of frequency: cannabis dependence; chronic bronchitis and respiratory infections; an increased risk of motor vehicle accidents, especially if used in combination with alcohol; an increased risk of respiratory cancers; an increased risk of giving birth to low birth-weight babies when used during pregnancy; and an increased risk of schizophrenia among those who are vulnerable. Many of these risks are shared with alcohol and tobacco.

On *current patterns of use*, cannabis poses a much less serious public health problem than alcohol and tobacco in Western societies. This is no cause for complacency, however. The public health impact of alcohol and tobacco are substantial, and the public health impact of cannabis would probably increase if daily cannabis use was as common among young adults as heavy alcohol use and daily tobacco smoking.

13

The benefits of cannabis use

In this chapter we consider four possible benefits of cannabis use; (1) the possible benefits of recreational cannabis use; (2) the possible mental health benefits of cannabis use; (3) the possibility that young people may use cannabis instead of other more harmful drugs, such as alcohol, heroin or cocaine; and (4) the possible medical uses of cannabis and cannabinoids.

The benefits of recreational cannabis use

The reasons that young people give for using cannabis are similar to the reasons they give for using alcohol. Among daily cannabis users, for example, Johnston (1981) found that most reported using it 'to feel good or get high' (94%) and 'to have a good time with my friends' (79%). Two-thirds said that they used it to relax. Johnston and O'Malley (1986) also found that the reasons given for using cannabis matched those given for drinking alcohol. If one accepts the operating assumption of economists that adults are the best judges of their own interests the fact that cannabis is widely used by adults for recreational reasons would show that it has benefits for many of those who use it. This is clearest for those cannabis users who do not report any adverse effects of their use, which the Australian National Survey of Mental Health and Wellbeing found was approximately two-thirds of adults who had used 5 or more times in the past year (Degenhardt and Hall, 2001).

Mental health benefits of cannabis use

Moderate alcohol use is associated with reduced mortality from cardiovascular disease (e.g. Chyou et al., 1997; Klatsky, 1999; Sacco et al., 1999). A number of studies have found a similar relationship between moderate alcohol use and mental health (Power et al., 1998; Rodgers et al., 2000; Degenhardt et al., 2001). Moderate alcohol users have lower rates of anxiety and affective disorders than abstainers or heavier users of alcohol but it is not yet clear whether moderate alcohol use is good for mental health or whether those with better mental health are more likely to drink moderately (Rodgers et al., 2000; Degenhardt et al., 2001).

The available evidence on the mental health of cannabis users does not suggest that moderate cannabis users have better mental health. Indeed, most studies suggest that heavier cannabis users have poorer mental health than non-users, with moderate users in between. The US National Longitudinal Alcohol Epidemiologic Survey (NLAES), a nationally representative survey of US adults (Grant and Harford, 1995), found that persons who met criteria for major depression within the past year were 6.4 times more likely to meet criteria for cannabis abuse or dependence than those who did not have major depression (6% vs 1% respectively) (Grant and Harford, 1995). Degenhardt et al. (2001) found higher rates of affective and anxiety disorders among cannabis users in a nationally representative sample of 10,641 Australian adults aged 18 years and over. Among those who were cannabis dependent, 14% had an affective disorder and 17% an anxiety disorder compared with 6% of persons who had not used cannabis. Regular cannabis users also reported more psychological distress and lower satisfaction with life than non-users (Degenhardt et al., 2000a) but adjustment for other drug use and neuroticism eliminated the difference in rates of disorders. It was still the case, however, that moderate cannabis users did not have better mental health than abstainers.

One study reported that experimentation with cannabis in adolescence was related to good social functioning (Shedler and Block, 1990). In a group of adolescents who were followed from childhood, those who had experimented with cannabis reported better social adjustment than both those who had never used cannabis and those who were heavy users. The authors suggested that experimentation with cannabis was a sign of better social adjustment because a minority had never tried cannabis (Shedler and Block, 1990). These relationships may reflect the very high prevalence of cannabis use in this birth cohort who went through adolescence during the peak period of cannabis use in the USA.

These findings have not been reported in other adolescent samples. A survey of a representative sample of Australians aged 13–17 years found that those who had used cannabis were three times more likely than those who had not to meet criteria for depression (Rey et al., 2002). Fergusson and colleagues (1997) examined the association between cannabis use and major depression using data from their birth cohort of 1265 children in Christchurch, New Zealand. They found that adolescents who had used cannabis 10 or more times by the age of 15–16 years were three times more likely to meet criteria for a mood disorder at that age (36%) than those who had never used cannabis (11%).

Similarly, the Zurich cohort study of young people (assembled when they were 20 years of age) found that by age 30 years, those who met criteria for depression over the period of the study were 2.3 times more likely to report weekly cannabis use (Angst, 1996). A study by Patton and colleagues (2002) of a cohort of young adults (aged 20–21 years) in Victoria found that 68% of females who reported daily cannabis use in the past year were depressed, a number eight times higher than non-users. Two other US longitudinal studies have reported conflicting results. Brook and colleagues (1998) found no relationship between cannabis use and DSM-III-R depressive disorders during 10 years of follow-up. A study of students aged 12–14 years found that those reporting cannabis use had higher depression scores, and 42% met criteria for DSM-IV major depression at some point in their lives (Kelder et al., 2001).

All considered, the available data does not indicate that moderate cannabis use is associated with better mental health. One study suggested that adolescents who experimented with cannabis use had better mental health than those who did not but most have found that more regular cannabis users have poorer mental health than non-users. It is unclear whether this means that cannabis use has an adverse effect on mental health, whether young people with mental disorders are more likely to use cannabis, or some combination of the two (which seems the more likely).

The benefits of drug substitution

The second possible benefit of cannabis use is that young people may use it instead of other more harmful drugs, such as alcohol, heroin or cocaine. The possibility that cannabis may be used instead of alcohol seems plausible because young adults give similar reasons for using the two drugs (Johnston and O'Malley, 1986). If cannabis use was less harmful than alcohol use (e.g. in terms of its contribution to motor vehicle accidents, injury and violence), then the substitution of cannabis for alcohol would benefit users and public health.

The epidemiology of alcohol and cannabis use raises some doubts about the substitution hypothesis because cannabis users are more likely to be regular alcohol users than non-users (Degenhardt and Hall, 2003). The typical sequence of involvement with drugs also seems inconsistent with the substitution hypothesis in that the use of alcohol usually precedes cannabis use and cannabis is typically added to the drug repertoire rather than replacing alcohol (see Chapters 3 and 10).

Most of the research examining the substitution between cannabis and other drugs comes from econometric analyses of the effects of policy changes (e.g. decriminalisation of cannabis, increasing taxes on alcohol and raising the drinking age) on the use of alcohol, cannabis and other drugs, or on indicators of alcohol and drug-related harm (see Kenkel, Mathios and Pacula, 2001 for a review). In the standard model of consumer demand, goods may be complements, substitutes, or unrelated. Two goods are economic complements if an increase in the price of the first good leads to a decrease in consumption of both the first good and second good. Two goods are economic substitutes if an increase in the price of the first good (that decreases its consumption) increases the consumption of the second good (e.g. electricity versus gas). Two goods are unrelated if changes in the price of the first good have no impact on the consumption of the second good.

Studies evaluating the nature of the relationship between the demands for cannabis and other substances have been severely limited because of the unavailability of good price data for cannabis. Measures of the legal risk of using cannabis are often used in the absence of price data. More recently, limited information on the price of cannabis has become available and its inclusion in these models has substantially improved our understanding of the relationship between demands for alcohol and cannabis.

DiNardo and Lemieux (1992) examined the relationship between demands for alcohol and cannabis using state-level data on high school seniors from 1980 to 1989 from the Monitoring the Future Surveys. They estimated the effects on alcohol and cannabis use of the price of alcohol, the minimum legal drinking age and cannabis decriminalisation. They found that decriminalisation was associated with reduced alcohol use by high school seniors but had no effect on cannabis use whereas raising the legal drinking age was associated with higher cannabis use. They interpreted these findings as evidence that alcohol and cannabis were economic substitutes among youth.

Chaloupka and Laixuthai (1997) confirmed DiNardo and Lemieux's (1992) earlier findings using individual level data on high school seniors from the 1982 and 1989 Monitoring the Future Surveys. They found that both the frequency of drinking and of heavy drinking were inversely related to beer prices and cannabis decriminalisation. This suggested that alcohol and cannabis were economic substitutes among youth.

Thies and Register (1993) used individual level data from the 1984 and 1988 National Longitudinal Survey of Youth to estimate predictors of demand for both alcohol and cannabis. They found decriminalisation of cannabis had a positive effect on alcohol (any use in the past 30 days) and cocaine use but no significant effect on cannabis use, raising doubts about its significance in predicting alcohol and cocaine use.

Pacula (1998) extended the analysis of Thies and Register (1993) by estimating demand for alcohol and cannabis use in the 1984 National Longitudinal Survey of Youth as functions of the full price of both substances. She found that increases in the beer tax or the legal drinking age decreased the demand for cannabis by at least as much as they decreased alcohol consumption, providing the first evidence of a complementary relationship between alcohol and cannabis.

Farrelly et al. (1999) explored the relationship between demand for alcohol and cannabis in different age groups using data on cannabis use in the past 30 days in youth (ages 12–20) and young adults (21–30) in the 1990–1996 NHSDA. They used state-level beer prices and several measures of the enforcement of the prohibition on cannabis use. Beer price was found to have a significant negative effect on cannabis use among youths (ages 12–20), suggesting a complementary relationship between alcohol and cannabis for this age group. There were no significant cross-price effects in young adults.

Cameron and Williams (2001) estimated the cross-price effects between alcohol and cannabis in Australia using survey data from the 1988, 1991, 1993, and 1995 National Drug Strategy Household Surveys. They took advantage of state-level variations in cannabis prices and the criminal status of cannabis to estimate past-year use of alcohol, cannabis and cigarettes. They found a positive and significant effect of the price of alcohol on cannabis use, suggesting that cannabis and alcohol were economic substitutes for Australians.

Saffer and Chaloupka (1999) have conducted the most comprehensive analysis of cross-price effects to date using data on alcohol, cannabis, cocaine and heroin use from the 1988, 1990 and 1991 NHSDA surveys. County-level alcohol prices and state-level cannabis decriminalisation laws were used as measures of price for alcohol and cannabis, respectively. State-level prices for cocaine and heroin were also included to control for any relationships between demand for alcohol and cannabis and demand for cocaine and heroin. They found strong complementary relationships across most of these substances. Alcohol and cannabis were found to be economic complements for all groups except Native Americans and Hispanics, among whom the two goods were substitutes. Cocaine and cannabis were also found to be economic complements, as higher cocaine prices reduced the likelihood of using cannabis in the past month and the past year, holding other factors constant. In addition, cannabis decriminalisation was generally associated with increased cocaine consumption. The relationship between cannabis and heroin use was undetermined as the findings were mixed.

Although existing findings are limited by the quality of the price data, these studies generally provide only limited support for a beneficial substitution effect, and then often only in some subpopulations. Most of the studies of youth that include some proxy for the monetary price of cannabis suggest that alcohol and cannabis are economic complements, not substitutes. Making cannabis more widely available would not reduce alcohol use among this population but increase it. The studies examining the relationship between alcohol and cannabis among adults appear to be sensitive to race/ethnicity and country of origin. Further investigation is clearly needed as are studies of the relationship between the demands for cannabis and other illicit drugs.

Therapeutic uses of cannabis

Cannabis has had a long history of medical and therapeutic use in India and the Middle East (Nahas, 1984; Mechoulam, 1986; Grinspoon and Bakalar, 1993) where it has been used for its analgesic, anti-convulsant, anti-spasmodic, anti-emetic, and hypnotic effects. Cannabis was used as an analgesic, anti-convulsant and anti-spasmodic in Britain and the USA throughout the latter half of the nineteenth century and the early part of the twentieth century.

The medical use of cannabis declined after the turn of the twentieth century as cannabis preparations that varied in purity and effectiveness were supplanted by pharmaceutically pure drugs that could be given in standardised doses to produce more dependable effects (Iversen, 2000). These included the opiates, aspirin, chloral hydrate, and the barbiturates (Nahas, 1984; Mechoulam, 1986). Many of these drugs could also be injected to provide rapid relief of symptoms whereas cannabis extracts had to be given orally (Iversen, 2000). After the introduction of international drug control agreements in the early part of the century, the medical use of cannabis preparations was discouraged by laws which treated cannabis as a 'narcotic' drug (Grinspoon and Bakalar, 1993).

THC was isolated in 1964 (Goani and Mechoulam, 1964), shortly before cannabis came to be widely used as a recreational drug by American youth. Its recreational use hindered pharmaceutical research into its therapeutic uses. The rediscovery of some of its therapeutic uses was largely serendipitous. Its value as an anti-emetic agent in the treatment of nausea was discovered by young adults who used cannabis recreationally while undergoing cancer chemotherapy (Grinspoon, 1990).

Cannabinoids and cannabis have primarily been advocated for medical uses to relieve symptoms of chronic diseases rather than as cures for specific diseases. The conditions for which cannabis has been most commonly advocated have been the symptomatic relief of nausea, vomiting, appetite loss, and chronic pain (Institute of Medicine, 1999).

Cannabinoids as anti-emetic agents

Profound nausea and vomiting during chemotherapy and radiotherapy for cancer may prompt patients to discontinue these potentially life-saving treatments (Institute of Medicine, 1999). The lack of effective treatments for chemotherapy-induced nausea prompted oncologists in the late 1970s and early 1980s to explore the anti-emetic properties of cannabinoids (Institute of Medicine, 1999). These anti-emetic effects made biological sense because there are cannabinoid receptors in the brain centres that control emesis (Institute of Medicine, 1999) and animal research has suggested that THC has anti-emetic effects (Institute of Medicine, 1999).

One of the earliest trials of the effectiveness of THC as an anti-emetic was prompted by patient reports that smoking marijuana relieved nausea and vomiting (Sallan et al., 1975). This study included 22 patients with a variety of cancers, 20 of whose nausea and vomiting had proven resistant to existing anti-emetic drugs. The study found greater anti-emetic effects of THC compared to placebo. Most patients (13/16) reported a 'high' after receiving THC that was correlated with the anti-emetic effect.

A trial by Chang et al. (1979) largely supported the findings of Sallan (1975). In this study 15 patients with osteogenic sarcoma served as their own controls during monthly high-dose methotrexate therapy. Eight patients had an excellent response, 6 a fair response, and one had no response. Few side effects were reported, with sedation the most common (12/15 patients). Four patients experienced dysphoric reactions but none of these lasted more than 30 minutes.

Since these early studies, controlled clinical studies have compared the effectiveness of THC with either a placebo or with other anti-emetic drugs (see Poster et al., 1981; Carey et al., 1983; Levitt, 1986 for reviews). Comparisons of oral THC with existing anti-emetic agents have been less consistent than the results of comparisons with placebo. The results generally indicated that THC was as effective as the anti-emetic drug prochlorperazine (Carey et al., 1983; Levitt, 1986). Their equivalence was demonstrated in one of the largest and best conducted studies (Ungerleider et al., 1982). Nonetheless the anti-emetic efficacy of cannabinoids was modest, with THC typically failing to stop nausea in two-thirds of patients.

Since these trials were conducted, newer anti-emetic drugs have been introduced that are much more effective than prochlorperazine (Hollister, 2001). These newer agents have dramatically reduced nausea and vomiting (Institute of Medicine, 1999; Campbell et al., 2001). Selective serotonin type 3 receptor agonists, such as ondansetron, achieve complete control over nausea induced by cisplatin in 75% of cases and up to 90% for less emetogenic chemotherapy compared with fewer than a third of patients receiving THC (Institute of Medicine, 1999). Side effects include headache and constipation but these are generally well tolerated.

Cannabinoids and AIDS-related wasting

Cannabinoids and cannabis have been used to reduce nausea, stimulate appetite and relieve pain in patients with AIDS-related wasting (Institute of Medicine, 1999). Such patients often experience nausea and weight loss, either while receiving antiviral drugs to suppress HIV, or as a direct effect of the AIDS-related diseases (Institute of Medicine, 1999).

THC in the form of dronabinol stimulates appetite in patients with AIDS-related wasting (Beal et al., 1995; Beal et al., 1997) and it has been registered for this purpose in the US. Some patients do not like dronabinol because of its psychoactive side effects, the difficulty of titrating the dose, the delayed onset of effects, and the prolonged duration of the effects (Institute of Medicine, 1999). There are anecdotal reports that smoked cannabis is also effective in the treatment of HIV/AIDS-associated anorexia and weight loss (Grinspoon and Bakalar, 1993; Clarke, 1995) but there have not been any controlled studies.

A major concern with the medical use of smoked cannabis in HIV-infected patients is that they might be more vulnerable than other cannabis users to any immunosuppressive effects of cannabis and to infectious micro-organisms found in cannabis plant material (Institute of Medicine, 1999). Recent epidemiological evidence allays this concern (see Chapter 5) in that a number of large prospective cohort studies of HIV/AIDS in homosexual and bisexual men have failed to find any relationship between cannabis use and the rate at which HIV-positive men develop clinical AIDS.

Cannabinoids as anti-glaucoma agents

Glaucoma is a leading cause of blindness in the United States, affecting 2,000,000 people and producing 300,000 new cases of blindness each year (Adler and Geller, 1986). In glaucoma, increasing intraocular pressure (IOP) progressively impairs vision and, if untreated, may damage the optic nerve, causing blindness (Adler and Geller, 1986).

The fact that cannabis reduced IOP was discovered in the 1970s by Hepler and his colleagues (Hepler et al., 1976; Hepler and Petrus, 1976) who observed a substantial decrease in IOP during cannabis intoxication. They demonstrated that both cannabis and oral THC reduced IOP in normal volunteers and in patients with glaucoma (Hepler and Petrus, 1971; Hepler et al., 1976; Hepler and Petrus, 1976). Subsequent research identified THC as the cause of this effect (Adler and Geller, 1986).

There have been case reports of the use of cannabis to manage glaucoma (e.g. Randall, 1990; Grinspoon and Bakalar, 1993) but there have not been any controlled clinical trials. THC is an effective anti-glaucoma agent when used acutely but there are doubts about its effectiveness with chronic use because tolerance develops to its effects on IOP (Jones et al., 1981). The Institute of Medicine (1999) concluded that evidence did not support the use of THC in glaucoma. It argued that its effects were too short-lived, and the high doses that were required to produce them caused side effects that precluded the lifelong use of cannabis or cannabinoids to treat glaucoma (Institute of Medicine, 1999).

Cannabinoids in neurological disorders

Cannabis has been reported to provide relief of symptoms in some neurological disorders, namely epilepsy; muscle spasticity, particularly in MS and spinal cord injury; and movement disorders such as Parkinson's and Huntington's disease and Tourette's syndrome (Institute of Medicine, 1999).

Cannabinoids and epilepsy

Cannabis was used as an anti-convulsant in the nineteenth century (O'Shaughnessy, 1842) to treat epilepsy, tetanus and rabies (Nahas, 1984). Animal studies provided some support for this use, with evidence that cannabidiol (CBD) is a potent anti-convulsant (Chesher and Jackson, 1974; Institute of Medicine, 1982; Consroe and Snider, 1986). There is very limited evidence on the therapeutic effects of cannabinoids in humans with epilepsy.

There are a small number of cases of individuals with epilepsy in whom the recreational use of cannabis appeared to enhance the effects of anti-convulsant medication (e.g. Consroe et al., 1975; Grinspoon and Bakalar, 1993). There is one randomised placebo-controlled study of CBD in 15 patients whose epilepsy was not controlled by conventional anti-convulsants. Four of the 8 patients who received CBD in addition to their usual anti-convulsant drugs were free of seizures throughout the study period and three were improved. Only 1 of 7 patients in the placebo condition showed any clinical improvement (Cunha et al., 1980). The anti-convulsant properties of cannabis appear to be attributable to cannabidiol rather than THC (Institute of Medicine, 1999).

Cannabinoids and muscle spasticity

Muscle spasticity is the increased resistance to passive stretch of muscles. Involuntary contractions can be painful and debilitating. About 90% of MS patients develop muscle stiffness, spasms, cramps, aches or pain.

There are anecdotal reports that cannabis reduces painful muscle spasms in patients with MS and spinal cord injuries (Miller and Walker, 1996; Glass et al., 1997). Animal research has found that THC reduces tremor and spasticity in diseased mice (Baker, 2000). A survey of 112 MS patients (Consroe et al., 1997) supported the use of cannabis for MS, as did some open studies (Petro and Ellenberger, 1981; Clifford, 1983; Ungerleider et al., 1987). The survey results suggest that it would be worth investigating the therapeutic value of cannabinoids in relieving symptoms associated with MS (Achirona et al., 2000) but there is insufficient evidence to judge efficacy at present (Killestein et al., 2002; Smith, 2002).

Muscle spasticity is also common in patients with spinal cord injuries. Surveys of these patients suggest that cannabis use reduces spasticity, nausea and insomnia. The clinical data are too limited to decide whether cannabis or cannabinoids have a role in the treatment of muscle spasticity. Carefully designed clinical trials of THC need to be done (House of Lords Select Committee on Science and Technology, 1998).

Cannabinoids and movement disorders

Movement disorders are caused by abnormalities in the brain cortex areas that control motor functions, resulting in abnormal muscle movements in the face, limbs and trunk. The disorders most often mentioned as candidates for medical cannabis use are dystonia, Huntington's disease, Parkinson's disease and Tourette's syndrome (Institute of Medicine, 1999).

There is limited research evidence that cannabis is useful for treating movement disorders in these conditions. There is evidence that the muscle spasms or 'tics' in persons with Tourette's syndrome are relieved by THC (e.g. Mueller-Vahl et al., 1999). Since stress often transiently exacerbates movement disorders, the anxiety-relieving effects of cannabis or cannabinoids might help some patients with movement disorders.

The evidence that cannabinoids have therapeutic effects in patients with movement disorders is largely anecdotal (e.g. Meinck et al., 1989; Grinspoon and Bakalar, 1993). Clifford (1983) reported a controlled evaluation of the effects of THC on tremor in 8 patients (4 male and 4 female) with advanced multiple sclerosis who had ataxia and tremor. Five patients reported subjective benefit from THC and there was objective evidence of benefit in two of these cases. Single-blind placebo challenge in these cases produced evidence that their clinical condition deteriorated when given placebo and improved when given THC.

The only controlled trial of a cannabinoid in a movement disorder has been an evaluation of the effects of CBD on severity of chorea in patients with advanced Huntington's disease (Consroe et al., 1991). In this study, 19 Huntington's patients were enrolled in a double-blind controlled trial in which they received six weeks administration of CBD or placebo in a cross-over design. There was no improvement in chorea on any of the clinical, self-report or motor measures.

Cannabinoids as anti-asthmatic agents

Smoked cannabis and oral THC have an acute bronchodilatory effect in persons with asthma (Tashkin et al., 1975; Tashkin et al., 1976), that is, they increase the lung's capacity to absorb oxygen. Cannabinoids have not been used therapeutically as anti-asthmatic agents (Tashkin, 1993). A major obstacle to therapeutic use has been that oral THC produces a smaller bronchodilator effect and after a longer delay than smoking cannabis. Smoking cannabis is an unsuitable way to administer a drug to patients with asthma (Tashkin, 1993). The unwanted psychoactive effects of cannabis have also been a barrier to its use.

Cannabinoids as analgesics

In animals cannabinoids have mild to moderate analgesic effects (Hollister, 2001). The CB_1 receptor acts on neural pathways that partially overlap with those affected by opioids but it acts through pharmacologically distinct mechanisms. Cannabinoids and opioids therefore probably have different side effects and may have additive effects or act synergistically to produce analgesia (Institute of Medicine, 1999).

There has been little clinical evidence of efficacy beyond its historical use for migraine, dysmenorrhoea, and neuralgia, and case histories of its use in chronic pain, dysmenorrhoea, labour pain, and migraine (Grinspoon and Bakalar, 1993). The few controlled studies of the analgesic efficacy in humans have been inconclusive. Three experimental pain studies in humans produced mixed results (Hill et al., 1974; Clark et al., 1981; Libman and Stern, 1985), but they were poorly controlled (Institute of Medicine, 1999). Two studies with acute clinical pain also had major limitations (Raft et al., 1977; Jain et al., 1981).

The most encouraging evidence on the effects of cannabinoids on chronic pain are three clinical studies of patients with severe cancer pain that was persistent and had resisted traditional analgesics (Noyes et al., 1975a; Noyes et al., 1975b; Staquet et al., 1978). These studies suggested that cannabinoids have analgesic effects equivalent to about 60 mg of codeine (Campbell et al., 2001; Bagshaw and Hagen, 2002). Some patients reported adverse psychoactive effects (Campbell et al., 2001; Bagshaw and Hagen, 2002) so researchers are hoping to develop synthetic cannabinoids with fewer adverse effects than THC (Walker and Huang, 2002). It may also be possible to achieve good analgesia by using smaller doses of cannabinoids in combination with other analgesics (Walker and Huang, 2002).

The limitations of anecdotal evidence

With the exception of anti-emetic and appetite-stimulant effects, the therapeutic uses of cannabis and cannabinoids depend upon anecdotal evidence. Such evidence is justifiably distrusted as evidence of therapeutic effectiveness in clinical medicine, especially in chronic conditions that have a fluctuating course. This is because it is difficult to be sure that apparent improvements in a patient's condition that follow their use of a drug (e.g. THC) are caused by its use. It is difficult in a single case to exclude the possibility that the use of the drug simply preceded an improvement in the patient's condition that would have occurred in its absence. In addition, there is the well-known placebo effect that is observed in many conditions and which may explain the apparent benefits of a drug or other treatment.

Grinspoon and Bakalar (1993) have defended anecdotal evidence for the therapeutic use of cannabinoids. They argue that a double standard has been applied to the appraisal of the safety and efficacy of cannabinoids: anecdotal evidence of harm has been readily accepted while anecdotal evidence of benefit has been discounted. Although at first glance 'double standards' may seem to describe the behaviour of the regulatory authorities, it is prudent to require stronger evidence of benefit than harm for putatively therapeutic drugs to ensure that the risks incurred by their therapeutic use do not outweigh their benefits. Moreover, this is not peculiar to the appraisal of cannabinoids; it is standard practice in the therapeutic appraisal of all drugs. Medical practitioners are encouraged to report possible adverse effects of prescribed drugs. These reports are treated as a noisy but necessary way of detecting rare but serious side effects of drugs that have not been detected in clinical trials or animal studies.

Obstacles to therapeutic cannabinoid use

Cannabinoids have not been widely used in clinical practice despite their safety under certain conditions of medical use and evidence of their efficacy as anti-emetics and appetite stimulants. Nor has much pharmacological research been undertaken to develop new synthetic cannabinoids for those indications (e.g. as anti-emetics). The main reasons for this are regulatory disincentives for pharmaceutical companies to develop and market cannabinoid drugs and the political and regulatory obstacles to the therapeutic use of cannabinoids. These are discussed in more detail in Appendix 1.

Summary

On the assumption that adults are the best judges of their own interests, the fact that a substantial proportion of adults in many developed societies use cannabis for recreational purposes is *ipso facto* evidence that some cannabis users benefit from its use. There is an absence of evidence for more specific benefits, such as improved mental health, as may be the case with moderate alcohol use. The epidemiological studies have typically found that heavier cannabis is correlated with poorer mental health. This relationship may not be attributable to cannabis use *per se* because it disappears when alcohol and tobacco use and neuroticism are controlled for.

The evidence is mixed on the extent to which cannabis use may substitute for the use of arguably more harmful drugs like alcohol. The epidemiology of alcohol and cannabis use are suggestive of a complementary relationship in that heavy consumers of alcohol are more likely to be cannabis users and vice versa. Much of the recent econometric evidence suggests that alcohol and cannabis are complements, particularly among youth who are at the greatest risk of misusing both substances. The evidence among adults is more mixed, with race, ethnicity and country of origin influencing the findings. It is possible that the relationship between these two substances is population-specific because of differences in cultures. If this is the case, then the claim that cannabis legalisation will reduce the use of other drugs is highly variable between at-risk populations. The evidence to date suggests that this would not be the case for youth.

A number of conclusions can be drawn on the therapeutic uses of cannabis. First, there is reasonable evidence for the therapeutic use of THC as an anti-emetic agent in the treatment of nausea and vomiting caused by cancer chemotherapy. More effective anti-emetic agents are now available so it remains to be seen how widely the cannabinoids will be used for this purpose. Second, there is reasonable evidence for the efficacy of THC in the treatment of AIDS-related wasting. Third, there is evidence that cannabinoids may have analgesic and anti-spasmodic properties that warrant further research into their effectiveness.

The effectiveness and costs of cannabis prohibition

Proponents of cannabis law reform (Kaplan, 1970; Nadelman, 1989) argue that cannabis prohibition should be repealed because like alcohol prohibition, it has failed to deter young people from using cannabis and its social costs outweigh its benefits (Kaplan, 1970; Wodak et al., 2002). The failures of alcohol prohibition are taken to be so uncontroversial that they do not require documentation (Kyvig, 1979; Tyrrell, 1997).

Historians suggest that American experience with alcohol prohibition was a little more complicated than this (Kyvig, 1979; Tyrrell, 1997). Alcohol consumption was substantially reduced during alcohol prohibition (Kyvig, 1979; Tyrrell, 1997). There was, for example, a 30% decline in alcohol consumption immediately after prohibition as indicated by a marked and sustained reduction in liver cirrhosis deaths, hospitalisations for alcoholic psychosis and arrests for drunkenness (Miron and Zweibel, 1991). By the late 1920s consumption recovered to 60%–70% of pre-prohibition levels (Miron and Zweibel, 1991) and there was a gradual increase in consumption after repeal in 1933 but consumption did not return to pre-prohibition levels for another decade (Miron and Zweibel, 1991; MacCoun and Reuter, 2001).

Alcohol prohibition did produce a large blackmarket in Chicago and New York where it contributed to widespread corruption of police and public officials (Kyvig, 1979; Tyrrell, 1997). It is unclear how widespread lawlessness was in the remainder of the US. The public perception of widespread lawlessness under alcohol prohibition may have been amplified by Hollywood gangster movies in much the same way that the US media amplified public perceptions of a crack cocaine epidemic in the mid-1980s (Reinarman and Levine, 1989). Historical hindsight also confers a sense of inevitability on the repeal of alcohol prohibition and makes the case for repeal seem clearer than it did for the American people at the time (Kyvig, 1979), or than it does to historians and economists who have analysed the data since (Kyvig, 1979; Miron and Zweibel, 1991; Tyrrell, 1997).

The complexities of the impacts of alcohol prohibition should prompt a more critical attitude towards similar claims that cannabis prohibition has manifestly failed to deter use and that the costs of the policy 'clearly' outweigh its benefits. In this section we provide a critical analysis of limited evidence on the effectiveness and costs of cannabis prohibition. In Chapter 14 we review the available evidence on the deterrent effect of cannabis prohibition on cannabis use. In Chapter 15 we consider the economic costs of enforcing the prohibition against cannabis use and the size of the cannabis blackmarket that has arisen to meet the demand for cannabis products in many developed countries. Chapter 16 completes the picture by enumerating the other costs of prohibition that have been identified by critics of cannabis prohibition, including less tangible costs that cannabis prohibition may have on individual liberty and respect for the law.

14

The impact of prohibition on cannabis use

The primary justification for criminalising the cultivation, sale, possession and use of cannabis is to *deter* its use in order to reduce the adverse health effects of cannabis use, especially long-term regular cannabis use. Critics of prohibition argue that the high rates of cannabis use, particularly among young adults, are clear evidence that the policy has failed to achieve its goal (Single et al., 1999; Lenton, 2000; Senate Special Committee on Illegal Drugs (Canada), 2002). The available survey data provides strong support for the claim (see Chapter 3).

In the United Kingdom in 2000, for example, 9% of persons between the ages of 16 and 59 reported using cannabis in the past year (Drugscope, 2001). Rates of use in the past year among youth (ages 16–19) and young adults (ages 20–24) were 25% and 27%, respectively (Drugscope, 2001). In the United States in 2000, 8% of the household population (ages 12 and older) reported using cannabis in the past year (Substance Abuse and Mental Health Services Administration, 2001). Rates among youth and young adults were 13% (ages 12 to 17) and 24% (ages 18 through 25) (Substance Abuse and Mental Health Services Administration, 2001). Rates of use in household surveys in Australia in 1998 were even higher, with 18% of individuals 14 years and older reporting use in the past year (Higgins et al., 2000). Estimates from other developed countries are similar to those presented here (see Chapter 3). All clearly show that prohibition of the sale and possession of cannabis has not eliminated the use of cannabis, rates of which are increasing in many of these countries.

Those who defend cannabis prohibition point out that very few laws eliminate an unwanted behaviour, whether it is income tax evasion, speeding, prostitution, gambling, abortion or substance use. The use of cannabis, they argue, would have been much higher if its use was not prohibited (e.g. Nahas and Latour, 1992). Research on lifetime patterns of cannabis use provide some support for this argument. This shows that most cannabis use (which is typically initiated in mid- to late adolescence) is intermittent and largely discontinued during the mid- to late twenties (see Chapter 3). The pattern of cannabis use differs from that for legal substances like alcohol and tobacco, which continue into later adult life (Chen and Kandel, 1995; Bachman et al., 1997). Household surveys in the USA, Great Britain and Australia are consistent with this pattern in finding that cannabis use is uncommon after the age of 30. These data suggest that although prohibition does not eliminate cannabis use, its illegality may moderate use and encourage young adults to stop using at an earlier age than may be the case if cannabis were legal.

A major obstacle to evaluating the deterrent effect of prohibition is the lack of consensus on a standard for evaluating its effectiveness. Critics argue that the goal of prohibition is the elimination of cannabis use, by which standard it has clearly failed. Those who recognise that few laws are ever effective at eliminating unwanted behaviours have to answer more complicated questions: How effective should we expect cannabis prohibition to be? How much should we expect it to reduce consumption? Should we expect cannabis prohibition to be more or less effective than laws prohibiting the use by or sale of alcohol to minors?

Even if we could agree on the answers to these questions, there are a number of major difficulties in deciding on the extent to which cannabis prohibition deters use. First, we have no way of estimating what rates of cannabis use would be in the absence of prohibition because all developed countries prohibit its sale, and rates of use were low and not assessed before it was prohibited. Second, survey data on rates of cannabis use provide poor indications of the deterrent effects of prohibition. Such data identify the proportion of the population who have *not* been deterred by the policy; people who do not report using cannabis include both those who are deterred by the policy and those who would not use cannabis even if it were legal. Third, it may be misleading to assume that rates of cannabis use would be similar to those of alcohol or tobacco if it were legal because cannabis has different effects that may make it more or less desirable. All of these reasons make it very difficult to decide to what degree prohibition has deterred people from using cannabis.

Do criminal sanctions deter use?

Most research on the impact of cannabis prohibition has addressed the more specific question: do criminal sanctions against cannabis use deter people from using cannabis? This is a much more specific question than the effect of cannabis prohibition because cannabis can be a prohibited substance even if there are no criminal sanctions for using it, as is discussed in more detail in Chapter 17.

This question has been addressed by a variety of study types such as cross-national comparisons and analyses over time within a country. All of these studies assess the effects of varying criminal penalties for cannabis possession and use offences on indicators of cannabis use. There is a problem with many of these studies that has only recently become clear: that they tend to take statutory penalties at face value, neglecting differences in the way that prohibition is enforced in the jurisdictions that are being compared. Two jurisdictions with the same written law, for example, might differ markedly in the way it is enforced, resulting in two very different policies. If these differences in enforcement are ignored, then the results of analyses can be misleading.

Recent evidence from an ethnographic study in Amsterdam, San Francisco and Bremen found striking similarities in cannabis use patterns among regular users despite differences in legal environments and enforcement practices. The authors use this finding to argue that government policy has no effect on cannabis use (Cohen and Kaal, 2001). Such a conclusion seems to be supported by some studies evaluating the effects of small changes in the legal penalties for possessing cannabis in the United States and Australia (Single, 1989; Christie, 1991; Thies and Register, 1993; Donnelly et al., 1995; McGeorge and Aitken, 1997).

More recent studies using large, nationally representative samples and more sophisticated statistical models suggest that criminal sanctions do affect reports of cannabis use (Cameron and Williams, 2001; Pacula et al., 2003; Williams, 2003). These studies show that the decision to use cannabis is affected by changes in the legal penalties for possession of cannabis when statistical models take account of individual differences in propensities to use, differences in the monetary price of cannabis, differences in enforcement patterns, and other factors. The quantity of cannabis used was not influenced by criminal penalties for possession of cannabis. In other words, criminal penalties may discourage some people from using *any* cannabis but they do not influence the quantity that is consumed by those who decide to use. Furthermore, the deterrent effect appears to be greatest for older individuals, particularly those over the age of 30 (Saffer and Chaloupka, 1999; Cameron and Williams, 2001).

These recent studies also highlight the difficulty in comparing results between studies and countries. The importance of decriminalisation as a variable, for example, depends on whether other aspects of the policy are included in the statistical model. For example, Williams (2003) shows that in Australia the impact of cannabis decriminalisation on cannabis use is very sensitive to the inclusion of data on the penalties imposed for use offences (that is, fines and imprisonment). Pacula et al. (2003) show that in policy studies in the United States the effects of legal penalties on cannabis use are influenced by measures of the way in which the law is enforced. The ability to control for the monetary price of cannabis is critical in evaluating the impact of reduced sanctions on rates of cannabis use. The purpose of legal penalties against possession or use is to raise the legal risk to the user/buyer. The legal risks to the seller are affected by penalties for the *sale* of cannabis, and it is this risk that is reflected in the market price of cannabis. Because the enforcement risk faced by buyers and sellers is likely to be positively correlated, ignoring the legal risk to the seller (reflected in the monetary cost of cannabis) results in the omission of an important variable and a misleading result (for more on this see Pacula et al., 2003).

All of these analyses have examined the effects of relatively small changes in the legal penalties for *possession* of cannabis. It is not surprising perhaps that these small variations in penalties for possession are associated with relatively small variations in rates of cannabis use. There may be a real deterrent effect of these laws, but the apparent effect in these studies is small because the policy change is small. One cannot use these studies to predict the effects of larger policy changes on rates of cannabis use. For example, the elimination of penalties for selling cannabis are likely to have a much larger impact on rates of use because it would influence not only willingness to try cannabis but also the price paid for it.

Caveats about comparisons between nations

There has been a tendency in the cannabis policy debate to evaluate the effects of different cannabis polices in different countries by comparing rates of cannabis use in them. We think that there are three good reasons why such cross-national comparisons should be interpreted very cautiously.

First, a common label for these policies often obscures the fact that the policies are *very* different. For example, in some states of Australia and the United States the possession of small amounts of cannabis has been 'decriminalised' but this label describes very different policies. In South Australia, for example, an individual can possess up to 100 grams of dried cannabis or 3 plants. If caught, he or she is given a citation that requires the defendant to pay a small fine within 60 days (Ali et al., 1999). Criminal proceedings only result if the individual fails to pay the fine and a criminal record is only given if the individual is found guilty. In the United States, 'decriminalisation' refers to the policies adopted in 11 states during the 1970s that eliminated imprisonment for possession of small amounts of cannabis (typically under one ounce) for first-time offenders (Pacula et al., 2003). Not all states eliminated criminal records for the offence. Cannabis cultivation was strictly prohibited in all of these US states. Comparisons of the effect of decriminalisation in Australia and the USA would accordingly be unwise. The same may even be true in comparing jurisdictions within the same country (as is the case in the United States).

A second reason for caution in comparing the deterrent effects of cannabis penalties between countries is even more important: the level of enforcement of cannabis laws also varies significantly between jurisdictions. Deterrent theory predicts that behaviour is most likely to be deterred by the prospect of certain, swift and severe punishment. The effectiveness of a policy is therefore defined by both the way that a law is enforced (which affects the certainty of punishment) and the penalties that are imposed (which affects swiftness and severity). If we only evaluate the impact of laws within particular jurisdictions and ignore the variability in enforcement across jurisdictions, we will miss a critical component of the policy and its impact on behaviour.

Unfortunately, many of the analyses of the impact of changes in criminal sanctions on cannabis use do not control for levels of enforcement across jurisdictions. Those that do often rely on data on arrests and imprisonment that confound information about enforcement with budgets, policing practices and adjudication processes, that are independent of cannabis policy. Some more recent studies have tried to account for unobserved differences in levels of enforcement statistically, but these models are also limited in that they assume that enforcement within a jurisdiction is constant over the time, which may not be the case. Future evaluations of the impact of criminal sanctions on cannabis use need to consider both penalties and the way that the law is enforced.

A final factor complicates comparisons of the deterrent effect of prohibition in different countries. This is that countries differ in many factors that affect demand for cannabis, including income, social norms, religiosity, family stability, and assumption of adult roles. Some of these factors are likely to reduce rates of cannabis use (e.g. religiosity, family stability), while others are likely to increase rates of use (e.g. greater disposable income). Two countries with the same cannabis policy (law and enforcement) can accordingly have very different rates of cannabis use. One should not expect, therefore, that a change in policy in one country with many protective factors would predict what would happen in a country that has fewer protective and more risk factors. More concretely, even if the rise in cannabis use in the Netherlands has been fairly small with the policy of tolerating cannabis use and sales in coffee shops, that does not mean that a similar policy would have the same effect in the United States, because of different patterns of protective and risk factors in the two populations.

The best way to evaluate the impact of changes in cannabis law on rates of use in a particular country is to conduct policy experiments within that country. By studying the effects of small changes in laws within a country we can better control for other factors that also influence individual decisions to use cannabis, such as enforcement, social norms, and other determinants of demand. This does not mean that nothing can be gained from cross-national comparisons; only that such comparisons should be made with the clear understanding that many uncontrolled factors may explain differences in rates of cannabis use between countries.

Summary

It is difficult to evaluate the success or failure of prohibition as a policy in the absence of a societal consensus on how we should judge success and because of the paucity of appropriate data to evaluate it. It is clear that prohibition has not eliminated use. It is also clear, however, that criminal sanctions on cannabis use have deterred some individuals from using cannabis, with the most impact on individuals over the age of 30 (Cameron and Williams, 2001). Neither of these 'facts' provides definitive evidence of prohibition's success or failure. We need better data to assess the impact of current policies on individuals' decisions that ideally should come from policy experiments within specific countries and from analyses that account for variations in enforcement and underlying determinants of cannabis use.

We also believe that evaluations of the deterrent effects of cannabis prohibition should move beyond rates of lifetime or past-year cannabis use. Indeed, our analysis of the harms caused by cannabis suggests that occasional and intermittent use by adults is unlikely to pose significant harms to the individual or society. It is regular use over long periods and inappropriate use (such as use before driving or while pregnant) that is likely to cause harm. It is a plausible hypothesis that prohibition deters regular, chronic or inappropriate use while having much less effect on experimentation or occasional cannabis use. Existing research on lifetime or past-year use does not speak to this question despite its greater relevance in evaluating the effectiveness of cannabis policy. We believe that future research needs to address this question.

15

The monetary cost of enforcing prohibition

It is widely understood that it is expensive to enforce a policy of prohibition, whether the prohibition is on the sale of cannabis or just the simple possession and use of cannabis. Critics of cannabis prohibition, and some judges and law enforcement officers, have criticised the allocation of scarce police and judicial resources to the prosecution and judicial processing of minor cannabis offences (e.g. Kaplan, 1970). The fact that prohibition is an expensive policy to pursue, coupled with a belief that it has not been successful at reducing cannabis use, has led some countries to consider alternative policies that are believed to result in lower overall societal costs (Senate Standing Committee on Social Welfare, 1977; Canadian Senate Special Committee on Illegal Drugs, 2002). Most of the alternative models that have been tried to date are models that retain a prohibition on the sale/supply of cannabis but reduce penalties for possession and use. They therefore eliminate the costs associated with enforcing a prohibition against users but retain the costs associated with enforcing a prohibition against supply.

Although there is general agreement among its critics that prohibition is an expensive policy, there is surprisingly little information on the costs of implementing it in any country. In fact, in a recent summary of cannabis policies in Europe, Australia and the United States, the Canadian Senate Report was unable to identify any studies that could quantify the total cost of prohibiting the supply and demand of cannabis for any of the countries it examined (Canadian Senate Special Committee on Illegal Drugs, 2002). Instead, estimates were made by attributing some fraction of the total drug budget for a country to cannabis prohibition. For reasons discussed below, this type of estimate presents a very poor assessment of the real cost of prohibiting cannabis sale and use.

In the absence of any good estimates of the cost of prohibiting cannabis we should not assume that these costs are trivial. Indeed, estimates have been made of the costs of enforcing specific aspects of prohibition, such as adjudicating and imprisoning offenders. These suggest that the cost of enforcing the prohibition may be very high. The limitations of these studies highlight the difficulty in trying to construct a reliable estimate of the cost of enforcing prohibition. They often make assumptions, implicitly or explicitly, about the opportunity costs of the resources that are used to enforce cannabis prohibition.

A policy of prohibition imposes monetary cost on society for at least two reasons. First, it requires the allocation of limited societal resources to the enforcement of cannabis prohibition and away from alternative uses of those resources. The economic value of the use of these resources in their most productive alternative use is what economists refer to as the 'opportunity cost' of these resources. Second, because prohibition does not eliminate cannabis use, blackmarkets emerge to meet demand. These impose additional costs on society by disrupting neighbourhoods, generating violence and crime, and creating a loss of taxation revenue. The level of costs imposed on a particular country or jurisdiction will depend upon a number of factors, including the form of cannabis prohibition that is adopted, the degree to which it is implemented within specific jurisdictions, and the level of use within that jurisdiction.

The cost of enforcing prohibition on cannabis use and sale

There is substantial variation in the type of prohibitions that have been implemented in developed countries. Although all developed countries prohibit the supply of cannabis for recreational purposes, countries differ in the way they treat users. Some countries, including the United States and Canada, impose a prohibition on the use (or possession) of cannabis, thereby imposing criminal sanctions upon individuals who are caught possessing cannabis. Other countries such as Spain, Italy and Portugal have eliminated criminal sanctions for the simple possession and/or use of cannabis although they maintain small administrative fines or penalties. Other countries, such as Australia and Great Britain, have adopted policies that are somewhere in between full sanctions against users and decriminalisation of all use. The costs associated with enforcing prohibition in each of these countries differ because of these differences in the treatment of users.

The cost of prohibiting use

The most readily available data on the costs of cannabis prohibition concern the costs of enforcing the prohibition on possession and use of cannabis. This is true in large part because critics of current policy in many Western countries have criticised expenditure of large amounts of money on apprehending, adjudicating and imprisoning non-violent drug users in general, and cannabis users in particular. As can be seen in Figure 15.1, several Western countries experienced a rise in cannabis use-related arrests during the 1990s. These rises were consistent across countries despite significant differences in policies towards cannabis use.

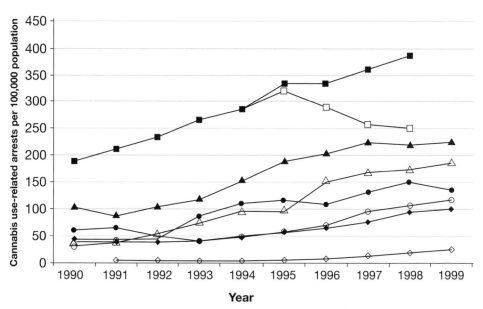

Fig. 15.1   Per capita cannabis possession arrests. Reprinted from Kilmer, B. (2002) Do cannabis
possession laws influence cannabis use? In I. P. Spruit (ed.), *Cannabis 2002 Report:
Technical Report of the International Scientific Conference*, Brussels: Rodin Foundation
and the Ministry of Public Health of Belgium. http://www.trimbos.nl/trimbos/
Cannabis2002%20Report.pdf. The plot with black squares indicates Switzerland, the plot
with white squares indicates Australia, the plot with black triangles represents the United
States, the plot with black circles indicates the United Kingdom, the plot with white
triangles indicates Austria, the plot with white circles indicates France, the plot with black
diamonds indicates Germany, and the plot with white diamonds indicates Portugal.

In the United States the number of cannabis possession arrests where cannabis
possession was identified as the primary offence more than doubled between
1992 and 1998, accounting for 38% of all drug arrests by 1998 (Federal Bureau of
Investigation, 2001). Over the same period the National Household Survey on
Drug Abuse shows that the prevalence of cannabis use in the general population
(ages 12 and older) rose very slightly from 7.9% in 1992 to 8.6% in 1998
(Substance Abuse and Mental Health Services Administration, 2001). Critics of
US policies argue that the enormous increase in cannabis possession arrests is the
result of a law enforcement crackdown on non-violent drug offenders (Thomas,
1999; Gettman, 2000). Such a claim seems to be substantiated by the fact that of
the 1,579,466 drug arrests in the US in 2000, 5.6% were for cannabis sales or cultivation and 40.9% were for simple possession (Federal Bureau of Investigation,
2001). Although no estimates of the policing cost of this policy have been

provided, Thomas (1999) used information on the estimated number of cannabis possession offenders who were imprisoned in 1997 to estimate the cost of imprisoning these offenders at US$1.2 billion a year.

Several recent ethnographic studies suggest that the rise in cannabis arrests in the United States is not due to a specific crackdown on cannabis use. Rather they are the result of a renewed focus among police agencies on quality-of-life policing (Eck and Maguire, 2000; Reuter et al., 2000; Johnson and Golub, 2001). Quality-of-life policing is a policing strategy that focuses on visible public nuisances, such as drunk and disorderly conduct, traffic violations, vagrancy and other misdemeanours. Data on circumstances of arrest in one large Maryland county found that 85% of all cannabis possession offences resulted from a traffic stop or direct observation by police rather than targeting of cannabis offenders (Reuter et al., 2000).

The situation in Canada appears to parallel that of the United States. Although rates of cannabis use have been relatively stable in Canada, rates of use and arrests have risen among youth during the 1990s. The fraction of 10th grade girls reporting lifetime use of cannabis rose from 24% in 1990 to 41% in 1998, while lifetime prevalence among 10th grade boys rose from 26% in 1990 to 44% in 1998 (King et al., 1999). This rise in consumption was also reflected in arrest statistics that showed in 2001 that youth comprised 18% of all cannabis-related charges (Savoie, 2002).

Interviews with police throughout Canada suggest that these arrests are incidental to other enforcement activities, including traffic stops, general drug enforcement activity, disorderly conduct and other patrol activities (Canadian Senate Special Committee on Illegal Drugs, 2002). Nonetheless, in 21,381 charges in 1999 possession of cannabis was the most serious offence. These charges had to be dealt with by the courts (Canadian Senate Special Committee on Illegal Drugs, 2002). Using limited information on the disposition and sentencing of drug offence cases, the Senate Report estimated that the cost of prosecuting cannabis possession offenses in 1999 was approximately CAN$5 million, or roughly 10% of the total budget for prosecuting all drug-related offences (p. 387).

Switzerland provides an interesting example of the cost of prohibiting use and possession of cannabis because the prohibition against the use and supply of cannabis for recreational purposes occurs within a legal, regulated cannabis market for industrial hemp. The fact that cannabis production is licit for some purposes and illicit for others poses an enormous challenge for law enforcement officials who have to distinguish licit behaviour from illicit behaviour, and to prove this to the satisfaction of a court. Law enforcement officials in some cantons have chosen not to enforce cannabis prohibition because of the difficulty of proving illegal intent (Swiss Federal Commission for Drug Issues, 1999). In the German-speaking cantons, for example, arrest data suggest that the police focus much more on heroin and cocaine users than on cannabis users. Nonetheless, arrests for cannabis use in some cantons have increased substantially, thus raising the national average (Swiss Federal Commission for Drug Issues, 1999, p. 50). Data on court decisions in 6 cantons shows that between 1991 and 1994 the number of convictions for illegal consumption of cannabis rose by 68% to 14,168. Although the majority of these cases received a fine, some custodial sentences were also imposed (Swiss Federal Commission for Drug Issues, 1999, p. 52).

It is clear that the prohibition on recreational use of cannabis still imposes a significant burden on the Swiss judicial and correctional systems. However, the burden appears to be borne unequally because of the significant variation in arrests and prosecutions for cannabis offences across cantons (Estermann and Rônez, 1995). The variation between cantons in the implementation of this policy has led Swiss authorities to conclude that prohibition has an additional cost: inequality in the administration of justice.

A recent study in Australia estimates that 13% of all criminal justice and police resources were devoted to detecting, arresting, and prosecuting Australian cannabis users (McDonald and Atkinson, 1995). There is substantial variation in the criminality of cannabis use across jurisdictions within Australia, however, that provides more useful information regarding the cost of prohibition versus alternative policies. Data from South Australia shows that the simple elimination of criminal penalties for cannabis use does not mean that criminal justice resources will be completely freed with the decriminalisation of possession offences.

In 1987 South Australia adopted a policy of prohibition with civil penalties, known as the Cannabis Expiation Notice (CEN) system. This eliminated criminal penalties for cannabis possession offences for individuals possessing up to 100 grams or growing a small number of plants for their own use (originally 10 plants, later reduced to 3). Individuals who are cited under the CEN system have 60 days to pay a small fine (varying from Australian $50 to Australian $150) to expiate (or remove) the charge. Failure to pay can result in criminal proceedings. If convicted, a criminal record and higher fines (to cover court costs) are imposed. Hence, under the CEN scheme it is not a criminal offence to possess or grow small amounts of cannabis, unless penalties are not paid but it is still illegal to possess and grow cannabis.

Studies examining citations and arrests in South Australia showed that the number of minor cannabis offences rose under the CEN scheme, from 6,000 in 1987–1988 to approximately 17,000 in 1993–1994 and later years. This reflected a change in policing practices rather than an increase in rates of cannabis use (Christie, 1999). Although significant declines in court costs were anticipated, they were not fully realised because only 50% of persons who were fined paid the expiation fees. The total burden on the court system under the CEN system was reduced, however, and an economic evaluation of the scheme estimated that the income from fines was greater than the cost incurred by the courts and corrections system (Ali et al., 1999).

The experience of these four countries provides some insights into the cost of policies prohibiting the use of cannabis. First, there are large costs incurred in prosecuting and imprisoning people for cannabis possession offences. The decriminalisation of cannabis use will probably reduce these costs, but, as can be seen by the Australian experience, it will not necessarily eliminate them. Criminal justice resources will still be required to handle individuals who do not comply with civil penalties. As such, it is unclear how to evaluate the opportunity cost of these criminal justice resources given that we do not know the extent to which resources can actually be used in more productive ways under a decriminalised regime. Second, one must be careful in identifying the policing costs that are incurred by the prohibition of cannabis use because the US and Canadian experience suggests that such offenders are primarily identified in the course of regular policing activities, not through activities targeted at cannabis users. If this is the case, then there would not necessarily be a reallocation of police resources to alternative purposes with a change in policy. There may be some savings in terms of time spent processing cannabis offenders, which could translate into more time spent conducting other police responsibilities, but it is unclear at this point whether this represents substantial cost savings. Further work on this is clearly needed.

The cost of prohibiting the supply of cannabis

It is even more difficult to estimate the cost of prohibiting the supply of cannabis than it is the cost of prohibiting use. It might seem simple to estimate the cost of enforcement activities targeting the cultivation, trafficking or distribution of cannabis, but this is a much more difficult task than one might expect. According to the US Drug Control Budget, for example, the National Guard committed US$34.7 million to cannabis eradication efforts in 2002 (Office of National Drug Control Policy, 2002). However, additional funds for eradicating cannabis plants came from the Agricultural Research Service, Forest Service, Bureau of Indian Affairs, Bureau of Land Management, the US Fish and Wildlife Service and the National Parks system. The total funds budgeted for these purposes across these departments is never presented and is impossible to calculate from the information in the report. Similarly, budgets by US Customs, Coast Guard and other departments do not indicate how much of their interdiction budget is devoted to cannabis-specific activities. Justice budgets do not identify funds allocated to prosecuting cannabis cultivation, sales, trafficking and distributing offences. Hence, any attempt to estimate the real cost of prohibiting the supply of cannabis in the US would be at best an educated guess.

The frustration in conducting what should be a simple budgeting exercise is not unique to the US. In a recent summary of cannabis policies in Europe, Australia and the US, the Canadian Senate Report was unable to quantify the cost of prohibiting the supply of cannabis for any of the countries it examined. Costs were most often reported in terms of total drug budgets, or components thereof, rather than the costs specifically related to cannabis. Many estimates were made by attributing a fraction of the total drug control budget to cannabis use (with the fraction estimated from arrest, seizure and/or use data). These estimates are unreliable, however, for at least two reasons. First, they ignore the economies of scale that are achieved by using the same resources (police, judicial and corrections resources) to prohibit cannabis distribution as to prohibit the distribution of other substances. Second, they assume that the allocation of resources to prohibiting each drug reflects rates of use rather than the social costs its use imposes on society.

There are some economies of scale that may occur as a result of the enforcing of cannabis prohibition in conjunction with prohibitions of other substances. These are possibly substantial. When border patrol agents are hired to check for drugs coming through a border, for example, they are trained to look for multiple substances. Adding another drug to the list of things to check has minimal cost implications and imposes no opportunity cost in terms of alternative uses of the agents' time. Similarly, undercover police who are employed to identify drug dealers may, in the course of their normal activities, identify individuals who sell cannabis. Because resources such as these are shared across objectives, and because many policing activities benefit policies aimed at all illegal substances, the assignment of the cost of these agents solely to the prohibition of cannabis would dramatically overstate the real opportunity cost of the policy.

It is clear that the social harms from cocaine and heroin far exceed the known social harms of cannabis use even though use rates for cannabis are far greater than those of the other two drugs (Harwood et al., 1998; Caulkins et al., 2002). Thus from a cost-benefit perspective, a government should allocate more resources to deterring the use of those drugs that generate the highest social cost. High arrest rates for cannabis do not necessarily mean that more resources are being dedicated to cannabis-specific enforcement strategies. Instead, it is more likely a reflection of the fact that cannabis enforcement benefits from general policing efforts that target all drugs and from general quality-of-life policing (Reuter et al., 2000; Johnson and Golub, 2001).

Because of uncertainties about the extent to which shared resources are used to enforce cannabis and other drug prohibitions, it is very difficult to try to estimate the costs of enforcing a prohibition against cannabis. It is clear, however, that simple estimates based on arbitrarily assigned fractions of national drug law enforcement budgets do not identify the cost of prohibiting the supply of cannabis because we do not know (a) what resources are dedicated exclusively to enforcing cannabis prohibition, and (b) what general law enforcement resources are used to enforce the cannabis prohibition. Future attempts to quantify the costs of prohibition, therefore, should improve upon existing estimates by making their assumptions more explicit and by examining the sensitivity of these estimates to plausible alternative assumptions.

The costs of the cannabis blackmarket

Cannabis prohibition makes cannabis a much more expensive commodity than it would be if it were sold at a price that merely reflected its costs of production and distribution. This is because the monetary price of cannabis in the blackmarket also reflects the economic value of the legal risks incurred by sellers who bring the product to market (Criminal Justice Commission, 1994; MacCoun and Reuter, 2001). Because different sellers face different risks over time, and because buyers have imperfect information about the quality and price of cannabis in the market at any time, sellers in the blackmarket can gain positive economic profit. Accounting profits, which ignore the monetary value of the legal risk incurred by the seller, are substantial for all sellers. These large accounting profits, combined with a readily identifiable demand, motivate sellers to continue providing the illegal substance.

Market-related violence

In general, blackmarkets are believed to impose social costs on a community for a number of reasons. First, blackmarkets often generate violence and crime in neighbourhoods where they operate. Violence and crime emerge because buyers and sellers are unable to use legal channels to enforce contracts, ensure the quality of goods sold, and protect an individual's right to do business in a given area. Second, when enormous accounting profits can be earned, blackmarkets enable criminals to corrupt law enforcement officials, thus undermining society's ability to enforce laws. Third, blackmarkets can impose additional costs to users involved in these markets because of the uncertain quality of goods that are being purchased, an inability to regulate sales to minors, and the possible introduction of the user to other harmful goods. Fourth, blackmarkets represent 'lost production' in that the value of the goods and services sold in the blackmarket are not included in national accounts and, more importantly, do not generate taxable income.

Cannabis blackmarkets share some of these characteristics of other blackmarkets but they generate very little violence in the United States (Goldstein et al., 1989; United States Office of National Drug Control Policy, 2001. See Appendix 2.). This is because they differ in a number of ways from blackmarkets for other drugs, particularly heroin and cocaine. The markup in the price of cannabis in illegal markets, although substantial, is nowhere near that for cocaine and other hard drugs. This reduces systemic crime (Kleiman, 1992). The supply chain for cannabis is also far more decentralised with ethnographic reports that cannabis sellers are more likely than other illicit drug sellers to operate independently than as part of an organised dealing operation (Office of National Drug Control Policy, 2002). The majority of sales are conducted in private, so dealers do not see their competitors, making turf wars less likely (Taylor et al., 2001; United States Office of National Drug Control Policy, 2001). Finally, cannabis users can supply their own drug because the plant is relatively easy to grow naturally or indoors at minimal expense. Indeed, at least one study shows that at the lower levels of production and supply, some heavy cannabis users grow their own cannabis and sell their surplus to fund their own use (Reilly et al., 1998).

These factors substantially reduce the amount of violence and crime that is generated by the cannabis blackmarket in the United States. The non-violent nature of the cannabis blackmarket does not appear to be unique to the United States. We are unaware of any country that has reported violence as a common problem in cannabis blackmarkets.

Corruption of law enforcement officials

Significant profits are generated by the cannabis blackmarket and it is possible that these monies could be used to corrupt law enforcement officials. However, the way in which cannabis is typically supplied makes corruption of law enforcement officials less likely to occur in cannabis markets than in markets for other illicit drugs. Because cannabis is easily grown indoors it is very difficult for police to prevent its cultivation. There is accordingly less need for cannabis growers to corrupt law enforcement officials to protect themselves from detection. In addition, because the supply is more decentralised and run by independent operators, profits are more diffused, which makes it unlikely that any one seller commands sufficient resources to corrupt many officials. This does not mean that corruption is not a problem in the case of cannabis; it only means that it is unlikely to occur on a similar scale to that of other illegal (or even heavily regulated) substances.

Lack of regulation

The inability to control the quality of the product brought to the blackmarket is a potential problem in the case of cannabis. Inexperienced and even experienced users can inadvertently purchase bags of cannabis that are cut with other, more harmful, substances. Variations in actual THC content may lead to unexpected reactions to the drug among neophyte users. Minors are also able to purchase cannabis in the absence of any age restrictions on sales in the blackmarket.

A related concern expressed by critics of cannabis prohibition is that the retail cannabis blackmarket is not separated from the retail blackmarket for other, more dangerous illicit drugs such as cocaine and heroin (Cohen, 1976). Individuals seeking to buy cannabis may be introduced to other illicit substances that they otherwise would not know how to obtain and might not have the opportunity to try. Some researchers argue that it is this market opportunity that explains the association between regular cannabis use and the use of other illegal drugs rather than any pharmacologically mediated 'gateway effect' (Lenton, 2001; Morral et al., 2002). Apart from some ethnographic research on cannabis markets there is very little information on the extent of overlap between retail cannabis and other illicit drug markets.

Forgone tax revenue

The social consequences of the blackmarket are likely to be non-trivial: the largest monetary consequence of a cannabis blackmarket is the forgone revenue that could be obtained if cannabis sales were legal and taxed in some way. Although it is reasonable to assume from current rates of cannabis use that the forgone tax revenue is significant, it is difficult to provide a reasonable estimate of what tax revenues could be in a legal regime. This is for two main reasons. First, we do not have any reliable estimates of the size of current blackmarkets in most developed countries. Second, the total revenue obtained in current blackmarkets does not necessarily reflect the total revenue that would be raised if cannabis use and sales were legal (see Chapter 18).

Conservative estimates in Australia suggest that the blackmarket for cannabis is very large. In the Australian state of Queensland in 1994, cannabis had an estimated annual turnover of AU$600 million. This made it an agricultural crop second in wholesale value to sugar and many times more valuable than tobacco (Criminal Justice Commission, 1994). An earlier and more conservative estimate of the value of cannabis in Australia in 1988 was AU$1.9 billion (Parliamentary Joint Committee on the National Crime Authority, 1989). US estimates of expenditure on illicit drugs are larger by an order of magnitude. In 1995, cannabis users in the USA were estimated to have spent US$7 billion on cannabis as against US$10 billion on heroin (Office of National Drug Control Policy, 1997).

Even if we accept these estimates of the size of the blackmarket, we cannot simply assume that the taxation revenue from cannabis under a legal market would be some percentage of the estimated market value under a blackmarket. This would assume that total revenues would be the same in a legal market as they are in the blackmarket. Total revenue (the average price of cannabis per unit multiplied by the quantity consumed), would depend on how much price and consumption changed in a legal market. As is explained in greater detail in Chapter 18, it is unlikely that the price of cannabis in a legal market would be as high as it is in a blackmarket. This is because sellers do not need to be compensated for risk in a legal market, eliminating the reason for the markup in blackmarkets. The average cannabis price would therefore fall, reducing total revenue. Consumption, however, is likely to go up because those individuals who were previously deterred by prohibition may no longer be deterred. Further, as price falls, consumption rises (Pacula et al., 2001). Without knowing how sensitive consumption is to changes in price (the elasticity of demand), it is unclear whether total revenue would rise or fall if it were legal to use and sell cannabis.

Summary

Cannabis law enforcement in Australia, the USA and in many other developed societies presents something of a paradox. Although most cannabis users are not arrested, the majority of drug-related offences dealt with by the courts are for cannabis possession and use. In Australia, for example, between 70% and 90% of 61,000 drug offences appearing before state courts in 1991–1993 were for cannabis possession and use (McDonald and Atkinson, 1995). In the USA in 1995, half a million people appeared before the courts on cannabis offences and 83% of these offences were for possession (Zimmer and Morgan, 1997).

It is clear that a policy of prohibition imposes a significant burden on criminal justice resources in numerous countries. It is difficult, however, to accurately quantify those costs. Current attempts to estimate the cost of prohibiting just the use of cannabis ignore a number of factors, including the cost of policing strategies targeting users, the flexibility of prosecutors to change the charges brought against defendants, and the variability in actual sentences imposed on offenders. Furthermore, these estimates ignore the fact that at least some of the resources dedicated to enforcing the current prohibition against cannabis use would still need to be used to enforce cannabis regulations in a legal regime (see Chapter 18). The most likely effect of ignoring these factors is to overstate the costs of cannabis prohibition. Attempts to calculate the cost of prohibiting the supply of cannabis are similarly unreliable because they make unreasonable assumptions about how drug budgets are allocated and they ignore the economies of scale that are achieved by pursuing a cannabis prohibition in conjunction with prohibitions on other substances.

Given the difficulties in trying to obtain a reliable assessment of the total cost of any specific prohibitionist policy, it is difficult to estimate the cost savings that would flow from a modest or a more significant change in cannabis policy. Future research needs to provide better estimates of the incremental costs of specific aspects of cannabis prohibition (e.g. on use versus sales) so that policy-makers have a better idea of where the most substantial cost savings can be made. For some countries, the bulk of the savings might come from the decriminalisation of the use of cannabis while retaining the prohibition on supply. For other countries, it may be the cost of restricting supply that imposes the greatest burden on their budgets.

16

Other costs of cannabis prohibition

The previous two chapters have considered evidence relevant to claims that cannabis prohibition fails to deter cannabis use and is a costly policy to enforce. The economic costs of enforcement and a blackmarket do not exhaust the costs identified by critics of cannabis prohibition. For the sake of completeness, this chapter briefly reviews other costs of cannabis prohibition that have been identified by its critics. Where available, evidence on these costs is reviewed. For the most part, however, many of these putative costs are either intangible or they have not been researched. These can be thought of as topics that require more detailed research as part of the overall task of evaluating cannabis policy.

Loss of liberty

A clear cost of prohibition is that adults are deprived of the liberty to enjoy any of the benefits of cannabis use, such as euphoria, relaxation, sociability and so on. These benefits of recreational cannabis use reported might be crudely quantified in terms of the number of current cannabis users who use the drug without experiencing problems of abuse or dependence. In Australia in 1997 this was 7.1% of all adults who used cannabis 5 or more times in the past year (Degenhardt et al., 2000).

According to libertarians, the prohibition on the recreational use of any drug is an unacceptable infringement of individual liberty (Szasz, 1997). The English philosopher John Stuart Mill gave this idea its most famous expression in his statement of the 'harm principle' as the basis for criminal law:

> ... the sole end for which mankind are warranted, individually or collectively, in interfering with the liberty of action of any of their number, is self-protection ... [i.e.] to prevent harm to others. His own good, either physical or moral, is not a sufficient warrant. (Mill, 1975, pp. 9–10)

Since a major justification of cannabis prohibition has been to protect the health and well-being of all cannabis users, including adults, cannabis prohibition is contrary to Mill's principle. According to libertarian theory, cannabis prohibition should be abolished (Szasz, 1997). The only role for the state, according to libertarians, is to regulate the sale of drugs to adults to ensure drug quality and purity and to prevent sales to minors, who could be prevented from using in accordance with Mill's principle (Szasz, 1997). Any cannabis user whose behaviour harmed others would be subject to criminal and civil laws (Szasz, 1997). For libertarians, the fact that cannabis prohibition infringes individual liberty trumps all other arguments. For non-libertarians, the loss of adult liberty entailed by prohibition is one cost that has to be weighed in the scale against any reduction in cannabis use and harm.

An unjust and disproportionate penalty

Some critics of cannabis prohibition argue that it is unjust to impose a custodial penalty for using a substance that largely harms the user (Husak, 2002). Others argue that a criminal penalty is disproportionate to the seriousness of the offence of using cannabis (Kaplan, 1970; Criminal Justice Commission, 1994).

The argument that criminal penalties for cannabis use are disproportionate has special force in jurisdictions in which the statutory penalty for cannabis use is a prison sentence of up to 15 years. This is true in some Australian states which, by contrast, do not impose a prison sentence for driving a motor vehicle while intoxicated by alcohol, conduct that clearly endangers the health and safety of others. There is no mandatory criminal penalty for drunk driving in Australia because the use of random breath testing and fines for drunk driving have deterred people from engaging in this behaviour (Homel, 1990). Advocates of civil penalties argue that the same approach should be adopted towards cannabis-use offences (McDonald et al., 1994).

According to Husak (2002), criminal penalties are unjust because there is no justification for imposing a criminal penalty for an offence that only harms the individual. Criminal penalties, Husak argues, require a demonstration that offenders' conduct harms others. He also claims that there is no justification for criminal prosecution of the minority of cannabis users who come to police attention in order to discourage the majority who use without detection. In his view, the injustice of prosecuting cannabis users is compounded by making an example of the unlucky few who have the misfortune to be detected.

Critics of cannabis prohibition claim that prosecution, conviction and the acquisition of a criminal record have an adverse effect on the lives of otherwise law-abiding cannabis users who are caught up in the criminal justice system; these consequences, they argue, are more serious than any harms that may be caused to users by their own cannabis use (Kaplan, 1970; Wodak et al., 2002). The limited research on the consequences of a cannabis conviction (Erickson, 1980; Lenton et al., 1999a; Lenton et al., 1999b) suggests that a substantial proportion of persons convicted of these offences have no other criminal records. For them a criminal conviction for a cannabis offence has an adverse effect on their lives in terms of employment and reputation, while having no impact on their level of cannabis use (Lenton et al., 1999a; Lenton et al., 1999b).

Unequal application of the law

There are numerous claims that the law does not get uniformly applied, thereby imposing a further cost to society. There is significant evidence, for example, that the criminal law on cannabis is not enforced against middle-class cannabis users in many developed countries (Kaplan, 1970; Criminal Justice Commission, 1994). Kaplan (1970) observed in California in the late 1960s that although college students had some of the highest rates of cannabis use in the community they were rarely arrested for cannabis offences. Two more recent reports show that cannabis arrest rates in the United States are disproportionately higher for Hispanic and Black minorities when compared to rates of use (Gettman, 2000; Human Rights Watch, 2000). Arrest data in the Uniform Crime Reports show that in 1995 Blacks were 2.5 times more likely to get arrested than whites for cannabis-related offences (Gettman, 2000). Another report by the Human Rights Watch Group shows that Blacks comprise 62.7% of all drug offenders admitted to state prisons but only 36.7% of the population (Human Rights Watch, 2000). Neither the arrest nor the sentencing patterns bear any resemblance to patterns of use, which show that Whites are much more likely to use illicit drugs than Blacks (Substance Abuse and Mental Health Services Administration, 2001).

Similarly findings have been shown in other countries. In the Australian state of Queensland, for example, a 1994 study showed that cannabis offenders appearing before the criminal courts were more likely to be unemployed and socially disadvantaged males than were the people who report cannabis use in community surveys in that state (Advisory Committee on Illicit Drugs, 1993). Analyses of self-reported arrests for cannabis offences in the Christchurch birth cohort provide clear evidence of discriminatory enforcement of cannabis prohibition in New Zealand against Maoris and young males with criminal records (Fergusson et al., 2003).

The unequal application of the law is not limited to issues just related to race and ethnicity. As discussed in the previous chapter, there is concern that variations in the application of the law across jurisdictions within the same country produce inequality in the administration of justice. In Switzerland, for example, Estermann and Ronez (1995) estimate that the proportion of prosecutions for cannabis use varied from 24% to 90% between cantons. Substantial variation in the arrest and adjudication of cannabis offenders has also been reported in Canada (Canadian Senate

Special Committee on Illegal Drugs, 2002). This variation in the enforcement of the policy generates an inequality in the application of the law, which has been taken very seriously by politicians and policy-makers in both of these countries.

Disrespect for the law

In countries like Australia and the USA which have a high prevalence of cannabis use, fewer than one in 50 users is arrested in any year. The proportion of cannabis users arrested in any one year was: 2% in Queensland in 1990 (Advisory Committee on Illicit Drugs, 1993), 1.5% in Western Australia in 1998 (Lenton, 2000), 2% in Canada in the early 1970s (Canadian Government Commission of Inquiry, 1970) and 2% in the USA in 1995 (MacCoun and Reuter, 2001). The low probability of arrest for cannabis use is the most likely explanation of the modest deterrent effects of cannabis prohibition in these jurisdictions (Lenton, 2000).

There is evidence too that the criminal law fails to deter use in the minority of cannabis users who are arrested and prosecuted. Erickson (1980) reported that one year after being convicted for a cannabis offence, 92% of her sample of cannabis users in Ontario were still using cannabis at the same level as before their arrest. The same was true of convicted cannabis users in South Australia and Western Australia (Erickson, 1980; Lenton et al., 1999a; Lenton et al., 1999b).

The low rate of detection and prosecution reduces the force of the criticism that the criminal law is being used to punish self-harmful behaviour but it prompts another criticism: that the failure to enforce a widely broken criminal law brings the criminal law into disrepute among the many young adults (the majority in Australia) who break the law without being prosecuted (Kaplan, 1970). There is no research on the impact of disobedience to cannabis prohibition on public attitudes towards the rule of law but this is a plausible hypothesis that deserves more investigation.

Health education about cannabis and other drugs

Accurate health education about the health effects of cannabis has been a casualty of the policy debate in many countries. In Australia and the USA, for example, the public have been presented with polarised views of the health risks of cannabis use, based upon selective and biased citation of research evidence by partisans for one or another cannabis policy, as some examples will show. In countries such as Sweden, where a more consistent view of the health risks is expressed in community educa-tion, some argue that it has been at the cost of exaggerating the risks of cannabis use by misrepresenting the evidence on its health risks (Van Solinge, 1997).

A cost of the cannabis policy debate is dishonest and selective citation of evi-dence on the health effects of cannabis. This prevents an intelligent and informed public debate about cannabis use. Like the boy who cried 'wolf', exaggerated claims about the adverse health effects of cannabis that are not borne out by personal or vicarious experience engender scepticism among the young about any information about the adverse health effects of cannabis. This must be counted as a cost of prohibition, as must the lack of a societal consensus on what type of health information to give young people about the risks of cannabis use.

A related concern is the impact that exaggerated claims about the health effects of cannabis may have on the perceived risks of using other illicit drugs (Zimmer and Morgan, 1997). The argument is that it is counterproductive to teach young people that the health risks of cannabis are similar to those of injected drugs like heroin and cocaine (United Kingdom Police Foundation, 2000). When young people find from experience that occasional cannabis use does not have the adverse effects claimed, they may become sceptical about the claimed adverse health effects of other more dangerous drugs. This argument has apparent validity but there is not a lot of direct evidence to support it. The fact that most cannabis users do *not* try other drugs would suggest otherwise but it is harder to exclude the possibility that less well-educated and well-informed cannabis users may do so. This too is an issue that deserves to be better researched by health educators.

The loss of medical uses of cannabis

Critics of cannabis prohibition have argued that it prevents patients with life-threatening and chronic illnesses, such as AIDS and cancer, from using cannabis for therapeutic purposes (Grinspoon and Bakalar, 1993; Zimmer and Morgan, 1997). They cite evidence that cannabinoids are effective as anti-nausea agents, appetite stimulants in patients with AIDS-related wasting, anti-spasmodic agents in neurological disorders such as multiple sclerosis, and analgesics for pain that is unrelieved by existing analgesics (WHO Program on Substance Abuse, 1997; House of Lords Select Committee on Science and Technology, 1998; Institute of Medicine, 1999).

In the US there is very little evidence on which to judge the seriousness of this cost of cannabis prohibition. We do not have credible estimates of the number of US patients who may benefit from the medical uses of cannabinoids, the number who currently smoke cannabis for medical purposes or the number who would be prepared to use cannabis for medical reasons if it were legal to do so (Institute of Medicine, 1999). A recent US General Accounting Office Report evaluating the implementation of state medical marijuana policies in just four states determined that in spring 2002 there were 2450 people in Alaska, Hawaii and Oregon who registered as medical marijuana users (US General Accounting Office, 2002). These registered users represent 0.05% of the combined population for these three states.

Over 75% of the registered users in Oregon and Hawaii used cannabis for severe pain and muscle spasms, such as those associated with multiple sclerosis (US General Accounting Office, 2002). Estimates were not available for California.

An estimate of the number of potential beneficiaries in the Australian state of New South Wales suggested that there were conservatively 14,000 patients with cancer and AIDS-related wasting, nausea induced by cancer chemotherapy and neurological disorders in a population of approximately 5,000,000 adults (Hall et al., 2001). This is likely to be an overestimate of the number of actual medical users of cannabis because the symptoms of many of these patients would be relieved by existing treatments and not all those whose symptoms were unrelieved would be interested in using cannabis. The numbers of medical cannabis users may be comparatively small, but, as Gable has pointed out, the current laws produce an inequitable access to cannabis (Gable, 1997). Younger recreational cannabis users are unlikely to be deterred by the legal prohibition on cannabis use and likely to have ready access through their social networks to illicit supplies of the drug. Older adults with terminal illnesses, by contrast, are likely to be discouraged by the legal prohibition on cannabis use and will have less ready access to illicit cannabis supplies.

Conclusions

In addition to the economic costs of enforcing cannabis prohibition, its critics have pointed to other personal, social and economic costs. Many of these putative costs have not been quantified but they include: a loss of liberty by adults to use cannabis; loss of respect for the law among young adults; selective enforcement of the law; impairment of public education about the adverse health effects of cannabis; and the loss of medical uses of cannabis by patients with chronic and life-threatening conditions.

The case for cannabis liberalisation may not be as overwhelming as its advocates assert but they nonetheless raise important questions about the costs of cannabis prohibition. In making decisions about cannabis policy, the community needs to appreciate that a societal decision to continue with cannabis prohibition (which is often made by default) is an implicit decision to continue to bear these costs.

7

Policy alternatives

All developed countries today prohibit in some fashion the possession, use, cultivation, distribution and sale of cannabis and cannabis products. They vary in the type of behaviour that is proscribed, the resources that are devoted to enforcing the laws and the penalties that are imposed on those who break these laws. These variations in laws and their enforcement, which together determine policy, make it impossible to talk about cannabis prohibition as if it were a single policy. It is more accurate to think of prohibition as a range of policies that can be differentiated by their legal treatment of suppliers and users and, more importantly, by the ways in which laws are enforced and by the sanctions that are imposed on suppliers and users.

When discussing variations on prohibition, it is useful to distinguish between policies aimed at the supply of cannabis (cultivation, distribution and sale offences) and policies aimed at the user (possession and use offences). This distinction makes it easier to differentiate between legal and illegal markets. When the supply of cannabis is prohibited, then the market is operationally illegal because the government does not allow the drug to be brought to a marketplace. Technically, the term prohibition can be applied to any policy that prohibits the supply of cannabis, regardless of the way it treats users. This is the way we define prohibition in this section and throughout the book.

In Chapter 17, we discuss variants of prohibition that differ in the legal penalties that are imposed on users (e.g. no penalties, fines, diversion to treatment and gaol sentences). In Chapter 18, we consider different types of legal cannabis markets. These identify a range of possible legal and regulatory arrangements that would allow cannabis to be supplied by a legal market. We stress that some existing features of cannabis prohibition may remain in a legal market. These may include restrictions on: the types of cannabis products that can be sold, who can sell cannabis, how much they can sell, and to whom it can be sold. We treat these restrictions as forms of regulation rather than as variants of prohibition because they would be applied in an environment in which cannabis supply was sanctioned by the government.

There are many different models of regulated supply that could be discussed when considering an appropriate model for cannabis (Single, 1999). It is beyond the scope of this book, however, to discuss them all. Instead, we follow Kleiman (1989) in focusing on models that may minimise two important outcomes that are frequently used to evaluate prohibitionist policies: (1) rates of cannabis use, where use is measured by acute intoxication, heavy use (e.g. daily use), and chronic or long-term heavy use; and (2) the net social costs of cannabis use, with social costs broadly construed to include the harms caused by cannabis intoxication and long-term cannabis use as well as the social costs of cannabis-control policies.

We have three aims in describing options for a legal cannabis market. These are to highlight: (1) uncertainties about the impact of a legal cannabis market on cannabis use and the social costs of use and control policies; (2) uncertainties about whether the costs and benefits of a legal cannabis market will be better than those of existing prohibitionist models; (3) the necessity to make trade-offs between the costs of cannabis use and the costs of cannabis control (Kleiman, 1989; Kleiman, 1992). We think that these aims will be best met by an analysis of the difficulties in trying to design a legal market that comes closest to simultaneously minimising the costs of use and control.

17

Variations on prohibition

Prohibitionist policies towards cannabis use can be grouped into three broad categories: complete prohibition, partial decriminalisation, and full decriminalisation. These three categories (which are defined in detail below) are used to facilitate discussion; they are not necessarily distinctions recognised by law. We recognise that a great deal of confusion has been generated by the imprecise use of the term 'decriminalisation' in the past, but we think that our use accurately characterises the policy regimes that are usually included under this heading in public debate. It also clearly differentiates different prohibitionist policies.

Complete prohibition

We use the term 'complete prohibition' to refer to prohibitionist policies that prohibit the supply of cannabis, impose criminal sanctions on individuals who possess or use *any amount* of cannabis or any cannabis product. A criminal sanction is one in which a criminal charge, either misdemeanour or felony, is brought against the offender, and a record of the offence is maintained on public record for a specified period of time. Because possession and use offences are criminalised under this model an offender may be imprisoned for a specified period, although jurisdictions may allow some offenders (e.g. first offenders) to avoid imprisonment by participating in a drug treatment, drug education or community service program. The maintenance of a criminal record for all offenders, however, is key because these records have consequences for individuals after they serve their sentence, e.g. adverse effects on their reputation, employment opportunities, travel and housing (Lenton et al., 1999).

There are numerous examples of complete prohibition in developed countries, such as Canada, Sweden and the federal policy of the United States. Most of these policies, however, have only been in effect for a relatively short period of time. Although their policies are nominally similar in their treatment of users and possessors, they differ substantially in the penalties that are imposed. Levels of enforcement also differ across countries. The United States and Sweden provide perhaps the greatest contrast.

The United States model

Cannabis was a legal product in the United States throughout the nineteenth century. Although widely available in pharmacies, the recreational use of cannabis was not widespread until the turn of the century. The rise in use, according to Stephen Belenko, was attributed to two circumstances. First, there was a dramatic increase in the amount of cannabis smuggled into the Southern USA from Mexico and Cuba, particularly into Texas and Louisiana. Second, the passage of the Eighteenth Amendment prohibiting the sale of alcohol and the Volstead Act of 1920 made it much more difficult and expensive to obtain alcohol, which led many to turn to cannabis because it was relatively cheap (Belenko, 2000). The growing popularity of cannabis among immigrants, particularly Mexicans, and other under-class groups, raised concerns in cities with large Mexican populations that cannabis use would spread to youth and the wider population. These fears motivated local laws that initially prohibited the non-medical use of cannabis and later prohibited the possession of cannabis. Similar state legislation was introduced later.

By 1927, 15 states had enacted laws against the sale or possession of cannabis. In the next four years another 14 states banned the non-medical sale and use of cannabis (Belenko, 2000). Finally, in 1937, the federal government passed the Marihuana Tax Act, which prohibited the non-medical use, possession and sale of cannabis federally. The law allowed doctors to prescribe cannabis for medicinal purposes, but a series of administrative constraints limited physicians' ability to do so.

The strongly prohibitionist environment that sparked the 1937 Marihuana Tax Act continued to affect federal laws on drug trafficking and other drug offences, including cannabis, throughout the 1950s. Physicians were legally able to prescribe cannabis until the 1970 Comprehensive Drug Abuse Prevention and Control Act, better known as the federal Controlled Substance Act (CSA), which replaced the Harrison Act of 1914 and the Marihuana Tax Act. The CSA placed all controlled substances into five categories, or schedules, based on their potential for abuse and their recognised medical usefulness. Cannabis was categorised as a Schedule I drug which meant that it had no currently accepted medical use and it was illegal for doctors to prescribe it. The penalties for simple possession of cannabis, however, were actually reduced from a felony charge to a misdemeanour.

In 1972, a Presidential Commission on cannabis advocated scientific research on the use of cannabis for medicinal purposes and a reduction in criminal penalties for possession of cannabis (National Commission on Marihuana and Drug Abuse, 1972). Although the federal government did not change the law, 11 states reduced criminal sanctions for possession of small amounts of cannabis during the mid- and late 1970s. Individuals who were prosecuted in state courts (but not federal courts) received these lower penalties.

There was a hardening of policy towards cannabis and other illicit drugs under President Reagan during the 1980s, the impetus for which came from a parents' movement (Massing, 2000). The USA adopted a policy goal of a 'drug free society' and a number of states reintroduced criminal penalties for cannabis use (Massing, 2000). Since 1980 in the USA the enforcement of the prohibition against all illicit drugs has been vigorously enforced as part of the 'War on Drugs'. Because cannabis is the most widely used illicit drug in the USA, cannabis users have been among the illicit drug users who have been swept up in the prosecution of 'drug war' policies (Kleiman, 1989).

Today, first-time offenders prosecuted in federal courts for a simple possession offence face a misdemeanour charge with a minimum fine of $1000 and up to a year in prison, regardless of the quantity involved (Doyle, 2000). Repeat offenders face incrementally higher fines and longer periods of imprisonment, but the penalty remains the same regardless of the quantity involved. The penalties faced by offenders who appear in state courts differ substantially across states, as will be discussed in greater detail below (Chriqui et al., 2002).

The Swedish model

The current Swedish drug policy has evolved since the mid-1960s when illicit drug problems first became a public issue in Sweden. In the mid-1960s there was some experimentation with 'liberal' drug policies in the form of a medical prescription regime for dependent drug users. This was abandoned in 1967 because of the death of a 17-year-old girl who had used prescribed drugs that had been diverted. The experiment was later portrayed by Bejerot (1975) as the cause of an epidemic of amphetamine injecting in Stockholm. In 1968 custodial penalties were introduced for drug offences on the recommendation of a Committee on Treatment of Drug Abuse. Penalties for drug offences were progressively increased throughout the 1970s but the personal use of illicit drugs was not a criminal offence and the possession of quantities for personal use was not prosecuted during this period.

The goal of a 'drug-free society' was declared in 1977 and, thereafter, the police began to prosecute users for possession (Boekhout Van Solinge, 1997). Treatment places for addiction were substantially increased during the later 1970s to deal with heroin addicts and to respond to an AIDS epidemic among Swedish injecting drug users (Boekhout Van Solinge, 1997). Legislation to allow compulsory treatment for addiction was introduced in 1981 and custodial penalties were introduced for personal use of drugs in 1993 when police were given the power to urine-test suspected drug users (Boekhout Van Solinge, 1997). An economic recession in Sweden during the 1990s led to some winding back of resources allocated for treatment but the system has remained in place since then.

Today, the Swedes continue to pursue the goal of a 'drug-free society' (Swedish National Institute for Public Health, 1993, 1998) through three strategies. The first is to prevent the recruitment of new drug users by limiting the experimental use of drugs. Cannabis is a special focus of these efforts because experimental cannabis users 'form the recruitment base for those who later develop heavy drug abuse' (Swedish National Institute for Public Health, 1998, p. 6). This policy is pursued through school-based and public education about the dangers of illicit drugs, especially cannabis, and by the mobilisation of community hostility to drug use through social organisations.

The second strategy is to induce as many addicts as possible to 'kick the habit'. This is done by the generous provision of abstinence-based treatment services provided by non-governmental organisations and by using threats of prosecution to coerce addicts into seeking treatment. There is legal provision for compulsory treatment for adults and adolescents. These provisions are rarely invoked although the threat of their use is probably more frequently used to induce reluctant addicts to undergo 'voluntary' treatment.

The third strategy is the reduction of the supply of illicit drugs. The rationale is that experience with alcohol 'shows that there is a connection between availability and consumption and there is much to suggest that the same holds true where drugs are concerned.' (Swedish National Institute for Public Health, 1998, p. 6). Police and Customs make vigorous efforts to disrupt local drug markets and to harass drug users.

There are three degrees of penalties for drug offences: minor, ordinary and serious. The seriousness of the offence is based on the nature and quantity of drugs as well as other circumstances. Personal use of cannabis or possession for personal use of up to 50 grams is considered a minor offence and is generally punishable with a fine that is based on the offender's income. The individual may also be given up to six months' imprisonment, but several alternatives exist including probation, conditional sentence or compulsory treatment. Persons found with larger amounts are classified as an ordinary or serious offence and face potentially higher fines and longer periods of imprisonment (up to three years, and two to ten years of imprisonment for ordinary and serious crimes, respectively) (Swedish *Penal Code*). However, in practice, probation and conditional sentencing in connection with compulsory treatment are usually applied for drug offences of normal severity (Dorn and Jamieson, 2001, p. 191).

Partial decriminalisation

We use the term 'partial decriminalisation' to refer to legal systems in which it remains illegal to produce or supply cannabis but civil penalties are imposed for possession and/or use of specified quantities of cannabis. Penalties for individual users vary on the basis of the quantity of cannabis that they possess (or use) and their number of prior offences. For example, individuals who are caught in possession of small amounts of cannabis might receive civil penalties while those caught in possession of larger quantities may face criminal charges.

Partial decriminalisation represents an intermediate step for countries that wish to reduce some of the societal costs of complete cannabis prohibition while retaining some of the benefits of criminalising cannabis. This policy has received considerable attention from policy-makers in recent years in Australia, Canada, Germany, and the United States. Although the motivation for adopting these policies has generally been to reduce the social costs of imprisoning non-violent drug offenders, the implementation of these policies has varied with the political and social context.

Australia

Since 1986, the goal of Australia's national drug strategy has been to 'minimize the harmful effects of drugs on Australian society' (Blewett, 1987, p. 2). Efforts to achieve this goal include the provision of education, a significant expansion of treatment and the collection of national data on drug use and drug-related harms (Bammer et al., 2002). In the Australian federal system, states and territories are responsible for enacting legislation and implementing drug policies while the federal government can influence national policy by tying funding for drug programs to compliance with broadly agreed national goals. Consequently, although harm minimisation has been the national drug policy goal, there has been no uniform approach to cannabis and several Australian states and territories have experimented with their own cannabis policies (Bammer et al., 2002).

Since the mid-1980s, three Australian territories have replaced the criminal penalties associated with minor cannabis offences with administrative fines (referred to as expiation). South Australia was the first to adopt the Cannabis Expiation Notice (CEN) system in 1987, eight years after the South Australian Royal Commission into the Non-Medical Use of Drugs recommended that cannabis use not be treated as a criminal offence (Bammer et al., 2002). In 1992 and 1996, the Australian Capital Territory and Northern Territory, respectively, adopted similar systems. Other states in Australia have retained the criminal status of these minor cannabis offences, although diversion to education and treatment are now the most common outcome for first offenders in all states.

Under the CEN, possession of up to 100 grams of cannabis, 20 grams of cannabis resin, or equipment for consuming cannabis are all treated as minor cannabis offences that are punishable by a small fine ranging from AU$50 to AU$150. If this fee is paid within 30 to 60 days, there are no criminal proceedings and no offence is recorded. Failure to pay the fine leads to criminal proceedings and may result in imprisonment (Bammer et al., 2002). Possession of quantities larger than those specified remains a criminal offence subject to criminal sanctions.

Germany

Although the German federal government retains substantially more control over drug policy than that of Australia, in 1994 the German constitutional court gave significant power to the individual states when it ruled that criminal sentences could not be imposed for possession of hashish or cannabis for 'occasional private use and if there is no danger to third parties'. Power was given to the states because the court left it up to them to define 'occasional private use' and 'small quantities' (MacCoun and Reuter, 2001). MacCoun and Reuter (2001) describe the variation in interpretations of the maximum 'small quantity,' ranging from 35 grams in Hamburg and Baden–Württemberg to 6 grams in Bavaria (*Die Welt*, 1994; *Bild*, 1995; MacCoun and Reuter, 2001, p. 214). Very little information is available on the penalties imposed for other cannabis offences, although treatment instead of imprisonment and compulsory treatment are common for drug offences (MacCoun and Reuter, 2001).

The United States

During the late 1970s, 11 US states reduced the criminal penalties for possession of small amounts of cannabis. This policy was a significance change because the vast majority of all cannabis possession cases are tried in state courts under state law (Ostrom and Kauder, 1999). Although a few states raised their penalties during the Reagan Administration, the general trend in state laws has been to reduce the criminal status of cannabis possession offences. Recent analysis of state legal statutes shows that, by 1999, 15 states had eliminated the criminal status of cannabis possession offences for small quantities of cannabis (Pacula et al., 2003). Surprisingly, seven of the states that do not treat simple possession of small amounts of cannabis as a criminal offence are not recognised as having decriminalised cannabis. Another 13 states that have not decriminalised cannabis allow the criminal record to be expunged upon successful completion of diversion programs, such as education, treatment or community service (Pacula et al., 2003). Thus the penalty in these 13 states is *de facto* the same as in states that have decriminalised cannabis *de jure*. In total then, 28 of the 50 US states have decriminalised cannabis use offences in fact or in law.

In addition to differences in the criminal treatment of simple cannabis possession offences, states also differ in the typical penalty imposed. According to data collected under the ImpacTeen Initiative, by 1999 ten states used diversion to treatment as the mandatory penalty for possession of small amounts of cannabis. The maximum prison sentence for possession of up to 10 grams of cannabis ranged from 0 to 5 years, while the maximum fines varied between US$100 and US$150,000 (Chriqui et al., 2002).

A fundamental difference between the US experience and that of Australia and Germany is the fact that in the United States, state policy is in direct conflict with federal policy. If these same cannabis offenders were tried in federal court (and technically they could be) then they would face much stiffer penalties and a criminal charge. The conflict between state and federal law has not yet been explicitly dealt with by the courts, although the likelihood of this has increased with the recent passage of state laws that conflict with federal law in allowing medical uses of cannabis (Pacula et al., 2002).

Full decriminalisation

We use 'full decriminalisation' to refer to cannabis policies in which the simple possession or use of any amount of cannabis is not a crime. These offences remain illegal but have civil (or administrative) sanctions, typically involving mandatory treatment and a fine. The cultivation, distribution, and sale of cannabis in these jurisdictions, however, remain prohibited. In addition, some countries impose enhanced penalties for individuals possessing and/or using cannabis under specific conditions (e.g. driving, operating heavy machinery, or in public).

Several European countries have adopted policies of full decriminalisation, including Italy, Spain and Portugal, not just for cannabis but for hard drugs as well. With the exception of Spain, which adopted its policy in 1983, these policies are fairly new and so their impact on the harms and costs of cannabis use has not been evaluated. Italy decriminalised cannabis possession offences in 1993 and Portugal decriminalised possession of all drugs in 2001. As is the case with the other policies, there are differences in the way that these countries have implemented these policies. Portugal, for example, has constructed a unique regime by introducing a separate administrative council to oversee offences committed by drug offenders instead of using police and the courts.

Portugal

Upon the recommendation of the Commission for a National Drug Strategy (CNDS) in 1998, the Portuguese Parliament and Council of Ministers decriminalised the simple possession and use of cannabis, along with all other drugs, in July 2001. This decision was based on a broad policy of harm reduction that aims to reduce the harms to the drug-using individual as well as to society.

A central element of this harm-reduction strategy was the declaration that drug users were not to be cast out of society as criminals or pariahs, but were to be fully integrated members of society (van het Loo et al., 2002). This was demonstrated by the complete separation of drug offenders from the criminal justice system. If the police stop someone for using or possessing cannabis they do not arrest him. Instead they issue a citation to appear before the city's administrative committee, a three-person administrative body consisting of two medically qualified and one legal member. This committee decides on a course of action based on the evidence of the case, including the severity of the offence, the type of drug used, whether the use was public or private, if the person is an addict, whether the use is occasional or habitual and the personal circumstances of the user (van het Loo et al., 2002). The possible sanctions range from the suspension of individual rights (such as revocation of a professional licence, a driver's licence, or a ban on where the individual might travel) to fines. Sanctions can be removed or reduced after completion of voluntary treatment (van het Loo et al., 2002). Critics of the Portuguese policy claim that the police and criminal justice system is simply being replaced by a new system. Only time will tell if the system that is implemented realises the intentions of the policy-makers.

Summary

The prohibition of cannabis is a relatively recent policy in many developed countries. Models of prohibition vary substantially in the extent to which simple cannabis possession and use offences are criminalised. Countries with complete prohibition treat simple possession and use offences of even small amounts of cannabis as criminal offences with the result that individuals who are convicted of breaking these laws incur a criminal record even if they avoid prison. In countries with partial decriminalisation, casual users are separated from more involved users by laws that avoid criminal penalties for simple possession and use when the quantity of cannabis is lower than some specified amount. Casual users, therefore, do not have to incur criminal penalties. More involved cannabis users, who are more likely to be convicted of possessing larger quantities, are still treated as criminals rather than being referred to treatment. In models of full decriminalisation, all possession and use offences remain illegal but offenders receive administrative rather than criminal sanctions. In the case of Portugal, the administrative sanctions can be as severe as criminal sanctions (e.g. suspension of professional or driving licences) but coerced treatment is generally the most common outcome.

A fundamental limitation of the classification provided above is that it is based on differences in statutory laws and statutory penalties. It ignores the extent to which these statutory laws are enforced, in part because accurate measures of enforcement of these laws are not readily available in most countries. Thus, it is important to keep in mind that variations in enforcement of these laws may mean that laws as implemented may differ markedly from statutory law. It is this discrepancy between legal statutes and enforcement that has led some individuals to mistakenly assume that cannabis is a legal substance in some countries, such as the Netherlands and Switzerland. As will be explained in the next chapter, although these countries tolerate a *de facto* retail cannabis market, a fully legal cannabis market does not exist in these countries because their legal statutes still forbid such markets.

18

Cannabis as a legal substance

In economics, a market is defined as the voluntary exchange of products and services between sellers (suppliers) and buyers (consumers). A market is legal when the government sanctions the exchange of the good or service. Operationally, a market is legal when the government allows a good or service to be brought to a marketplace, or as economists' say 'supplied'. The supply of a good like cannabis might involve cultivation, production, distribution (including transporting, importing and exporting the good), wholesale trade, retail sale, promotion and advertising. Not all aspects of supply need to be legally sanctioned for a legal market to exist. A completely free market would allow all these aspects of supply without restriction. There are no such free markets for cannabis anywhere in the world today, in part because of the 1961 United Nation's Single Convention on Narcotic Drugs, which requires all signatory nations to take necessary steps to limit 'the production, manufacture, export, import, distribution of, trade in, use and possession of drugs' (MacCoun and Reuter, 2001). There are, however, a number of countries that have experimented with some aspects of a legal cannabis market.

The Netherlands

The most well-known experiment with a partially legal cannabis market has been in the Netherlands. In 1976 a formal written policy of non-enforcement made the possession and sale of up to 30 grams of cannabis *de facto* legal even though the Netherlands technically retained its prohibitionist policy against cannabis (Korf, 2002). The policy basically stated that prosecutors and police would refrain from enforcing the law in those cases where the quantity possessed or sold did not exceed 30 grams. They would also tolerate the sale of these small amounts in coffee shops (MacCoun and Reuter, 2001). By not enforcing the prohibition in these cases, the Dutch government in effect sanctioned the creation of a small retail cannabis market. It continues to aggressively enforce the prohibition against the sale, distribution and trafficking of larger quantities of cannabis. The government also prohibits the cultivation of cannabis for personal or industrial use.

In the following ten years a series of formal and informal guidelines emerged that effectively regulated the *de facto* retail cannabis market. These regulations prevent coffee shops that sell cannabis products from (1) advertising these products, (2) selling hard drugs, (3) selling cannabis to minors, (4) selling amounts greater than the legally specified quantity, and (5) allowing public disturbances (MacCoun and Reuter, 2001). In the 1990s, a licensing system was created that enables the government to limit the number and location of coffee shops, and hence to control where cannabis can be sold. In 1995, the formal non-enforcement policy was modified to reduce the quantity of cannabis that can be legally sold and/or possessed to 5 grams (Korf, 2002). Thus the Dutch policy has allowed a very small, moderately regulated retail cannabis market to develop as a result of non-enforcement of the law while maintaining a statutory prohibition on cannabis use and supply.

Switzerland

In Switzerland, the cultivation and production of cannabis for industrial purposes is legal but the production and use of cannabis as a drug is not. The country consequently has a widespread cannabis production network in place, including agricultural and private cultivation. It also has a national distribution network that supplies shops that sell cannabis products, commonly referred to as 'hemp shops'. Because it is fairly easy to divert cannabis from legal production to illegal products, many hemp shops sell both legal and illicit products. Enforcement of the prohibition on illegal use varies significantly from canton to canton. Ten of the 26 cantons have admitted to the federal government that they do not aggressively enforce the prohibition because of difficulties in doing so (Swiss Federal Commission for Drug Issues, 1999). The result has been *de facto* legalisation of cannabis use in some Swiss cantons.

Australia

A more subtle experiment has been tried in a number of Australian states and territories, where cultivation of small amounts of cannabis has been decriminalised. As in the case of the Netherlands, technically the sale, possession and cultivation of cannabis for any purpose is illegal in all of these territories. However, South Australia in 1987, the Australian Capital Territory in 1992, and the Northern Territory in 1996 introduced an expiation notice system that replaced criminal penalties with administrative fines for minor cannabis offences, if the expiation fee is paid within a specified amount of time (Ali et al., 1999). The cultivation of a small number of plants, initially set at 10 in South Australia (later reduced to 3), was included in the category of 'minor cannabis offences' in order to enable users to obtain cannabis without resorting to the blackmarket. No other aspect of a formal market is sanctioned, however, and the prohibition against home cultivation of larger than statutory amounts is still enforced as evidenced by a rise in the number of such cannabis offences detected (Christie, 1999).

Proposals for legalisation

Due in part to the perceived success of these models, alternative models of partial and/or limited legal markets are currently being considered by Switzerland, Canada, and parts of the United States. For example, in Canada in September 2002, a special committee of the Senate proposed a regulatory system that would grant licences for the production and sale of cannabis to individuals 16 years of age and older. Restrictions on use, including bans on consumption in public places and additional penalties for driving under the influence of cannabis, were proposed as ways of containing demand for cannabis under a legal regime (Senate Special Committee on Illegal Drugs (Canada), 2002).

In the United States, a ballot initiative in the state of Nevada in November 2002 proposed that it would be legal to sell up to 3 ounces of cannabis in state-licensed stores and the possession and use of these amounts would be decriminalised. This initiative was defeated, but still received one-third of the popular vote. In Switzerland, a proposal is being considered that would legalise the personal use and possession of cannabis and effectively allow for the production of cannabis for individual consumption. The legal distribution of cannabis would still be limited to adults and the THC content could not exceed a specified level. Advertising would be banned and all individuals cultivating the product for individual or industrial purposes would have to notify the authorities.

The concept of a legally sanctioned cannabis market is not a new one. Cannabis was a legally supplied good in most developed countries in the early and mid-1900s. However, use rates in these countries at those times were nowhere near their current levels (Belenko, 2000; MacCoun and Reuter, 2001). This suggests that there are social and cultural factors at work today that will affect the costs and benefits of creating a legal cannabis market. And just as cultural factors will influence the end result of a formal change in policy, so will the structure of the new market that is formed. There are a number of different alternative market structures that could be used to legally supply cannabis, each having very different implications for the use of cannabis and the social costs imposed by that use and by the policy. The best approach for a particular country will depend on the goals and objectives of that country as well as the underlying level of demand.

Potential models of legal markets

Our two main criteria for evaluating alternative cannabis policy regimes are: (1) their impact on rates of hazardous cannabis use and hence cannabis-related harm; and (2) the social costs of implementing the policy. Is it possible to create a legal cannabis market that can minimise the harms of both use and control policies? Proponents of cannabis decriminalisation and legalisation argue that these policies would dramatically reduce the costs of existing cannabis policies. Would these cost savings be offset by a rise in hazardous cannabis use and harmful consequences of use?

We begin by explaining why we believe that the change from prohibition to a legal cannabis market is likely to produce an increase in cannabis use. It seems undeniable to us that cannabis use will rise under a legal market although it is difficult to predict by how much. We recognise that it may be possible to use market regulations to minimise the increase in cannabis use, and particularly harmful cannabis use. We therefore consider models of regulated markets that might be effective in minimising the rise in cannabis use and cannabis-related harm. Our discussion makes it clear that an effective regulated cannabis market is not without enforcement costs because the operation of a legal market must be monitored and regulated.

The effects of a legal, regulated market on cannabis use

Economic theory predicts that a legal cannabis market will have two effects that will increase demand for cannabis. First, social norms governing the recreational use of cannabis will change from general disapproval to grudging acceptance, if not explicit approval. By legally sanctioning the cultivation and sale of cannabis, even if limited to adults, the government will send an implicit message that it is acceptable for adults to use cannabis. The simple change in legal status will prompt some adults to initiate use and may prompt others to continue using longer into adulthood (Weatherburn and Jones, 2001). In addition, a change in legal status may lead employers and sporting organisations to reconsider their opposition to cannabis use by eliminating non-criminal personal penalties for use. Finally, increased use by adults is also likely to affect the perceived harmfulness of cannabis use which may increase its use among youth (Bachman et al., 1988; Bachman et al., 1998; Pacula et al., 2001).

The second consequence of creating a legal cannabis market is that the price of cannabis will decline below current blackmarket prices. Cannabis is very cheap to produce, far less costly than is reflected in its blackmarket price. If we ignore the fixed cost of obtaining the plant, which in a legal market is likely to be no more than the cost of obtaining an orange or apple tree (approximately US$50 for a young tree), then the maintenance costs of producing cannabis in a growing season would be the cost of soil, good lighting, water, and nutrients (or pesticides if grown outdoors). These are the same 'inputs' needed to grow any other agricultural product that could be grown in a home garden for less than $25 a year.

When processing cannabis cultivators under federal law in the United States, US federal prosecutors treat one plant as the equivalent of one pound of dried cannabis, presumably because one plant can yield a pound of dried cannabis in a single growing season. If we use this as a conservative estimate of the annual yield from a cannabis plant, then the cost of growing a pound of cannabis in a legal market would be slightly more than $25 a year, assuming that a plant can easily produce more than one yield over the course of its lifetime and the fixed cost of the plant would be depreciated over its life. For our purposes we can reasonably assume that the cost of producing a pound of cannabis in a free market would be approximately US$25, based on the cost of home production. This will be an overestimate of costs if, as seems likely, there are economies of scale in cultivating cannabis on a large scale.

Data from the Drug Enforcement Agency's 19 Cities Report shows that a pound of commercial-grade cannabis sold in the United States in 2001 for anywhere between US$200 and US$4000, depending on location. Most of this blackmarket price reflects the monetary compensation for the legal risks incurred in growing, transporting and selling an illegal product (Caulkins, 1997; Chriqui et al., 2002). The monetary value of these risks is passed on to lower-end distributors who add their risk premium to their costs.

The difference between the blackmarket price and our estimated price of production (US$25) means that the government would have to impose a tax (or levy other fees for cultivation) of between US$150 and $3950 a pound if it wanted to keep cannabis prices at the same levels as in the existing blackmarket. Any such attempt to maintain the high blackmarket price of cannabis in a legal market would be problematic for two reasons.

First, a high legal price would provide an incentive for blackmarket sellers to stay in the market by undercutting the legal price chosen by the government. Much smaller profit margins have created blackmarkets and smuggling for legal products, such as cigarettes. In fact, the smuggling of cigarettes into Canadian provinces became such a big problem during the early 1990s, that the Canadian government had to cut its federal tax of CAN$10.36 per carton of 200 cigarettes to CAN$5.36 per carton in 1994. There were further cuts in some provinces after that (Gruber et al., 2002). Although blackmarket participants have to offer their product for a lower price than the legal market to entice customers from the legal market, they can still earn significant profits if the legal price is substantially larger than the cost of production, as can be seen for cigarettes. Thus, unless the level of enforcement against blackmarket suppliers remains high, the blackmarket suppliers will have incentive to supply cheaper cannabis to the market. As Jonathan Caulkins has pointed out to us, the costs of policing blackmarket cannabis production will probably be higher in a legal than an illegal market because the police and courts will have to use resources to distinguish legal from illegal cannabis supply.

Second, high taxes on cannabis products will provide a strong economic incentive to avoid taxes by reverting to home cultivation. With today's improved growing technology, it is relatively easy and inexpensive to grow good-quality cannabis at home and the legal risks of growing a small number of cannabis plants is fairly low when it is done indoors in a private dwelling. If societal norms changed towards cannabis use after legalisation, then home cultivation would probably increase. The government could only maintain a high price for legal cannabis by aggressive enforcement against blackmarket and home cultivation, thereby raising the social costs of legalisation and undercutting one of its putative benefits.

For these reasons we believe that the current blackmarket price for cannabis cannot be sustained by heavily taxing cannabis in a legal market. We think it is much more plausible that the price of cannabis will be allowed to fall well below the current blackmarket level. It may not necessarily fall to the cost of production, but it seems unlikely that a tax (or fee) could be imposed that was greater than twice the cost of production without encouraging a sizable blackmarket to remain.

Lower prices and a greater social acceptance of cannabis use will probably increase the number of cannabis users and the quantity of cannabis that they consume (Cameron and Williams, 2001; Pacula et al., 2001). Economic analyses conducted on Australian and US data, for example, show that cannabis users are responsive to changes in the price of cannabis and that lower prices increase use (Cameron and Williams, 2001; Pacula et al., 2001). These studies also show that the decision to use cannabis is price-sensitive, with lower cannabis prices resulting in a larger number of people being willing to use it. These studies only assessed the effects of small changes in cannabis price. This means that we cannot use their estimates of the price-sensitivity of cannabis consumption (the price elasticity of cannabis demand) to predict how much consumption would change if the price of cannabis dropped substantially. It is clear, however, that both the number of current cannabis users and the amount of cannabis consumed by existing users are likely to increase if a legal cannabis market is created.

For all these reasons we believe that the creation of a legal cannabis market will produce a rise in cannabis consumption compared to that under cannabis prohibition as a result of changes in social norms and a reduction in price. Exactly how much consumption increases will depend on how much these two factors change and the responsiveness of a country's demand to changes in each factor. Under a legal market, policies and regulations may be adopted that will reduce the amount of change in social norms and price. These policies and regulations require enforcement if they are to be effective and so have costs associated with them. We now turn to consider the form that these regulations may take.

Using market regulations to influence social norms about cannabis

All else being equal, a good that is visible, particularly in socially ('desirable situations, will be seen as more acceptable and its use as normative than one which is used in private. If our social policy goal is to reduce the chance that cannabis use is seen as socially benign, then governments would enact demand-and-supply-side policies that limited its visibility in positive social situations. Some demand-side policies that have been effective at accomplishing this goal for alcohol and tobacco include restrictions on product advertising, how the product can be used, and when the product can be used.

Influencing social norms by regulating demand

Experience with tobacco and alcohol suggests that advertising influences consumption and how these goods are perceived (Warner, 1986; Saffer, 1996). Advertising has large effects on adolescent alcohol and tobacco consumption despite the fact that adolescents do not have legal access to these drugs (Lewit et al., 1981; US Department of Health and Human Services et al., 1994). If the government wants to reduce the impact of cannabis legalisation on adolescent use it should accordingly ban all cannabis advertising, e.g. print, radio, internet, television, point-of-sale, and sponsorship.

As with alcohol and tobacco, warning labels could also be required on all cannabis products. These would advise consumers about the probable risks of regular and inappropriate cannabis use (e.g. respiratory effects, risks of use during pregnancy, effects on persons with schizophrenia and the risks of driving after using). These would need to be accompanied by an aggressive public health campaign that alerted users to the risks of inappropriate use, such as driving under the influence and use during pregnancy. Public health campaigns accompanied by aggressive law enforcement against drink driving have contributed to the decline in drink driving in the United States during the 1990s (Hingson et al., 1996; DeJong and Hingson, 1998). Public education campaigns against drunk driving and 'random breath testing' have reduced alcohol-related vehicle fatalities in Australia (Holman et al., 1988). These are examples of how public health media campaigns and tough law enforcement can minimise some of the harms associated with alcohol use. Similar efforts will be required if cannabis is legalised.

Governments can also reduce the 'normalisation' of cannabis use by imposing restrictions on when, where and by whom cannabis can be used ('restrictions on use'). Twenty years ago when cigarette smoking was allowed in almost every public place in the United States, social norms about smoking were positive, despite knowledge of the serious health risks associated with smoking after the US Surgeon General's report in 1964. Today in the United States, the social sentiment has completely changed, at least in part because of the growing number of restrictions on where cigarettes can be used (Chaloupka and Warner, 2000). It is easiest to enact restrictions on use when the majority of voters are non-smokers. The lessons learned from tobacco control should be implemented if the legal status of cannabis is changed by minimising public cannabis use and exposure to cannabis use among youth. In this way the government could reduce the likelihood that cannabis use is seen as normative.

Governments can use a variety of other restrictions to reduce the visibility of cannabis use and its risks to others. Restrictions on the use of cannabis in public places, including restaurants and bars, would reduce the number of people exposed to other people's cannabis smoke. Restrictions on cannabis use while driving or operating heavy machinery may reduce the risks of some types of accidents. Age restrictions on cannabis use and possession would make it more difficult for youth to obtain and use cannabis although it is unlikely that these restrictions will be any more effective at deterring cannabis use among high-risk youth than current restrictions are in restricting access to alcohol and tobacco. Nonetheless, if such restrictions were aggressively enforced as part of a comprehensive set of public policies to minimise cannabis use, they may reduce some of the adverse consequences of cannabis use among youth. They also send a clear message that not all cannabis use is harmless and socially acceptable.

Influencing social norms by regulating supply

Demand-side policies that limit the social acceptability of cannabis use will only be effective if they are implemented along with policies that aim to reduce cannabis supply. A good that is readily accessible is generally viewed as more acceptable or normative than one that is less accessible, even if restrictions are placed on its use (e.g. alcohol). Restricted availability has been a hallmark of alcohol and tobacco policy in a number of developed countries for this reason. The availability of a good is determined by a number of market characteristics that affect the size of the market and the amount of the good that is supplied. These include the quantities of cannabis that can be traded, the number of firms that are allowed to sell it, the type of cannabis products that can be traded, and restrictions on how and when cannabis can be sold.

If cannabis were supplied like coffee, then there would be: a market for farmers who grow the product; a market of distributors who transfer the farm product to various secondary markets; a group of wholesalers who buy in large quantities (either from farmers or distributors) to supply specific retailers or groups of retailers; and finally there would be the retail cannabis shops. Although some policy reformers have discussed options for limiting the number of retail shops in which cannabis could be sold (e.g. the Canadian suggestion of a licensure system), far less attention has been paid to the other levels of the supply chain under a legal cannabis market. A government that aims to limit the amount of cannabis that is supplied should be interested in limiting the levels of the supply chain. This enables government to maintain tighter control over the amount of cannabis that is produced and to reduce opportunities for large-scale diversion from legal to illegal markets.

A government can influence the size of the supply chain in one of two ways. The first, and simplest, is to create a government monopoly on supply. Government could have the tightest control on production and access if it was responsible for the cultivation, distribution and sale of cannabis through government-run retail outlets. This seems an unlikely option nowadays because in most modern market economies, very few special goods and services are government monopolies. Even public goods, such as transportation and health care, are usually provided through partial monopolies or private–public partnerships.

Relatively tight control could also be maintained over a cannabis market through a partial monopoly in which the government took responsibility for the wholesale and/or retail sale of the good but allowed private cultivation and packaging. Such a model is currently employed for alcohol in many parts of the world, including 18 states in the US (Alcohol Epidemiology Program, 2000). The government can influence the amount of cannabis that is delivered to particular areas/regions and dramatically reduce the opportunity for large-scale diversion to the blackmarket if it controls the wholesale distribution of cannabis. By controlling the retail sale of cannabis, the government can influence the number and location of outlets from which cannabis products can be purchased and the types and quantities of different cannabis products that can be sold to individuals.

A second way that a government could influence the supply chain is through a licensing system. It could impose restrictions on the quantities of cannabis that can be cultivated, purchased and sold by licence holders. A licensing system is useful for controlling the number of players involved in supply and where they are located. It does not, however, control the quantity of cannabis that can be traded at specified levels among these players. Additional restrictions on the amount of cannabis that can be sold and/or cultivated by licence holders would be necessary for the government to control (1) the supply chain, and (2) the amount of cannabis that is supplied to the market.

For example, restricting sales to less than 100 bulk grams would prevent the development of a wholesale market for cannabis because wholesale quantities could not be legally purchased or sold. Stores that wished to stock larger quantities of cannabis would have to buy from multiple suppliers (although the government could also restrict the amount of cannabis that retailers could hold in stock, as they do in the Netherlands). Alternatively, the government could construct a tiered quantity restriction system in which retailers who bought cannabis products to sell in their shops would face two quantity restrictions. The first would restrict purchases from wholesalers (e.g. no greater more 500 bulk grams) and the second would restrict the quantities that retailers could sell to individuals (e.g. no more than 10 bulk grams). Such a tiered restrictive licensing system could limit the size of sales occurring at a particular level in the market. However, it could also create incentive for wholesalers to divert excess product to the blackmarket. Restricting the quantity of cannabis that can be sold directly to consumers would be a useful way to influence availability by making it inconvenient for users to obtain large quantities and by eliminating bulk discounts at the retail level.

Another way to avoid large-scale cultivation of cannabis in a partial monopoly or restricted licensing system would be to license all individuals and/or companies involved in the cultivation and packaging of cannabis. The licences would impose quotas on the amount of cannabis that individuals could produce in a year, much like fishing-harvest quotas imposed on lakes and oceans to protect species. In a given season (year), a farmer would not be allowed to cultivate more than a specified amount of cannabis. Anyone who violated this quota would have his licence revoked and be subject to civil (or criminal) penalties. Strict and regular monitoring of all licensed individuals and/or companies would be necessary for such a system to work effectively and to reduce leakage to the black market. One way to ensure compliance and regular monitoring would be to impose time limits on licences, for example, a year. Interested parties would have to reapply for new licences and provide evidence of compliance with the regulations. The government could change the quantity that an individual could produce by changing the quota/licence that they were granted.

Evidence from the alcohol literature suggests that rates of cannabis use under a government monopoly, even a partial monopoly, would be lower than that under a licensing system. US studies have consistently shown that the amount of alcohol that is sold increases when a state relinquishes a monopoly on alcohol sales and allows alcohol to be sold through privately licensed stores (Toomey et al., 1993; Toomey and Wagenaar, 1999). It is not clear what causes the increase but some of the contributory factors are longer sale hours, lower prices, a greater number of stores, and increased marketing (Alcohol Epidemiology Program, 2000).

In either a partial monopoly or restricted licensing system the government could maintain relatively tight control on the types or forms of cannabis that could be sold in the legal market as well as its potency. This could be done either directly (in the case of a monopoly) or indirectly through licensing requirements. Limiting the types of cannabis that could be legally sold would be desirable for two reasons. First, limiting the types and/or forms of cannabis that can be sold reduces the exposure of consumers to cannabis products in general and limits the size of the cannabis market. Allowing a proliferation of different cannabis products would create incentives for producers of different products to compete more aggressively for market share. Even if formal advertising was banned, the tobacco industry has shown that numerous other marketing strategies can be used to sell products, including product placement in stores, in movies and on television, and two-for-one specials (Chaloupka and Warner, 2000).

The second reason why a government might want to restrict the type of cannabis products on the market would be to reduce the public health and safety risks of cannabis products. This is perhaps one of the motivations behind Switzerland's proposal to legalise only those cannabis products with a relatively low level of THC. However, it is very likely that any attempt to restrict the range of products available through the legal market would create an economic opportunity for the existing blackmarket to specialise in restricted goods. Aggressive enforcement of both legal and illicit markets would therefore need to be maintained.

Restrictions on sales, such as age, location or time of day restrictions, can have a substantial impact on perceived availability and social norms for use by specifying who can use and when and where they can use cannabis. Allowing cannabis to be purchased at coffee houses, restaurants, or convenience stores makes it far more accessible than restricting use to specialised locations with limited store hours. Although restrictions on sales can be legislated in any formal market, they can be more closely monitored and enforced in a government-run retail system, in which special retail stores are the only place that the product can be purchased. Although it is possible to set up a licensing system in which certain types of businesses (e.g. restaurants) would not be allowed to obtain a licence, other sales restrictions remain difficult to enforce, particularly restrictions on the age of purchasers. Sales of cigarettes to minors in the US were far more common prior to the 1996 Synar Amendment, which required states to run compliance checks of tobacco retailers or else lose federal dollars for treatment programs. Even after the passage of the Synar Amendment, however, retailer compliance with the age restrictions has remained low in many states (Di Franza, 2001). Real compliance only improved when the policy was aggressively monitored by state agencies.

Aspects of legal markets that influence the monetary price of cannabis

The availability of cannabis products in a legal market will affect the price at which they are sold. If large amounts of cannabis are allowed to be sold, then the equilibrium price of cannabis will be lower than if only small amounts of cannabis are allowed to be sold, everything else being equal. This is because of increased efficiencies with large-scale production, competition between suppliers, and the law of demand. Even if competition is minimised by only allowing a small number of suppliers, price will be lower in markets with greater supply because the only way that sellers can compete is by reducing their price (the law of demand). Conversely, cannabis price will be higher in markets where there is less cannabis supplied.

There are two ways in which the government can control the amount of cannabis supplied in the market, and several other mechanisms through which it can indirectly influence the final price of the good. The easiest way for a government to control the amount of cannabis on the market is by being its sole distributor (through a partial or full monopoly). If the government was solely responsible for selling cannabis to consumers, than it could directly control how much cannabis was available at any time. Price could be kept high, that is, by creating an artificial scarcity of cannabis products. The effectiveness of this policy would also depend on the government's ability to control the production of cannabis, because a scarcity of cannabis would provide a strong economic incentive for cultivators and producers to divert cannabis to illegal markets.

The government could also control the quantity of cannabis produced and brought to the market through a cultivation licensing system. This would impose tight restrictions on the amount of cannabis that can be produced by the holder of the licence, as described above. By limiting the amount that can be cultivated by each licensee, the government could control the maximum amount of cannabis produced in a year by limiting the number of licences that it grants. The maximum amount of cannabis produced in a given year would be a product of: (1) the number of licences granted; and (2) the licence-specific production quota for each licensee. By fixing the amount cultivated in a given year, the government could directly influence the amount of cannabis produced, and hence indirectly affect its price.

Other indirect methods for influencing price could be used in conjunction with the methods just described. For example, a licensing fee could be charged to all individuals and companies who applied for a cultivation or sales licence. This would raise the cost of selling cannabis that would translate into an increased price for the final product. Similarly, producers and wholesalers could be taxed on the quantities of goods sold to suppliers, again increasing the cost of bringing cannabis to market. All of these costs, which would be borne by the supplier, would produce a higher price for the final price paid by the consumer. Finally, the government could impose a sales tax on cannabis at point of purchase, directly raising the price that consumers have to pay.

There is a fundamental problem with all of these mechanisms for raising the price of cannabis: the higher they raise the price above production costs, the greater the economic incentive they create for illegal suppliers to remain in the market. Taxes and licensing fees can only be levied on participants of legal markets, and thus represent a price increase that is only imposed in these markets. If the price difference between the legal market and the blackmarket is large enough, than there is incentive for consumers to use the blackmarket and an incentive for illegal producers to continue to supply this market.

Proposals that presume taxes can be set so that the legal market price is equivalent to the current blackmarket prices are naïve in that they assume (1) that there is a single blackmarket price in any given location, (2) that the blackmarket price is fixed over time and across locations, and (3) that the enforcement risks associated with providing cannabis on the blackmarket would be the same in a legalised regime as they are in an illegal regime. Switzerland's experience with legalised industrial hemp demonstrates how easy it is to divert cannabis from legal markets (Swiss Federal Commission for Drug Issues, 1999). The Canadian–US experience with tax differentials on tobacco demonstrates how relatively small price differences between markets ($4.00 per pack of cigarettes) can induce significant smuggling across borders (Gruber et al., 2002). Therefore, any government that legalises cannabis will have a limited ability to maintain price substantially higher than production costs. Furthermore, if a government allowed home cultivation in order to undercut the blackmarket, it would give away its limited ability to keep prices artificially high.

A word of caution must be given about the regulatory models described above. Most of the ideas about how to regulate supply and demand are models that have been tried with either alcohol and/or cigarettes with only moderate success. Although it is feasible to design a system that might minimise the harms of a legal market, experience with the alcohol and cigarette industries suggests that none of them is easy to implement. Regulatory schemes as implemented by the political process can work very differently than as envisioned by their designers.

The likely impact of a legal cannabis market on social costs

Legalising cannabis would produce societal savings in the criminal justice system because fewer people would be arrested, prosecuted, and gaoled. As was discussed in Chapter 16, this change could produce significant cost savings in many countries. In addition, society would benefit if thousands of otherwise law-abiding citizens were no longer victims of the criminal justice system or stigmatised for having encountered it (Kleiman, 1992; Christie, 1999).

There will, however, still be social costs of a legal cannabis market. Whether these costs offset the cost savings in the criminal justice system will depend on the type of market that is adopted and the country's demand for cannabis. These costs are generated by (1) any increases in inappropriate use and abuse of cannabis, and

(2) the enforcement costs required to monitor the legal market and prevent the existing blackmarket from continuing or the creation of a new one.

The impact of a legal cannabis market on the social cost of cannabis use

We have already explained why we believe that cannabis use will increase under a legal regime, namely, that social norms will become more accepting of cannabis use and price will fall, both of which will increase the number of cannabis users and the quantity consumed. Regulations may be able to offset this rise to some degree but it is unlikely that they will be any more successful in deterring hazardous, heavy or long-term use of cannabis than similar regulations are at deterring cigarette smoking or the misuse of alcohol. Although current patterns of cannabis use do not appear to impose significant social costs (Caulkins et al., 2002, see Chapter 12), it would be optimistic to assume that a legal cannabis regime would only increase recreational and non-harmful patterns of cannabis use. Our experience with alcohol suggests that as more people use cannabis, we should expect to see more cannabis-related accidents and problems. Indeed, the limited research on US emergency room episodes shows that areas with lower penalties for possession of cannabis have higher levels of marijuana-related ER visits (Model, 1993).

An increase in even occasional cannabis use may not be wholly harmless if used in combination with other drugs, especially alcohol (see Chapter 4). Recent studies on the demand for alcohol and cannabis show that in the United States alcohol and cannabis are economic complements, particularly among youth (Pacula, 1998; Farrelly et al., 1999; Saffer and Chaloupka, 1999). This means that alcohol use may increase along with cannabis use. If alcohol use rose then cannabis legalisation would raise social costs even if the combined health and social effects of alcohol and cannabis were no worse than those of alcohol alone.

What market policies could be used to minimise the increase in these social costs of cannabis use? Given the absence of studies, we must rely on analogies drawn from what we have learned from studies of alcohol policy.

It is clear that heavy drinking, and in particular binge drinking, responds to changes in the price of alcohol (Grossman et al., 1994; Chaloupka and Wechsler, 1996; Kenkel, 1996). In addition, increasing or decreasing the price of alcohol has effects on: motor vehicle accidents and fatalities (Kenkel, 1993; Mullahy and Sindelar, 1994; Ruhm, 1996; Chaloupka and Laixuthai, 1997); liver cirrhosis mortality and other health consequences related to alcohol (Cook and Tauchen, 1982; Saffer, 1991); and alcohol-related mortality more generally (Sloan et al., 1994). Even alcohol-dependent individuals are sensitive to increases in the price of alcohol (Moore and Cook, 1995; Andrikopoulos et al., 1997). Hence, if one goal is to minimise the social costs of inappropriate, heavy or chronic cannabis use, then the alcohol literature suggests that it should be government policy to ensure that the price of cannabis remains as high as possible without encouraging the continuation of a blackmarket.

Experience with alcohol also indicates that restrictions on use can minimise the social costs of use and abuse. In particular, the government should prohibit the use of cannabis while driving or operating heavy machinery in the same way that alcohol use is restricted to reduce the risk of accidents while intoxicated. Although similar restrictions for alcohol have not completely eliminated these behaviours, they have reduced their incidence when laws are aggressively enforced (Kenkel, 1993; Wagenaar et al., 2001). Age restrictions could reduce the risk of intoxication among inexperienced youth and perhaps reduce the risks of dependence at an early age. Age restrictions on alcohol use are effective in reducing drinking among youth; they may also be effective in reducing cannabis use (Cook and Tauchen, 1984; Coate and Grossman, 1988; Chaloupka and Laixuthai, 1997).

In a legal market the government could regulate the quality and potency of cannabis that is sold to consumers. This would reduce users' exposure to harmful contaminants. More importantly, it would enable the government to limit the cannabis products sold to those with lower levels of THC. In the absence of research, the relationship between the THC content of cannabis and cannabis use and harm is not clear (Hall and Swift, 2000) but it is a plausible hypothesis that reducing the average THC content of cannabis would reduce the likelihood of experiencing severe acute health effects (e.g. panic and psychotic symptoms, and degree of psychomotor impairment) and, more speculatively, the chances of younger users becoming dependent on cannabis.

The impact of legal markets on the cost of enforcement

Although there are costs associated with enforcing criminal penalties for cannabis use and sale, estimated cost savings from legalising cannabis often overstate the real savings for two reasons.

First, most local law enforcement agencies do not have explicit budgets for enforcing cannabis laws. These enforcement activities are typically part of other general policing activities, including quality of life policing as well as general drug enforcement (Reuter et al., 2000; Senate Special Committee on Illegal Drugs (Canada), 2002). Hence a change in cannabis policy will not necessarily generate large savings associated with policing, at least at the local level. It may, however, allow some of those resources to be better used elsewhere.

Second, as should be clear by now, the removal of criminal sanctions for sale and possession of cannabis does not eliminate the need to monitor and enforce cannabis laws. It shifts some of these duties from the criminal justice system to a civil administration. Even those countries that have taken significant steps toward legal markets still aggressively enforce the remaining aspects of prohibition to ensure that use and sales do not get out of control (Christie, 1999; Swiss Federal Commission for Drug Issues, 1999; MacCoun and Reuter, 2001). Legalisation would therefore shift some, although not all, of the burden of enforcement to regulating and licensing agencies. These agencies would presumably create their own set of administrative, and perhaps criminal, sanctions for violations of rules or laws. The cost of enforcing these will depend on how these agencies and their policies develop.

Under a legal cannabis regime, law enforcement officials would still be responsible for ensuring that the regulations (e.g. age restrictions) are strictly enforced and for minimising the size of the remaining blackmarket. The size of a residual blackmarket will depend on a number of factors, such as the difference between the cost of producing cannabis and the price being charged in the legal market and the level of law enforcement. If there is economic incentive for the blackmarket to remain, and there is very little risk of detection or penalty for breaking the law, then the blackmarket will continue to be a problem. It will also occupy new market niches by selling cannabis products that are not permitted in the legal market or by selling to individuals who are not allowed to purchase legally (e.g. underage users).

Other issues raised by the legalisation of cannabis

There are two additional issues that will need to be addressed after the creation of a legal market for cannabis products. First, a government must decide whether to allow home cultivation. Second, the government must be prepared to deal with a rise in youth cannabis use, even if that use is prohibited under the legal system.

Home cultivation

As previously noted, jurisdictions in some parts of Australia and the USA allow a small number of cannabis plants to be cultivated for personal use even under a formal prohibition. This policy has two principal advantages when the sale and large-scale production of cannabis are still prohibited. First, it eliminates the need to purchase from the blackmarket, allowing otherwise law-abiding citizens to avoid dealers who might try to introduce them to substances other than cannabis. Second, it reduces the economic gain from the blackmarket by creating a cheap substitute and reducing the number of people going to the blackmarket for cannabis. These effects could be substantial if enough regular cannabis users cultivated cannabis for their own use.

Home cultivation also has some disadvantages. The primary one is that it makes cannabis easily accessible to anyone living in homes that cultivate it, including youth. If cannabis is available in the home, and it is not supervised, then adolescents are likely to use it. A second disadvantage would arise under a legal cannabis market: home cultivation would undermine government attempts to maintain high cannabis prices by allowing individuals to avoid taxes by growing their own cannabis at very little cost. The government could, of course, issue licences to grow, say, up to six cannabis plants for a fee. Enforcement would be difficult, however, because it would be impossible to ensure that individuals grew no more than six plants in the privacy of their own home without violating their civil rights. The advantages of allowing home cultivation under prohibition can become disadvantages under a legal market.

Adolescent cannabis use

There is little doubt that adolescent cannabis use will increase if cannabis becomes legal for adults. There are at least four reasons for saying this: (1) cannabis will be more readily available than it is under prohibition; (2) its price will fall and we know that youth consumption is responsive to price (Pacula et al., 2001); (3) adults will be seen using cannabis, reinforcing the behaviour; and (4) restricting cannabis use to adults only will encourage precociously mature youth to imitate the behaviour of adults, much as they do now with tobacco and alcohol use.

Existing alcohol and tobacco laws in the United States have been ineffective at restricting youth access to alcohol and tobacco, except in those states and areas in which the laws have been strictly enforced (Forster et al., 1994; Jason et al., 1996). Lifetime prevalence rates for cigarettes and alcohol among 8th graders in the United States in 2001 were 36.6% and 50.5%, respectively (Johnston et al., 2001). Further, 70.6% of 8th graders reported that it was 'easy' or 'fairly easy' to get alcohol compared to 48.1% who reported that it was 'easy' or 'fairly easy' to get cannabis. Fundamental questions that advocates of a legal cannabis market need to answer are: how do we develop a system for restricting youth access to cannabis that is more effective than that for alcohol and cigarettes? And how do we enforce these laws without being overly punitive toward youth? Although we can borrow from current models used with alcohol and cigarettes, we must realistically evaluate their limitations. Any move to a legal cannabis market will need to be accompanied by policies that ensure that cannabis use among youth does not become an even greater problem in a legal market than it is under prohibition.

Summary

We have suggested that two types of restrictive, highly regulated markets – partial government monopoly and a licensing system – may be the best ways to minimise the impact of cannabis legalisation on rates of use and cannabis-related harm. We have also argued that neither system will be able to maintain the high price charged on the existing blackmarket. Hence, the creation of a legal market will probably lead to a fall in cannabis price and a rise in cannabis use, particularly among young adults and youth. It is unclear whether heavy and chronic cannabis use will increase in proportion to rising use but experience with alcohol and tobacco suggests that they will rise as the result of declining price, if not from a change in social norms. Neither of the regulatory systems proposed is likely to prevent cannabis use from increasing but they should prevent it from rising as high as it would in a completely free market.

The impact of these alternative market regimes on social harms is also unclear. Although any change to a legal market would dramatically reduce the current criminal justice expenditure on cannabis offences (Kleiman, 1989), these costs will not be simply saved. First, the need to enforce cannabis regulation will remain and may actually be greater under a legal system because more agencies may have to police violations of the regulatory system. Second, violators of the regulated system will presumably be prosecuted (although it is not clear to what extent criminal or civil sanctions will be needed or used). Finally, targeting of blackmarket suppliers of cannabis will be necessary to ensure that a change to a legal market does not merely provide shelter and lower risk to those who are already supplying cannabis in the blackmarket.

Any rise in cannabis use is likely to be accompanied by an increase in accidents and other acute adverse effects of cannabis use. These may not be large increases but they will not diminish under a legal market. We think it is likely that the criminal justice savings from reduced incarceration should more than offset the rise in acute health care costs but we cannot cite any evidence to support this assertion. We do not know to what extent cannabis-related health costs will increase under a legal market, as a result of increased rates of regular long-term cannabis use. One benefit of a liberalisation of cannabis policy is that it would make it possible to quantify many of the unknowns identified in this and previous chapters. But, this benefit comes at a cost that will only become apparent after the policy is implemented. By then the policy will be difficult, if not impossible, to reverse.

19

Summing up

In many developed countries the debate about cannabis policy has been simplified in the popular media to a choice of two options: (1) we should legalise cannabis, or at the very least decriminalise its use, because its use is harmless (or at least much less harmful than alcohol); or (2) we should continue to prohibit cannabis use because it is harmful to users. We have argued that this simplification has distorted the policy debate and evaluations of the health risks of cannabis use.

Our aim has been to broaden the cannabis policy debate to take account of the problems caused by our efforts to control cannabis use. The fact that we have devoted much more space to the adverse health effects of cannabis than we have to the effectiveness and costs of cannabis prohibition reflects the power of the policy simplification to direct research investment. We support recent proposals for more research on the effectiveness of drug policy (Manski et al., 2001) which may address the current imbalance in research investment.

The health and psychological effects of cannabis use

Acute psychological and health effects

The main reason why people use cannabis is to feel good, relax, and be sociable. These effects come at the cost of impaired attention, short-term memory, and psychomotor performance. The most frequent unpleasant effects of cannabis use are anxiety and panic reactions. These most often occur in users who are unfamiliar with the drug's effects. Psychotic symptoms such as delusions and hallucinations may be experienced following very high doses. There are no cases of fatal cannabis poisoning in the human medical literature and the fatal dose in humans is likely to exceed what recreational users can ingest.

Psychomotor effects and driving

Cannabis intoxication impairs a wide range of cognitive and behavioural functions that are involved in driving an automobile or operating machinery. It has been difficult until recently to decide whether these impairments increase the risk of being involved in motor vehicle accidents. Studies of the effect of cannabis on driving performance on the road have found only modest impairments because cannabis-intoxicated drivers drive more slowly, and take fewer risks, than alcohol-intoxicated drinkers. More recent evidence from large, well-controlled longitudinal and case-control studies suggests that driving after using cannabis on its own approximately doubles the risk of accidental injury in a motor vehicle accident.

Cannabinoids are found in substantial proportions of motor vehicle accident fatalities but these findings are difficult to evaluate. We do not know whether persons with cannabinoids are over-represented among accident victims and we do not know whether drivers with cannabinoids in their blood were intoxicated at the time of the accident. Cannabis used alone seems to make very little contribution to accidents but cannabis used in combination with alcohol may do so.

The health effects of chronic cannabis use
Cellular effects and cancers

Cannabis *smoke* is a potential cause of cancer because it contains many of the same carcinogenic substances as cigarette smoke. Cancers have been reported in the aerodigestive tracts of young adults who were daily cannabis smokers and a case-control study has found an association between cannabis smoking and head and neck cancer. A prospective cohort study of 64,000 adults did not find any increase in rates of head and neck or respiratory cancers so further studies are needed to clarify the issue.

Three studies of different types of cancer have reported an association with maternal cannabis use during pregnancy. There have also not been any increases in the rates of these cancers that parallel increases in rates of cannabis use.

Immunological effects

High doses of cannabinoids impair cell-mediated and humoral immunity and reduce resistance to infection by bacteria and viruses in rodents. Cannabis smoke impairs the functioning of alveolar macrophages, the first line of the body's immune defence system in the lungs. The doses required to produce these effects have been very high, and extrapolation to the doses used by humans is complicated by the fact that tolerance may develop to these effects. There is as yet no epidemiological evidence that rates of infectious disease are increased among chronic heavy cannabis users. Several large prospective studies of HIV-positive homosexual men have not found that cannabis use increases progression to AIDS.

Reproductive effects

Chronic administration of THC disrupts male and female reproductive systems in animals, reducing testosterone secretion, and sperm production, motility, and viability in males, and disrupting ovulation in females. It is uncertain whether cannabis use has these effects in humans because of the limited research on human males and females.

The use of cannabis during pregnancy is associated with smaller birthweight but does not appear to increase the risk of birth defects. In some studies, infants exposed to cannabis during pregnancy show behavioural and developmental effects during the first few months after birth. These effects are smaller than those seen after tobacco use during pregnancy.

The cardiovascular system

The changes that cannabis smoking causes in heart rate and blood pressure are unlikely to harm healthy young adults but may harm patients with hypertension, cerebrovascular disease and coronary atherosclerosis. One controlled study suggests that cannabis use can precipitate heart attacks in middle-aged cannabis users who have atherosclerosis in the heart, brain and peripheral blood vessels.

The respiratory system

Regular cannabis smoking impairs the functioning of the large airways and causes chronic bronchitis. Given that tobacco and cannabis smoke contain similar carcinogenic substances, it is likely that chronic cannabis smoking increases the risks of respiratory cancer.

Gastrointestinal system

There is no human or animal evidence that cannabinoids adversely affect liver function or the gastrointestinal system. The most dependable gastrointestinal effect of cannabis is to stimulate appetite which may have therapeutic use in cancer and AIDS patients.

Psychological effects of chronic cannabis use

A dependence syndrome

A cannabis dependence syndrome occurs in heavy chronic users of cannabis. Regular cannabis users develop tolerance to THC, some experience withdrawal symptoms on cessation of use, and some report problems controlling their cannabis use. The risk of dependence is about one in ten among those who ever use the drug, between one in five and one in three among those who use cannabis more than a few times, and around one in two among daily users. The prevalence of drug-related problems is lower than in alcohol dependence and there appears to be a high rate of remission of cannabis dependence without treatment.

Cognitive effects

Long-term daily cannabis use does not severely impair cognitive function but it may more subtly impair memory, attention and the integration of complex information.

It remains uncertain whether these effects are due to the cumulative effect of regular cannabis use on cannabinoid receptors in the brain or they are the residual effects of THC that will disappear after an extended period of abstinence.

Psychotic disorders

There is now good evidence that chronic cannabis use may precipitate a psychosis in vulnerable individuals. It is unlikely that cannabis use can cause psychosis *de novo* because the incidence of schizophrenia has either remained stable, or declined, while cannabis use has increased among young adults.

The effects of adolescent cannabis use

The gateway hypothesis

Among adolescents in developed societies alcohol and tobacco have typically been used used before cannabis, which in turn, has been used before hallucinogens, amphetamine, heroin and cocaine. Generally, the earlier the age of first use, and the greater the involvement with any drug in the sequence, the more likely a young person is to use the next drug in the sequence. The role played by cannabis in this sequence remains controversial. The hypothesis that cannabis use has a pharmacological effect that increases the risk of using later drugs in the sequence is not strongly supported. More plausible hypotheses are that it is due to a combination of: (1) early recruitment into cannabis use of nonconforming and deviant adolescents who are likely to use alcohol, tobacco and illicit drugs; (2) a shared genetic vulnerability to dependence on alcohol, tobacco and cannabis; and (3) socialisation of cannabis users within an illicit drug-using subculture which increases the opportunity and the encouragement to use other illicit drugs.

Adolescent psychosocial outcomes

Cannabis use is associated with non-completion of high school, early family formation, poor mental health, and involvement in drug-related crime. In the case of each of these outcomes the strong associations in cross-sectional data are more modest when account is taken of the fact that cannabis users show characteristics before they use cannabis which predict these outcomes, e.g. have lower academic aspirations and poorer school performance than peers who do not use. Nonetheless, the evidence increasingly suggests that regular cannabis use adds to the risk of these outcomes in adolescents who are at risk for other reasons.

Health effects and cannabis policy

Any fair appraisal of the adverse health effects of cannabis use complicates the cannabis policy debate by undermining the leading policy simplification. Supporters of cannabis prohibition are often troubled by the fact that the adverse health consequences are not manifestly more serious than those of alcohol and tobacco. The fact that there are adverse health effects also complicates the case for cannabis law reform. Proponents of reform are often reluctant to concede that cannabis use has any adverse effects (e.g. Zimmer and Morgan, 1997) because to do so is to give up the compelling argument for reform that cannabis use is harmless.

As we have argued, it does not necessarily follow that cannabis use should be prohibited simply because it harms some users. We have to argue that criminal penalties are the best way to discourage cannabis use and decrease the harms that it causes. We also have to consider the social costs entailed in using the criminal law to deter people from using cannabis. As a society, we have to decide what social costs we are prepared to bear in order to discourage cannabis use by young people. For all these reasons, policy debates should consider the costs of cannabis prohibition along with the harms of cannabis use.

Has prohibition deterred cannabis use?

The high rates of cannabis use among young people in many developed societies have weakened the case for cannabis prohibition by showing that criminal penalties have failed to deter young people from trying cannabis (e.g. Fischer et al., 1998; Single et al., 1999; Lenton, 2000). Cannabis prohibition has probably still had some deterrent effects. If cannabis prohibition was repealed then more people would probably use cannabis, regular cannabis use would probably be more common and cannabis use would probably continue later into adult life than is the case under prohibition. If we allow that this is true, we must: (1) examine the economic and social costs of cannabis prohibition in order make a societal judgement about whether the deterrent effects of existing cannabis policy justify the social costs of its continuance; and (2) critically examine the likely costs and benefits of the alternative cannabis policies that are often proposed, namely, decriminalisation of cannabis use and the creation of a legal cannabis market.

The costs of cannabis prohibition

Opponents of cannabis prohibition argue that it causes greater costs to users, society and its institutions than any adverse health effects that cannabis use causes to those who use it (Zimmer and Morgan, 1997; Lenton, 2000; Wodak et al., 2002).

Economic costs of enforcing prohibition

There are substantial economic costs in enforcing cannabis prohibition by policing cannabis laws, arresting, processing, adjudicating, and punishing cannabis users who are caught. As we have shown, it is not as straightforward as it may seem to estimate these costs. It would also be unwise to assume that all of these costs will be averted if cannabis use is made legal.

A related argument is that it is inefficient to use scarce law enforcement and crim-inal justice resources to prosecute cannabis users. Critics argue that these resources would be better used policing more violent and serious property offences and other types of drug offence (Advisory Committee on Illicit Drugs, 1993; McDonald et al., 1994). Removing criminal penalties would provide an opportunity for this reallo-cation of resources to occur; it does not guarantee that it will happen.

Social costs of enforcing prohibition

There are a number of inter-related concerns about the social costs of enforcing cannabis prohibition. First, some argue that a prison sentence is a severe penalty for conduct that largely harms the user (Criminal Justice Commission, 1994). This is difficult to dispute in jurisdictions that have a statutory penalty for cannabis use of up to 15 years in prison. The fact that prison sentences are rarely imposed does not disarm this criticism; severe statutory penalties that are not enforced bring the law into disrepute.

Second, social costs are incurred by the fact that fewer than 2% of cannabis users are ever prosecuted in most developed societies. A widely broken law that is not enforced brings the law into disrepute and may undermine the deterrent effect of criminal penalties (Advisory Committee on Illicit Drugs, 1993; United Kingdom Police Foundation, 2000).

Third, there are also concerns that the criminal law is enforced in a discrimina-tory way (Advisory Committee on Illicit Drugs, 1993). Cannabis users who are arrested in some jurisdictions are more likely to be unemployed, socially disadvan-taged and criminally involved than are cannabis users in community surveys (Advisory Committee on Illicit Drugs, 1993; Fergusson et al., 2003).

Fourth, Canadian and Australian research suggests that the criminal record received by cannabis users who come to police attention has an adverse effect on their employment prospects and reputation, without reducing their cannabis use (Erickson, 1980; Lenton et al., 1999a; Lenton et al., 1999b).

Effects of a cannabis blackmarket

The widespread use of cannabis by young adults in many developed countries has created a demand for cannabis products that has been met by a blackmarket con-trolled by criminals. The existence of a blackmarket has a number of undesirable effects. First, cannabis is sold without any controls on THC potency or restrictions on sales to minors. Second, the cannabis industry is run by, and for, criminals who derive substantial profit from it (Carney et al., 1991). Third, criminals may use these profits to corrupt law enforcement officials (Lenton, 2000). Fourth, because cannabis is an illegal commodity the government forgoes a potentially large source of tax revenue (Kaplan, 1970; Kleiman, 1992). Fifth, governments are also unable to use their taxation powers to reduce demand for cannabis (Criminal Justice Commission, 1994). These are all undeniable consequences of prohibition although good estimates of the scale of the cannabis blackmarket are needed.

Loss of benefits of cannabis use

Cannabis prohibition deprives adults of the right to enjoy any benefits of recreational cannabis use, such as, euphoria, relaxation, and increased sociability. For libertarians, this prohibition is an unacceptable infringement of individual liberty (Szasz, 1985; Husak, 1992). If we assume that adults are the best judges of their own interests, the fact that a substantial proportion of adults in developed societies use cannabis is *ipso facto* evidence that there are benefits from such use.

There is no evidence that recreational cannabis use improves mental health, as may be the case with moderate alcohol use. Regular cannabis is correlated with poorer mental health and occasional users do not have better mental health than non-users. The evidence is also mixed on whether cannabis may be used instead of more harmful drugs like alcohol. Early econometric studies provided evidence of substitution of cannabis for alcohol but the results of more recent studies have found that the two drugs tend to be used together.

There is better evidence for the therapeutic use of cannabis. There is reasonable evidence that THC is effective in the treatment of nausea and vomiting caused by cancer chemotherapy and stimulates appetite in patients with AIDS-related wasting. THC and other cannabinoids have analgesic and anti-spasmodic effects that warrant further research. Estimates for the Australian State of New South Wales in 2000 (Hall et al., 2001) suggest that cannabis could be used medically by 3 adults in a thousand.

Health education about cannabis and other drugs

Some critics have argued that one casualty of cannabis prohibition has been accurate health education about the health effects of cannabis (United Kingdom Police Foundation, 2000). Others have argued that exaggerated claims about the adverse effects of cannabis undermine the credibility of education about the health risks of heroin and cocaine (Zimmer and Morgan, 1997). These are plausible hypotheses that deserve further investigation.

Reform options

Cannabis decriminalisation

The reform proposal with the greatest public support in many countries is decriminalisation (e.g. Bowman and Sanson-Fisher, 1994). Decriminalisation may be achieved by imposing a fine for first-time offenders or by diverting first time cannabis offenders into treatment and education instead of charging them with a criminal offence.

The major advantages claimed for decriminalisation are that it reduces the costs of prohibition to users and the criminal justice system without reducing the deterrent effect of prohibition (e.g. Wodak et al., 2002). Decriminalisation may have another advantage: it may reduce pressure for more radical cannabis law reform and thereby provide a breathing space for a more considered examination of the risks and benefits of cannabis use and different cannabis control regimes. The major disadvantages of decriminalisation are that it does not address the issue of cannabis supply and it does not, in itself, address any of the harms caused by cannabis use.

Does decriminalisation reduce the costs of cannabis prohibition?

Decriminalisation is assumed to reduce the costs of enforcing cannabis prohibition but the issue has only been evaluated in two jurisdictions, South Australia (Ali et al., 1999) and California (Aldrich and Mikuriya, 1988). The South Australian study was prompted by the observation that the number of offenders fined under the decriminalisation regime was substantially higher than the number who appeared before the courts on cannabis offences under the old law. Recent US research has similarly found that the number of offenders fined can increase when penalties are reduced, suggesting that decriminalisation cannot be assumed to reduce costs; this needs to be demonstrated. The same could be said for the assumption that decriminalisation reduces the effects of prohibition on users. To date only one study (Lenton, 2000) has suggested that this may be true.

Does cannabis decriminalisation still deter?

The decriminalisation of cannabis use in 11 US states does not appear to have had a *large* effect on the decline in rates of cannabis use observed between 1980 and 1992 (Single, 1989; Johnston et al., 1994a; Johnston et al., 1994b). Cannabis use in Australian states that have decriminalised use does not appear to have increased at a faster rate than states which have not done so (Ali et al., 1999). These findings do not necessarily mean that decriminalisation has had no impact on cannabis use because econometric analyses suggest that longer gaol terms are associated with lower rates of cannabis use and with smaller amounts of cannabis consumed. It may mean that small changes in criminal penalties do not have *large* effects on cannabis use in the short to medium term. Many of the studies on the impact of law changes on rates of cannabis use have had low statistical power to detect small to moderate changes in rates of use and the longest period over which effects have been examined is 16 years.

The issue of cannabis supply

Cannabis supply is the major issue that is not resolved by the decriminalisation of cannabis use. It remains illegal to produce and sell cannabis so cannabis users cannot legally obtain the drug without resort to the blackmarket. This has prompted proposals to allow home cultivation of cannabis. This could be through a licensing system that would require growers to fill out a form, subject themselves to random checks on the number of plants cultivated, and go through a background check. A licensing system that required a fee and strictly regulated the number of plants that could be cultivated for home use (e.g. 2 plants) would reduce the profitability of the blackmarket (although it could open up a host of other regulatory and law-enforcement problems). A simpler option that has been adopted in South Australia is to impose a fine on people who grow less than a specific number of plants and to impose gaol penalties on those who grow more plants. It remains to be seen how easy it is to enforce these regulatory schemes and what impact they have on the size of the cannabis blackmarket.

Reducing the harms of cannabis use under decriminalisation

The introduction of civil penalties for cannabis use would need to be accompanied by other policies if it is to reduce harms from cannabis use (Swift et al., 2000). For those who are concerned about the increased sale of more potent forms of cannabis, these could include graduated civil or criminal penalties for the production and sale of cannabis with a high THC content. This may reduce the incentives for the blackmarket to produce more potent forms of cannabis but there would be enforcement and adjudication costs (e.g. testing the THC content of cannabis).

Educational efforts would be needed to deter young adults from driving after using cannabis. This could be done as part of campaigns to discourage driving after drinking alcohol. Effective enforcement of any laws against driving after using cannabis requires better methods of detecting recent cannabis use that could sustain convictions in a court of law.

The development of more effective education of adolescents about the risks of cannabis use would be a priority. Such education should focus on cannabis users at high risk of experiencing adverse effects: daily or near-daily users. A sensible strategy for communicating the health risks of cannabis would be to capitalise on the community's knowledge of the adverse health effects of alcohol and tobacco. For example, the chronic respiratory risks of marijuana and tobacco smoking are reasonably well understood but some cannabis users believe that it is safer to smoke cannabis than tobacco. Information on the respiratory risks of cannabis smoking could be included in health educational materials about tobacco smoking.

Epidemiological research on the health and psychological consequences of cannabis use should be a priority. This should include prospective studies of the effects of cannabis use on adolescent development and clinical trials of therapeutic interventions for cannabis dependence in primary care and specialist treatment (WHO Program on Substance Abuse, 1997). Epidemiological research should examine the correlates and consequences of heavy sustained cannabis use, especially among young people who initiate use early, and who display symptoms of dependence on cannabis. Longitudinal studies of large and representative cohorts of cannabis users (Sidney et al., 1997) are needed to assess the effects that cannabis use has on rarer adverse health outcomes, such as serious accidental injury, psychosis, respiratory tract cancer, respiratory disease and premature death. Such research may be easier to conduct if cannabis use is no longer a criminal offence.

Legalisation of cannabis use

The legalisation of cannabis would make it legal for any adult to use cannabis and would make it legal to produce and sell cannabis. The main roles for government under a legal cannabis regime would be to: control the quantity and quality of cannabis products, regulate the behaviour of manufacturers and distributors; tax cannabis sales; and restrict sales to minors. We should expect government to be as effective (or ineffective) in regulating a cannabis market as it is in regulating alcohol and tobacco markets. This is more realistic than optimistic policy projections in which cannabis legalisation removes all the economic and social costs of enforcing prohibition and increases government revenue, without increasing cannabis use or the harms that it causes.

Legal obstacles to cannabis legalisation

Cannabis legalisation faces formidable obstacles to its implementation. It does not enjoy widespread public support even in countries like Australia (Bowman and Sanson-Fisher, 1994; Criminal Justice Commission, 1994) and the Netherlands (Korf et al., 1999) where there is majority support for liberalisation of the law. In these countries, fewer than 25% of adults support the legalisation of cannabis.

The legalisation of cannabis would also contravene international treaties on illicit drugs, such as the Single Convention, which has been signed by most developed countries (Moffit et al., 1998). This Convention obliges all signatories to criminalise the use, possession, production and sale of cannabis drugs although it allows some latitude in the penalties that are imposed for use and possession. Signatories can, for example, decide not to impose a prison sentence on first offenders and still comply with the Convention (Working Party of the Royal College of Psychiatrists and the Royal College of Physicians, 2000).

These drug-control treaties would either have to be amended by the agreement of all signatories or they would have to be abrogated by any country that decided to legalise cannabis use (Single et al., 1999; Swiss Federal Commission for Drug

Issues, 1999). Given the strength of international sentiment in favour of the treaties, it is unlikely that there will be majority support for removing cannabis from the list of controlled substances.

Effects of legalisation on rates of cannabis use

No country has to date implemented *de jure* cannabis legalisation. There is consequently no contemporary evidence on the effects of such a policy on rates of cannabis use or cannabis-related harm. The experience most often appealed to as a guide to the likely effects of cannabis legalisation is that of the Netherlands. It has implemented a *de facto* legal retail cannabis market in its largest cities while continuing to nominally prohibit cannabis use and sale. Rates of cannabis use have increased in the Netherlands but researchers debate whether the rate of increase has been higher in the Netherlands than in countries that have continued to enforce prohibition (MacCoun and Reuter, 2001; Korf, 2002).

A reasonable prediction from economics is that cannabis use will increase because the creation of a legal cannabis market will change social norms towards use and result in cannabis being sold at a lower price than at present. These predictions are also consistent with our experience with alcohol (Edwards et al., 1994). Both suggest that legalising cannabis sales will lead to greater experimentation with cannabis, more regular use, and cannabis being used for a longer period during adult lives (Chen and Kandel, 1995; Bachman et al., 1997). Our historical experience with alcohol also suggests that more regular use would probably mean more cannabis-related health and psychological problems among users, such as dependence, impaired school performance among adolescents, and exacerbation of psychoses in the population (Hall, 1995).

Reducing the harms of cannabis use under legalisation

Legalisation allows government to use a cannabis tax as a policy lever to reduce cannabis use and related harms. A high tax could, in principle, reduce cannabis use but, as we have argued, it is unlikely for a number of reasons that the taxation of cannabis under a legal regime could maintain the same price paid under prohibition. Any attempt by the government to do so (either by taxation or regulatory schemes for ensuring the scarcity of cannabis) will create incentives for a cannabis blackmarket to continue. The government could also tax cannabis on its THC content or otherwise regulate THC content.

A legal regime would restrict adolescent access to cannabis, although experience with tobacco and alcohol suggests that the legalisation of cannabis will increase adolescent access to cannabis. Making it legal for adults to use cannabis will reinforce the identification of cannabis use with adult status that makes alcohol use attractive to adolescents.

Health education about the health effects of cannabis would be easier in some ways under a legal regime. There would, for example, not be the problems that are experienced under full or modified prohibition in acknowledging that cannabis is used, nor would health educators have to preface all information the health effects of cannabis with statements that it is illegal to use the drug. We would expect that governments in developed societies would be prepared to invest similar resources in health education about cannabis as they do for alcohol and tobacco. And we would expect that these efforts would be about as effective in reducing adolescent cannabis use and harm, that is, modest at best (Caulkins et al., 1999).

It is difficult to predict the size of any increase in cannabis use or problems that may occur under a legal cannabis regime but some increase seems likely (MacCoun and Reuter, 2001). The increase would be much larger under a liberal legal regime that allowed cannabis to be sold by a wide variety of outlets (e.g. liquor stores, bars, pubs, supermarkets) with a minimum of restrictions. The increase would be larger still if cannabis could be advertised and promoted in the same way as alcohol. We believe that a liberal regime with minimal restrictions on sale, promotion and access to cannabis use would be the worst possible regime from the point of view of minimising cannabis use and cannabis-related harm. A government monopoly or a partial monopoly via a licensing system would provide the greatest policy leverage to minimise cannabis use and cannabis-related harm but at the cost of increased regulatory and enforcement costs. Such regulatory schemes are also very much out of favour in most developed countries in which governments have generally retreated from the regulation of most goods and services over the past few decades.

Cannabis policy: a choice of evils

The use of cannabis causes harm to some users, and less certainly, to the broader society. So does the use of the criminal law to deter its use. The harms caused by chronic cannabis use are not well understood but they probably include: an increased risk of motor vehicle accidents; respiratory disease; dependence; adverse effects on adolescent development; and the exacerbation of psychosis.

The harms caused by cannabis prohibition are less tangible and more contested but they include: the loss of liberty to use cannabis; the creation of a blackmarket; disrespect for a widely broken and minimally enforced law; harms to the reputation of cannabis users who are prosecuted; impaired health education about cannabis and other drugs; loss of benefits from cannabis use including medical use; and an inefficient use of law-enforcement resources.

If one is a utilitarian, then selecting a policy towards cannabis involves a choice of evils. All of the policy options under discussion, including prohibition, impose costs on cannabis users and the community. Many of these costs and benefits are difficult to quantify, although we can make more informed estimates about the probable health costs to users than we can about many of the costs of prohibition.

Even if all these costs could be quantified, in deciding upon a cannabis policy our societies have to accept trade-offs between incommensurable values. We have to decide what weight we should give to: the adverse effects that cannabis use has on the health and well-being of adolescent and adult users and the community; the individual liberty of adult cannabis users; the economic costs of enforcing pro-hibition; the adverse effects on public respect for the law; the social effects of a large and profitable industry that is outside the law; and the loss of taxation rev-enue. In liberal democracies, these trade-offs are, and ought to be, made by elected politicians acting in the community's best interests and informed by the best avail-able information on the costs of competing policies.

Given the lack of community support for cannabis legalisation, the most likely change in policy is the decriminalisation of cannabis possession and use. Decriminalisation probably reduces some of the costs of enforcing prohibition, while having modest effects on deterrence. It has other advantages too: it provides a breathing space that *may* allow research into the adverse effects of cannabis use; may provide more credible health education about its risks; and it would be more easily reversed than the legalisation of cannabis. Decriminalisation does not, how-ever, address the problem of blackmarket supply unless users are also allowed to grow cannabis for their own use and it requires additional measures to reduce the harms caused by cannabis use.

Cannabis legalisation faces formidable obstacles. These include a lack of public support for the policy, its being in contravention of international drug control treaties, and reasonable community concerns that making cannabis legally avail-able will increase its use and the harms that it causes. Legalisation is an unlikely but not an impossible outcome. It could occur by degrees if cannabis use was decriminalised, and if cannabis use became even more entrenched in the youth culture of developed societies. Cannabis legalisation could also occur quickly if the liberal democracies' retreat from government regulation of markets were to extend to illicit drug policy. The regulation of the currently illicit drugs is one of the last bastions for governmental regulation that is supported by free market liberals, even if it involves regulation by criminal rather than by civil law.

A way forward?

We need cannabis policies that are more responsive to evidence on both the adverse heath effects of cannabis and the costs and effectiveness of cannabis control poli-cies. We need to know more about the adverse effects of cannabis but an equal imperative is more critical evaluations of the effectiveness and costs of variations on cannabis prohibition and the current examples of *de facto* legal retail cannabis markets.

Better public policy on cannabis will require investments in both epidemiological research on the long-term health consequences of cannabis use (WHO Program on Substance Abuse, 1997; Kalant et al., 1999) and in rigorous research on the costs and benefits of current and alternative cannabis policy options (e.g. Ali et al., 1999). The epidemiological research need not be costly if cannabis use is routinely inquired about in prospective studies of adolescent development (e.g. Fergusson and Horwood, 1997) and in adult health (Sidney et al., 1997). Both types of evaluations should use a consistent standard in appraising evidence (Hall et al., 1999).

The larger public health and social policy communities also need to be more involved in the cannabis policy debate. We need assessments of the health effects of cannabis and of the impact of cannabis policies that are less contaminated by their assessors' views on legal policy options. Cannabis policies are too important to be left, as they so often have been, to partisans of the falsely simplified forced choices that are usually represented in public debates on cannabis policy.

The medical marijuana debate

The evidence reviewed in Chapter 13 shows that THC is moderately effective in treating nausea and vomiting and appetite loss and it may be useful in treating acute and chronic pain. Advocates for the medical use of cannabis argue that patients should be allowed to smoke cannabis to relieve these symptoms because smoked marijuana is superior to oral THC (Grinspoon and Bakalar, 1993).

We review various 'medical marijuana initiatives' that have been proposed to achieve this goal in this appendix (rather than in the book proper) for the following reasons. First, if cannabis was legalised (or its use was decriminalised) then anyone who wanted to could use it for therapeutic purposes (Grinspoon and Bakalar, 1993). The debate about whether cannabis use should or should not be legalised is therefore more fundamental. Second, cannabis is unlikely to be legalised simply because it has medical uses. Legalisation requires a much stronger political justification. Third, some proponents of 'medical marijuana' have arguably used citizen-initiated referenda as a way to legalise cannabis by stealth and to embarrass intransigent defenders of prohibition who refuse to concede that cannabis may have any therapeutic uses. There are, however, ways in which patients could be given access to cannabis or cannabinoids for medical use without removing the prohibition on recreational cannabis use. We describe these and their limitations in this appendix.

Why can't patients use pharmaceutical cannabinoids?

If cannabis or cannabinoids are shown to have medical uses it would seem a simple matter of registering them for medical use. Dronabinol (THC) and nabilone have been registered for medical use as anti-emetics and appetite stimulants in the USA and the UK respectively. They have not been widely used in clinical practice because patients find it difficult to titrate doses of these drugs (Institute of Medicine, 1999).

Recent work on the biology of the cannabinoid system (Iversen, 2000) raises the prospects of new therapeutic cannabinoids being developed but pharmaceutical companies face substantial disincentives to develop and market new cannabinoids (Institute of Medicine, 1999). First, the research and development costs of cannabinoids are similar to neuropharmaceuticals which are costly to develop and register. Second, only synthetic cannabinoids can be patented, naturally occurring ones like THC cannot. Third, the markets for cannabinoids are more like those for orphan drugs than for drugs that are 'blockbuster' drugs used to treat common disorders like depression, hypertension, and arthritis. Fourth, effective drugs are already available to treat many of the symptoms for which cannabinoids are indicated. Fifth, in the USA strict regulatory requirements must be met to register a drug that is derived from, or chemically related to, a prohibited substance.

New formulations of cannabis are currently being developed and trialled in the UK (GW Pharmaceuticals, 2002) and there is a renewed interest in developing synthetic therapeutic cannabinoids and 'cannabinergics' (Goutoloplis and Makriyannis, 2002). Until these drugs and new formulations have been marketed, however, the only choice that patients with these conditions have is to use oral THC or to smoke cannabis.

Why not register cannabis for medical use?

There are two sources of opposition to the registration of cannabis for medicinal purposes. The first is the medical objection that cannabis smoke delivers a variable mixture of THC and other cannabinoids, carcinogens, and other biologically toxic substances to the lungs (Institute of Medicine, 1999; Tashkin, 2001). Although the smoking risks may not be a major concern when dealing with terminal illnesses (such as cancer and AIDS), the risks are a consideration when used for indications that are not life-threatening (e.g. glaucoma, pain). The risks of smoking could be avoided by using alternatives ways of delivering THC or cannabis extracts, such as, lozenges, sublingually, inhaling it, suppositories or skin patches (Institute of Medicine, 1999; GW Pharmaceuticals, 2002). To date it has proven difficult to find such alternative routes. The transpulmonary route used with opioid drugs, for example, cannot deliver THC because it is not water soluble (Institute of Medicine, 1999). Nonetheless, science continues to advance and it is conceivable that some alternative delivery device could be developed.

The second major source of opposition against smoking cannabis for medical reasons is political. Opponents are concerned that doing so will increase the recreational use of cannabis (Institute of Medicine, 1999). They argue that since some proponents of 'medical marijuana' are also advocates of cannabis legalisation (e.g. NORML) 'medical marijuana' is a Trojan horse for legalising cannabis (DuPont,

1999). One cannot help but see their point when some communities, predominantly located in California, set extremely liberal allowances for the number of plants that may be legally cultivated for medical use (e.g. up to 72 plants indoors and 40 plants outdoors). Allowing cultivation of such large quantities makes it difficult to distinguish patients from drug traffickers and does surely send the 'wrong message' to youth (DuPont, 1999).

Medical marijuana initiatives in the United States

The Marijuana Tax Act of 1937 prohibited the use of marijuana for recreational purposes in the United States but physicians were still able to legally prescribe marijuana until it was classified as a Schedule I substance under the 1970 Comprehensive Drug Abuse Prevention and Control Act, now known as the Federal Controlled Substance Act (Pacula et al., 2002). In 1972, a petition was submitted to the forerunner of the Drug Enforcement Agency to reschedule marijuana as Schedule II so that physicians would be legally able to prescribe it (Marijuana Policy Project, 2001). The same year, the National Commission on Marihuana and Drug Abuse advocated scientific research on the use of marijuana for medicinal purposes and a reduction in criminal penalties for marijuana possession (National Commission on Marihuana and Drug Abuse, 1972).

In 1975, in part in response to a court case brought by Robert Randall, the US federal government began a small Individual Patient Investigational New Drug (IND) program. The IND enabled physicians to prescribe marijuana to enrolled patients on a trial basis so long as strict scientific protocols were followed. Between 1975 and 1992 the federal government provided eight patients with compassionate access to cannabis under this program. These patients had a limited range of medicinal conditions and received their marijuana from the federal government to avoid the need for home cultivation which had been a major issue in the Randall case.

Within this political environment a number of US states enacted their own legislation allowing the medical use of marijuana in the late 1970s. By the end of 1982, 31 states and the District of Columbia had passed legislation that allowed the medical use of marijuana (Markoff, 1997). The majority (n = 22) legislated to permit Therapeutic Research Programs (TRPs), scientific research programs modelled on the federal IND program that enabled physicians to prescribe marijuana to their patients provided that strict research protocols were followed that were consistent with the Federal IND.

Another six states reclassified marijuana below a Schedule I controlled substance within their state's controlled substance act, thereby in theory enabling physicians to prescribe it as medicine. Because these acts were inconsistent with overriding federal laws regulating the prescription of medicines, physicians who prescribed cannabis would not be protected from federal prosecution or the loss of their licence to prescribe.

Nine other states enacted 'physician prescription provisions' that enabled physicians to prescribe marijuana for medicinal use, authorised them to discuss the potential benefits of cannabis use with patients, or provided them with a defence against state prosecution for prescribing or discussing cannabis. Some of these early laws were repealed or allowed to expire in the mid-1980s when it became clear that the federal government would not change its position on medicinal marijuana and when Marinol, a synthetic form of THC, was approved for medical use by the FDA.

A second wave of medical marijuana legislation began in the mid-1990s and continues today. It has been prompted by claims that smoked cannabis was effective in treating in patients with cancer and AIDS-related wasting. This second wave occurred in the face of federal government intransigence on the medical value of marijuana. These laws attempt to allow the prescription and distribution of cannabis to qualified patients.

Eight states enacted new medical marijuana laws between 1 January 1996 and 31 December 2000. All of these new laws, except for Arizona's, have provisions that protect physicians from prosecution and provide medical necessity defences to protect patients from prosecution for possessing and using marijuana. Prior to 1996, only Louisiana, New Hampshire, Virginia, and Wisconsin had physician prescription laws and only Virginia included a medical necessity defence. All of these state laws specify that marijuana can be used for a broad range of illnesses and symptoms, including 'pain management'. Finally, home cultivation of cannabis for medicinal purposes is enabled by all of these state statutes. Only six of the state statutes specify a maximum allowable number of plants (six or less).

State medical marijuana policies and US federal law conflict in two ways. The first is in the physician's ability to prescribe cannabis. States can protect physicians against prosecution in state courts but not from prosecution by the federal government, which is responsible for licensing the prescription of medicines. Unless there is a formal change in the federal scheduling of marijuana, physicians who prescribe marijuana are not protected from federal sanctions, including loss of their licence to prescribe (Barnes, 2000). The federal government has threatened to prosecute physicians or strip them of their licence to practise if they prescribe cannabis. Physicians are also concerned about their legal liability for any harm that may be caused to patients for whom they prescribe cannabis (Pacula et al., 2002). In the absence of data from controlled trials, physicians find it difficult to decide to whom they should prescribe cannabis, in what amounts and for how long (Reuter and Burnam, 1997).

The second source of conflict between state and federal law arises over cannabis cultivation. Because the federal government prohibits the cultivation of cannabis, patients and caregivers who cultivate cannabis in states that permit this are at risk of federal prosecution. To date, only patients and caregivers living in communities that have set very broad guidelines on home cultivation have come under federal prosecution. For example, the Californian counties of Oakland, Santa Cruz and Humbolt all allow cultivation of up to 72 indoor plants and 20 outdoor plants for medicinal purposes. These very liberal guidelines are permitted because California state law does not specify a maximum allowable number of plants. It is not surprising that the federal government has prosecuted individuals in these communities who grow large numbers of plants claiming a medical defence. The courts have not explicitly resolved the issue of medical necessity but the US Supreme Court ruled in 2001 that third-party organisations that sell or supply cannabis for medicinal purposes (e.g. cannabis buyers' clubs) are not protected from federal prosecution by state laws (Pacula et al., 2002).

In 1996 the federal–state conflict over medical cannabis use prompted the Office of National Drug Control Policy to ask the Institute of Medicine (IOM) to review the evidence on medical uses of cannabis. In 1999 the IOM Committee concluded that there was sufficient evidence of safety and efficacy to warrant clinical trials of cannabis and cannabinoids for less than six months in a number of clinical conditions (Institute of Medicine, 1999). The IOM recommended that cannabis should be provided on compassionate grounds through an IND system until the clinical trials were completed. This would allow access to cannabis (that would be supplied by the US government) to patients who had failed to respond to conventional treatment and for whom there was a reasonable expectation of benefit (Institute of Medicine, 1999).

The IOM recommendations on compassionate provision were not accepted by the US government. Conflict continues between US federal and state governments with the consequences that medical practitioners remain uncertain about the legality of prescribing cannabis, and patients risk federal prosecution for using cannabis in states that have legislated to allow it to be medically prescribed.

Gieringer has recently reported data on the number of patients who have registered to use medicinal marijuana in the US states that allow its use (Gieringer, 2003). He estimated that 35,000 Americans were legally registered to use cannabis for medicinal purposes on the recommendations of 2500 physicians. Rates of registration (per 100,000 population) varied from 89 in California and 79 in Oregon to 3 in Colorado. The percentage of physicians who were prepared to recommend marijuana varied from 2% in California to 5% in Oregon. Registration rates varied markedly between Northern and Southern California, with the highest rates (1% of adults in Mendicino County) in Northern California (the centre for illegal cannabis cultivation) where law-enforcement officials were sympathetic to medical cannabis use.

These data suggest that patients in the US have relatively low rates of access to medical marijuana even in states that have the most liberal laws on medical use of marijuana. The reluctance of physicians to recommend the medical use of cannabis to their patients may be as much a constraint on access as conflict between federal and state laws.

Medical cannabis initiatives in the United Kingdom

In 1998 the House of Lords Select Committee on Science and Technology (SCOST) examined proposals to allow the medical use of cannabis in the United Kingdom (House of Lords Select Committee on Science and Technology, 1998). SCOST concluded that there was enough anecdotal evidence to convince it that cannabis had 'genuine medical applications … in treating the painful muscular spasms and other symptoms of multiple sclerosis (MS) and in the control of other forms of pain' (House of Lords Select Committee on Science and Technology, 1998, section 8.2). It recommended clinical trials of cannabis in these conditions and research into 'alternative modes of administration (e.g. inhalation, sub-lingual, rectal) which would retain the benefit of rapid absorption offered by smoking, without its adverse effects. Until such trials had been completed, it recommended that doctors be allowed to prescribe cannabis as an unlicensed medicine on a named-patient basis.

The UK government did not accept the Committee's recommendations on the rescheduling of cannabis for medical use. The Medical Research Council, however, has funded several large-scale clinical trials of THC and cannabis preparations to manage post-operative pain and muscle spasticity in multiple sclerosis (Moffat, 2002).

Medical cannabis initiatives in Australia

In August 1999 the New South Wales Premier appointed a Working Party to advise: (a) whether cannabis and cannabinoid drugs had any medical uses, and (b) if they did, how cannabis or cannabinoids could be used for medical purposes without decriminalising recreational cannabis use. The Working Party (New South Wales Working Party, 2000) concluded that THC was useful in treating HIV- and cancer-related wasting and nausea caused by cancer chemotherapy. It also noted suggestive evidence that THC may relieve painful muscle spasms in neurological disorders and pain that has not responded to conventional analgesics. It recommended further research on the therapeutic use of cannabis and cannabinoid drugs in all of these conditions.

The Working Party also concluded that smoked cannabis would not meet criteria for registration as a therapeutic good (a pre-condition for medical use in

Australia). Until new medicinal cannabinoids were developed, the Working Party recommended that patients be given compassionate access to cannabis by exempting them from criminal prosecution if they were medically certified to have certain medical conditions. These would be patients who had been certified by an approved medical practitioner to suffer from: HIV- or cancer-related wasting; nausea caused by cancer chemotherapy; muscle spasm in neurological disorders or spinal cord injury; and pain unrelieved by conventional analgesia.

Certification had to be obtained *prior* to medical cannabis use to enable practitioners to: counsel the patient about alternative treatments; explain the risks of smoking cannabis; and review their health. The certificate would have to be renewed after six months. Patients would be allowed to grow a small number of cannabis plants for their own use. Seriously ill and debilitated patients could nominate a carer to grow the same small number of cannabis plants on their behalf. The effects of this compassionate provision scheme were to be evaluated after a two-year trial period.

The New South Wales Premier cautiously welcomed the Working Party's report and media reaction was generally positive, apart from some concerns expressed about diversion. The government appointed a committee to advise on implementation of the recommendations and, three years after the report was released, announced that legislation would be introduced.

Medical marijuana initiatives in Canada

In April 2001 the Canadian Government legislated to allow patients compassionate access to cannabis while awaiting the results of clinical trials of its efficacy (to take effect on 30 July 2001). The cannabis could be supplied by the government (who sourced it from a commercial supplier), or it could be grown under licence by the patient or by a person designated by the patient.

Patients with three broad medical indications were eligible for the scheme: (1) those with a terminal illness and a life expectancy of less than 12 months; (2) patients with MS, spinal cord injury or disease, cancer pain, AIDS, arthritis and epilepsy; and (3) patients 'who have symptoms associated with a serious medical condition other than those described in categories 1 and 2 where among other things conventional treatments have failed to relieve symptoms of the medical condition or its treatment' (Health Canada Office of Cannabis Medical Access, 2002).

To date 798 applications for compassionate access have been approved, allowing patients to grow cannabis for their own use. No patients have so far been supplied with cannabis under the government program, however (Abraham, 2002). In August 2002, the new Minister for Health delayed the full operation of the scheme until clinical trials have demonstrated the safety and efficacy of cannabis in treating the indicated disorders (Abraham, 2002). One reason for this decision was the fact that the Canadian Medical Association (CMA) and the Canadian Medical Protective Association both advised physicians not to prescribe cannabis (Abraham, 2002). They argued that there was no clinical evidence that cannabis was effective for most of the indications for which it could be prescribed and they claimed that medical practitioners who prescribed cannabis would be legally liable for any adverse effects experienced by their patients.

The conundrums of medical marijuana initiatives

Different types of medical marijuana initiative face different practical and legal problems. Research trials obviate the need for complex legislation and enforcement but at the cost of only providing legal access to cannabis for very small numbers of patients, at substantial cost (e.g. it cost US$250,000 to provide cannabis to eight patients in the US) (Conboy, 2000). Patients who do not wish to participate in such trials do not have legal access to cannabis.

Laws that allow physicians to prescribe cannabis (as in some US states and as has been proposed in Canada and the UK) face a number of problems. In the USA state prescription laws conflict with federal laws, exposing physicians and patients to the risk of federal criminal prosecution. Even in the absence of prosecution (as in Canada), physicians have been reluctant to prescribe cannabis because of uncertainty about the indications for its use. The organised medical profession also fears incurring legal liability for any harms that may be caused by chronic cannabis smoking (New South Wales Working Party, 2000).

Securing legal supply of cannabis is the third problem for patients under medical prescription schemes. One option is for the government to supply cannabis (as proposed in Canada). This can be expensive and involves the government directly in cannabis supply which may raise issues of legal liability for harm. Alternatively, patients (or carers) may be allowed to grow cannabis for their own medical use (as proposed in New South Wales and permitted in Canada). Governments who want to supply cannabis to patients or allow patients to cultivate it face criticisms about sending the 'wrong message' to young people about cannabis.

Governments face political difficulties in granting patients exemptions from criminal prosecution or allowing medical necessity defences. These are attacked by supporters of cannabis prohibition as 'back-door' legalisation that sends the wrong message to youth. Governments also find it hard to reassure the public about the risks of diversion, even if this is likely to be a trivial issue by comparison with the scale of the blackmarket that already exists to meet the demand for recreational cannabis use (Hall et al., 2001).

Conclusions

All of the conundrums raised by 'medical marijuana' initiatives would disappear if synthetic cannabinoids were registered for medical use or if there were medically acceptable and efficient ways of delivering THC. The IOM (1999) was pessimistic about the prospects of any such product reaching the US market which, because of its size, has a large impact on the pharmaceutical industry world-wide. The IOM emphasised the small market for such products, the lack of incentives provided by a patent system for naturally occurring cannabinoids, and the regulatory obstacles to the medical use of drugs that produce similar effects to a plant that is classified as having no medical uses.

The best prospects of delivering therapeutic cannabinoids currently rest with researchers at a small UK pharmaceutical company which has been trialling novel methods of delivering THC and cannabis extracts. Success in this research would enable the medical and broader community to make a fairer evaluation of the therapeutic usefulness of THC and other cannabinoids and the pharmaceutical size of the market for THC. We hope that this and other research over the next decade will enable a more informed answer than has the inconclusive 30 years' debate about medical marijuana in the USA.

Cannabis use and crime

The assumption that drugs and crime are causally related is a major reason for prohibiting the use of illicit drugs in many developed countries. In the case of cannabis, however, the evidence for this assumption is much less compelling than it is for heroin and cocaine.

Cannabis, like most other illegal substances, may be associated with crime for two reasons. The first possibility is that cannabis use generates crime. The second reason is a simple consequence of cannabis prohibition: because cannabis use is illegal its use is a crime by definition. We focus on the first of these possibilities in this appendix.

Studies in the United States, England and Australia all show that approximately 60% of arrestees test positive for cannabis (Taylor and Bennett, 1999; Makkai et al., 2000). These data indicate that criminals use cannabis but they do not necessarily mean that cannabis is a cause of crime. First, very few arrestees *only* test positive for cannabis; most also use other illicit drugs and alcohol that may motivate criminal behaviour (Taylor et al., 2001). Second, a positive urine sample for THC only indicates that the drug has been used in the past month; it does not indicate that cannabis was used at or near the time of the criminal activity that led to arrest.

Surprisingly few studies have examined the relationship between cannabis use and crime. Most of these have examined the relationships between crime and other illegal drugs that have been more closely linked to crime, namely, heroin and cocaine. We review this limited evidence in the light of four hypotheses that have been used to describe the relationship between crime and other illicit drugs (Goldstein, 1985).

The psychopharmacological model

According to the psychopharmacological model, drug users engage in crime because of the acute psychoactive effects of the substance (Goldstein, 1985). There is very little support for this model in the case of cannabis. Laboratory studies generally show that cannabis, unlike alcohol, temporarily inhibits aggression and violence (Miczek et al., 1994; White and Gorman, 2000). These findings raise doubts about the psychopharmacological hypothesis.

Although it is quite likely that cannabis temporarily inhibits aggression in the general population, it is possible that cannabis use increases aggression in some individuals. In controlled laboratory studies, for example, the relationship between alcohol use and aggression is influenced by subject characteristics, such as gender, aggressive tendencies, and cognitive abilities, as well as experimental conditions, such as whether the subject was provoked (Bushman, 1997). There may be similar variations in response among cannabis users. In a study comparing cannabis users in Amsterdam, San Francisco and Bremen, for example, 4.6% of users reported that the cannabis made them more aggressive (Cohen and Kaal, 2001). The US National Research Council recently concluded after reviewing the literature that while short-term use of cannabis appears to inhibit aggressive behaviour in humans, long-term use may alter the nervous system in ways that promote violence (National Research Council, 1993).

There is more consistent evidence of a link between frequent cannabis use and violent crime among juveniles (Dembo et al., 1991; Salmelainen, 1995; Baker, 1998). In a study of 10,441 secondary students in New South Wales, Australia, students who were frequent cannabis users were two times more likely to participate in assault and malicious damage of property than students who did not use cannabis. The relationship persisted after adjusting for differences in developmental characteristics, demographic and other substance use (Baker, 1998). Further investigation of the characteristics of these users, and the prevalence of any such effects in the general population, would be useful in understanding the seriousness of this risk.

There is some evidence that cannabis use may increase the chances of being the victim of a crime. Markowitz (2000) examined US data on the relationship between state decriminalisation of cannabis (as a proxy for lower penalties for possessing cannabis) and data from the 1992–1994 National Criminal Victimization Survey. She found that there was a higher probability of being assaulted in states that had decriminalised cannabis than in states that had not. Chaloupka and Saffer (1992) also found a positive and statistically significant association between cannabis decriminalisation in the United States and assaults, using state-level data on crimes from the Uniform Crime Reports. These findings suggest that cannabis use, like other intoxicants that may impair judgement, may increase the risks of being victimised.

Economically motivated crime

Economic crime is motivated by the need to fund one's drug use. It is the combined result of the desired pharmacological effects of these drugs and their high cost under prohibition (Goldstein, 1985). By comparison with other illicit drugs, cannabis dos not typically produce compulsive patterns of use and it is much less expensive than other illicit drugs. As noted in Chapter 7, the physical withdrawal symptoms from cannabis are milder than those for heroin or alcohol and the average cost per unit of intoxication is much lower for cannabis than alcohol (Kleiman, 1992). Hence the pharmacological properties of the drug do not generally induce economic compulsive crime (MacCoun and Reuter, 2001). In their ethnographic study of regular cannabis users in Amsterdam, San Francisco and Bremen, Cohen and Kaal (2001) found that fewer than 5% committed offences to obtain cannabis and the most frequent offence was selling cannabis.

The same may not be true among youth. Among juvenile offenders in the United States and Australia, frequent cannabis users report greater involvement in theft than non-users (Dembo et al., 1991; Salmelainen, 1995; Stevenson and Forsythe, 1998). In addition, higher cannabis involvement was correlated with higher rates of offending for property crimes (Salmelainen, 1995; Stevenson and Forsythe, 1998). The relationship was supported by a school-based survey of 10,441 secondary students in New South Wales, Australia, in which frequent cannabis users were almost five times more likely to report participation in acquisitive property crime than non-users, even after controlling for individual characteristics, family background, and other substance use (Baker, 1998). Findings from these studies support a possible economic-compulsive relationship between cannabis use and crime among young offenders. Further investigation is necessary to understand how generalisable these findings are to other settings.

Systemic crime

Systemic violence arises when violence is used to enforce contracts or to resolve 'turf wars' in illicit drug markets. This violence is motivated by the enormous profits that are generated by illicit drug sales and the absence of legitimate law enforcement to resolve disputes. It is more likely to occur in outdoor blackmarkets where consumers who have a propensity to resolve personal disputes by violence make frequent small purchases of their drug. These are common features of markets for heroin and cocaine in many US cities.

It is doubtful that the experience of violence in heroin and cocaine markets is applicable to cannabis markets. Most cannabis sales occur through friendship networks in private dwellings rather than in outdoor street markets. Although there is a significant mark-up in the cannabis market, it is nowhere near the mark-up for cocaine and other hard drugs. The relatively low price reduces the importance of the cannabis blackmarket as a generator of economic crime by users or systemic crime (Kleiman, 1992, p. 92).

Cannabis markets have generated violence in a few places in the United States but this has been extremely rare and very localised (Goldstein et al., 1989; Reuter et al., 2000; United States Office of National Drug Control Policy, 2001). For example, Goldstein et al. (1989) found in their assessment of 414 drug-related homicides in New York City that only 6 were related to cannabis. Ethnographic research on the cannabis market in New York City showed that although cannabis dealers used outdoor parks and streets during the early 1980s, the market was not associated with the violence seen in the crack market. In the United States today, the majority of cannabis sales are done in private so dealers do not see their competitors (Johnston et al., 2000; Taylor et al., 2001; United States Office of National Drug Control Policy, 2001). The majority of arrestees report purchasing cannabis indoors (71%) with the proportion who made outdoor purchases of marijuana exceeding 50% in only 4 sites (Taylor et al., 2001).

Ethnographers report that cannabis sellers are more likely to operate independently than as part of an organised dealing operation, although formal organised structures exist in a few cities (United States Office of National Drug Control Policy, 2002). There is also a greater opportunity to supply one's own cannabis because cannabis is a relatively hearty plant that grows naturally in many areas as well as indoors. The low frequency of violence in the cannabis blackmarket does not appear to be unique to the United States. We are not aware of any country that has reported violence as a common problem in cannabis blackmarkets.

Common causes

Cannabis use and criminal behaviour appear to be associated because both have a common cause, such as personal characteristics of individuals that motivate them to become involved in both (Hirschi and Gottfredson, 1988; Fagan, 1990; White, 1990; Fergusson and Horwood, 2000). Among the common factors that have been hypothesised to produce the association are: gang involvement (Fagan, 1990), peer effects (Gorman and White, 1995), problem behaviour during adolescence (Jessor and Jessor, 1977), and common environments and situational causes (Skogan, 1990; Fagan, 1993). The evidence that cannabis use and delinquent behaviour share many common causes or predictors is reviewed in more detail in Chapter 11, which indicates that many of the childhood risk factors for violence, such as hyperactivity, impulsiveness, risk-taking, early school failure, peer rejection, and inability to delay gratification, are also risk factors for cannabis use among adolescents and young adults.

References

Introduction

Advisory Committee on Drug Dependence (1968). *Cannabis: report,* London: HMSO.

Beauchamp, T. L. and Childress, J. F. (2001). *Principles of Biomedical Ethics,* 5th edn. New York: Oxford University Press.

Canadian Government Commission of Inquiry (1970). *The Non-Medical Use of Drugs,* Ottawa: Information Canada.

Cook, T. D. and Campbell, D. T. (1979). *Quasi-Experimentation: Design and Analysis Issues for Field Settings,* Chicago: Rand McNally.

Edwards, G., Anderson, P., Babor, T. F., Casswell, S., Ferrence, R., Geisbrecht, N., Godfrey, C., Holder, H. D., Lemmens, P., Makela, K., Midanik, L. T., Norstrom, T., Osterberg, E, Romelsjo, A., Room, R., Simpura, J. and Skog, O. J. (1994). *Alcohol Policy and the Public Good.* Oxford: Oxford University Press.

Ellard, J. (1992). The ninth crusade: the crusade against drugs. *Modern Medicine,* **35** (4), 58–61, 64–68.

Fehr, K. and Kalant, H. (1983). *Cannabis and Health Hazards,* Toronto: Addiction Research Foundation.

Goodin, R. E. (1995). *Utilitarianism as Public Philosophy,* Cambridge: Cambridge University Press.

Grinspoon, L. and Bakalar, J. (1993). *Marihuana, the forbidden medicine,* New Haven: Yale University Press.

Hall, W. D. (1997). The recent Australian debate about the prohibition on cannabis use. *Addiction,* **92** (9), 1109–15.

Hall, W. D., Johnston, L. and Donnelly, N. (1999). Epidemiology of cannabis use and its consequences. In *The Health Effects of Cannabis,* ed. H. Kalant, W. Corrigal, W. D. Hall and R. Smart, pp. 69–125. Toronto: Centre for Addiction and Mental Health.

Hall, W. D. and Nelson, J. (1995). *Public perceptions of health and psychological consequences of cannabis use,* Canberra: Australian Government Publishing Service.

Husak, D. (2002). *Legalize This! The Case for Decriminalising Drugs,* London: Verso.

Institute of Medicine (1999). *Marijuana and Medicine: Assessing the Science Base,* Washington, DC: National Academy Press.

Kaplan, J. (1970). *Marijuana: The New Prohibition,* New York: World Publishing Company.

Kleiman, M. A. R. (1992). *Against Excess: Drug Policy for Results,* New York: Basic Books.

MacCoun, R. and Reuter, P. (2001). *Drug War Heresies: Learning from Other Vices, Times and Places,* Cambridge: Cambridge University Press.

Machado, T. (1994). *Culture and Drug Abuse in Asian Settings: Research for Action,* Bangalore: St John's Medical College.

Manderson, D. (1993). *From Mr Sin to Mr Big: A History of Australian Drug Laws,* Melbourne: Oxford University Press.

Manski, C. F., Pepper, J. V. and Petrie, C. V. (eds) (2001). *Informing America's Policy on Illegal Drugs: What We Don't Know Keeps Hurting Us,* Washington, DC, National Academy Press.

McAllister, I. and Makkai, T. (1991). Whatever happened to marijuana? Patterns of marijuana use in Australia, 1985–1988. *International Journal of the Addictions,* **26** (5), 491–504.

McAllister, W. B. (2000). *Drug Diplomacy in the Twentieth Century: An International History,* London: Routledge.

Moore, M. H. and Gerstein, D. C. (1981). *Alcohol and Public Policy: Beyond the Shadow of Prohibition,* Washington, DC: National Academy Press.

Nahas, G. and Latour, C. (1992). The human toxicity of marijuana. *Medical Journal of Australia,* **156** (7), 495–97.

National Commission on Marihuana and Drug Abuse (1972). *Marihuana: A Signal of Misunderstanding,* Washington, DC: US Government Printing Office.

Room, R. (1984). Alcohol and ethnography: a case of problem deflation? *Current Anthropology,* **25,** 169–91.

Senate Standing Committee on Social Welfare (1977). *Drug Problems in Australia: An Intoxicated Society,* Canberra: Australian Government Printing Office.

Walters, E. (1993). *Marijuana: an Australian crisis,* Malvern, Vic: E. Walters.

WHO Program on Substance Abuse (1997). *Cannabis: A Health Perspective and Research Agenda,* Geneva: Division of Mental Health and Prevention of Substance Abuse, World Health Organisation.

Zimmer, L. and Morgan, J. P. (1997). *Marijuana Myths, Marijuana Facts: A Review of the Scientific Evidence,* New York: The Lindesmith Center.

Section 1: Cannabis the drug and how it is used

Adams, I. B. and Martin, B. R. (1996). Cannabis: pharmacology and toxicology in animals and humans. *Addiction,* **91** (11), 1585–614.

Adlaf, E. M., Paglia, A., Ivis, F. J. and Ialomiteanu, A. (2000). Nonmedical drug use among adolescent students: highlights from the 1999 Ontario Student Drug Use Survey. *Canadian Medical Association Journal,* **162** (12), 1677–80.

Adlaf, E. M. and Smart, R. G. (1991). Drug use among adolescent students in Canada and Ontario: the past, present and future. *Journal of Drug Issues,* **21,** 59–72.

Agurell, S., Halldin, M., Lindgren, J., Ohlsson, A., Widman, M., Gillespie, H. and Hollister, L. (1986). Pharmacokinetics and metabolism of Δ-9-tetrahydrocannabinol and other cannabinoids with emphasis on man. *Pharmacological Reviews,* **38** (1), 21–43.

Australian Institute of Health and Welfare (2002). *2001 National Drug Strategy Household Survey: Detailed Findings,* Drug Statistics, Vol. 11, Canberra: Australian Institute of Health and Welfare.

Bachman, J. G., Wadsworth, K. N., O'Malley, P. M., Johnston, L. D. and Schulenberg, J. (1997). *Smoking, drinking, and drug use in young adulthood: the impacts of new freedoms and new responsibilities,* Mahwah, NJ: Lawrence Erlbaum.

Brenneisen, R. (2002). Pharmacokinetics. In *Cannabis and Cannabinoids: Pharmacology, Toxicology and Therapeutic Potential,* ed. F. Grotenhermen and E. Russo, pp. 67–72. London: Haworth.

Chen, K. and Kandel, D. B. (1995). The natural history of drug use from adolescence to the mid-thirties in a general population sample. *American Journal of Public Health,* **85** (1), 41–47.

Chen, K. and Kandel, D. B. (1998). Predictors of cessation of marijuana use: an event history analysis. *Drug and Alcohol Dependence,* **50** (2), 109–21.

Chesher, G. and Hall, W. D. (1999). Effects of cannabis on the cardiovascular and gastrointestinal systems. In *The Health Effects of Cannabis,* ed. H. Kalant, W. Corrigall, W. D. Hall and R. Smart, pp. 435–58. Toronto: Centre for Addiction and Mental Health.

Clarke, R. C. and Watson, D. P. (2002). The botany of natural cannabis medicines. In *Cannabis and Cannabinoids: Pharmacology, Toxicology and Therapeutic Potential,* ed. F. Grotenhermen and E. Russo, pp. 3–14. New York: Haworth Press.

Degenhardt, L., Lynskey, M. and Hall, W. D. (2000). Cohort trends in the age of initiation of drug use in Australia. *Australian and New Zealand Journal of Public Health,* **24** (4), 421–26.

Devane, W., Hanus, L., Breuer, A., Pertwee, R., Stevenson, L., Griffin, G., Gibson, D., Mandelbaum, A., Etinger, A. and Mechoulam, R. (1992). Isolation and structure of a brain constituent that binds to the cannabinoid receptor. *Science,* **258**, 1946–49.

Donnelly, N. and Hall, W. D. (1994). *Patterns of Cannabis Use in Australia,* Canberra: Australian Government Publishing Service.

Ellis, G., Mann, M., Judson, B., Scramm, N. and Tashchian, A. (1985). Excretion patterns of cannabinoid metabolites after last use in a group of chronic users. *Clinical Pharmacology and Therapeutics,* **38**, 572–78.

ElSohly, M. A. (2002). Chemical constituents of cannabis. In *Cannabis and Cannabinoids: Pharmacology, Toxicology and Therapeutic Potential,* ed. F. Grotenhermen and E. Russo, pp. 27–36. London: Haworth.

ElSohly, M. A., Ross, S. A., Mehmedic, Z., Arafat, R., Yi, B. and Banahan, B. F. (2000). Potency trends of delta(9)-THC and other cannabinoids in confiscated marijuana from 1980–1997. *Journal of Forensic Sciences,* **45** (1), 24–30.

European Monitoring Centre for Drugs and Drug Addiction (2002). *Annual Report on the State of the Drugs Problem in the European Union, 2001,* Lisbon: European Monitoring Centre for Drugs and Drug Addiction.

Ghodse, A. H. (1986). Cannabis psychosis. *British Journal of Addiction,* **81** (4), 473–78.

Hall, W. D. (1999). Assessing the health and psychological effects of cannabis use. In *The Health Effects of Cannabis,* ed. H. Kalant, W. Corrigall, W. D. Hall and R. Smart, pp. 1–17. Toronto: Centre for Addiction and Mental Health.

Hall, W. D. and Swift, W. (2000). The THC content of cannabis in Australia: evidence and implications. *Australian and New Zealand Journal of Public Health,* **24** (5), 503–08.

Harkin, A., Anderson, P. and Goos, P. (1997). *Smoking, Drinking and Drug Taking in the European Region,* Copenhagen: WHO Regional Office for Europe.

Harvey, D. J. (1999). Absorption, distribution and biotransformation of the cannabinoids. In *Marihuana and Medicine,* ed. G. Nahas, K. M. Sutin, D. Harvey and S. Agurell, pp. 91–103. Towa, NJ: Humana Press.

Hawks, R. (1982). The constituents of cannabis and the disposition and metabolism of cannabinoids. In *The Analysis of Cannabinoids in Biological Fluids*, ed. R. Hawks, pp. 125–37. Rockville, MD: US Department of Health and Human Services.

Heustis, M. A., Gorelick, D. A., Heishman, S. J., Preston, K. L., Nelson, R. A., Moochan, E. T. and Frank, R. A. (2001). Blockade of effects of smoked marijuana by the CB1-selective cannabinoid receptor antagonist SR141716. *Archives of General Psychiatry*, **58**, 322–28.

Heustis, M. A., Henningfield, J. E. and Cone, E. J. (1992). Blood cannabinoids II. Models for the prediction of marijuana exposure from plasma concentrations of D9-Tetrahydrocannabinol (THC) and 11-nor-9-carboxy-D9-tetrahydrocannabinol (THCCOOH). *Journal of Analytical Toxicology*, **16**, 283–90.

Howlett, A., Bidaut-Russell, M., Devane, W., Melvin, L., Johnson, M. and Herkenham, M. (1990). The cannabinoid receptor: biochemical, anatomical and behavioral characterization. *Trends in Neuroscience*, **13** (10), 420–23.

Hunt, C. and Jones, R. (1980). Tolerance and disposition of tetrahydrocannabinol in man. *Journal of Pharmacology and Experimental Therapeutics*, **215** (1), 35–44.

Institute of Medicine (1999). *Marijuana and Medicine: Assessing the Science Base*, Washington, DC: National Academy Press.

Iversen, L. (2000). *The Science of Marijuana*, Oxford: Oxford University Press.

Ivis, F. J. and Adlaf, E. M. (1999). A comparison of trends in drug use among students in the USA and Ontario, Canada: 1975–1997. *Drugs, Education Prevention and Policy*, **6**, 17–27.

Johansson, E., Agurell, S., Hollister, L. E. and Halldin, M. M. (1988). Prolonged apparent half-life of delta 1-tetrahydrocannabinol in plasma of chronic marijuana users. *Journal of Pharmacy and Pharmacology*, **40** (5), 374–75.

Johansson, E., Sjovall, J., Noren, K., Agurell, S., Hollister, L. and Halldin, M. (1987). Analysis of delta9-tetrahydrocannabinol (delta9-THC) in human plasma and fat after smoking. In *Marijuana: An International Research Report*, ed. G. B. Chesher, P. Consroe and R. Musty, pp. 291–96. Canberra: Australian Government Publishing Service.

Johnston, L., Bachman, J. and O'Malley, P. (1981). *Highlights from Student Drug Use in America, 1975–1981*, Rockville, MD: National Institute on Drug Abuse.

Johnston, L. D., O'Malley, P. M. and Bachman, J. G. (1994a). *National Survey Results on Drug Use from the Monitoring the Future Study, 1975–1993. College Students and Young Adults*, Vol. 2, Rockville, MD: National Institute on Drug Abuse.

Johnston, L. D., O'Malley, P. M. and Bachman, J. G. (1994b). *National Survey Results on Drug Use from the Monitoring the Future Study, 1975–1993. Secondary School Students*, Vol. 1, Rockville, MD: National Institute on Drug Abuse.

Johnston, L. D., O'Malley, P. M. and Bachman, J. G. (2001). *Monitoring the Future: National Results on Adolescent Drug Use, Overview of Key Findings 2000*, Rockville, MD: National Institute on Drug Abuse.

Lynskey, M. and Hall, W. D. (1999). *Cannabis use among Australian youth: prevalence and correlates of use*, Sydney: National Drug and Alcohol Research Centre, University of New South Wales.

Makkai, T. and McAllister, I. (1997). *Marijuana Use in Australia: Patterns and Attitudes*, Canberra: Australian Government Publishing Service.

Makkai, T. and McAllister, I. (1998). *Patterns of Drug Use in Australia, 1985–1995*, Canberra: Australian Government Publishing Service.

Martin, B. and Cone, E. (1999). Chemistry and pharmacology of cannabis. In *The Health Effects of Cannabis*, ed. H. Kalant, W. Corrigal, W. D. Hall and R. G. Smart, pp. 19–68. Toronto: Centre for Addiction and Mental Health.

Menkes, D., Howard, R., Spears, G. and Cairns, E. (1991). Salivary THC following cannabis smoking correlates with subjective intoxication and heart rate. *Psychopharmacology*, **103**, 277–79.

National Institute on Drug Abuse (1985). Consensus report: drug concentrations and driving impairment. *Journal of the American Medical Association*, **254** (18), 2618–2621.

National Institute on Drug Abuse (1992). *National Survey of Drug Abuse: Population Estimates 1991 – Revised November 20, 1992*, Rockville, MD: National Institute on Drug Abuse.

O'Malley, P., Bachman, J.G. and Johnston, L. (1983). Reliability and consistency of self-reports of drug use. *International Journal of the Addictions*, **18**, 805–24.

Ohlsson, A., Lindgren, J.-E., Wahlen, A., Agurell, S., Hollister, L. and Gillespie, H. (1980). Plasma delta-9-tetrahydrocannabinol concentrations and clinical effects after oral and intravenous administration and smoking. *Clinical Pharmacology and Therapeutics*, **28** (3), 409–16.

Perez-Reyes, M., Di Giuseppi, S., Davis, K., Schindler, V. and Cook, C. (1982). Comparison of effects of marihuana cigarettes of three different potencies. *Clinical Pharmacology and Therapeutics*, **31** (5), 617–24.

Pertwee, R. (1999). Cannabinoid receptors and their ligands in brain and other tissues. In *Marijuana and Medicine*, ed. G. Nahas, K. Sutin, D. Harvey and S. Agurell, pp. 177–85. Totowa, NJ: Humana Press.

Pertwee, R. (2002). Sites and mechanism of action. In *Cannabis and Cannabinoids: Pharmacology, Toxicology and Therapeutic Potential*, ed. F. Grotenhermen and E. Russo, pp. 73–88. London: Haworth.

Smart, R. G. and Ogborne, A. C. (2000). Drug use and drinking among students in 36 countries. *Addictive Behaviors*, **25** (3), 455–60.

Substance Abuse and Mental Health Services Administration (2001). *Summary of Findings from the 2000 National Household Survey on Drug Abuse*, Washington, DC: Department of Health and Social Services.

United Nations Office for Drug Control and Crime Prevention (2002). *Global Illicit Drug Trends, 2002*, New York: United Nations Office for Drug Control and Crime Prevention.

Walsh, G. W. and Mann, R. E. (1999). On the high road: driving under the influence of cannabis in Ontario. *Canadian Journal of Public Health*, **90** (4), 260–63.

Wiley, J. L. and Martin, B. R. (2002). Cannabinoid pharmacology: implications for additional cannabinoid receptor types. *Chemistry and Physics of Lipids*, **121**, 57–63.

Williams, B., Chang, K. and Van Truong, M. (1992). *Canadian Profile: Alcohol and Other Drugs 1992*, Canada: Addiction Research Foundation Publications.

Section 2: Health effects

Abel, E. (1985). Effects of prenatal exposure to cannabinoids. In *Current Research on the Consequences of Maternal Drug Abuse*, ed. T. Pinkert, pp. 20–35. Rockville, MD: US Department of Health and Human Services.

Adlaf, E. M., Mann, R. E. and Paglia, A. (2003). Drinking, cannabis use and driving among Ontario students. *Canadian Medical Association Journal*, **168**, 565–66.

Altman, D. G., Machin, D., Bryant, T. N. and Gardner, M. J. (2000). *Statistics With Confidence*, 2nd edn. London: BMJ Books.

Andreasson, S. and Allebeck, P. (1990). Cannabis and mortality among young men: a longitudinal study of Swedish conscripts. *Scandinavian Journal of Social Medicine*, **18**, 9–15.

Aronow, W. and Cassidy, J. (1974). Effect of marihuana and placebo marihuana smoking on angina pectoris. *New England Journal of Medicine*, **291**, 65–67.

Bachman, J. G., Wadsworth, K. N., O'Malley, P. M., Johnston, L. D. and Schulenberg, J. (1997). *Smoking, drinking, and drug use in young adulthood: the impacts of new freedoms and new responsibilities*, Mahwah, NJ: Lawrence Erlbaum.

Bachs, L. and Morland, H. (2001). Acute cardiovascular fatalities following cannabis use. *Forensic Science International*, **124** (2–3), 200–3.

Barsky, S. H., Roth, M. D., Kleerup, E. C., Simmons, M. and Tashkin, D. P. (1998). Histopathologic and molecular alterations in bronchial epithelium in habitual smokers of marijuana, cocaine, and/or tobacco. *Journal of the National Cancer Institute*, **90**, 1198–205.

Bates, M. N. and Blakely, T. A. (1999). Role of cannabis in motor vehicle crashes. *Epidemiologic Reviews*, **21**, 222–32.

Beardsley, P. and Kelly, T. (1999). Acute effects of cannabis on human behavior and central nervous system functions. In *The Health Effects of Cannabis*, ed. H. Kalant, W. Corrigall, W. D. Hall and R. Smart, pp. 127–265. Toronto: Centre for Addiction and Mental Health.

Benowitz, N. and Jones, R. (1975). Cardiovascular effects of prolonged delta-9-tetrahydrocannabinol ingestion. *Clinical Pharmacology and Therapeutics*, **18** (3), 287–89.

Blackard, C. and Tennes, K. (1984). Human placental transfer of cannabinoids. *New England Journal of Medicine*, **311**, 797.

Bloch, E. (1983). Effects of marijuana and cannabinoids on reproduction, endocrine function, development, and chromosomes. In *Cannabis and Health Hazards*, ed. K. Fehr and H. Kalant, pp. 355–432. Toronto: Addiction Research Foundation.

Bloom, J., Kaltenborn, W., Paoletti, P., Camilli, A. and Lebowitz, M. (1987). Respiratory effects of non-tobacco cigarettes. *British Medical Journal*, **295**, 1516–18.

Brown, T. T. and Dobs, A. S. (2002). Endocrine effects of marijuana. *Journal of Clinical Pharmacology*, **42** (11), 90S–96S.

Cabral, G. A., Mishkin, E. M., Marciano Cabral, F., Coleman, P., Harris, L. and Munson, A. E. (1986). Effect of delta 9-tetrahydrocannabinol on herpes simplex virus type 2 vaginal infection in the guinea pig. *Proceedings of the Society for Experimental Biology and Medicine*, **182** (2), 181–86.

Cabral, G. A. and Pettit, D. A. D. (1998). Drugs and immunity: cannabinoids and their role in decreased resistance to infectious disease. *Journal of Neuroimmunology*, **83** (1–2), 116–23.

Caplan, G. A. and Brigham, B. A. (1990). Marijuana smoking and carcinoma of the tongue: is there an association? *Cancer*, **66** (5), 1005–6.

Carter, W. E. (1980). *Cannabis in Costa Rica : A Study of Chronic Marihuana Use*, Philadelphia: Institute for the Study of Human Issues.

Cates, W., Jr and Pope, J. N. (1977). Gynecomastia and cannabis smoking: a nonassociation among U.S. Army soldiers. *American Journal of Surgery*, **134** (5), 613–15.

Chan, P. C., Sills, R. C., Braun, A. G., Haseman, J. K. and Bucher, J. R. (1996). Toxicity and carcinogenicity of delta 9-tetrahydrocannabinol in Fischer rats and B6C3F1 mice. *Fundamental and Applied Toxicology*, **30** (1), 109–17.

Chesher, G. (1995). Cannabis and road safety: an outline of research studies to examine the effects of cannabis on driving skills and actual driving performance. In *The Effects of Drugs (Other than Alcohol) on Road Safety*, ed. Parliament of Victoria Road Safety Committee, pp. 67–96. Melbourne: Road Safety Committee.

Chesher, G. and Hall, W. D. (1999). Effects of cannabis on the cardiovascular and gastrointestinal systems. In *The Health Effects of Cannabis*, ed. H. Kalant, W. Corrigall, W. D. Hall and R. Smart, pp. 435–58. Toronto: Centre for Addiction and Mental Health.

Cimbura, G., Lucas, D., Bennet, R., Warren, R. and Simpson, H. (1982). Incidence and toxicological aspects of drugs detected in 484 fatally injured drivers and pedestrians in Ontario. *Journal of Forensic Science*, 27, 855–67.

Compton, D. R., Dewey, W. L. and Martin, B. R. (1990). Cannabis dependence and tolerance production. *Advances in Alcohol and Substance Abuse*, 9 (1–2), 129–47.

Cornelius, M. D., Goldschmidt, L., Day, N. L. and Larkby, C. (2002). Alcohol, tobacco and marijuana use among pregnant teenagers: 6-year follow-up of offspring growth effects. *Neurotoxicology and Teratology*, 24 (6), 703–10.

Dax, E., Pilotte, N., Adler, W., Nagel, J. and Lange, W. (1989). The effects of 9-ENE-tetrahydrocannabinol on hormone release and immune function. *Journal of Steroid Biochemistry*, 34, 263–70.

Day, N. L., Richardson, G. A., Goldschmidt, L., Robles, N., Taylor, P.M., Stoffer, D.S., Cornelius, M.D. and Geva, D. (1994). Effect of prenatal marijuana exposure on the cognitive development of offspring at age three. *Neurotoxicology and Teratology*, 16 (2), 169–75.

Day, N. L., Wagener, D. and Taylor, P. (1985). Measurement of substance use during pregnancy: methodologic issues. In *Current Research on the Consequences of Maternal Drug Abuse*, ed. T. Pinkert, pp. 36–47. Rockville, MD: US Department of Health and Human Services.

DiFranco, M., Sheppard, H., Hunter, D., Tosteson, T. and Ascher, M. (1996). The lack of association of marijuana and other recreational drugs with progression to AIDS in the San Francisco Men's Health Study. *Annals of Epidemiology*, 6 (4), 283–89.

Doll, R. and Peto, R. (1980). *The Causes of Cancer*, Oxford: Oxford University Press.

Donald, P. (1991). Marijuana and upper aerodigestive tract malignancy in young patients. In *Physiopathology of Illicit Drugs: Cannabis, Cocaine, Opiates*, ed. G. Nahas and C. Latour, pp. 39–54. Oxford: Pergamon.

Drew, W., Miller, L. and Wikler, A. (1972). Effects of delta-9-THC on the open field activity of the rat. *Psychopharmacology*, 23, 289–99.

Drummer, O. H. (1994). *Drugs in drivers killed in Australian road traffic accidents: the use of responsibility analysis to investigate the contribution of drugs to fatal accidents*, Melbourne: Victorian Institute of Forensic Medicine, Monash University.

Drummer, O. H. (1998). *Involvement of Drugs in Accident Causation*, Canberra: Federal Office of Road Safety.

English, D., Holman, C., Milne, E., Winter, M., Hulse, G., Codde, S., Corti, B., Dawes, V., De Klerk, N., Knuiman, M., Kurinczuk, J., Lewin, G. and Ryan, G. (1995). *The Quantification of Drug Caused Morbidity and Mortality in Australia, 1995*, Canberra: Commonwealth Department of Human Services and Health.

English, D., Hulse, G., Milne, E., Holman, C. and Bower, C. (1997). Maternal cannabis use and birth weight: a meta-analysis. *Addiction*, 92, 1553–60.

Eyler, F. D. and Behnke, M. (1999). Early development of infants exposed to drugs prenatally. *Clinics in Perinatology*, 26 (1), 107.

Fergusson, D. M. and Horwood, L. J. (1997). Early onset cannabis use and psychosocial adjustment in young adults. *Addiction*, **92** (3), 279–96.

Fergusson, D. M. and Horwood, L. J. (2001). Cannabis use and traffic accidents in a birth cohort of young adults. *Accident Analysis and Prevention*, **33** (6), 703–11.

Fergusson, D. M., Horwood, L. J. and Northstone, K. (2002). Maternal use of cannabis and pregnancy outcome. *British Journal of Obstetrics and Gynaecology*, **109** (1), 21–27.

Fligiel, S., Beals, T., Venkat, H., Stuth, S., Gong, H. and Tashkin, D. P. (1988). Pulmonary pathology in marijuana smokers. In *Marijuana: An International Research Report*, ed. G. B. Chesher, P. Consroe and R. Musty, pp. 44–48. Canberra: Australian Government Publishing Service.

Fried, P. A. (1980). Marihuana use by pregnant women: neurobehavioral effects in neonates. *Drug and Alcohol Dependence*, **6** (6), 415–24.

Fried, P. A. (1985). Postnatal consequences of maternal marijuana use. In *Current Research on the Consequences of Maternal Drug Abuse*, ed. T. Pinkert, pp. 61–72. Rockville, MD: National Institute on Drug Abuse.

Fried, P. A. (1991). Marijuana use during pregnancy: consequences for the offspring. *Seminars in Perinatology*, **15** (4), 280–87.

Fried, P. A. (1996). Behavioral outcomes in preschool and school-age children exposed prenatally to marijuana: a review and speculative interpretation. In *Behavioral Studies of Drug-Exposed Offspring: Methodological Issues in Human and Animal Research*, pp. 242–60. Rockville, MD: National Institute on Drug Abuse.

Fried, P. A., O'Connell, C. M. and Watkinson, B. (1992). 60- and 72-month follow-up of children prenatally exposed to marijuana, cigarettes, and alcohol: cognitive and language assessment. *Journal of Developmental and Behavioral Pediatrics*, **13** (6), 383–91.

Fried, P. A. and Smith, A. R. (2001). A literature review of the consequences of prenatal marihuana exposure: an emerging theme of a deficiency in aspects of executive function. *Neurotoxicology and Teratology*, **23** (1), 1–11.

Fried, P.A. and Watkinson, B. (1990). 36- and 48-month neurobehavioral follow-up of children prenatally exposed to marijuana, cigarettes, and alcohol. *Journal of Developmental and Behavioral Pediatrics*, **11** (2), 49–58.

Fried, P. A. and Watkinson, B. (2000). Visuoperceptual functioning differs in 9- to 12-year olds prenatally exposed to cigarettes and marihuana. *Neurotoxicology and Teratology*, **22** (1), 11–20.

Gable, R. S. (1993). Toward a comparative overview of dependence potential and acute toxicity of psychoactive substances used nonmedically. *American Journal of Drug and Alcohol Abuse*, **19** (3), 263–81.

Gerberich, S. G., Sidney, S., Braun, B. L., Tekawa, I. S., Tolan, K. K. and Quesenberry, C. P. (2003) Marijuana use and injury events resulting in hospitalisation. *Annals of Epidemiology*, 13, 230–37.

Gibson, G., Baghurst, P. and Colley, D. (1983). Maternal alcohol, tobacco and cannabis consumption and the outcome of pregnancy. *Australian and New Zealand Journal of Obstetrics and Gynaecology*, **23**, 15–19.

Goldschmidt, L., Day, N. L. and Richardson, G. A. (2000). Effects of prenatal marijuana exposure on child behavior problems at age 10. *Neurotoxicology and Teratology*, **22** (3), 325–36.

Gong, H., Fligiel, S., Tashkin, D. P. and Barbers, R. (1987). Tracheobronchial changes in habitual, heavy smokers of marijuana with and without tobacco. *American Review of Respiratory Disease*, **136**, 142–49.

Gottschalk, L., Aronow, W. and Prakash, R. (1977). Effect of marijuana and placebo-marijuana smoking on psychological state and on psychophysiological and cardiovascular functioning in angina patients. *Biological Psychiatry,* **12** (2), 255–66.

Greenland, S., Staisch, K., Brown, N. and Gross, S. (1982). The effects of marijuana use during pregnancy, I. A preliminary epidemiologic study. *American Journal of Obstetrics and Gynaecology,* **143**, 408–13.

Grufferman, S., Schwartz, A. G., Ruymann, F. B. and Maurer, H. M. (1993). Parents' use of cocaine and marijuana and increased risk of rhabdomyosarcoma in their children. *Cancer Causes and Control,* **4** (3), 217–24.

Gurney, J., Smith, M. A. and Bunin, C. (2000a). CNS and miscellaneous intracranial and intraspinal neoplasms. In *SEER Cancer Statistics Review, 1973–1997,* ed. L. Reis, M. Eisner, C. Kosary, B. Hankey, B. Miller, L. Clegg and B. Edwards, pp. 51–63. Bethesda, MD: National Cancer Institute.

Gurney, J., Young, J., Roffers, S., Smith, M. A. and Bunin, C. (2000b). Soft tissue sarcomas. In *SEER Cancer Statistics Review, 1973–1997,* ed. L. Reis, M. Eisner, C. Kosary, B. Hankey, B. Miller, L. Clegg and B. Edwards, pp. 11–123. Bethesda, MD: National Cancer Institute.

Hall, W. D. (1987). A simplified logic of causal inference. *Australian and New Zealand Journal of Psychiatry,* **21** (4), 507–13.

Hall, W. D., Degenhardt, L. and Lynskey, M. (2001). *The Health and Psychological Effects of Cannabis Use,* National Drug Strategy Monograph, Vol. 44, Canberra: Commonwealth Department of Health and Aged Care.

Hall, W. D. and Einfeld, S. (1990). On doing the 'impossible': inferring that a putative causal relationship does not exist. *Australian and New Zealand Journal of Psychiatry,* **24** (2), 217–26.

Hall, W. D. and MacPhee, D. (2002). Cannabis use and cancer. *Addiction,* **97** (3), 243–47.

Ham, M. and DeJon, J. (1975). Effects of delta-9-tetrahydrocannabinol and cannabidiol on blood glucose concentrations in rabbits and rats. *Pharmaceutisch Weekblad,* **110**, 1157–61.

Hansteen, R., Miller, R., Lonero, L., Reid, L. and Jones, B. (1976). Effects of cannabis and alcohol on automobile driving and psychomotor tracking. *Annals of the New York Academy of Sciences,* **282**, 240–56.

Harmon, J. and Aliapoulios, M. (1972). Gynecomastia in marihuana users. *New England Journal of Medicine,* **287**, 936.

Hatch, E. and Bracken, M. (1986). Effect of marijuana use in pregnancy on fetal growth. *American Journal of Epidemiology,* **124**, 986–93.

Hill, A. (1977). *A Short Textbook of Statistics,* London: Hodder and Stoughton.

Hingson, R., Alpert, J., Day, N., Dooling, E., Kayne, H., Morelock, S., Oppenheimer, E. and Zuckerman, B. (1982a). Effects of maternal drinking and marijuana use on fetal growth and development. *Pediatrics,* **70**, 539–46.

Hingson, R., Heeren, T., Mangione, T., Morelock, S. and Mucatel, M. (1982b). Teenage driving after using marijuana or drinking and traffic accident involvement. *Journal of Safety Research,* **13**, 33–37.

Hollister, L. (1992). Marijuana and immunity. *Journal of Psychoactive Drugs,* **24**, 159–64.

Hollister, L. E. (1986). Health aspects of cannabis. *Pharmacological Reviews,* **38** (1), 1–20.

Huber, G., Griffith, D. and Langsjoen, P. (1988). The effects of marihuana on the respiratory and cardiovascular systems. In *Marijuana: An International Research Report,* ed. G. Chesher, P. Consroe and R. Musty, pp. 3–18. Canberra: Australian Government Publishing Service.

Hutchings, D. and Fried, P. A. (1999). Cannabis during pregnancy: neurobehavioural effects in animals and humans. In *The Health Effects of Cannabis*, ed. H. Kalant, W. Corrigall, W. D. Hall and R. Smart, pp. 401–34. Toronto: Centre for Addiction and Mental Health.

Institute of Medicine (1999). *Marijuana and Medicine: Assessing the Science Base*, Washington, DC: National Academy Press.

International Agency on Cancer (1990). *Cancer: Causes, Occurrence and Control*, Lyon: International Agency on Cancer.

Iversen, L. (2000). *The Science of Marijuana*, Oxford: Oxford University Press.

Jaffe, J. (1985). Drug addiction and drug abuse. In *The Pharmacological Basis of Therapeutics*, ed. A. Gilman, L. Goodman and F. Murad, pp. 532–81. New York: Macmillan.

Janowsky, D., Meacham, M., Blaine, J., Schoor, M. and Bozzetti, L. (1976). Marijuana effects on simulated flying ability. *American Journal of Psychiatry*, **133**, 384–88.

Jones, R. T. (1987). Drug of abuse profile: cannabis. *Clinical Chemistry*, **33** (11B), 72B–81B.

Jones, R. T. (2002). Cardiovascular system effects of marijuana. *Journal of Clinical Pharmacology*, **42** (11 Supplement), 58S–63S.

Jones, R. T., Benowitz, N. and Herning, R. (1976). The 30-day trip: clinical studies of cannabis use tolerance and dependence. In *The Pharmacology of Marijuana*, Vol. 2, ed. M. Braude and S. Szara, pp. 627–42. New York: Academic Press.

Kandel, D. B., Davies, M., Karus, D. and Yamaguchi, K. (1986). The consequences in young adulthood of adolescent drug involvement: an overview. *Archives of General Psychiatry*, **43** (8), 746–54.

Kandel, D. B. and Logan, J. A. (1984). Patterns of drug use from adolescence to young adulthood: I. Periods of risk for initiation, continued use, and discontinuation. *American Journal of Public Health*, **74** (7), 660–6.

Kaslow, R. A., Blackwelder, W. C., Ostrow, D. G., Yerg, D., Palenicek, J., Coulson, A. H. and Valdiserri, R.O. (1989). No evidence for a role of alcohol or other psychoactive drugs in accelerating immunodeficiency in HIV-1-positive individuals: a report from the Multicenter AIDS Cohort Study. *Journal of the American Medical Association*, **261** (23), 3424–29.

Klein, T. W., Friedman, H. and Specter, S. (1998). Marijuana, immunity and infection. *Journal of Neuroimmunology*, **83** (1–2), 102–15.

Klein, T. W., Newton, C. A. and Friedman, H. (2001). Cannabinoids and the immune system. *Pain Research and Management*, **6**, 95–101.

Klonoff, H. (1974). Effects of marijuana on driving in a restricted area and on city streets: driving performance and physiological changes. In *Marijuana: Effects on Human Behavior*, ed. L. Miller, pp. 359–97. New York: Academic Press.

Kolodny, R. C., Masters, W. H., Kolodner, R. M. and Toro, G. (1974). Depression of plasma testosterone levels after chronic intensive marihuana use. *New England Journal of Medicine*, **290** (16), 872–4.

Kuijten, R. R., Bunin, G. R., Nass, C. C. and Meadows, A. T. (1992). Parental occupation and childhood astrocytoma – results of a case control study. *Cancer Research*, **52** (4), 782–86.

Leirer, V. O., Yesavage, J. A. and Morrow, D. G. (1989). Marijuana, aging, and task difficulty effects on pilot performance. *Aviation, Space, and Environmental Medicine*, **60** (12), 1145–52.

Leirer, V. O., Yesavage, J. A. and Morrow, D. G. (1991). Marijuana carry-over effects on aircraft pilot performance. *Aviation, Space, and Environmental Medicine*, **62** (3), 221–27.

Leuchtenberger, C. (1983). Effects of marihuana (cannabis) smoke on cellular biochemistry of in vitro test systems. In *Cannabis and Health Hazards*, ed. K. Fehr and H. Kalant, pp. 177–224. Toronto: Addiction Research Foundation.

Linn, S., Schoenbaum, S., Monson, R., Rosnber, R., Stubblefield, P. and Ryan, K. (1983). The association of marijuana use with outcome of pregnancy. *American Journal of Public Health*, 73 (10), 1161–64.

Longo, M. C., Hunter, C. E., Lokan, R. J., White, J. M. and White, M. A. (2000). The prevalence of alcohol, cannibinoids, benzodiazepines and stimulants amongst injured drivers and their role in driver culpability. Part II: the relationship between drug prevalence and drug concentration, and driver culpability. *Accident Analysis and Prevention*, 32 (5), 623–32.

MacPhee, D. (1999). Effects of marijuana on cell nuclei: a review of the literature relating to the genotoxicity of cannabis. In *The Health Effects of Cannabis*, ed. H. Kalant, W. Corrigall, W. D. Hall and R. Smart, pp. 291–309. Toronto: Centre for Addiction and Mental Health.

Marselos, M. and Karamanakos, P. (1999). Mutagenicity, developmental toxicity and carcinogeneity of cannabis. *Addiction Biology*, 4 (1), 5–12.

Mason, A. P. and McBay, A. J. (1984). Ethanol, marijuana, and other drug use in 600 drivers killed in single-vehicle crashes in North Carolina, 1978–1981. *Journal of Forensic Sciences*, 29 (4), 987–1026.

Masur, J., Martz, R., Korte, F. and Beieniek, D. (1971). Influence of (-) delta-9-trans-tetrahydrocannabinol and mescaline on the behavior of rats submitted to food competition situations. *Psychopharmacologia*, 22, 187–94.

Maykut, M. (1984). *Health Consequences of Acute and Chronic Marihuana Use*, Oxford: Pergamon Press.

McBay, A. (1986). Drug concentrations and traffic safety. *Alcohol, Drugs and Driving*, 2, 51–59.

Mendelson, J. H., Kuehnle, J., Ellingboe, J. and Babor, T. F. (1974). Plasma testosterone levels before, during and after chronic marihuana smoking. *New England Journal of Medicine*, 291 (20), 1051–55.

Milman, D. (1982). Psychological effects of cannabis in adolescence. In *Marijuana and Youth: Clinical Observations on Motivation and Learning*, pp. 27–38. Rockville, MD: National Institute on Drug Abuse.

Mittleman, M. A., Lewis, R. A., Maclure, M., Sherwood, J. B. and Muller, J. E. (2001). Triggering myocardial infarction by marijuana. *Circulation*, 103, 2805–9.

Mishkin, E. M. and Cabral, G. A. (1985). Delta-9-Tetrahydrocannabinol decreases host resistance to herpes simplex virus type 2 vaginal infection in the B6C3F1 mouse. *Journal of General Virology*, 66 (Pt 12), 2539–49.

Morahan, P. S., Klykken, P. C., Smith, S. H., Harris, L. S. and Munson, A. E. (1979). Effects of cannabinoids on host resistance to *Listeria monocytogenes* and herpes simplex virus. *Infection and Immunity*, 23 (3), 670–74.

Munson, A. E. and Fehr, K. (1983). Immunological effects of cannabis. In *Cannabis and Health Hazards*, ed. K. Fehr and H. Kalant, pp. 257–353. Toronto: Addiction Research Foundation.

Mura, P., Kintz, P., Ludes, B., Gaulier, J. M., Marquet, P., Martin-Dupont, S., Vincent, F., Kaddour, A., Goulle, J. P., Nouveau, J., Moulsma, M., Tilhet-Coartet, S. and Pourrat, O. (2003) Comparison of the prevalence of alcohol, cannabis and other drugs between 900 injured drivers and 900 control subjects: results of a French collaborative study. *Forensic Science International*, 133, 79–85.

Murphy, L. (1999). Cannabis effects on endocrine and reproductive function. In *The Health Effects of Cannabis*, ed. H. Kalant, W. Corrigall, W. D. Hall and R. Smart, pp. 375–400. Toronto: Centre for Addiction and Mental Health.

Nahas, G. and Latour, C. (1992). The human toxicity of marijuana. *Medical Journal of Australia*, **156** (7), 495–97.

Nahas, G. G. (1984). Toxicology and pharmacology. In *Marihuana in Science and Medicine*, ed. G. G. Nahas, pp. 102–247. New York: Raven Press.

National Institute on Drug Abuse (1985). Consensus report: drug concentrations and driving impairment. *Journal of the American Medical Association*, **254** (18), 2618–21.

Newcomb, M. D. and Bentler, P. M. (1988). *Consequences of adolescent drug use: impact on the lives of young adults*, Thousand Oaks, CA: Sage.

Peck, R., Biasotti, A., Boland, P., Mallory, C. and Reeve, V. (1986). The effects of marijuana and alcohol on actual driving performance. *Alcohol, Drugs and Driving*, **2**, 135–54.

Perez-Reyes, M. (1990). Marijuana smoking: factors that influence the bioavailability of tetrahydrocannabinol. In *Research Findings on Smoking of Abused Substances*, ed. C. N. Chiang and R. Hawks, pp. 42–62. Rockville, MD: National Institute on Drug Abuse.

Plasse, T., Gorter, R., Krasnow, S., Lane, M., Shepard, K. and Wadleigh, R. (1991). Recent clinical experience with dronabinol. *Pharmacology, Biochemistry, and Behaviour*, **40**, 695–700.

Polen, M. R., Sidney, S., Tekawa, I. S., Sadler, M. and Friedman, G. D. (1993). Health care use by frequent marijuana smokers who do not smoke tobacco. *Western Journal of Medicine*, **158** (6), 596–601.

Ramaekers, J. G., Robbe, H. W. J. and O'Hanlon, J. F. (2000). Marijuana, alcohol and actual driving performance. *Human Psychopharmacology – Clinical and Experimental*, **15** (7), 551–58.

Robbe, H. W. J. (1994). *Influence of Marijuana on Driving*, Maastricht: Institute for Human Psychopharmacology, University of Limberg.

Robbe, H. W. J. and O'Hanlon, J. (1993). Marijuana's effect on actual driving: summary of a 3-year experimental program. In *Alcohol, Drugs and Traffic Safety*, Vol. 2, ed. H. Utzelmann, G. Berghaus and G. Kroj, pp. 603–11. Köln: Verlag TUV Rheinland.

Rosenkrantz, H. (1983). Cannabis, marijuana and cannabinoid toxicological manifestations in man and animals. In *Cannabis and Health Hazards*, ed. K. Fehr and H. Kalant, pp. 91–175. Toronto: Addiction Research Foundation.

Rosenkrantz, H. (1985). Cannabis components and responses of neuroendocrine-reproductive targets: an overview. In *Marihuana '84: Proceedings of the Oxford Symposium on Cannabis*, ed. D. J. Harvey, W. Paton and G. Nahas, pp. 457–505. Oxford: IRL Press.

Roth, M. D., Baldwin, G. C. and Tashkin, D. P. (2002). Effects of delta-9-tetrahydrocannabinol on human immune function and host defense. *Chemistry and Physics of Lipids*, **121** (1–2), 229–39.

Rubin, V. and Comitas, L. (1975). *Ganja in Jamaica: A Medical Anthropological Study of Chronic Marihuana Use*, The Hague: Mouton.

Sherman, M. P., Campbell, L. A., Gong, H., Roth, M. D. and Tashkin, D. P. (1991). Antimicrobial and respiratory burst characteristics of pulmonary alveolar macrophages recovered from smokers of marijuana alone, smokers of tobacco alone, smokers of marijuana and tobacco, and nonsmokers. *American Review of Respiratory Disease*, **144** (6), 1351–56.

Sherrill, D. L., Kryzanowski, J. W., Bloom, J. and Lebowitz, M. D. (1991). Respiratory effects of non-tobacco cigarettes: a longitudinal study in general population. *International Journal of Epidemiology*, **20**, 132–37.

Sidney, S. (2002). Cardiovascular consequences of marijuana use. *Journal of Clinical Pharmacology,* **42** (11 Suppl), 64S–70S.

Sidney, S., Beck, J. E., Tekawa, I. S., Quesenberry, C. P. and Friedman, G. D. (1997a). Marijuana use and mortality. *American Journal of Public Health,* **87** (4), 585–90.

Sidney, S., Quesenberry, C. P., Jr, Friedman, G. D. and Tekawa, I. S. (1997b). Marijuana use and cancer incidence (California, United States). *Cancer Causes and Control,* **8** (5), 722–28.

Siler, J., Sheep, W. and Bates, L. (1933). Marijuana smoking in Panama. *Military Surgery,* **73,** 269–80.

Simpson, H.M. (1986). Epidemiology of road accidents involving marijuana. *Alcohol, Drugs and Driving,* **2,** 15–30.

Smart, R. and Fejer, D. (1976). Drug use and driving among high school students. *Accident Analysis and Prevention,* **8,** 33–38.

Smiley, A. (1986). Marijuana: on road and driving simulator studies. *Alcohol, Drugs and Driving,* **2,** 121–34.

Smiley, A. (1999). Marijuana: on road and driving simulator studies. In *The Health Effects of Cannabis,* ed. H. Kalant, W. Corrigall, W. D. Hall and R. Smart, pp. 171–91. Toronto: Centre for Addiction and Mental Health.

Smith, D. E. (1968). Acute and chronic toxicity of marijuana. *Journal of Psychedelic Drugs,* **2,** 37–47.

Smith, M. A., Gloekler-Reiss, L. A., Gurney, J. and Ross, J. (2000). Leukemia. In *SEER Cancer Statistics Review, 1973–1997,* ed. L. Reis, M. Eisner, C. Kosary, B. Hankey, B. Miller, L. Clegg and B. Edwards, pp. 17–34. Bethesda, MD: National Cancer Institute.

Snyder, S. (1970). *Use of Marijuana,* New York: Oxford University Press.

Soderstrom, C., Triffilis, A., Chankar, B., Clark, W. and Cowley, R. (1988). Marijuana and alcohol use among 1023 trauma patients. *Archives of Surgery,* **123,** 733–37.

Solowij, N. (1998). *Cannabis and Cognitive Functioning,* Cambridge, UK: Cambridge University Press.

Sprauge, R., Rosenkrantz, H. and Braude, M. (1973). Cannabinoid effects on liver glucogen stores. *Life Sciences,* **12,** 409–16.

Stefanis, C., Dornbush, R. and Fink, M. (1977). *Hashish: Studies of Long-Term Use,* New York: Raven Press.

Tart, C. (1970). Marijuana intoxication: common experiences. *Nature,* **226,** 701–04.

Tashkin, D. P. (1988). Summary of the session on pulmonary effects. In *Marijuana: An International Research Report,* ed. G. B. Chesher, P. Consroe and R. Musty, pp. 49–52. Canberra: Australian Government Publishing Service.

Tashkin, D. P. (1999). Effects of cannabis on the respiratory system. In *The Health Effects of Cannabis,* ed. H. Kalant, W. Corrigall, W. D. Hall and R. Smart, pp. 311–45. Toronto: Centre for Addiction and Mental Health.

Tashkin, D. P., Baldwin, G. C., Sarafian, T., Dubinett, S., and Roth, M. D. (2002). Respiratory and immunologic consequences of marijuana smoking. *Journal of Clinical Pharmacology,* 42(11), 71S–81S.

Tashkin, D. P., Coulson, A. H., Clark, V. A., Simmons, M., Bourque, L., Duann, S., Spivey, G. and Gong, H. (1987). Respiratory symptoms and lung function in habitual heavy smokers of marijuana alone, smokers of marijuana and tobacco, smokers of tobacco alone, and non-smokers. *American Review of Respiratory Disease,* **135,** 209–16.

Tashkin, D. P., Fligiel, S., Wu, T., Gong, H., Barbers, R., Coulson, A., Simmons, M. and Beals, T. (1990). Effects of habitual use of marijuana and/ or cocaine on the lung. In *Research Findings on Smoking of Abused Substances*, ed. C. N. Chiang and R. Hawks, pp. 63–87. Rockville, MD: National Institute on Drug Abuse.

Taylor, D. R., Fergusson, D. M., Milne, B. J., Horwood, L. J., Moffitt, T. E., Sears, M. R. and Poulton, R. (2002). A longitudinal study of the effects of tobacco and cannabis exposure on lung function in young adults. *Addiction*, **97** (8), 1055–61.

Taylor, D. R., Poulton, R., Moffitt, T., Ramankutty, P. and Sears, M. (2000). The respiratory effects of cannabis dependence in young adults. *Addiction*, **95**, 1669–77.

Taylor, I. F. (1988). Marijuana as a potential respiratory tract carcinogen: a retrospective analysis of a community hospital population. *Southern Medical Journal*, **81** (10), 1213–16.

Tennant, F. S. (1983). Clinical toxicology of cannabis use. In *Cannabis and Health Hazards*, ed. K. Fehr and H. Kalant. Toronto: Addiction Research Foundation.

Tennant, F. S., Jr (1980). Histopathologic and clinical abnormalities of the respiratory system in chronic hashish smokers. *Substance and Alcohol Actions/ Misuse*, **1** (1), 93–100.

Tennes, K., Aritable, N., Blackard, C., Boyles, C., Hasoun, B., Holmes, L. and Kreye, M. (1985). Marihuana: prenatal and postnatal exposure in the human. In *Current Research on the Consequences of Maternal Drug Abuse*, ed. T. Pinkert, pp. 48–60. Rockville, MD: US Department of Health and Human Services.

Terhune, K. (1986). Problems and methods in studying drug crash effects. *Alcohol, Drugs and Driving*, **2**, 1–13.

Thomas, H. (1993). Psychiatric symptoms in cannabis users. *British Journal of Psychiatry*, **163**, 141–49.

Tindall, B., Cooper, D. A., Donovan, B., Barnes, T., Philpot, C. R., Gold, J. and Penny, R. (1988). The Sydney AIDS Project: development of acquired immunodeficiency syndrome in a group of HIV seropositive homosexual men. *Australian and New Zealand Journal of Medicine*, **18** (1), 8–15.

Van Hoozen, B. E. and Cross, C. E. (1997). Marijuana: respiratory tract effects. *Clinical Reviews in Allergy and Immunology*, **15** (3), 243–69.

Vokes, E. E., Weichselbaum, R. R., Lippman, S. M. and Hong, W. K. (1993). Head and neck cancer. *New England Journal of Medicine*, **328** (3), 184–94.

Walsh, G. W. and Mann, R. E. (1999). On the high road: driving under the influence of cannabis in Ontario. *Canadian Journal of Public Health*, **90** (4), 260–63.

Weil, A. T. (1970). Adverse reactions to marihuana: classification and suggested treatment. *New England Journal of Medicine*, **282** (18), 997–1000.

Williams, A., Peat, M., Crouch, D., Wells, J. and Finkle, B. (1985). Drugs in fatally injured young male drivers. *Public Health Reports*, **100**, 19–25.

Wu, T., Tashkin, D. P., Djahed, B. and Rose, E. (1988). Pulmonary hazards of smoking marijuana as compared with tobacco. *New England Journal of Medicine*, **318**, 347–51.

Yesavage, J., Leirer, V.-O., Denari, M. and Hollister, L. (1985). Carry-over effects of marijuana intoxication on aircraft pilot performance: a preliminary report. *American Journal of Psychiatry*, **142**, 1325–29.

Zhang, Z. F., Morgenstern, H., Spitz, M. R., Tashkin, D. P., Yu, G. P., Marshall, J. R., Hsu, T. C. and Schantz, S. P. (1999). Marijuana use and increased risk of squamous cell carcinoma of the head and neck. *Cancer Epidemiology Biomarkers and Prevention*, **8** (12), 1071–8.

Zimmerman, E., Yaeger, E., Soares, J., Hollister, L. and Reeve, V. (1983). Measurement of delta-9-tetrahydrocannabinol (THC) in whole blood samples from impaired motorists. *Journal of Forensic Sciences*, **28**, 957–62.

Zuckerman, B. (1985). Developmental consequences of maternal drug use during pregnancy. In *Current Research on the Consequences of Maternal Drug Abuse*, ed. T. Pinkert, pp. 96–106. Rockville, MD: US Department of Health and Human Services.

Zuckerman, B., Frank, D. A., Hingson, R., Amaro, H., Levenson, S. M., Kayne, H., Parker, S., Vinci, R., Aboagye, K., Fried, L. E. and et al. (1989). Effects of maternal marijuana and cocaine use on fetal growth. *New England Journal of Medicine*, **320** (12), 762–8.

Section 3: The psychological effects of chronic cannabis use

Aceto, M., Scates, S., Lowe, A. and Martin, B. (1996). Dependence studies on delta-9-tetrahydrocannabinol: studies on precipitated and abrupt withdrawal. *Journal of Pharmacology and Experimental Therapeutics*, **278**, 1290–95.

Adams, I. B. and Martin, B. R. (1996). Cannabis: pharmacology and toxicology in animals and humans. *Addiction*, **91** (11), 1585–614.

Agarwal, A., Sethi, B. and Gupta, S. (1975). Physical and cognitive effects of chronic bhang (cannabis) intake. *Indian Journal of Psychiatry*, **17**, 1–17.

Allebeck, P. (1991). Cannabis and schizophrenia: is there a causal association? In *Physiopathology of Illicit Drugs: Cannabis, Cocaine, Opiates*, ed. G. G. Nahas and C. Latour, pp. 23–31. Oxford: Pergamon Press.

American Psychiatric Association (1994). *Diagnostic and Statistical Manual of Mental Disorders*, 4th edn. Washington, DC: American Psychiatric Association.

Andreasson, S., Allebeck, P. and Rydberg, U. (1989). Schizophrenia in users and nonusers of cannabis: a longitudinal study in Stockholm County. *Acta Psychiatrica Scandinavica*, **79** (5), 505–10.

Andreasson, S., Engstrom, A., Allebeck, P. and Rydberg, U. (1987). Cannabis and schizophrenia: a longitudinal study of Swedish conscripts. *Lancet*, **2** (8574), 1483–86.

Anthony, J. C. and Helzer, J. E. (1991). Syndromes of drug abuse and dependence. In *Psychiatric Disorders in America: The Epidemiologic Catchment Area*, ed. L. N. Robins and D. A. Regier, pp. 116–54. New York: Free Press.

Anthony, J. C., Warner, L. and Kessler, R. (1994). Comparative epidemiology of dependence on tobacco, alcohol, controlled substances and inhalants: basic findings from the National Comorbidity Survey. *Experimental and Clinical Psychopharmacology*, **2** (3), 244–68.

Arndt, S., Tyrrell, G., Flaum, M. and Andreasen, N. C. (1992). Comorbidity of substance abuse and schizophrenia: the role of premorbid adjustment. *Psychological Medicine*, **22** (2), 379–88.

Arseneault, L., Cannon, M., Poulton, R., Murray, R., Caspi, A. and Moffitt, T. E. (2002). Cannabis use in adolescence and risk for adult psychosis: longitudinal prospective study. *British Medical Journal*, **325** (7374), 1212–13.

Bachman, J. G., Wadsworth, K. N., O'Malley, P. M., Johnston, L. D. and Schulenberg, J. (1997). *Smoking, drinking, and drug use in young adulthood: the impacts of new freedoms and new responsibilities*, Mahwah, NJ: Lawrence Erlbaum.

Bell, D. S. (1973). The experimental reproduction of amphetamine psychosis. *Archives of General Psychiatry,* **29** (1), 35–40.

Bernhardson, G. and Gunne, L. M. (1972). Forty-six cases of psychosis in cannabis abusers. *International Journal of the Addictions,* **7** (1), 9–16.

Blanchard, J. J., Brown, S. A., Horan, W. P. and Sherwood, A. R. (2000). Substance use disorders in schizophrenia: review, integration, and a proposed model. *Clinical Psychology Review,* **20** (2), 207–34.

Bland, R. C., Newman, S. C. and Orn, H. (1987). Schizophrenia: lifetime comorbidity in a community sample. *Acta Psychiatrica Scandinavica,* **75** (4), 383–91.

Block, R. I. (1996). Does heavy marijuana use impair human cognition and brain function? *Journal of the American Medical Association,* **275** (7), 560–61.

Block, R. I., Farnham, S., Braverman, K., Noyes, R. and Ghoneim, M. M. (1990). Long-term marijuana use and subsequent effects on learning and cognitive functions related to school achievement: preliminary study. *NIDA Research Monograph,* **101**, 96–111.

Block, R. I., O'Leary, D. S., Ehrhardt, J. C., Augustinack, J. C., Ghoneim, M. M., Arndt, S. and Hall, J. A. (2000a). Effects of frequent marijuana use on brain tissue volume and composition. *Neuroreport,* **11** (3), 491–96.

Block, R. I., O'Leary, D. S., Hichwa, R. D., Augustinack, J. C., Ponto, L. L. B., Ghoneim, M. M., Arndt, S., Ehrhardt, J. C., Hurtig, R. R., Watkins, G. L., Hall, J. A., Nathan, P. E. and Andreasen, N. C. (2000b). Cerebellar hypoactivity in frequent marijuana users. *Neuroreport,* **11** (4), 749–53.

Bolla, K. I., Brown, K., Eldreth, D., Tate, K. and Cadet, J. L. (2002). Dose-related neurocognitive effects of marijuana use. *Neurology,* **59** (9), 1337–43.

Bowers, M. B., Mazure, C. M., Nelson, J. C. and Jatlow, P. I. (1990). Psychotogenic drug use and neuroleptic response. *Schizophrenia Bulletin,* **16** (1), 81–85.

Bowie, P., Branton, T. and Holmes, J. (1999). Should the Mini Mental State Examination be used to monitor dementia treatments? *Lancet,* **354** (9189), 1527–28.

Bowman, M. and Pihl, R. O. (1973). Cannabis: psychological effects of chronic heavy use. A controlled study of intellectual functioning in chronic users of high potency cannabis. *Psychopharmacologia,* **29** (2), 159–70.

Brill, H. and Nahas, G. G. (1984). Cannabis intoxication and mental illness. In *Marihuana in Science and Medicine,* ed. G. G. Nahas, pp. 263–305. New York: Raven Press.

Bromet, E. J., Dew, M. A. and Eaton, W. (1995). Epidemiology of psychosis with special reference to schizophrenia. In *Textbook of Psychiatric Epidemiology,* ed. M. T. Tsuang, M. Tohen and G. E. P. Zahner, pp. 283–300. New York: Wiley-Liss.

Brook, J. S., Cohen, P., Whiteman, M. and Gordon, A. S. (1992). Psychosocial risk factors in the transition from moderate to heavy use or abuse of drugs. In *Vulnerability to Drug Abuse,* ed. M. D. Glantz, pp. 359–88. Washington, DC: American Psychological Association.

Budney, A. J., Higgins, S. T., Radonovich, K. J. and Novy, P. L. (2000). Adding voucher-based incentives to coping skills and motivational enhancement improves outcomes during treatment for marijuana dependence. *Journal of Consulting and Clinical Psychology,* **68** (6), 1051–61.

Budney, A. J., Hughes, J. R., Moore, B. A. and Novy, P. L. (2001). Marijuana abstinence effects in marijuana smokers maintained in their home environment. *Archives of General Psychiatry,* **58** (10), 917–24.

Budney, A. J. and Moore, B. A. (2002). Development and consequences of cannabis dependence. *Journal of Clinical Pharmacology,* **42** (11), 28S–33S.

Budney, A. J., Radonovich, K. J., Higgins, S. T. and Wong, C. J. (1998). Adults seeking treatment for marijuana dependence: a comparison with cocaine-dependent treatment seekers. *Experimental and Clinical Psychopharmacology,* **6** (4), 419–26.

Campbell, I. (1976). The amotivational syndrome and cannabis use with emphasis on the Canadian scene. *Annals of the New York Academy of Sciences,* **282**, 33–36.

Carlin, A. S. (1986). Neuropsychological consequences of drug abuse. In *Neuropsychological Assessment of Neuropsychiatric Disorders*, ed. I. Grant and K. M. Adams, pp. 478–97. New York: Oxford University Press.

Carney, M., Bacelle, L. and Robinson, B. (1984). Psychosis after cannabis use. *British Medical Journal,* **288**, 1047.

Carter, W. E. (1980). *Cannabis in Costa Rica: A Study of Chronic Marihuana Use,* Philadelphia: Institute for the Study of Human Issues.

Childers, S. R. and Breivogel, C. S. (1998). Cannabis and endogenous cannabinoid systems. *Drug and Alcohol Dependence,* **51** (1–2), 173–87.

Chopra, G. S. and Smith, J. W. (1974). Psychotic reactions following cannabis use in East Indians. *Archives of General Psychiatry,* **30**, 24–27.

Cleghorn, J. M., Kaplan, R. D., Szechtman, B., Szechtman, H., Brown, G. M. and Franco, S. (1991). Substance abuse and schizophrenia: effect on symptoms but not on neurocognitive function. *Journal of Clinical Psychiatry,* **52** (1), 26–30.

Cohen, S. (1976). The 94-day cannabis study. *Annals of the New York Academy of Sciences,* **282**, 211–110.

Cohen, S. (1986). Marijuana research: selected recent findings. *Drug Abuse and Alcoholism Newsletter,* **15**, 1–3.

Compton, D. R., Dewey, W. L. and Martin, B. R. (1990). Cannabis dependence and tolerance production. *Advances in Alcohol and Substance Abuse,* **9** (1–2), 129–47.

Cook, S. A., Lowe, J. A. and Martin, B. R. (1998). CB1 receptor antagonist precipitates withdrawal in mice exposed to delta9-tetrahydrocannabinol. *Journal of Pharmacology and Experimental Therapeutics,* **285** (3), 1150–56.

Copeland, J. and Conroy, A. (2001). Australian National Minimum Data Set for Clients of Alcohol and Other Drug Treatment Services: findings of the national pilot and developments in implementation. *Drug and Alcohol Review,* **20** (3), 295–98.

Copeland, J., Swift, W. and Rees, V. (2001a). Clinical profile of participants in a brief intervention program for cannabis use disorder. *Journal of Substance Abuse Treatment,* **20** (1), 45–52.

Copeland, J., Swift, W., Roffman, R. and Stephens, R. (2001b). A randomized controlled trial of brief cognitive-behavioral interventions for cannabis use disorder. *Journal of Substance Abuse Treatment,* **21** (2), 55–64.

Crowley, T. J., Macdonald, M. J., Whitmore, E. A. and Mikulich, S. K. (1998). Cannabis dependence, withdrawal, and reinforcing effects among adolescents with conduct symptoms and substance use disorders. *Drug and Alcohol Dependence,* **50** (1), 27–37.

Cuffel, B. J., Heithoff, K. A. and Lawson, W. (1993). Correlates of patterns of substance abuse among patients with schizophrenia. *Hospital and Community Psychiatry,* **44** (3), 247–51.

Degenhardt, L. and Hall, W. D. (2001). The association between psychosis and problematical drug use among Australian adults: findings from the National Survey of Mental Health and Wellbeing. *Psychological Medicine,* **31** (4), 659–68.

Dennis, M., Babor, T. F., Roebuck, M. C. and Donaldson, J. (2002). Changing the focus: the case for recognizing and treating cannabis use disorders. *Addiction, 97*, 4–15.

Der, G., Gupta, S. and Murray, R. M. (1990). Is schizophrenia disappearing? *Lancet, 335* (8688), 513–16.

Dixon, L., Haas, G., Weiden, P., Sweeney, J. and et al. (1990). Acute effects of drug abuse in schizophrenic patients: clinical observations and patients' self-reports. *Schizophrenia Bulletin, 16* (1), 69–79.

Donnelly, N. and Hall, W. D. (1994). *Patterns of Cannabis Use in Australia,* Canberra: Australian Government Publishing Service.

Dornbush, R. L. (1972). 21-day administration of marijuana in male volunteers. In *Current Research in Marijuana,* ed. M. F. Lewis, pp. 115–28. Oxford, UK: Academic Press.

Edwards, G., Arif, A. and Hadgson, R. (1981). Nomenclature and classification of drug- and alcohol-related problems: a WHO Memorandum. *Bulletin of the World Health Organization, 59* (2), 225–42.

Edwards, G. and Gross, M. M. (1976). Alcohol dependence: provisional description of a clinical syndrome. *British Medical Journal, 1* (6017), 1058–61.

European Monitoring Centre for Drugs and Drug Addiction (1998). *Annual Report on the State of the Drugs Problem in the European Union, 1998,* Lisbon: European Monitoring Centre for Drugs and Drug Addiction.

Eva, J. (1992). Cannabis psychosis. *Psychiatric Bulletin, 16*, 310–11.

Fergusson, D. M., Horwood, J. L. and Swain-Campbell, N. R. (2003). Cannabis dependence and psychotic symptoms in young people. *Psychological Medicine, 33*, 15–21.

Fletcher, J. M., Page, J. B., Francis, D. J., Copeland, K., Naus, M. J., Davis, C. M., Morris, R., Krauskopf, D. and Satz, P. (1996). Cognitive correlates of long-term cannabis use in Costa Rican men. *Archives of General Psychiatry, 53* (11), 1051–57.

Frank, I., Lessin, P., Tyrell, E., Hahn, P. and Szara, S. (1976). Acute and cumulative effects of marihuana smoking in hospitalised subjects: a 36 day study. In *The Pharmacology of Marihuana,* Vol. 2, ed. M. Braude and S. Szara, pp. 673–80. New York: Raven Press.

Fried, P. A., Watkinson, B., James, D. and Gray, F. (2002). Current and former marijuana use: preliminary findings of a longitudinal study of effects on IQ in young adults. *Canadian Medical Association Journal, 166* (7), 887–91.

Georgotas, A. and Zeidenberg, P. (1979). Observations on the effects of four weeks of heavy marihuana smoking on group interaction and individual behavior. *Comprehensive Psychiatry, 20* (5), 427–32.

Ghodse, A. H. (1986). Cannabis psychosis. *British Journal of Addiction, 81* (4), 473–78.

Gonzales, R., Carey, C. and Grant, I. (2002). Nonacute (residual) neuropsychological effects of cannabis use: a qualitative analysis and systematic review. *Journal of Clinical Pharmacology, 42*, 48S–57S.

Gottesman, I. I. (1991). *Schizophrenia Genesis: The Origins of Madness,* New York: W. H. Freeman.

Gruber, A. J. and Pope, H. G. (1994). Cannabis psychotic disorder: does it exist? *American Journal on Addictions, 3* (1), 72–83.

Halikas, J. A., Weller, R. A., Morse, C. and Shapiro, T. (1982). Incidence and characteristics of amotivational syndrome, including associated findings, among chronic marijuana users. In *Marijuana and Youth: Clinical Observations on Motivation and Learning,* pp. 11–26. Rockville, MD: National Institute on Drug Abuse.

Hall, W. D. (1987). A simplified logic of causal inference. *Australian and New Zealand Journal of Psychiatry*, **21** (4), 507–13.

Hall, W. D. (1998). Cannabis use and psychosis. *Drug and Alcohol Review*, **17** (4), 433–44.

Hall, W. D., Solowij, N. and Lemon, J. (1994). *The Health and Psychological Consequences of Cannabis Use*, National Drug Strategy Monograph, Vol. 25, Canberra: Australian Government Publishing Service.

Hall, W. D., Teesson, M., Lynskey, M. and Degenhardt, L. (1998). *The Prevalence in the Past Year of Substance Use and ICD-10 Substance Use Disorders in Australian Adults: Findings from the National Survey of Mental Health and Wellbeing*, NDARC Technical Report, Vol. 63, Sydney: National Drug and Alcohol Research Centre, University of New South Wales.

Hall, W. D., Teesson, M., Lynskey, M. and Degenhardt, L. (1999). The 12-month prevalence of substance use and ICD-10 substance use disorders in Australian adults: Findings from the National Survey of Mental Health and Wellbeing. *Addiction*, **94** (10), 1541–50.

Hambrecht, M. and Hafner, H. (1996). Substance abuse and the onset of schizophrenia. *Biological Psychiatry*, **40** (11), 1155–63.

Hamera, E., Schneider, J. K. and Deviney, S. (1995). Alcohol, cannabis, nicotine and caffeine use and symptom distress in schizophrenia. *Journal of Nervous and Mental Disease*, **183** (9), 559–65.

Haney, M., Ward, A. S., Comer, S. D., Foltin, R. W. and Fischman, M. W. (1999a). Abstinence symptoms following oral THC administration to humans. *Psychopharmacology*, **141** (4), 385–94.

Haney, M., Ward, A. S., Comer, S. D., Foltin, R. W. and Fischman, M. W. (1999b). Abstinence symptoms following smoked marijuana in humans. *Psychopharmacology*, **141** (4), 395–404.

Harding, T. and Knight, F. (1973). Marihuana-modified mania. *Archives of General Psychiatry*, **29** (5), 635–37.

Harshman, R., Crawford, H. and Hecht, E. (1976). Marihuana, cognitive style, and lateralised hemisphere. In *The Therapeutic Potential of Marihuana*, ed. S. Cohen and R. Stillman, pp. 205–54. New York: Plenum Press.

Heather, N. and Tebbutt, J. (1989). *An Overview of the Effectiveness of Treatment for Drug and Alcohol Problems*, NCADA Monograph, Vol. 11, Canberra: Australian Government Publishing Service.

Helzer, J. E., Burnham, A. and McEvoy, L. (1991). Alcohol abuse and dependence. In *Psychiatric Disorders in America*, ed. L. Robins and D. Regier, pp. 81–115. New York: Free Press, Macmillan.

Hwu, H. G. and Compton, W. M. (1994). Comparison of major epidemiological surveys using the Diagnostic Interview Schedule. *International Review of Psychiatry*, **6** (4), 309–27.

Imade, A. T. and Ebie, J. C. (1991). A retrospective study of symptom patterns of cannabis-induced psychosis. *Acta Psychiatrica Scandinavica*, **83** (2), 134–36.

Inghe, G. (1969). The present state of abuse and addiction to stimulant drugs in Sweden. In *Abuse of Central Stimulants*, ed. F. Sjoqvist and M. Tottie, pp. 19–27. New York: Raven Press.

Jablensky, A. (1999). Schizophrenia: epidemiology. *Current Opinion in Psychiatry*, **12** (1), 19–28.

Jablensky, A., Sartorius, N. and Ernberg, G. (1992). Schizophrenia: manifestations, incidence and course in different cultures, a World Health Organization 10-country study. *Psychological Medicine Monograph*, **Supplement**, 20.

Jerrell, J. M. and Ridgely, M. S. (1995). Comparative effectiveness of three approaches to serving people with severe mental illness and substance abuse disorders. *Journal of Nervous and Mental Disease*, **183** (9), 566–76.

Jones, R. T., Benowitz, N. and Herning, R. (1976). The 30-day trip: clinical studies of cannabis use tolerance and dependence. In *The Pharmacology of Marijuana*, Vol. 2, ed. M. Braude and S. Szara, pp. 627–42. New York: Academic Press.

Jones, R. T., Benowitz, N. and Herning, R. (1981). The clinical relevance of cannabis tolerance and dependence. *Journal of Clinical Pharmacology*, **21** (8–9 Supplement), 143S–52S.

Joyce, P. R. (1987). Changing trends in first admissions and readmissions for mania and schizophrenia in New Zealand, 1974 to 1984. *Australian and New Zealand Journal of Psychiatry*, **21** (1), 82–86.

Kandel, D. and Faust, R. (1975). Sequence and stages in patterns of adolescent drug use. *Archives of General Psychiatry*, **32** (7), 923–32.

Kandel, D. B. and Davies, M. (1992). Progression to regular marijuana involvement: phenomenology and risk factors for near-daily use. In *Vulnerability to Drug Abuse*, ed. M. D. Glantz, pp. 211–53. Washington, DC: American Psychological Association.

Kavanagh, D. J. (1995). An intervention for substance abuse in schizophrenia. *Behaviour Change*, **12** (1), 20–30.

Kendell, R. E., Malcolm, D. E. and Adams, W. (1993). The problem of detecting changes in the incidence of schizophrenia. *British Journal of Psychiatry*, **162**, 212–18.

Kokkevi, A. and Dornbush, R. (1977). Psychological test characteristics of long term hashish users. In *Hashish: Studies of Long-Term Use*, ed. C. Stefanis, R. Dornbush and M. Fink, pp. 43–47. New York: Raven Press.

Kolansky, H. and Moore, W. T. (1971). Effects of marihuana on adolescents and young adults. *Journal of the American Medical Association*, **216** (3), 486–92.

Kouri, E. M. and Pope, H. G. (2000). Abstinence symptoms during withdrawal from chronic marijuana use. *Experimental and Clinical Psychopharmacology*, **8** (4), 483–92.

Kovasznay, B., Bromet, E., Schwartz, J. E., Ram, R., Lavelle, J. and Brandon, L. (1993). Substance abuse and onset of psychotic illness. *Hospital and Community Psychiatry*, **44** (6), 567–71.

Leavitt, J., Webb, P., Norris, G., Struve, F., Straumanis, J., Fitz-Gerald, J., Nixon, F., Patrick, G. and Manno, J. (1993). Performance of chronic daily marijuana users on neuropsychological tests. In *Problems of Drug Dependence 1992*, ed. L. S. Harris, pp. 179. Washington, DC: US Government Printing Office.

Leavitt, J., Webb, P., Norris, G., Struve, F., Straumanis, J., Patrick, G., Fitz-Gerald, J. and Nixon, F. (1992). Differences in complex reaction time between THC users and non-user controls. In *Problems of Drug Dependence 1991*, ed. L. S. Harris, pp. 452. Washington, DC: U.S. Government Printing Office.

Lehman, A. F., Herron, J. D., Schwartz, R. P. and Myers, C. P. (1993). Rehabilitation for adults with severe mental illness and substance use disorders: a clinical trial. *Journal of Nervous and Mental Disease*, **181** (2), 86–90.

Linszen, D. H., Dingemans, P. M. and Lenior, M. E. (1994). Cannabis abuse and the course of recent-onset schizophrenic disorders. *Archives of General Psychiatry*, **51** (4), 273–79.

Lyketsos, C. G., Garrett, E., Liang, K. Y. and Anthony, J. C. (1999). Cannabis use and cognitive decline in persons under 65 years of age. *American Journal of Epidemiology*, **149** (9), 794–800.

Maldonado, R. (2002). Study of cannabinoid dependence in animals. *Pharmacology and Therapeutics*, **95**, 153–64.

Martinez-Arevalo, M. J., Calcedo-Ordonez, A. and Varo-Prieto, J. R. (1994). Cannabis consumption as a prognostic factor in schizophrenia. *British Journal of Psychiatry*, **164**, 679–81.

McGlothlin, W. H. and West, L. J. (1968). The marihuana problem: an overview. *American Journal of Psychiatry*, **125** (3), 370–78.

McGuire, P. K., Jones, P., Harvey, I., Bebbington, P., Toone, B., Lewis, S. and Murray, R. M. (1994). Cannabis and acute psychosis. *Schizophrenia Research,* **13** (2), 161–67.

McGuire, P. K., Jones, P., Harvey, I., Williams, M., McGuffin, P. and Murray, R. M. (1995). Morbid risk of schizophrenia for relatives of patients with cannabis-associated psychosis. *Schizophrenia Research,* **15** (3), 277–81.

Mendelson, J., Rossi, M. and Meyer, R. (1974). *The Use of Marihuana: A Psychological and Physiological Inquiry,* New York: Plenum.

Miller, L. L. and Branconnier, R. J. (1983). Cannabis: effects on memory and the cholinergic limbic system. *Psychological Bulletin,* **93** (3), 441–56.

Miller, W. and Hester, R. (1986). The effectiveness of alcoholism treatment: what research reveals. In *Treating Addictive Behaviors: Processes of Change*, ed. W. Miller and N. Heather, pp. 121–74. New York: Plenum Press.

Moore, H., West, A. R. and Grace, A. A. (1999). The regulation of forebrain dopamine transmission: relevance to the pathophysiology and psychopathology of schizophrenia. *Biological Psychiatry,* **46** (1), 40–55.

Mueser, K. T., Bellack, A. S. and Blanchard, J. J. (1992). Comorbidity of schizophrenia and substance abuse: implications for treatment. *Journal of Consulting and Clinical Psychology,* **60** (6), 845–56.

Negrete, J. C. (1989). Cannabis and schizophrenia. *British Journal of Addiction,* **84** (4), 349–51.

Negrete, J. C., Knapp, W. P., Douglas, D. E. and Smith, W. B. (1986). Cannabis affects the severity of schizophrenic symptoms: results of a clinical survey. *Psychological Medicine,* **16** (3), 515–20.

Newcomb, M. D. (1992). Understanding the multidimensional nature of drug use and abuse: the role of consumption, risk factors, and protective factors. In *Vulnerability to Drug Abuse*, ed. M. D. Glantz, pp. 255–97. Washington, DC: American Psychological Association.

Noordsy, D. L., Drake, R. E., Teague, G. B., Osher, F. C., Hulbut, S., Beaudett, M. and Paskus, T. (1991). Subjective experiences related to alcohol use among schizophrenics. *Journal of Nervous and Mental Disease,* **179** (7), 410–14.

Nunez, L. A. and Gurpegui, M. (2002). Cannabis-induced psychosis: a cross-sectional comparison with acute schizophrenia. *Acta Psychiatrica Scandinavica,* **105** (3), 173–78.

Page, J. B., Fletcher, J. and True, W. R. (1988). Psychosociocultural perspectives on chronic cannabis use – the Costa Rican follow-up. *Journal of Psychoactive Drugs,* **20** (1), 57–65.

Peralta, V. and Cuesta, M. J. (1992). Influence of cannabis abuse on schizophrenic psychopathology. *Acta Psychiatrica Scandinavica,* **85** (2), 127–30.

Phillips, L. J., Curry, C., Yung, A. R., Yuen, H. P., Adlard, S. and McGorry, P. D. (2002). Cannabis use is not associated with the development of psychosis in an 'ultra' high-risk group. *Australian and New Zealand Journal of Psychiatry,* **36**, 800–06.

Poole, R. and Brabbins, G. (1996). Drug induced psychosis. *British Journal of Psychiatry,* **168** (2), 135–38.

Pope, H. G. (2002). Cannabis, cognition, and residual confounding. *Journal of the American Medical Association,* **287** (9), 1172–74.

Pope, H. G., Gruber, A. J., Hudson, J. I., Huestis, M. A. and Yurgelun-Todd, D. (2001). Neuropsychological performance in long-term cannabis users. *Archives of General Psychiatry,* **58** (10), 909–15.

Pope, H. G., Gruber, A. J. and Yurgelun-Todd, D. (1995). The residual neuropsychological effects of cannabis: the current status of research. *Drug and Alcohol Dependence,* **38** (1), 25–34.

Pope, H. G. and Yurgelun-Todd, D. (1996). The residual cognitive effects of heavy marijuana use in college students. *Journal of the American Medical Association*, **275** (7), 521–27.

Regier, D. A., Farmer, M. E., Rae, D. S., Locke, B. Z., Keith, S. J., Judd, L. L. and Goodwin, F. K. (1990). Comorbidity of mental disorders with alcohol and other drug abuse: results from the Epidemiologic Catchment Area (ECA) Study. *Journal of the American Medical Association*, **264** (19), 2511–18.

Robins, L. N. and Reiger, D. A. (eds.) (1991). *Psychiatric Disorders in America: The Epidemiological Catchment Area Study*, New York: The Free Press.

Roffman, R. A., Stephens, R. S., Simpson, E. E. and Whitaker, D. L. (1988). Treatment of marijuana dependence: preliminary results. *Journal of Psychoactive Drugs*, **20** (1), 129–37.

Rottanburg, D., Robins, A. H., Ben-Arie, O., Teggin, A. and Elk, R. (1982). Cannabis-associated psychosis with hypomanic features. *Lancet*, **2** (8312), 1364–6.

Rubin, V. and Comitas, L. (1975). *Ganja in Jamaica: A Medical Anthropological Study of Chronic Marihuana Use*, The Hague: Mouton.

Russell, J. M., Newman, S. C. and Bland, R. C. (1994). Drug abuse and dependence. *Acta Psychiatrica Scandinavica*, **89**, 54–62.

Satz, P., Fletcher, J. and Sutker, L. (1976). Neuropsychologic, intellectual and personality correlates of chronic marijuana use in native Costa Ricans. *Annals of the New York Academy of Sciences*, **282**, 266–306.

Schneier, F. R. and Siris, S. G. (1987). A review of psychoactive substance use and abuse in schizophrenia: patterns of drug choice. *Journal of Nervous and Mental Disease*, **175** (11), 641–52.

Shedler, J. and Block, J. (1990). Adolescent drug use and psychological health: a longitudinal inquiry. *American Psychologist*, **45** (5), 612–30.

Smith, J. and Hucker, S. (1994). Schizophrenia and substance abuse. *British Journal of Psychiatry*, **165**, 13–21.

Smith, N. T. (2002). A review of the published literature into cannabis withdrawal symptoms in human users. *Addiction*, **97** (6), 621–32.

Solomons, K., Neppe, V. M. and Kuyl, J. M. (1990). Toxic cannabis psychosis is a valid entity. *South African Medical Journal*, **78** (8), 476–81.

Solowij, N. (1995). Do cognitive impairments recover following cessation of cannabis use? *Life Sciences*, **56** (23–24), 2119–26.

Solowij, N. (1998). *Cannabis and Cognitive Functioning*, Cambridge: Cambridge University Press.

Solowij, N. (1999). Long-term effects of cannabis on the central nervous system. I. Brain function and neurotoxicity. II. Cognitive functioning. In *The Health Effects of Cannabis*, ed. H. Kalant, W. Corrigal, W. Hall and R. Smart, pp. 195–265. Toronto: Centre for Addiction and Mental Health.

Solowij, N., Michie, P. T. and Fox, A. M. (1991). Effects of long-term cannabis use on selective attention: an event-related potential study. *Pharmacology Biochemistry and Behavior*, **40** (3), 683–88.

Solowij, N., Michie, P. T. and Fox, A. M. (1995). Differential impairments of selective attention due to frequency and duration of cannabis use. *Biological Psychiatry*, **37** (10), 731–39.

Solowij, N., Stephens, R. S., Roffman, R. A., Babor, T., Kadden, R., Miller, M., Christiansen, K., McRee, B. and Vendetti, J. (2002). Cognitive functioning of long-term heavy cannabis users seeking treatment. *Journal of the American Medical Association*, **287** (9), 1123–31.

Soueif, M. I. (1971). The use of cannabis in Egypt: a behavioural study. *Bulletin on Narcotics*, **23** (4), 17–28.

Stahl, S. M. and Muntner, N. (1996). *Essential Psychopharmacology: Neuroscientific Basis and Clinical Applications*, Cambridge: Cambridge University Press.

Stephens, R. S., Babor, T. F., Kadden, R. and Miller, M. (2002). The Marijuana Treatment Project: rationale, design and participant characteristics. *Addiction*, **97**, 109–24.

Stephens, R. S., Roffman, R. A. and Curtin, L. (2000). Comparison of extended versus brief treatments for marijuana use. *Journal of Consulting and Clinical Psychology*, **68** (5), 898–908.

Stephens, R. S., Roffman, R. A. and Simpson, E. E. (1993). Adult marijuana users seeking treatment. *Journal of Consulting and Clinical Psychology*, **61** (6), 1100–04.

Stephens, R. S., Roffman, R. A. and Simpson, E. E. (1994). Treating adult marijuana dependence – a test of the relapse prevention model. *Journal of Consulting and Clinical Psychology*, **62** (1), 92–99.

Swift, W., Hall, W. D. and Copeland, J. (1998a). Characteristics of long-term cannabis users in Sydney, Australia. *European Addiction Research*, **4** (4), 190–97.

Swift, W., Hall, W. D. and Copeland, J. (2000). One year follow-up of cannabis dependence among long-term users in Sydney, Australia. *Drug and Alcohol Dependence*, **59** (3), 309–18.

Swift, W., Hall, W. D., Didcott, P. and Reilly, D. (1998b). Patterns and correlates of cannabis dependence among long-term users in an Australian rural area. *Addiction*, **93** (8), 1149–60.

Swift, W., Hall, W. D. and Teesson, C. (2001). Characteristics of DSM-IV and ICD-10 cannabis dependence among Australian adults: results from the National Survey of Mental Health and Wellbeing. *Drug and Alcohol Dependence*, **63** (2), 147–53.

Tanda, G., Pontieri, F. E. and Di Chiara, G. (1997). Cannabinoid and heroin activation of mesolimbic dopamine transmission by a common mu1 opioid receptor mechanism. *Science*, **276** (5321), 2048–50.

Thacore, V. R. and Shukla, S. R. (1976). Cannabis psychosis and paranoid schizophrenia. *Archives of General Psychiatry*, **33** (3), 383–86.

Thomas, H. (1996). A community survey of adverse effects of cannabis use. *Drug and Alcohol Dependence*, **42** (3), 201–07.

Thornicroft, G. (1990). Cannabis and psychosis: is there epidemiological evidence for association? *British Journal of Psychiatry*, **157**, 25–33.

Tien, A. Y. and Anthony, J. C. (1990). Epidemiological analysis of alcohol and drug use as risk factors for psychotic experiences. *Journal of Nervous and Mental Disease*, **178** (8), 473–80.

Tims, F. M., Dennis, M. L., Hamilton, N., Buchan, B. J., Diamond, G., Funk, R. and Brantley, L. B. (2002). Characteristics and problems of 600 adolescent cannabis abusers in outpatient treatment. *Addiction*, **97**, 46–57.

Torres, M., Mattick, R., Chen, R. and Baillie, A. (1995). *Clients of Treatment Service Agencies: March 1995 Census Findings*, Canberra: Commonwealth Department of Human Services and Health.

Turner, W. M. and Tsuang, M. T. (1990). Impact of substance abuse on the course and outcome of schizophrenia. *Schizophrenia Bulletin*, **16** (1), 87–95.

United States Office of National Drug Control Policy (1998). *Pulse Check: National Trends in Drug Abuse. Winter 1998*, Washington, DC: Office of National Drug Control Policy.

van Os, J., Bak, M., Hanssen, M., Bijl, R.V., de Graaf, R. and Verdoux, H. (2002). Cannabis use and psychosis: a longitudinal population-based study. *American Journal of Epidemiology*, **156** (4), 319–27.

Verdoux, H., Gindre, C., Sorbara, F., Tournier, M. and Swendsen, J. (2002). Cannabis use and the expression of psychosis vulnerability in daily life. *European Psychiatry*, **17**, 180S–80S.

Warner, R., Taylor, D., Wright, J., Sloat, A., Springett, G., Arnold, S. and Weinberg, H. (1994). Substance use among the mentally ill: prevalence, reasons for use, and effects on illness. *American Journal of Orthopsychiatry*, **64** (1), 30–39.

Webster, P., Mattick, R. and Baillie, A. (1992). Characteristics of clients receiving treatment in Australian drug and alcohol agencies: a national census. *Drug and Alcohol Review*, 11, 111–19.

Weil, A. T. (1970). Adverse reactions to marihuana: classification and suggested treatment. *New England Journal of Medicine*, **282** (18), 997–1000.

Wells, J., Bushnell, J., Joyce, P. R., Oakley-Browne, M. and Hornblow, A. (1992). Problems with alcohol, drugs and gambling in Christchurch, New Zealand. In *Alcohol and Drug Dependence and Disorders of Impulse Control*, ed. M. Abbot and K. Evans, pp. 3–13. Auckland: Alcohol Liquor Advisory Council.

Wert, R. C. and Raulin, M. L. (1986). The chronic cerebral effects of cannabis use 1: methodological issues and neurological findings. *International Journal of the Addictions*, 21 (6), 605–28.

Wiesbeck, G. A., Schuckit, M. A., Kalmijn, J. A., Tipp, J. E., Bucholz, K. K. and Smith, T. L. (1996). An evaluation of the history of a marijuana withdrawal syndrome in a large population. *Addiction*, **91** (10), 1469–78.

Wig, N. N. and Varma, V. K. (1977). Patterns of long-term heavy cannabis use in North India and its effects on cognitive functions: a preliminary report. *Drug and Alcohol Dependence*, 2 (3), 211–19.

Wylie, A. S., Scott, R. T. A. and Burnett, S. J. (1995). Psychosis due to 'skunk'. *British Medical Journal*, 311 (6997), 125–25.

Zammit, S., Allebeck, P., Andreasson, S., Lundberg, I. and Lewis, G. (2002). Self reported cannabis use as a risk factor for schizophrenia in Swedish conscripts of 1969: historical cohort study. *British Medical Journal*, 325 (7374), 1199–201.

Zisook, S., Heaton, R., Moranville, J., Kuck, J., Jernigan, T. and Braff, D. (1992). Past substance abuse and clinical course of schizophrenia. *American Journal of Psychiatry*, 149 (4), 552–53.

Section 4: Effects on adolescent development

Allebeck, P. and Allgulander, C. (1990). Psychiatric diagnoses as predictors of suicide: a comparison of diagnosis at conscription and in psychiatric care in a cohort of 50,465 young men. *British Journal of Psychiatry*, 157, 339–44.

Andreasson, S. and Allebeck, P. (1990). Cannabis and mortality among young men: a longitudinal study of Swedish conscripts. *Scandinavian Journal of Social Medicine*, 18, 9–15.

Angst, J. (1996). Comorbidity of mood disorders: a longitudinal prospective study. *British Journal of Psychiatry*, 168, 31–37.

Arseneault, L., Moffitt, T. E., Caspi, A., Taylor, P. J. and Silva, P. A. (2000). Mental disorders and violence in total birth cohort: results from the Dunedin study. *Archives of General Psychiatry*, 57, 979–86.

Bailey, S. L., Flewelling, R. L. and Rachal, J. V. (1992). Predicting continued use of marijuana among adolescents: the relative influence of drug-specific and social context factors. *Journal of Health and Social Behavior*, 33 (1), 51–66.

Baumrind, D. and Moselle, K. A. (1985). A developmental perspective on adolescent drug abuse. *Advances in Alcohol and Substance Abuse,* **4** (3–4), 41–67.

Beautrais, A. L., Joyce, P. R. and Mulder, R. T. (1999). Cannabis abuse and serious suicide attempts. *Addiction,* **94** (8), 1155–64.

Borges, G., Walters, E. E. and Kessler, R. C. (2000). Associations of substance use, abuse and dependence with subsequent suicidal behavior. *American Journal of Epidemiology,* **151**, 781–89.

Botvin, G. J., Scheier, L. M. and Griffin, K. W. (2002). Preventing the onset and developmental progression of adolescent drug use: implications for the gateway hypothesis. In *Stages and Pathways of Drug Involvement: Examining the Gateway Hypothesis,* ed. D. B. Kandel, pp. 115–38. New York: Cambridge University Press.

Brook, J. S., Balka, E. B. and Whiteman, M. (1999). The risks for late adolescence of early adolescent marijuana use. *American Journal of Public Health,* **89** (10), 1549–54.

Brook, J. S., Cohen, P. and Brook, D. W. (1998). Longitudinal study of co-occurring psychiatric disorders and substance use. *Journal of the American Academy of Child and Adolescent Psychiatry,* **37** (3), 322–30.

Brook, J. S., Cohen, P., Whiteman, M. and Gordon, A. S. (1992). Psychosocial risk factors in the transition from moderate to heavy use or abuse of drugs. In *Vulnerability to Drug Abuse,* ed. M. D. Glantz, pp. 359–88. Washington, DC: American Psychological Association.

Cadoni, C., Pisanu, A., Solinas, M., Acquas, E. and Di Chiara, G. (2001). Behavioural sensitization after repeated exposure to [Delta]9-tetrahydrocannabinol and cross-sensitization with morphine. *Psychopharmacology,* **158** (3), 259–66.

Caulkins, J. P., Rydell, C. P., Everingham, S. M. S., Chiesa, J. R. and Bushway, S. (1999). *An Ounce of Prevention, a Pound of Uncertainty: The Cost-Effectiveness of School-Based Drug Prevention Programs,* Santa Monica, CA: Rand Corporation.

Chen, K. and Kandel, D. B. (1995). The natural history of drug use from adolescence to the mid-thirties in a general population sample. *American Journal of Public Health,* **85** (1), 41–47.

Cohen, S. (1972). Drug use: religion and secularization. *American Journal of Psychiatry,* **129** (1), 97.

DeSimone, J. (1988). Is marijuana a gateway drug? *Eastern Economic Journal,* **24**, 149–64.

Donnelly, N. and Hall, W. D. (1994). *Patterns of Cannabis Use in Australia,* Canberra: Australian Government Publishing Service.

Donovan, J. E. and Jessor, R. (1983). Problem drinking and the dimension of involvement with drugs: a Guttman scalogram analysis of adolescent drug use. *American Journal of Public Health,* **73** (5), 543–52.

Donovan, J. E. and Jessor, R. (1985). Structure of problem behavior in adolescence and young adulthood. *Journal of Consulting and Clinical Psychology,* **53** (6), 890–904.

Duncan, S. C., Duncan, T. E., Biglan, A. and Ary, D. (1998). Contributions of the social context to the development of adolescent substance use: a multivariate latent growth modeling approach. *Drug and Alcohol Dependence,* **50** (1), 57–71.

DuPont, R. L. (1984). *Getting Tough on Gateway Drugs: a Guide for the Family,* Washington, DC: American Psychiatric Press.

Ellickson, P., Bui, K., Bell, R. and McGuigan, K. A. (1998). Does early drug use increase the risk of dropping out of high school? *Journal of Drug Issues,* **28** (2), 357–80.

Fergusson, D. M. and Horwood, L. J. (1997). Early onset cannabis use and psychosocial adjustment in young adults. *Addiction,* **92** (3), 279–96.

Fergusson, D. M. and Horwood, L. J. (1999). Prospective childhood predictors of deviant peer affiliations in adolescence. *Journal of Child Psychology and Psychiatry and Allied Disciplines,* **40** (4), 581–92.

Fergusson, D. M. and Horwood, L. J. (2000). Does cannabis use encourage other forms of illicit drug use? *Addiction,* **95** (4), 505–20.

Fergusson, D. M., Horwood, L. J. and Northstone, K. (2002a). Maternal use of cannabis and pregnancy outcome. *British Journal of Obstetrics and Gynaecology,* **109** (1), 21–27.

Fergusson, D. M., Horwood, L. J. and Swain-Campbell, N. (2002b). Cannabis use and psycho-social adjustment in adolescence and young adulthood. *Addiction,* **97**, 1123–35.

Fergusson, D. M., Lynskey, M. T. and Horwood, L. J. (1996). The short-term consequences of early onset cannabis use. *Journal of Abnormal Child Psychology,* **24** (4), 499–512.

Gerstein, D. R. and Green, L. W. (eds.) (1993). *Preventing Drug Abuse: What Do We Know?* Washington, DC, National Academy Press.

Golub, A. and Johnson, B. D. (2002). Substance use progression and hard drug use in inner-city New York. In *Stages and Pathways of Drug Involvement: Examining the Gateway Hypothesis,* ed. D. B. Kandel, pp. 90–112. Cambridge, UK: Cambridge University Press.

Goode, E. (1974). Marijuana use and the progression to dangerous drugs. In *Marijuana: Effects on Human Behavior,* ed. L. L. Miller, pp. 303–38. New York: Academic Press.

Han, C., McGue, M. K. and Iacono, W. G. (1999). Lifetime tobacco, alcohol and other substance use in adolescent Minnesota twins: univariate and multivariate behavioral genetic analyses. *Addiction,* **94** (7), 981–93.

Hawkins, J. D., Catalano, R. F. and Miller, J. Y. (1992). Risk and protective factors for alcohol and other drug problems in adolescence and early adulthood: implications for substance abuse prevention. *Psychological Bulletin,* **112** (1), 64–105.

Heath, A. C. (1995). Genetic influences on alcoholism risk: a review of adoption and twin studies. *Alcohol Health and Research World,* **19** (3), 166–71.

Hillman, S. D., Silburn, S. R., Green, A. and Zubrick, S. R. (2000). *Youth Suicide in Western Australia Involving Cannabis and Other Drugs,* Perth: Western Australian Drug Abuse Strategy Office.

Hundleby, J. D. and Mercer, G. W. (1987). Family and friends as social environments and their relationship to young adolescents' use of alcohol, tobacco, and marijuana. *Journal of Marriage and the Family,* **49** (1), 151–64.

Jessor, R. (1976). Predicting time of onset of marijuana use: a developmental study of high school youth. *Journal of Consulting and Clinical Psychology,* **44** (1), 125–34.

Jessor, R. and Jessor, S. L. (1977). *Problem Behavior and Psychosocial Development: A Longitudinal Study of Youth,* New York: Academic Press.

Jessor, R. and Jessor, S. L. (1978). Theory testing in longitudinal research on marijuana use. In *Longitudinal Research on Drug Use: Empirical Findings and Methodological Issues,* ed. D. B. Kandel, pp. 41–71. New York: John Wiley.

Johnston, L. D., O'Malley, P. M. and Eveland, L. K. (1978). Drugs and delinquency: a search for causal connections. In *Longitudinal Research on Drug Use: Empirical Findings and Methodological Issues,* ed. D. B. Kandel, pp. 137–56. New York: John Wiley.

Jones, S. P. and Heaven, P. C. L. (1998). Psychosocial correlates of adolescent drug-taking behaviour. *Journal of Adolescence,* **21** (2), 127–34.

Kandel, D. (1975). Stages in adolescent involvement in drug use. *Science,* **190**, 912–14.

Kandel, D. B. (1978). Convergences in prospective longitudinal surveys of drug use in normal populations. In *Longitudinal Research on Drug Use: Empirical Findings and Methodological Issues,* ed. D. B. Kandel, pp. 3–38. New York: John Wiley.

Kandel, D. B. (1980). Drug and drinking behavior among youth. *Annual Review of Sociology,* **6**, 235–85.

Kandel, D. B. (1984). Marijuana users in young adulthood. *Archives of General Psychiatry,* **41** (2), 200–9.

Kandel, D. B. (1988). Issues of sequencing of adolescent drug use and other problem behaviors. *Drugs and Society,* **3** (1–2), 55–76.

Kandel, D. B. (ed.) (2002). *Stages and Pathways of Drug Involvement: Examining the Gateway Hypothesis,* New York, Cambridge University Press.

Kandel, D. B. and Davies, M. (1992). Progression to regular marijuana involvement: phenomenology and risk factors for near-daily use. In *Vulnerability to Drug Abuse,* ed. M. D. Glantz, pp. 211–53. Washington, DC: American Psychological Association.

Kandel, D. B., Davies, M., Karus, D. and Yamaguchi, K. (1986). The consequences in young adulthood of adolescent drug involvement: an overview. *Archives of General Psychiatry,* **43** (8), 746–54.

Kandel, D. B. and Logan, J. A. (1984). Patterns of drug use from adolescence to young adulthood: I. Periods of risk for initiation, continued use, and discontinuation. *American Journal of Public Health,* **74** (7), 660–66.

Kandel, D. B. and Yamaguchi, K. (2002). Stages of drug involvement in the U.S. population. In *Stages and Pathways of Drug Involvement: Examining the Gateway Hypothesis,* ed. D. B. Kandel, pp. 65–89. New York: Cambridge University Press.

Kaplan, H. B. and Johnson, R. J. (1992). Relationships between circumstances surrounding initial illicit drug use and escalation of drug use: moderating effects of gender and early adolescent experiences. In *Vulnerability to Drug Abuse,* ed. M. D. Glantz and R. W. Pickens, pp. 299–358. Washington, DC: American Psychological Association.

Kaplan, H. B., Martin, S. S. and Robbins, C. (1984). Pathways to adolescent drug use: self-derogation, peer influence, weakening of social controls, and early substance use. *Journal of Health and Social Behavior,* **25** (3), 270–89.

Kelder, S. H., Murray, N. G., Orpinas, P., Prokhorov, A., McReynolds, L., Zhang, Q. and Roberts, R. (2001). Depression and substance use in minority middle-school students. *American Journal of Public Health,* **91** (5), 761–66.

Kelly, D. and Balch, R. W. (1971). Social origins and school failure: a re-examination of Cohen's theory of working-class delinquency. *Pacific Sociological Review,* **14**, 413–30.

Kendler, K. S. and Prescott, C. A. (1998). Cannabis use, abuse, and dependence in a population-based sample of female twins. *American Journal of Psychiatry,* **155** (8), 1016–22.

Kenkel, D., Mathios, A. D. and Pacula, R. L. (2001). Economics of youth drug use, addiction and gateway effects. *Addiction,* **96** (1), 151–64.

Kleiman, M. A. R. (1992). *Against Excess: Drug Policy for Results,* New York: Basic Books.

Krohn, M. D., Lizotte, A. J. and Perez, C. M. (1997). The interrelationship between substance use and precocious transitions to adult statuses. *Journal of Health and Social Behavior,* **38** (1), 87–103.

Lamarque, S., Taghzouti, K. and Simon, H. (2001). Chronic treatment with [Delta] 9-tetrahy-drocannabinol enhances the locomotor response to amphetamine and heroin: implications for vulnerability to drug addiction. *Neuropharmacology,* **41** (1), 118–29.

Lifrak, P. D., McKay, J. R., Rostain, A., Alterman, A. I. and O'Brien, C. P. (1997). Relationship of perceived competencies, perceived social support, and gender to substance use in young adolescents. *Journal of the American Academy of Child and Adolescent Psychiatry,* **36** (7), 933–40.

Lynskey, M. (2002). An alternative model is feasible, but the gateway hypothesis has not been invalidated: comments on Morral et al. *Addiction,* **97** (12), 1505–7.

Lynskey, M. and Hall, W. D. (2000). The effects of adolescent cannabis use on educational attainment: a review. *Addiction,* **96** (3), 433–43.

Lynskey, M., White, V., Hill, D., Letcher, T. and Hall, W. D. (1999). Prevalence of illicit drug use among youth: results from the Australian school students' alcohol and drugs survey. *Australian and New Zealand Journal of Public Health,* **23** (5), 519–24.

Lynskey, M. T., Heath, A. C., Bucholz, K. K. and Slutske, W. S. (2003). Escalation of drug use in early-onset cannabis users vs. co-twin controls. *Journal of the American Medical Association,* **289** (4), 427–33.

MacCoun, R. (1998). In what sense (if any) is marijuana a gateway drug? *FAS Drug Policy Analysis Bulletin,* **4**.

Manski, C. F., Pepper, J. V. and Petrie, C. V. (eds) (2001). *Informing America's Policy on Illegal Drugs: What We Don't Know Keeps Hurting Us,* Washington, DC, National Academy Press.

McGee, R. and Feehan, M. (1993). Cannabis use among New Zealand adolescents. *New Zealand Medical Journal,* **106** (961), 345.

McGee, R., Williams, S., Poulton, R. and Moffitt, T. (2000). A longitudinal study of cannabis use and mental health from adolescence to early adulthood. *Addiction,* **95**, 491–503.

McGregor, I. S., Issakidis, C. N. and Prior, G. (1996). Aversive effects of the synthetic cannabinoid CP 55,940 in rats. *Pharmacology Biochemistry and Behavior,* **53** (3), 657–64.

Mensch, B. and Kandel, D. B. (1992). Drug use as a risk factor for premarital teen pregnancy and abortion in a national sample of young white women. *Demography,* **29** (3), 409–29.

Morral, A. R., McCaffrey, D. F. and Paddock, S. M. (2002). Reassessing the marijuana gateway effect. *Addiction,* **97** (12), 1493–504.

Nahas, G. G. (1990). *Keep off the grass,* 5th edn. Middlebury, VT: Paul Eriksson.

Negrete, J. C. (1988). What's happened to the cannabis debate? *British Journal of Addiction,* **83** (4), 359–72.

Newcomb, M. D. (1992). Understanding the multidimensional nature of drug use and abuse: the role of consumption, risk factors, and protective factors. In *Vulnerability to Drug Abuse,* ed. M. D. Glantz, pp. 255–97. Washington, DC: American Psychological Association.

Newcomb, M. D. and Bentler, P. M. (1988). *Consequences of adolescent drug use: impact on the lives of young adults,* Thousand Oaks, CA: Sage.

Newcomb, M. D. and Bentler, P. M. (1989). Substance use and abuse among children and teenagers. *American Psychologist,* **44** (2), 242–48.

Novins, D. K. and Mitchell, C. M. (1998). Factors associated with marijuana use among American Indian adolescents. *Addiction,* **93** (11), 1693–702.

O'Donnell, J. A. and Clayton, R. R. (1982). The stepping stone hypothesis: marijuana, heroin, and causality. *Chemical Dependencies: Behavioral and Biomedical Issues,* **4** (3), 229–41.

Osgood, D. W., Johnston, L. D., O'Malley, P. M. and Bachman, J. G. (1988). The generality of deviance in late adolescence and early adulthood. *American Sociological Review,* 53 (1), 81–93.

Pacula, R. L. (1997). Women and substance use: are women more susceptible to addiction? *American Economic Review,* 87 (2), 454–59.

Patton, G. C., Coffey, C., Carlin, J. B., Degenhardt, L., Lynskey, M. and Hall, W. D. (2002). Cannabis use and mental health in young people: cohort study. *British Medical Journal,* 325 (7374), 1195–98.

Patton, G. C., Harris, J. B., Schwartz, M. and Bowes, G. (1997). Adolescent suicidal behaviors: a population-based study of risk. *Psychological Medicine,* 27, 715–24.

Polich, J. M., Ellickson, P. L., Reuter, P. and Kahan, J. P. (1984). *Strategies for Controlling Adolescent Drug Use,* Santa Monica, CA: Rand Corporation.

Resnick, M. D., Bearman, P. S., Blum, R. W., Bauman, K. E., Harris, K. M., Jones, J., Tabor, J., Beuhring, T., Sieving, R. E., Shew, M., Ireland, M., Bearinger, L. H. and Udry, J. R. (1997). Protecting adolescents from harm: findings from the National Longitudinal Study on Adolescent Health. *Journal of the American Medical Association,* 278 (10), 823–32.

Rey, J. M., Sawyer, M. G., Raphael, B., Patton, G. C. and Lynskey, M. (2002). Mental health of teenagers who use cannabis: results of an Australian survey. *British Journal of Psychiatry,* 180, 216–21.

Robins, L., Darvish, H. S. and Murphy, G. E. (1970). The long-term outcome for adolescent drug users: a follow-up study of 76 users and 146 nonusers. In *The Psychopathology of Adolescence,* ed. J. Zubin and A. M. Freedman, pp. 159–80. New York: Grune and Stratton.

Robins, L. N. (1993). Vietnam veterans' rapid recovery from heroin addiction: a fluke or normal expectation? *Addiction,* 88 (8), 1041–54.

Rosenbaum, E. and Kandel, D. B. (1990). Early onset of adolescent sexual behavior and drug involvement. *Journal of Marriage and the Family,* 52 (3), 783–98.

Rutter, M. (1988). Longitudinal data in the study of causal processes: some uses and some pitfalls. In *Studies of Psychosocial Risk: The Power of Longitudinal Data,* ed. M. Rutter, pp. 12–19. Cambridge, UK: Cambridge University Press.

Salmelainen, P. (1995). *The correlates of offending frequency: a study of juvenile theft offenders in detention,* Sydney: New South Wales Bureau of Crime Statistics and Research.

Scheier, L. M. and Newcomb, M. D. (1991). Psychosocial predictors of drug use initiation and escalation: an expansion of the multiple risk factors hypothesis using longitudinal data. *Contemporary Drug Problems,* 18 (1), 31–73.

Schwenk, C. R. (1998). Marijuana and job performance: comparing the major streams of research. *Journal of Drug Issues,* 28 (4), 941–70.

Shedler, J. and Block, J. (1990). Adolescent drug use and psychological health: a longitudinal inquiry. *American Psychologist,* 45 (5), 612–30.

Smith, D. E. (1968). Acute and chronic toxicity of marijuana. *Journal of Psychedelic Drugs,* 2, 37–47.

Solowij, N. (1998). *Cannabis and Cognitive Functioning,* Cambridge, UK: Cambridge University Press.

Swaim, R. C., Beauvais, F., Chavez, E. L. and Oetting, E. R. (1997). The effect of school dropout rates on estimates of adolescent substance use among three racial/ethnic groups. *American Journal of Public Health,* 87 (1), 51–55.

Tanda, G., Pontieri, F. E. and Di Chiara, G. (1997). Cannabinoid and heroin activation of mesolimbic dopamine transmission by a common mu1 opioid receptor mechanism. *Science,* **276** (5321), 2048–50.

Tanner, J., Davies, S. and O'Grady, B. (1999). Whatever happened to yesterday's rebels? Longitudinal effects of youth delinquency on education and employment. *Social Problems,* **46** (2), 250–74.

Trimboli, L. and Coumarelos, C. (1998). Cannabis and crime: treatment programs for adolescent cannabis use. *Crime and Justice Bulletin,* **41** (December), 1–16.

True, W. R., Heath, A. C., Scherrer, J. F., Xian, H., Lin, N., Eisen, S. A., Lyons, M. J., Goldberg, J. and Tsuang, M. T. (1999). Interrelationship of genetic and environmental influences on conduct disorder and alcohol and marijuana dependence symptoms. *American Journal of Medical Genetics,* **88** (4), 391–97.

Wagner, F. A. and Anthony, J. C. (2002). Into the world of illegal drug use: exposure opportunity and other mechanisms linking the use of alcohol, tobacco, marijuana, and cocaine. *American Journal of Epidemiology,* **155** (10), 918–25.

Walters, E. (1993). *Marijuana: an Australian crisis,* Malvern, Vic: E. Walters.

Wickelgren, I. (1997). Marijuana: harder than thought? *Science,* **276** (5321), 1967–68.

Yamaguchi, K. and Kandel, D. B. (1984a). Patterns of drug use from adolescence to young adulthood: II. Sequences of progression. *American Journal of Public Health,* **74** (7), 668–72.

Yamaguchi, K. and Kandel, D. B. (1984b). Patterns of drug use from adolescence to young adulthood: III. Predictors of progression. *American Journal of Public Health,* **74** (7), 673–81.

Zimmer, L. and Morgan, J. P. (1997). *Marijuana Myths, Marijuana Facts: A Review of the Scientific Evidence,* New York: The Lindesmith Center.

Section 5: Harms and benefits of cannabis use

Achiron, A., Miron, S., Lavie, V., Margalit, R. and Biegon, A. (2000). Dexanabinol (HU-211) effect on experimental autoimmune encephalomyelitis: implications for the treatment of acute relapses of multiple sclerosis. *Journal of Neuroimmunology,* **192**, 26–31.

Adler, M. W. and Geller, E. B. (1986). Ocular effects of cannabinoids. In *Cannabinoids as Therapeutic Agents,* ed. R. Mechoulam, pp. 51–70. Boca Raton, FL: CRC Press.

Anderson, P., Cremona, A., Paton, A., Turner, C. and Wallace, P. (1993). The risk of alcohol. *Addiction,* **88** (11), 1493–508.

Andreasson, S., Engstrom, A., Allebeck, P. and Rydberg, U. (1987). Cannabis and schizophrenia: a longitudinal study of Swedish conscripts. *Lancet,* **2** (8574), 1483–86.

Angst, J. (1996). Comorbidity of mood disorders: a longitudinal prospective study. *British Journal of Psychiatry,* **168**, 31–37.

Anthony, J. C., Warner, L. and Kessler, R. (1994). Comparative epidemiology of dependence on tobacco, alcohol, controlled substances and inhalants: basic findings from the National Comorbidity Survey. *Experimental and Clinical Psychopharmacology,* **2** (3), 244–68.

Ashton, C. H. (2001). Pharmacology and effects of cannabis: a brief review. *British Journal of Psychiatry,* **178**, 101–6.

Bachman, J. G., Wadsworth, K. N., O'Malley, P. M., Johnston, L. D. and Schulenberg, J. (1997). *Smoking, drinking, and drug use in young adulthood: the impacts of new freedoms and new responsibilities*, Mahwah, NJ: Lawrence Erlbaum.

Bagshaw, S. M. and Hagen, N. A. (2002). Medical efficacy of cannabinoids and marijuana: a comprehensive review of the literature. *Journal of Palliative Care*, 18 (2), 111–22.

Baker, D. (2000). Reply: a sanguine approach to cannabis. *Trends in Pharmacological Sciences*, 21 (6), 197.

Bates, M. N. and Blakely, T. A. (1999). Role of cannabis in motor vehicle crashes. *Epidemiologic Review*, 21, 222–32.

Beal, J., Olson, R., Lefkowitz, L., Laubenstein, L., Bellman, P., Yangco, B., Morales, J., Murphy, R., Powderly, W., Plasse, T., Mosdell, K. and Shepard, K. (1997). Long-term efficacy and safety of dronabinol for acquired immunodefiency syndrome-associated anorexia. *Journal of Pain and Symptom Management*, 14, 7–14.

Beal, J., Olson, R., Morales, J., Bellman, P., Yangco, B., Lefkowitz, L., Plasse, T. and Shepard, K. (1995). Dronabinol as a treatment for anorexia associated with weight loss in patients with AIDS. *Journal of Pain and Symptom Management*, 10, 89–97.

Brook, J. S., Cohen, P. and Brook, D. W. (1998). Longitudinal study of co-occurring psychiatric disorders and substance use. *Journal of the American Academy of Child and Adolescent Psychiatry*, 37 (3), 322–30.

Cameron, L. and Williams, J. (2001). Cannabis, alcohol and cigarettes: substitutes or complements? *Economic Record*, 77 (236), 19–34.

Campbell, F. A., Tramer, M. R., Carroll, D., Reynolds, D. J., Moore, R. A. and McQuay, H. J. (2001). Are cannabinoids an effective and safe treatment option in the management of pain? A qualitative systematic review. *British Medical Journal*, 323 (7303), 13–16.

Carey, M. P., Burish, T. G. and Brenner, D. E. (1983). Delta-9-tetrahydrocannabinol in cancer chemotherapy: research problems and issues. *Annals of Internal Medicine*, 99, 196–14.

Chaloupka, F. J. and Laixuthai, A. (1997). Do youths substitute alcohol and marijuana? Some econometric evidence. *Eastern Economic Journal*, 23 (3), 253–76.

Chang, A. E., Shiling, D. J., Stillman, R. C., Goldberg, N. H., Seipp, C. A., Barofsky, I., Simon, R. M. and Rosenberg, S. A. (1979). Delta-9-tetrahydrocannabinol as an antiemetic in cancer patients receiving high-dose methotrexate. *Annals of Internal Medicine*, 91, 819–24.

Chesher, G. B. and Jackson, D. M. (1974). Anticonvulsant effects of cannabinoids in mice: drug interactions within cannabinoids, and cannabinoid interactions with phenytoin. *Psychopharmacologia*, 37, 255–64.

Chyou, P. H., Burchfiel, C. M., Yano, K., Sharp, D. S., Rodriguez, B. L., Curb, J. D. and Nomura, A. M. (1997). Obesity, alcohol consumption, smoking, and mortality. *Annals of Epidemiology*, 311–17.

Clark, W. C., Janal, M. N., Zeidenberg, P. and Nahas, G. G. (1981). Effects of moderate and high doses of marihuana on thermal pain: a sensory decision theory analysis. *Journal of Clinical Pharmacology*, 21 (8–9 Suppl), 299S–310S.

Clarke, R. (1995). *Marijuana Botany, An Advanced Study: The Propagation and Breeding of Distinctive Cannabis*, Berkeley: Ronin.

Clifford, D. B. (1983). Tetrahydrocannabinol for tremor in multiple sclerosis. *Annals of Neurology*, 13 (6), 669–71.

Cohen, S. (1986). Marijuana research: selected recent findings. *Drug Abuse and Alcoholism Newsletter*, 15, 1–3.

Collins, D. and Lapsley, H. (1991). *Estimating the Economic Costs of Drug Abuse in Australia,* Canberra: Australian Government Publishing Service.

Collins, D. and Lapsley, H. (1996). *The Social Costs of Drug Abuse in Australia in 1988 and 1992,* Canberra: Australian Government Publishing Service.

Consroe, P., Laguna, J., Allender, J., Snider, S., Stern, L., Sandyk, R., Kennedy, K. and Schram, K. (1991). Controlled clinical trial of cannabidiol in Huntington's disease. *Pharmacology Biochemistry and Behavior,* **40** (3), 701–8.

Consroe, P., Musty, R., Rein, J., Tillery, W. and Pertwee, R. (1997). The perceived effects of smoked cannabis on patients with multiple sclerosis. *European Neurology,* **38** (1), 44–48.

Consroe, P. and Snider, S. R. (1986). Therapeutic potential of cannabinoids in neurological disorders. In *Cannabinoids as Therapeutic Agents,* ed. R. Mechoulam, pp. 21–50. Boca Raton, FL: CRC Press.

Consroe, P. F., Wood, G. C. and Buchsbaum, H. (1975). Anticonvulsant nature of marihuana smoking. *Journal of the American Medical Association,* **234** (3), 306–7.

Cook, P. J. and Moore, M. J. (1993). Economic perspectives on reducing alcohol-related violence. In *Alcohol and Interpersonal Violence: Fostering Multidisciplinary Perspectives,* ed. S. E. Martin, pp. 193–212. Rockville, MD: US Department of Health and Human Services.

Cunha, J. M., Carlini, E. A., Pereira, A. E., Ramos, O. L., Pimentel, C., Gagliardi, R., Sanvito, W. L., Lander, N. and Mechoulam, R. (1980). Chronic administration of cannabidiol to healthy volunteers and epileptic patients. *Pharmacology,* **21** (3), 175–85.

Degenhardt, L. and Hall, W. D. (2001). The association between psychosis and problematical drug use among Australian adults: findings from the National Survey of Mental Health and Wellbeing. *Psychological Medicine,* **31** (4), 659–68.

Degenhardt, L. and Hall, W. D. (2003). Patterns of comorbidity between alcohol use and other substance use in the Australian population. *Drug and Alcohol Review,* **22**, 7–13.

Degenhardt, L., Hall, W. D. and Lynskey, M. (2000a). *Cannabis Use and Mental Health among Australian Adults: Findings from the National Survey of Mental Health and Wellbeing,* NDARC Technical Report, Vol. 98, Sydney: National Drug and Alcohol Research Centre, University of New South Wales.

Degenhardt, L., Hall, W. D. and Lynskey, M. (2001). Alcohol, cannabis and tobacco use among Australians: a comparison of their associations with other drug use, other drug use disorders, affective and anxiety disorders, and psychosis. *Addiction,* **96**, 1603–14.

Degenhardt, L., Lynskey, M. and Hall, W. D. (2000b). Cohort trends in the age of initiation of drug use in Australia. *Australian and New Zealand Journal of Public Health,* **24** (4), 421–26.

Der, G., Gupta, S. and Murray, R. M. (1990). Is schizophrenia disappearing? *Lancet,* **335** (8688), 513–16.

DiNardo, J. and Lemieux, T. (1992). *Alcohol, Marijuana, and American Youth: The Unintended Effects of Government Regulation,* NBER Working Paper, Vol. 4212, Cambridge, MA: National Bureau of Economic Research.

Drummond, C. (2002). Cannabis control: costs outweigh the benefits. Against. *British Medical Journal,* **324** (7329), 107–8.

Edwards, G. (1983). Psychopathology of a drug experience. *British Journal of Psychiatry,* **143**, 139–42.

Edwards, G., Anderson, P., Babor, T. F., Casswell, S., Ferrence, R., Giesbrecht, N., Godfrey, C., Holder, H., Lemmens, P., Makela, K., Midanik, L., Norstrom, T., Osterberg, E., Romelsjo, A.,

Room, R., Simpura, J. and Skog, O. (1994). *Alcohol Policy and the Public Good,* Oxford: Oxford University Press.

Edwards, G., Marshall, E. J. and Cook, C. C. H. (1997). *The Treatment of Drinking Problems,* 3rd edn. Cambridge: Cambridge University Press.

ElSohly, M. A. and Ross, S. A. (1999). *Quarterly report: potency monitoring project. Report 69: January 1, 1999–March 31, 1999,* University, MS: National Center for Development of Natural Products, University of Mississippi.

ElSohly, M. A., Ross, S. A., Mehmedic, Z., Arafat, R., Yi, B. and Banahan, B. F. (2000). Potency trends of delta(9)-THC and other cannabinoids in confiscated marijuana from 1980–1997. *Journal of Forensic Sciences,* **45** (1), 24–30.

English, D., Holman, C., Milne, E., Winter, M., Hulse, G., Codde, S., Corti, B., Dawes, V., De Klerk, N., Knuiman, M., Kurinczuk, J., Lewin, G. and Ryan, G. (1995). *The Quantification of Drug Caused Morbidity and Mortality in Australia, 1995,* Canberra: Commonwealth Department of Human Services and Health.

Ezzati, M., Lopez, A. D., Rodgers, A., Vander Hoorn, S. and Murray, C. J. L. (2002). Selected major risk factors and global and regional burden of disease. *Lancet,* **360** (9343), 1347–60.

Farrelly, M., Bray, J., Zarkin, G., Wendling, B. and Pacula, R. (1999). *The Effects of Prices and Policies on the Demand for Marijuana: Evidence from the National Household Surveys on Drug Abuse,* NBER Working Paper, Vol. 6940, Cambridge, MA: National Bureau of Economic Research.

Fergusson, D. M. and Horwood, L. J. (1997). Early onset cannabis use and psychosocial adjustment in young adults. *Addiction,* **92** (3), 279–96.

Ghodse, H. (1996). When too much caution can be harmful. *Addiction,* **91** (6), 764–66.

Glass, M., Dragunow, M. and Faull, R. L. M. (1997). Cannabinoid receptors in the human brain: a detailed anatomical and quantitative autoradiographic study in the fetal, neonatal and adult human brain. *Neuroscience,* **77** (2), 299–318.

Goani, Y. and Mechoulam, R. (1964). Isolation, structure and partial synthesis of an active constituent of hashish. *Journal of the American Chemical Society,* **86,** 1646–47.

Grant, B. F. and Harford, T. C. (1995). Comorbidity between DSM-IV alcohol use disorders and major depression: results of a national survey. *Drug and Alcohol Dependence,* **39** (3), 197–206.

Grinspoon, L. (1990). Testimony of Lester Grinspoon, MD. In *Cancer Treatment and Marijuana Therapy,* ed. R. C. Randall, pp. 5–12. Washington, DC: Galen Press.

Grinspoon, L. and Bakalar, J. (1993). *Marihuana, the forbidden medicine,* New Haven: Yale University Press.

Hall, W. D. and Babor, T. F. (2000). Cannabis use and public health: assessing the burden. *Addiction,* **95** (4), 485–90.

Hall, W. D., Solowij, N. and Lemon, J. (1994). *The Health and Psychological Consequences of Cannabis Use,* National Drug Strategy Monograph, Vol. 25, Canberra: Australian Government Publishing Service.

Hall, W. D. and Swift, W. (2000). The THC content of cannabis in Australia: evidence and implications. *Australian and New Zealand Journal of Public Health,* **24** (5), 503–8.

Hall, W. D. and Zador, D. (1997). The alcohol withdrawal syndrome. *Lancet,* **349** (9069), 1897–900.

Hepler, R. S., Frank, I. M. and Petrus, R. (1976). Ocular effects of marihuana smoking. In *The Pharmacology of Marihuana,* Vol. 2, ed. M. C. Braude and S. Szara, pp. 815–24. New York: Raven Press.

Hepler, R. S. and Petrus, R. J. (1971). Marihuana smoking and intraocular pressure. *Journal of the American Medical Association*, **217**, 1392.

Hepler, R. S. and Petrus, R. J. (1976). Experiences with administration of marihuana to glaucoma patients. In *The Therapeutic Potential of Marihuana*, ed. S. Cohen and R. C. Stillman, pp. 63–75. New York: Plenum.

Hill, S. Y., Schwin, R., Goodwin, D. W. and Powell, B. J. (1974). Marihuana and pain. *Journal of Pharmacology and Experimental Therapeutics*, **188** (2), 415–18.

Hollister, L.E. (2001). Marijuana (cannabis) as medicine. *Journal of Cannabis Therapeutics*, **1**, 5–27.

Holman, C., Armstrong, B. K., Arias, L. N., Martin, C. A., Hatton, W. M., Hayward, L. D., Salmon, M. A., Shean, R. E. and Waddell, V. P. (1988). *The Quantification of Drug-Caused Morbidity and Mortality in Australia 1988*, Canberra: Commonwealth Department of Community Services and Health.

House of Lords Select Committee on Science and Technology (1998). *Cannabis: The Scientific and Medical Evidence*, London: House of Lords, The Stationery Office.

Institute of Medicine (1982). *Marijuana and Health*, Washington, DC: National Academy Press.

Institute of Medicine (1987). *Causes and Consequences of Alcohol Problems: An Agenda for Research*, Washington, DC: National Academy Press.

Institute of Medicine (1999). *Marijuana and Medicine: Assessing the Science Base*, Washington, DC: National Academy Press.

Iversen, L. (2000). *The Science of Marijuana*, Oxford: Oxford University Press.

Jain, A. K., Ryan, J. R., McMahon, F. G. and Smith, G. (1981). Evaluation of intramuscular levonantradol and placebo in acute postoperative pain. *Journal of Clinical Pharmacology*, **21** (8–9 Suppl), 320S–26S.

Johnson, R. A. and Gerstein, D. R. (1998). Initiation of use of alcohol, cigarettes, marijuana, cocaine, and other substances in US birth cohorts since 1919. *American Journal of Public Health*, **88** (1), 27–33.

Johnston, L. D. (1981). Frequent marijuana use: correlates, possible effects, and reasons for using and quitting. In *Treating the Marijuana Dependent Person*, ed. R. deSilva, R. Dupont and R. Russell, pp. 8–14. New York: American Council on Marijuana and Other Psychoactive Drugs.

Johnston, L. D. and O'Malley, P. M. (1986). Why do the nation's students use drugs and alcohol? Self-reported reasons from 9 national surveys. *Journal of Drug Issues*, **16** (1), 29–66.

Jones, R. T., Benowitz, N. L. and Herning, R. I. (1981). Clinical relevance of cannabis tolerance and dependence. *Journal of Clinical Pharmacology*, **21** (8–9 Suppl), 143S–52S.

Kelder, S. H., Murray, N. G., Orpinas, P., Prokhorov, A., McReynolds, L., Zhang, Q. and Roberts, R. (2001). Depression and substance use in minority middle-school students. *American Journal of Public Health*, **91** (5), 761–66.

Killestein, J., Hoogervorst, E. L. J., Reif, M., Kalkers, N. F., van Loenen, A. C., Staats, P. G. M., Gorter, R. W., Uitdehaag, B. M. J. and Polman, C. H. (2002). Safety, tolerability, and efficacy of orally administered cannabinoids in MS. *Neurology*, **58** (9), 1404–7.

Klatsky, A. L. (1999). Moderate drinking and reduced risk of heart disease. *Alcohol Research and Health*, **23** (1), 15–23.

Lenke, L. (1990). *Alcohol and Criminal Violence – Time Series Analyses in a Comparative Perspective*, Stockholm: Almqvist and Wiksell.

Levitt, M. (1986). Cannabinoids as antiemetics in cancer chemotherapy. In *Cannabinoids as Therapeutic Agents*, ed. R. Mechoulam, pp. 71–83. Boca Raton, FL: CRC Press.

Libman, E. and Stern, M. H. (1985). The effects of delta-9 THC on cutaneous sensitivity and its relation to personality. *Personality and Individual Differences,* **6** (2), 169–74.

Mathers, C., Vos, T. and Stevenson, C. (1999). *The Burden of Disease and Injury in Australia.,* Canberra: Australian Institute of Health and Welfare.

Mechoulam, R. (1986). The pharmacohistory of *Cannabis sativa*. In *Cannabinoids as Therapeutic Agents,* ed. R. Mechoulam, pp. 1–19. Boca Raton, FL: CRC Press.

Meinck, H. M., Schonle, P. W. and Conrad, B. (1989). Effect of cannabinoids on spasticity and ataxia in multiple-sclerosis. *Journal of Neurology,* **236** (2), 120–22.

Miller, A. S. and Walker, J. M. (1996). Electrophysiological effects of a cannabinoid on neural activity in the globus pallidus. *European Journal of Pharmacology,* **304** (1–3), 29–35.

Mueller-Vahl, K., Kolbe, H., Schneider, U. and Emrich, H.M. (1999). Cannabis in movement disorders. *Research in Complementary Medicine,* **6** (Supplement 3), 23–27.

Murray, C. J. L. and Lopez, A. D. (1997). Global mortality, disability, and the contribution of risk factors: Global Burden of Disease Study. *Lancet,* **349** (9063), 1436–42.

Nahas, G. G. (1984). Toxicology and pharmacology. In *Marihuana in Science and Medicine,* ed. G. G. Nahas, pp. 102–247. New York: Raven Press.

Negrete, J. C. (1988). What's happened to the cannabis debate? *British Journal of Addiction,* **83** (4), 359–72.

Noyes, R., Brunk, F., Avery, D. H. and Canter, A. (1975a). The analgesic properties of delta-9-tetrahydrocannabinol and codeine. *Clinical Pharmacology and Therapeutics,* **18**, 84–89.

Noyes, R., Brunk, S., Baram, D. and Canter, A. (1975b). Analgesic effect of delta-9-tetrahydrocannabinol. *Journal of Clinical Pharmacology,* **15** (2–3), 139–43.

O'Shaughnessy, W. (1842). On the preparation of the Indian hemp, or gunjah (*Cannabis indica*) and their effects on the animal system in health and their utility in the treatment of tetanus and other convulsive disorders. *Transcripts of the Medical Physicians' Society of Calcutta,* **8**, 421–61.

Pacula, R. L. (1998). Does increasing the beer tax reduce marijuana consumption? *Journal of Health Economics,* **17** (5), 557–85.

Patton, G. C., Coffey, C., Carlin, J. B., Degenhardt, L., Lynskey, M. and Hall, W. D. (2002). Cannabis use and mental health in young people: cohort study. *British Medical Journal,* **325** (7374), 1195–98.

Petro, D. J. and Ellenberger, C., Jr (1981). Treatment of human spasticity with delta 9-tetrahydrocannabinol. *Journal of Clinical Pharmacology,* **21** (8–9 Suppl), 413S–16S.

Poster, D. S., Penta, J. S., Bruno, S. and Macdonald, J.S. (1981). Delta 9-tetrahydrocannabinol in clinical oncology. *Journal of the American Medical Association,* **245** (20), 2047–51.

Power, C., Rodgers, B. and Hope, S. (1998). U-shaped relation for alcohol consumption and health in early adulthood and implications for mortality. *Lancet,* **352** (9131), 877–77.

Raft, D., Gregg, J., Ghia, J. and Harris, L. (1977). Effects of intravenous tetrahydrocannabinol on experimental and surgical pain. Psychological correlates of the analgesic response. *Clinical Pharmacology and Therapeutics,* **21** (1), 26–33.

Randall, R. C. (1990). *Cancer Treatment and Marijuana Therapy,* Washington, DC: Galen Press.

Rey, J. M., Sawyer, M. G., Raphael, B., Patton, G. C. and Lynskey, M. (2002). Mental health of teenagers who use cannabis: results of an Australian survey. *British Journal of Psychiatry,* **180**, 216–21.

Ridolfo, B. and Stevenson, C. (2001). *The quantification of drug-caused mortality and morbidity in Australia, 1998,* Canberra: Australian Institute of Health and Welfare.

Rodgers, B., Korten, A. E., Jorm, A. F., Jacomb, P. A., Christensen, H. and Henderson, A. S. (2000). Non-linear relationships in associations of depression and anxiety with alcohol use. *Psychological Medicine,* 30 (2), 421–32.

Room, R. (1983). Alcohol and crime: behavioral aspects. In *Encyclopaedia of Crime and Justice,* Vol. 1, ed. S. H. Kadish, pp. 35–44. New York: Free Press.

Room, R. (2001). Intoxication and bad behaviour: understanding cultural differences in the link. *Social Science and Medicine,* 53 (2), 189–98.

Sacco, R. L., Elkind, M., Boden-Albala, B., Lin, I. F., Kargman, D. E., Hauser, W. A., Shea, S. and Paik, M. C. (1999). The protective effect of moderate alcohol consumption on ischemic stroke. *Journal of the American Medical Association,* 281 (1), 53–60.

Saffer, H. and Chaloupka, F. J. (1999). Demographic differentials in the demand for alcohol and drugs. In *The Economic Analysis of Substance Use and Abuse,* ed. F. J. Chaloupka, M. Grossman, W. K. Bickel and H. Saffer, pp. 187–211. Chicago: University of Chicago Press.

Sallan, S. E., Zinberg, N. E. and Frei, E., III (1975). Antiemetic effect of delta-9-tetrahydrocannabinol in patients receiving cancer chemotherapy. *New England Journal of Medicine,* 293 (16), 795–97.

Shedler, J. and Block, J. (1990). Adolescent drug use and psychological health: a longitudinal inquiry. *American Psychologist,* 45 (5), 612–30.

Smith, N. T. (2002). A review of the published literature into cannabis withdrawal symptoms in human users. *Addiction,* 97 (6), 621–32.

Staquet, M., Gantt, C. and Machin, D. (1978). Effect of a nitrogen analog of tetrahydrocannabinol on cancer pain. *Clinical Pharmacology and Therapeutics,* 23, 397–401.

Tashkin, D. P. (1993). Is frequent marijuana smoking harmful to health? *Western Journal of Medicine,* 158 (6), 635–37.

Tashkin, D. P., Shapiro, B. J. and Frank, I. M. (1976). Acute effects of marihuana on airway dynamics in spontaneous and experimentally induced bronchial asthma. In *The Pharmacology of Marihuana,* ed. M. C. Braude and S. Szara, pp. 63–87. New York: Raven Press.

Tashkin, D. P., Shapiro, B. J., Lee, Y. E. and Harper, C. E. (1975). Effects of smoked marijuana in experimentally induced asthma. *American Review of Respiratory Disease,* 112 (3), 377–86.

Thies, C. F. and Register, C. A. (1993). Decriminalization of marijuana and the demand for alcohol, marijuana and cocaine. *Social Science Journal,* 30 (4), 385–99.

Thomas, H. (1993). Psychiatric symptoms in cannabis users. *British Journal of Psychiatry,* 163, 141–49.

Ungerleider, J. T., Andrysiak, T., Fairbanks, L., Goodnight, J., Sarna, G. and Jamison, K. (1982). Cannabis and cancer chemotherapy: a comparison of oral delta-9-THC and prochlorperazine. *Cancer,* 50 (4), 636–45.

Ungerleider, J. T., Andrysiak, T., Fairbanks, L., Ellison, G. W. and Myers, L. W. (1987). Delta-9-THC in the treatment of spasticity associated with multiple sclerosis. *Advances in Alcohol and Substance Abuse,* 7 (1), 39–50.

Walker, J. M. and Huang, S. M. (2002). Cannabinoid analgesia. *Pharmacology and Therapeutics,* 95 (2), 127–35.

Xie, X., Rehm, J., Single, E. and Robson, L. (1996). *The Economic Costs of Alcohol, Tobacco and Illicit Drug Abuse in Ontario: 1992,* Toronto: Addiction Research Foundation.

Zimmer, L. and Morgan, J. P. (1997). *Marijuana Myths, Marijuana Facts: A Review of the Scientific Evidence,* New York: The Lindesmith Center.

Section 6: The effectiveness and costs of cannabis prohibition

Advisory Committee on Illicit Drugs (1993). *Cannabis and the Law in Queensland: A Discussion Paper,* Brisbane: Queensland Criminal Justice Commission.

Ali, R., Christie P., Lenton, S., Hawks, D., Sutton, A., Hall, W. D. and Allsop, S. (1999). *The Social Impacts of the Cannabis Expiation Notice Scheme in South Australia. Summary report presented to the Ministerial Council on Drug Strategy,* National Drug Strategy Monograph, Vol. 34, Canberra: Commonwealth Department of Health and Aged Care.

Bachman, J. G., Wadsworth, K. N., O'Malley, P. M., Johnston, L. D. and Schulenberg, J. (1997). *Smoking, drinking, and drug use in young adulthood: the impacts of new freedoms and new responsibilities,* Mahwah, NJ: Lawrence Erlbaum.

Cameron, L. and Williams, J. (2001). Cannabis, alcohol and cigarettes: substitutes or complements? *Economic Record,* 77 (236), 19–34.

Canadian Government Commission of Inquiry (1970). *The Non-Medical Use of Drugs,* Ottawa: Information Canada.

Canadian Senate Special Committee on Illegal Drugs (2002). *Cannabis – our position for a Canadian public policy. Summary Report of the Senate Special Committee on Illegal Drugs,* Ottawa: Parliament of Canada.

Caulkins, J., L., P. R., Paddock, S. and Chiesa, J. (2002). *School Based Drug Prevention: What Kind of Drug Use Does It Prevent?* Santa Monica, CA: Rand Corporation.

Chen, K. and Kandel, D. B. (1995). The natural history of drug use from adolescence to the mid-thirties in a general population sample. *American Journal of Public Health,* 85 (1), 41–47.

Christie, P. (1991). *The Effects of Cannabis Legislation in South Australia on Levels of Cannabis Use,* Adelaide: Drug and Alcohol Services Council.

Christie, P. (1999). *Cannabis Offences Under the Cannabis Expiation Notice Scheme in South Australia,* National Drug Strategy Monograph, Vol. 35, Canberra: Commonwealth Department of Health and Aged Care.

Cohen, P. D. A. and Kaal, H. L. (2001). *The Irrelevance of Drug Policy: Patterns and Careers of Experienced Cannabis Use in the Populations of Amsterdam, San Francisco and Bremen,* Amsterdam: Centrum voor Drugsonderzoek, University of Amsterdam.

Cohen, S. (1976). The 94-day cannabis study. *Annals of the New York Academy of Sciences,* **282,** 211–110.

Criminal Justice Commission (1994). *Report on Cannabis and the Law in Queensland,* Brisbane: Criminal Justice Commission, Queensland.

Degenhardt, L., Hall, W. D. and Lynskey, M. (2000). *Cannabis Use and Mental Health among Australian Adults: Findings from the National Survey of Mental Health and Wellbeing,* NDARC Technical Report, Vol. 98, Sydney: National Drug and Alcohol Research Centre, University of New South Wales.

Donnelly, N., Hall, W. D. and Christie, P. (1995). The effects of partial decriminalisation on cannabis use in South Australia, 1985 to 1993. *Australian Journal of Public Health,* **19** (3), 281–87.

Drugscope (2001). *Annual Report of the UK Drug Situation: 2001,* http://www.drugscope. org.uk/druginfo/drugreport.asp (7 April 2003).

Eck, J. E. and Maguire, E. R. (2000). Have changes in policing reduced violent crime? An assessment of the evidence. In *The Crime Drop in America,* ed. A. Blumstein and J. Wallman, pp. 207–65. Cambridge, UK: Cambridge University Press.

Erickson, P. G. (1980). *Cannabis Criminals: The Social Effects of Punishment on Drug Users,* Toronto: Addiction Research Foundation.

Estermann, J. and Rônez, S. (1995). *Drogen und Strafrecht in der Schweiz: Zeitreihen zu Verzeigungen, Strafurteilen und Strafvollzug,* Berne: Swiss Federal Statistical Office.

Federal Bureau of Investigation (2001). *Crime in the United States 2000,* Uniform Crime Reports, Washington, DC: U.S. Department of Justice.

Fergusson, D. M., Swain-Campbell, N. R. and Horwood, L. J. (2003). Arrests and convictions for cannabis-related offences in a New Zealand birth cohort. *Drug and Dependence,* **70**, 53–63.

Gable, R. S. (1997). Opportunity costs of drug prohibition. *Addiction,* **92**, 1179–82.

Gettman, J. (2000). *United States Marijuana Arrests, Part Two: Racial Differences in Drug Arrests,* National Organization for the Reform of Marijuana Laws. http://www.norml.org/ index.cfm?Group_ID=5326 (4 April 2002).

Goldstein, P. J., Brownstein, H. H., Ryan, P. J. and Bellucci, P. A. (1989). Crack and homicide in New York City, 1988: a conceptually based event analysis. *Contemporary Drug Problems,* **16**, 651–87.

Grinspoon, L. and Bakalar, J. (1993). *Marihuana, the forbidden medicine,* New Haven: Yale University Press.

Hall, W. D., Degenhardt, L. and Currow, D. (2001). Allowing the medical use of cannabis. *Medical Journal of Australia,* **175**, 39–40.

Harwood, H. J., Fountain, D. and G., L. (1998). *The economic costs of alcohol and drug abuse in the United States, 1992,* Rockville, MD: National Institute on Drug Abuse.

Higgins, K., Cooper-Stanbury, M. and Williams, P. (2000). *Statistics on drug use in Australia 1998,* Drug Statistics, Vol. 8, Canberra: Australian Institute of Health and Welfare.

Homel, R. (1990). Crime on the roads: drinking and driving. In *Alcohol and Crime,* ed. J. Veron, pp. 67–82. Canberra: Australian Institute of Criminology.

House of Lords Select Committee on Science and Technology (1998). *Cannabis: The Scientific and Medical Evidence,* London: House of Lords, The Stationery Office.

Human Rights Watch (2000). Punishment and prejudice: racial disparities in the war on drugs. *Human Rights Watch Report,* **12** (2). http://www.hrw.org/reports/2000/usa/ (4 April 2003)

Husak, D. (2002). *Legalize This! The Case for Decriminalising Drugs,* London: Verso.

Institute of Medicine (1999). *Marijuana and Medicine: Assessing the Science Base,* Washington, DC: National Academy Press.

Johnson, B. D. and Golub, A. (2001). *Measuring the impacts of QOL policing in New York City,* National Institute of Justice Research in Progress videotape, No. NCJ 190638.

Kaplan, J. (1970). *Marijuana: The New Prohibition,* New York: World Publishing Company.

King, A. J. C., Boyce, W. F. and King, M. A. (1999). *Trends in the Health of Canadian Youth: Health Behaviour in School-Aged Children, a World Health Organization Cross-National Study,* Ottawa: Health Canada.

Kleiman, M. A. R. (1992). *Against Excess: Drug Policy for Results*, New York: Basic Books.

Kyvig, D. E. (1979). *Repealing National Prohibition*, Chicago: University of Chicago Press.

Lenton, S. (2000). Cannabis policy and the burden of proof: is it now beyond reasonable doubt that cannabis prohibition is not working? *Drug and Alcohol Review, 19* (1), 95–100.

Lenton, S. (2001). Cannabis as a gateway drug: comments on Fergusson and Horwood (2000). *Addiction, 96*, 511–13.

Lenton, S., Bennett, M. and Heale, P. (1999a). *The Social Impact of a Minor Cannabis Offence Under Strict Prohibition : The Case of Western Australia*, Perth: National Centre for Research into the Prevention of Drug Abuse.

Lenton, S., Christie, P., Humeniuk, R., Brooks, A., Bennet, M. and Heale, P. (1999b). *Infringement Versus Conviction: The Social Impact of a Minor Cannabis Offence Under A Civil Penalties System and Strict Prohibition in Two Australia States*, National Drug Strategy Monograph, Vol. 36, Canberra: Commonwealth Department of Health and Aged Care.

MacCoun, R. and Reuter, P. (2001). *Drug War Heresies: Learning from Other Vices, Times and Places*, Cambridge: Cambridge University Press.

McDonald, D. and Atkinson, L. (1995). *Social Impacts of the Legislative Options for Cannabis in Australia. Phase 1 Research*, Canberra: Australian Institute of Criminology.

McDonald, D., Moore, R., Norberry, J., Wardlaw, G. and Ballenden, N. (1994). *Legislative Options for Cannabis In Australia*, National Drug Strategy Monograph, Vol. 26, Canberra: Australian Government Publishing Service.

McGeorge, J. and Aitken, C. K. (1997). Effects of cannabis decriminalization in the Australian Capital Territory on university students' patterns of use. *Journal of Drug Issues, 27*, 785–93.

Mill, J. S. (1975). *On Liberty*, ed. D. Spitz. Norton Critical Edition. New York, Norton.

Miron, J. A. and Zweibel, J. (1991). Alcohol consumption during prohibition. *American Economic Review, 81*, 242–46.

Morral, A. R., McCaffrey, D. F. and Paddock, S. M. (2002). Reassessing the marijuana gateway effect. *Addiction, 97* (12), 1493–504.

Nadelman, E. (1989). Drug prohibition in the United States: costs, consequences and alternatives. *Science, 245*, 939–47.

Nahas, G. and Latour, C. (1992). The human toxicity of marijuana. *Medical Journal of Australia, 156* (7), 495–97.

Office of National Drug Control Policy (1997). *What America's Users Spend on Illegal Drugs, 1988–1995*, Rockville, MD: Office of National Drug Control Policy.

Office of National Drug Control Policy (2002). Pulse Check: Trends in Drug Abuse, November 2002.

Pacula, R. L., Chriqui, J. F. and King, J. (2003). Decriminalization in the United States: what does it mean? National Bureau of Economic Research Working Paper, Vol. 8401. Cambridge, MA: National Bureau of Economic Research.

Pacula, R. L., Grossman, M., Chaloupka, F. J., O'Malley, P. M., Johnston, L. and Farrelly, M. C. (2001). Marijuana and youth. In *Risky Behavior Among Youths: An Economic Analysis*, ed. J. Gruber, pp. 271–326. Chicago: University of Chicago Press.

Parliamentary Joint Committee on the National Crime Authority (1989). *Drugs, Crime and Society*, Canberra: Australian Government Publishing Service.

Reilly, D., Didcott, P., Swift, W. and Hall, W. D. (1998). Long-term cannabis use: characteristics of users in an Australian rural area. *Addiction, 93*, 837–46.

Reinarman, C. and Levine, H. G. (1989). The crack attack: politics and media in America's latest drug scare. In *Images of Issues: Typifying Contemporary Social Problems*, ed. J. Best, pp. 115–37. Hawthorn, NY: Aldine de Gruyter.

Reuter, P., Hirschfield, P. and Davies, C. (2000). *Assessing the crack-down on marijuana in Maryland*, Unpublished paper, University of Maryland.

Saffer, H. and Chaloupka, F. J. (1999). The demand for illicit drugs: effects of decriminalization. *Economic Inquiry*, 37 (3), 401–18.

Savoie, J. (2002). Crime statistics in Canada, 2001. In *Juristat*, Vol. 22 No. 6. Ottawa: Statistics Canada, Canadian Center for Justice Statistics.

Senate Special Committee on Illegal Drugs (Canada) (2002). *Cannabis: Summary Report*, Ottawa: Parliament of Canada.

Senate Standing Committee on Social Welfare (1977). *Drug Problems in Australia: An Intoxicated Society*, Canberra: Australian Government Printing Office.

Single, E., Christie, P. and Ali, R. (1999). *The Impact of Cannabis Decriminalisation in Australia and the United States*, Adelaide: Drug and Alcohol Services Council.

Single, E. W. (1989). The impact of marijuana decriminalization: an update. *Journal of Public Health Policy*, 9 (4), 456–66.

Substance Abuse and Mental Health Services Administration (2001). *Summary of Findings from the 2000 National Household Survey on Drug Abuse*, Washington, DC: Department of Health and Social Services.

Swiss Federal Commission for Drug Issues (1999). *Cannabis Report*, Bern: Swiss Federal Commission for Drug Issues.

Szasz, T. (1997). *Ceremonial Chemistry: The Ritual Persecution of Drugs, Addicts and Pushers*, Revised edn. Holmes Beach, FL: Learning Publications.

Taylor, B. G., Fitzgerald, N., Hunt, D., Reardon, J. A. and Brownstein, H. H. (2001). *ADAM Preliminary 2000 Findings on Drug Use and Drug Markets – Adult Male Arrestees*, Washington, DC: National Institute of Justice.

Thies, C. F. and Register, C. A. (1993). Decriminalization of marijuana and the demand for alcohol, marijuana and cocaine. *Social Science Journal*, 30 (4), 385–99.

Thomas, C. (1999). Marijuana arrests and incarceration in the United States. *FAS Drug Policy Analysis Bulletin*, 7 (June), 5–7.

Tyrrell, I. (1997). The US prohibition experiment: myths, history and implications. *Addiction*, 92, 1405–9.

United Kingdom Police Foundation (2000). *Drugs and the Law: Report of the Independent Inquiry into the Misuse of Drugs Act 1971*, London: The United Kingdom Police Foundation.

United States Office of National Drug Control Policy (2001). *Pulse Check: Trends in Drug Abuse. November 2001*, Washington, DC: Office of National Drug Control Policy.

US General Accounting Office (2002). *Marijuana: Early Experiences with Four States' Laws that Allow Use for Medical Purposes*, Washington, DC: General Accounting Office.

Van Solinge, B. (1997). *The Swedish Drug Control System: An In-depth Review and Analysis*, Amsterdam: Uitgeverij Jan Mets and University of Amsterdam.

WHO Program on Substance Abuse (1997). *Cannabis: A Health Perspective and Research Agenda*, Geneva: Division of Mental Health and Prevention of Substance Abuse, World Health Organization.

Williams, J. (2003). The effects of price and policy on marijuana use: what can be learned from the Australian experience? *Health Economics,* published online in advance of print 28 February 2003: DOI (Digital Object Identifier) No. 10.1002/hec.796.

Wodak, A., Reinarman, C. and Cohen, P. (2002). Cannabis control: costs outweigh benefits. *British Journal of Medicine,* **324,** 105–6.

Zimmer, L. and Morgan, J. P. (1997). *Marijuana Myths, Marijuana Facts: A Review of the Scientific Evidence,* New York: The Lindesmith Center.

Section 7: Policy alternatives

Alcohol Epidemiology Program (2000). *Alcohol Policies in the United States: Highlights from the 50 States,* Minneapolis: University of Minnesota.

Ali, R., Christie P., Lenton, S., Hawks, D., Sutton, A., Hall, W. D. and Allsop, S. (1999). *The Social Impacts of the Cannabis Expiation Notice Scheme in South Australia. Summary report presented to the Ministerial Council on Drug Strategy,* National Drug Strategy Monograph, Vol. 34, Canberra: Commonwealth Department of Health and Aged Care.

Andrikopoulos, A. A., Brox, J. A. and Carvalho, E. (1997). The demand for domestic and imported alcoholic beverages in Ontario, Canada: a dynamic simultaneous equation approach. *Applied Economics,* **29,** 945–53.

Bachman, J. G., Johnston, L. D. and O'Malley, P. M. (1998). Explaining recent increases in students' marijuana use: impacts of perceived risks and disapproval, 1976 through 1996. *American Journal of Public Health,* **88** (6), 887–92.

Bachman, J. G., Johnston, L. D., O'Malley, P. M. and Humphrey, R. H. (1988). Explaining the recent decline in marijuana use: differentiating the effects of perceived risks, disapproval and general lifestyle factors. *Journal of Health and Social Behavior,* **29,** 92–112.

Bammer, G., Hall, W. D., Hamilton, M. and Ali, R. (2002). Harm minimisation in a prohibition context: Australia. *Annals of the American Academy of Political and Social Sciences,* **58,** 80–93.

Bejerot, N. (1975). Drug abuse and drug policy. An epidemiological and methodological study of drug abuse of intravenous type in the Stockholm police arrest population 1965–1970 in relation to changes in drug policy. *Acta Psychiatrica Scandinavica,* **Suppl 256,** 3–277.

Belenko, S. R. (2000). *Drugs and drug policy in America,* Westport, CT: Greenwood Press.

Blewett, N. (1987). *National Campaign Against Drug Abuse: Assumptions, Arguments and Aspirations,* Canberra: Australian Government Publishing Service.

Boekhout Van Solinge, T. (1997). *The Swedish Drug Control System: An In-Depth Review and Analysis,* Amsterdam: Uitgeverij Jan Mets and University of Amsterdam.

Cameron, L. and Williams, J. (2001). Cannabis, alcohol and cigarettes: substitutes or complements? *Economic Record,* **77** (236), 19–34.

Caulkins, J., Pacula, L. R., Paddock, S. and Chiesa, J. (2002). *School Based Drug Prevention: What Kind of Drug Use Does It Prevent?,* Santa Monica, CA: Rand Corporation.

Caulkins, J. P. (1997). Modeling the domestic distribution network for illicit drugs. *Management Science,* **43** (10), 1364–71.

Chaloupka, F. J. and Warner, K. E. (2000). The economics of smoking. In *The Handbook of Health Economics,* ed. J. P. Newhouse and A. J. Cuyler, pp. 1539–1627. New York: Elsevier.

Chaloupka, F. J. and Wechsler, H. (1996). Binge drinking in college: the impact of price, availability, and alcohol control policies. *Contemporary Economic Policy,* **14** (4), 112–24.

Chriqui, J. F., Pacula, R. L., McBride, D. C., Reichmann, D. A., Van der Waal, C .J. and Terry-McElrath, Y. (2002). *Illicit Drug Policies: Selected Laws from the 50 States,* Berrien Springs, MI: Andrews University.

Christie, P. (1999). *Cannabis Offences Under the Cannabis Expiation Notice Scheme in South Australia,* National Drug Strategy Monograph, Vol. 35, Canberra: Commonwealth Department of Health and Aged Care.

Coate, D. and Grossman, M. (1988). Effects of alcoholic beverage prices and legal drinking ages on youth alcohol use. *Journal of Law and Economics,* **31** (1), 145–71.

Cook, P. J. and Tauchen, G. (1982). The effect of liquor taxes on heavy drinking. *Bell Journal of Economics,* **13** (2), 379–90.

Cook, P. J. and Tauchen, G. (1984). The effect of minimum drinking age legislation on youthful auto fatalities, 1970–77. *Journal of Legal Studies,* **13**, 169–90.

DeJong, W. and Hingson, R. (1998). Strategies to reduce driving under the influence of alcohol. *Annual Review of Public Health,* **19**, 359–78.

Di Franza, J. R. (2001). State and federal compliance with the Synar Amendment: federal fiscal year 1998. *Archives of Pediatric and Adolescent Medicine,* **155** (5), 546–47.

Dorn, N. and Jamieson, A. (2001). *European Drug Laws: The Room for Manoeuvre,* London: DrugScope.

Doyle, C. (2000). *Drug Offences: Maximum Fines and Terms of Imprisonment for Violation of the Federal Controlled Substances Act and Related Laws,* Washington, DC: Library of Congress Congressional Research Service.

Farrelly, M., Bray, J., Zarkin, G., Wendling, B. and Pacula, R. (1999). *The Effects of Prices and Policies on the Demand for Marijuana: Evidence from the National Household Surveys on Drug Abuse,* NBER Working Paper, Vol. 6940, Cambridge, MA: National Bureau of Economic Research.

Forster, J. L., McGovern, P. G., Wagenaar, A. C., Wolfson, M., Perry, C. L. and Anstine, P. S. (1994). The ability of young people to purchase alcohol without age identification in northeastern Minnesota, USA. *Addiction,* **89**, 699–705.

Grossman, M., Chaloupka, F. J., Saffer, H. and Laixuthai, A. (1994). Alcohol price policy and youths: a summary of economic research. *Journal of Research on Adolescence,* **4**, 347–64.

Gruber, J., Sen, A. and Stabile, M. (2002). *Estimating Price Elasticities When There is Smuggling: The Sensitivity of Smoking to Price in Canada,* National Bureau of Economic Research Working Paper, Vol. 8962, Cambridge, MA: National Bureau of Economic Research.

Hall, W. D. and Swift, W. (2000). The THC content of cannabis in Australia: evidence and implications. *Australian and New Zealand Journal of Public Health,* **24** (5), 503–08.

Hingson, R., McGovern, T., Howland, J., Heeren, T., Winter, M. and Zakocs, R. (1996). Reducing alcohol impaired driving in Massachusetts: the Saving Lives program. *American Journal of Public Health,* **86**, 791–97.

Holman, C., Armstrong, B. K., Arias, L. N., Martin, C. A., Hatton, W. M., Hayward, L. D., Salmon, M. A., Shean, R. E. and Waddell, V. P. (1988). *The Quantification of Drug Caused Morbidity and Mortality in Australia 1988,* Canberra: Commonwealth Department of Community Services and Health.

Jason, L. A., Billows, W. D., Schnopp-Wyatt, D. L. and King, C. (1996). Long-term findings from Woodridge in reducing illegal cigarette sales to older minors. *Evaluation and the Health Professions,* **19**, 3–13.

Johnston, L. D., O'Malley, P. M. and Bachman, J. G. (2001). *Monitoring the Future: National Results on Adolescent Drug Use, Overview of Key Findings 2000,* Rockville, MD: National Institute on Drug Abuse.

Kenkel, D. S. (1993). Drinking, driving and deterrence: the effectiveness and social costs of alternative policies. *Journal of Law and Economics,* **36**, 877–914.

Kenkel, D. S. (1996). New estimates of the optimal tax on alcohol. *Economic Inquiry,* **34**, 296–319.

Kleiman, M. (1989). *Marijuana: Costs of Abuse, Costs of Controls,* New York: Greenwood.

Kleiman, M. A. R. (1992). *Against Excess: Drug Policy for Results,* New York: Basic Books.

Korf, D. J. (2002). Dutch coffee shops and trends in cannabis use. *Addictive Behaviors,* **27** (6), 851–66.

Lenton, S., Christie, P., Humeniuk, R., Brooks, A., Bennet, M. and Heale, P. (1999). *Infringement Versus Conviction: The Social Impact of a Minor Cannabis Offence Under A Civil Penalties System and Strict Prohibition in Two Australia States,* National Drug Strategy Monograph, Vol. 36, Canberra: Commonwealth Department of Health and Aged Care.

Lewit, E. M., Coate, D. and Grossman, M. (1981). The effects of government regulation on teenage smoking. *Journal of Law and Economics,* **24** (3), 545–69.

MacCoun, R. and Reuter, P. (2001). *Drug War Heresies: Learning from Other Vices, Times and Places,* Cambridge: Cambridge University Press.

Massing, M. (2000). *The Fix,* Berkeley: University of California Press.

Model, K. E. (1993). The effect of marijuana decriminalization on hospital emergency room drug episodes: 1975–1978. *Journal of the American Statistical Association,* **88** (423), 737–47.

Moore, M. J. and Cook, P. J. (1995). *Habit and Heterogeneity in the Youthful Demand for Alcohol,* National Bureau of Economic Research Working Paper, Vol. 5152: National Bureau of Economic Research.

Mullahy, J. and Sindelar, J. L. (1994). Do drinkers know when to say when? An empirical analysis of drunk driving. *Economic Inquiry,* **32**, 383–94.

National Commission on Marihuana and Drug Abuse (1972). *Marihuana: A Signal of Misunderstanding,* Washington, DC: US Government Printing Office.

Ostrom, B. and Kauder, N. (1999). Drug crime: the impact on state courts. *National Center for State Courts Caseload Highlights,* **5** (1). Available online at http://www.ncsonline.org/D_Research/csp/Highlights/DrugsV5%20No1.pdf

Pacula, R. L. (1998). Does increasing the beer tax reduce marijuana consumption? *Journal of Health Economics,* **17** (5), 557–85.

Pacula, R. L., Chriqui, J. F. and King, J. (2003). Decriminalization in the United States: what does it mean? National Bureau of Economic Research Working Paper, Vol. 8401. Cambridge, MA: National Bureau of Economic Research.

Pacula, R. L., Grossman, M., Chaloupka, F. J., O'Malley, P. M., Johnston, L. and Farrelly, M. C. (2001). Marijuana and youth. In *Risky Behavior Among Youths: An Economic Analysis,* ed. J. Gruber, pp. 271–326. Chicago: University of Chicago Press.

Reuter, P., Hirschfield, P. and Davies, C. (2000). *Assessing the crack-down on marijuana in Maryland,* Unpublished paper, University of Maryland.

Ruhm, C. J. (1996). Alcohol policies and highway vehicle fatalities. *Journal of Health Economics*, 15, 435–54.

Saffer, H. (1991). Alcohol advertising bans and alcohol abuse: an international perspective. *Journal of Health Economics*, 10 (1), 65–79.

Saffer, H. (1996). Studying the effects of alcohol advertising on consumption. *Alcohol Health and Research World*, 20 (4), 266–72.

Saffer, H. and Chaloupka, F. J. (1999). The demand for illicit drugs: effects of decriminalization. *Economic Inquiry*, 37 (3), 401–18.

Senate Special Committee on Illegal Drugs (Canada) (2002). *Cannabis: Summary Report*, Ottawa: Parliament of Canada.

Single, E. (1999). Options for cannabis reform. *International Journal of Drug Policy*, 10, 281–90.

Sloan, F. A., Reilly, B. A. and Schenzler, C. (1994). Effects of prices, civil and criminal sanctions, and law enforcement on alcohol-related mortality. *Journal of Studies on Alcohol*, 55, 454–65.

Swedish National Institute for Public Health (1993). *A Restrictive Policy: The Swedish Experience.*, Stockholm: Swedish National Institute for Public Health.

Swedish National Institute for Public Health (1998). *A Preventive Strategy: Swedish Drug Policy in the 1990s*, Stockholm: Swedish National Institute for Public Health.

Swiss Federal Commission for Drug Issues (1999). *Cannabis Report*, Bern: Swiss Federal Commission for Drug Issues.

Toomey, T. L., Jones-Webb, R. J. and Wagenaar, A. C. (1993). Policy: alcohol. *Annual Review of Addiction, Research and Treatment*, 3, 279–92.

Toomey, T. L. and Wagenaar, A. C. (1999). Policy options for prevention: the case of alcohol. *Journal of Public Health Policy*, 20 (2), 192–213.

US Department of Health and Human Services, Public Health Service, Centers for Disease Control, National Center for Chronic Disease Prevention and Health Promotion and Office on Smoking and Health (1994). *Preventing Tobacco Use Among Young People: A Report of the Surgeon General*, Washington, DC: US Government Printing Office.

van het Loo, M., van Beusekom, I. and Kahan, J. P. (2002). Decriminalization of drug use in Portugal: the development of a policy. *Annals of the American Academy of Political and Social Science*, 582, 49–63.

Wagenaar, A. C., O'Malley, P. and LaFond, C. (2001). Very low legal BAC limits for young drivers: effects on drinking, driving, and driving-after-drinking behaviors in 30 states. *American Journal of Public Health*, 91 (5), 801–04.

Warner, K. E. (1986). *Selling Smoke: Cigarette Advertising and Public Health*, Washington, DC: American Public Health Association.

Weatherburn, D. and Jones, C. (2001). *Does prohibition deter cannabis use?* Crime and Justice Bulletin, Vol. 58, Sydney: Bureau of Crime Statistics and Research, New South Wales Attorney General's Department.

Summing up

Advisory Committee on Illicit Drugs (1993). *Cannabis and the Law in Queensland: A Discussion Paper*, Brisbane: Queensland Criminal Justice Commission.

Aldrich, M. R. and Mikuriya, T. (1988). Savings in California marijuana law enforcement costs attributable to the Moscone Act of 1976: a summary. *Journal of Psychoactive Drugs*, 20, 75–81.

Ali, R., Christie P., Lenton, S., Hawks, D., Sutton, A., Hall, W. D. and Allsop, S. (1999). *The Social Impacts of the Cannabis Expiation Notice Scheme in South Australia. Summary report presented to the Ministerial Council on Drug Strategy,* National Drug Strategy Monograph, Vol. 34, Canberra: Commonwealth Department of Health and Aged Care.

Bachman, J. G., Wadsworth, K. N., O'Malley, P. M., Johnston, L. D. and Schulenberg, J. (1997). *Smoking, drinking, and drug use in young adulthood: the impacts of new freedoms and new responsibilities,* Mahwah, NJ: Lawrence Erlbaum.

Bowman, J. and Sanson-Fisher, R. (1994). *Public Perceptions of Cannabis Legalisation,* National Drug Strategy Monograph, Vol. 28, Canberra: Australian Government Publishing Service.

Carney, T., Drew, L., Mathews, J., Mugford, S. and Wodak, A. (1991). *An Unwinnable War Against Drugs: The Politics of Decriminalisation,* Leichhardt, NSW: Pluto Press.

Caulkins, J. P., Rydell, C. P., Everingham, S. M. S., Chiesa, J. R. and Bushway, S. (1999). *An Ounce of Prevention, a Pound of Uncertainty: The Cost-Effectiveness of School-Based Drug Prevention Programs,* Santa Monica, CA: Rand Corporation.

Chen, K. and Kandel, D. B. (1995). The natural history of drug use from adolescence to the mid-thirties in a general population sample. *American Journal of Public Health,* 85 (1), 41–47.

Criminal Justice Commission (1994). *Report on Cannabis and the Law in Queensland,* Brisbane: Criminal Justice Commission, Queensland.

Edwards, G., Anderson, P., Babor, T. F., Casswell, S., Ferrence, R., Giesbrecht, N., Godfrey, C., Holder, H., Lemmens, P., Makela, K., Midanik, L., Norstrom, T., Osterberg, E., Romelsjo, A., Room, R., Simpura, J. and Skog, O. (1994). *Alcohol Policy and the Public Good,* Oxford: Oxford University Press.

Erickson, P. G. (1980). *Cannabis Criminals: The Social Effects of Punishment on Drug Users,* Toronto: Addiction Research Foundation.

Fergusson, D. M., Horwood, J. L. and Swain-Campbell, N. R. (2003). Cannabis dependence and psychotic symptoms in young people. *Psychological Medicine,* 33, 15–21.

Fergusson, D. M. and Horwood, L. J. (1997). Early onset cannabis use and psychosocial adjustment in young adults. *Addiction,* 92 (3), 279–96.

Fischer, B., Single, E., Room, R., Poulin, C., Sawka, E., Thompson, H. and Topp, J. (1998). Cannabis use in Canada: Policy options for control. *Policy Options/Options Politiques,* 19 (October), 34–38.

Hall, W. D. (1995). The public health implications of cannabis use. *Australian Journal of Public Health,* 19, 235–42.

Hall, W. D., Degenhardt, L. and Currow, D. (2001). Allowing the medical use of cannabis. *Medical Journal of Australia,* 175, 39–40.

Hall, W. D., Johnston, L. D. and Donnelly, N. (1999). Assessing the health and psychological effects of cannabis use. In *The Health Effects of Cannabis,* ed. H. Kalant, W. Corrigal, W. D. Hall and R. Smart, pp. 1–17. Toronto: Centre for Addiction and Mental Health.

Husak, D. N. (1992). *Drugs and Rights,* Cambridge: Cambridge University Press.

Johnston, L. D., O'Malley, P. M. and Bachman, J. G. (1994a). *National Survey Results on Drug Use from the Monitoring the Future Study, 1975–1993. College Students and Young Adults,*Vol. 2, Rockville, MD: National Institute on Drug Abuse.

Johnston, L. D., O'Malley, P. M. and Bachman, J. G. (1994b). *National Survey Results on Drug Use from the Monitoring the Future Study, 1975–1993. Secondary School Students,*Vol. 1, Rockville, MD: National Institute on Drug Abuse.

Kalant, H., Corrigal, W., Hall, W. D. and Smart, R. (Eds.) (1999). *The Health Effects of Cannabis,* Toronto, Center for Addiction and Mental Health.

Kaplan, J. (1970). *Marijuana: The New Prohibition,* New York: World Publishing Company.

Kleiman, M. A. R. (1992). *Against Excess: Drug Policy for Results,* New York: Basic Books.

Korf, D. J. (2002). Dutch coffee shops and trends in cannabis use. *Addictive Behaviors,* **27** (6), 851–66.

Korf, D. J., Riper, H. and Bullington, B. (1999). Windmills in their minds? Drug policy and drug research in the Netherlands. *Journal of Drug Issues,* **29** (3), 451–72.

Lenton, S. (2000). Cannabis policy and the burden of proof: is it now beyond reasonable doubt that cannabis prohibition is not working? *Drug and Alcohol Review,* **19** (1), 95–100.

Lenton, S., Bennett, M. and Heale, P. (1999a). *The Social Impact of a Minor Cannabis Offence Under Strict Prohibition: The Case of Western Australia,* Perth: National Centre for Research into the Prevention of Drug Abuse.

Lenton, S., Christie, P., Humeniuk, R., Brooks, A., Bennet, M. and Heale, P. (1999b). *Infringement Versus Conviction: The Social Impact of a Minor Cannabis Offence Under A Civil Penalties System and Strict Prohibition in Two Australia States,* National Drug Strategy Monograph, Vol. 36, Canberra: Commonwealth Department of Health and Aged Care.

MacCoun, R. and Reuter, P. (2001). *Drug War Heresies: Learning from Other Vices, Times and Places,* Cambridge: Cambridge University Press.

Manski, C.F., Pepper, J.V. and Petrie, C.V. (Eds.) (2001). *Informing America's Policy on Illegal Drugs: What We Don't Know Keeps Hurting Us,* Washington, DC, National Academy Press.

McDonald, D., Moore, R., Norberry, J., Wardlaw, G. and Ballenden, N. (1994). *Legislative Options for Cannabis In Australia,* National Drug Strategy Monograph, Vol. 26, Canberra: Australian Government Publishing Service.

Moffit, A., Malouf, D. and Johnson, C. (1998). *Drug Precipice,* Sydney: University of New South Wales Press.

Sidney, S., Quesenberry, C. P., Jr, Friedman, G. D. and Tekawa, I. S. (1997). Marijuana use and cancer incidence (California, United States). *Cancer Causes and Control,* **8** (5), 722–28.

Single, E., Christie, P. and Ali, R. (1999). *The Impact of Cannabis Decriminalization in Australia and the United States,* Adelaide: Drug and Alcohol Services Council.

Single, E. W. (1989). The impact of marijuana decriminalization: an update. *Journal of Public Health Policy,* **9** (4), 456–66.

Swift, W., Hall, W. D. and Copeland, J. (2000). One year follow-up of cannabis dependence among long-term users in Sydney, Australia. *Drug and Alcohol Dependence,* **59** (3), 309–18.

Swiss Federal Commission for Drug Issues (1999). *Cannabis Report,* Bern: Swiss Federal Commission for Drug Issues.

Szasz, T. (1985). *Ceremonial Chemistry: The Ritual Persecution of Drugs, Addicts, and Pushers,* Holmes Beach, FL: Learning Publications.

United Kingdom Police Foundation (2000). *Drugs and the Law: Report of the Independent Inquiry into the Misuse of Drugs Act 1971,* London: The United Kingdom Police Foundation.

WHO Programme on Substance Abuse (1997). *Cannabis: A Health Perspective and Research Agenda,* Geneva: Division of Mental Health and Prevention of Substance Abuse, World Health Organization.

Wodak, A., Reinarman, C. and Cohen, P. (2002). Cannabis control: costs outweigh benefits. *British Journal of Medicine,* **324,** 105–6.

Working Party of the Royal College of Psychiatrists and the Royal College of Physicians (2000). *Drugs: Dilemmas and Choices,* London: Gaskell.

Zimmer, L. and Morgan, J. P. (1997). *Marijuana Myths, Marijuana Facts: A Review of the Scientific Evidence,* New York: The Lindesmith Center.

Appendix 1: The medical marijuana debate

Abraham, C. (2002). Medicinal-marijuana harvest on hold, *The Globe and Mail,* 22 April 2002, A4.

Barnes, R. E. (2000). Reefer madness: legal and moral issues surrounding the medical prescription of marijuana. *Bioethics,* **14,** 16–41.

Conboy, J. R. (2000). Smoke screen: America's drug policy and medical marijuana. *Food and Drug Law Journal,* **55,** 601–17.

DuPont, R. L. (1999). Examining the debate on the use of medical marijuana. *Proceedings of the Association of American Physicians,* **111** (2), 166–72.

Gieringer, D. (2003). The acceptance of medicinal marijuana in the US. *Journal of Cannabis Therapeutics,* **3** (1), 53–66.

Goutoloplis, A. and Makriyannis, A. (2002). From cannabis to cannabinergics: new therapeutic opportunities. *Pharmacology and Therapeutics,* **95,** 103–17.

Grinspoon, L. and Bakalar, J. (1993). *Marihuana, the forbidden medicine,* New Haven: Yale University Press.

GW Pharmaceuticals (2002). *Drug Delivery Technologies,* http://www.gwpharm.com/rese_drug_index.html (12 March 2002).

Hall, W. D., Degenhardt, L. and Currow, D. (2001). Allowing the medical use of cannabis. *Medical Journal of Australia,* **175,** 39–40.

Health Canada Office of Cannabis Medical Access (2002). *Medical Access to Marijuana: How the Regulations Work,* http://www.hc-sc.gc.ca/hecs-sesc/ocma/bckdr_1-0601.htm (4 April 2002).

House of Lords Select Committee on Science and Technology (1998). *Cannabis: The Scientific and Medical Evidence,* London: House of Lords, The Stationery Office.

Institute of Medicine (1999). *Marijuana and Medicine: Assessing the Science Base,* Washington, DC: National Academy Press.

Iversen, L. (2000). *The Science of Marijuana,* Oxford: Oxford University Press.

Marijuana Policy Project (2001). *Medical Marijuana Briefing Paper,* Washington, DC: Marijuana Policy Project.

Markoff, S. C. (1997). *State-by-State Medical Marijuana Laws,* Washington, DC: Marijuana Policy Project.

Moffat, A. C. (2002). The legalisation of cannabis for medical use. *Science and Justice: Journal of the Forensic Science Society,* **42,** 55–57.

National Commission on Marihuana and Drug Abuse (1972). *Marihuana: A Signal of Misunderstanding,* Washington, DC: US Government Printing Office.

New South Wales Working Party (2000). *Report of the Working Party on the Use of Cannabis for Medical Purposes,* Sydney: New South Wales Working Party.

Pacula, R. L., Chriqui, J. F., Reichman, D. A. and Terry-McElrath, Y. (2002). State medical marijuana laws: understanding the laws and their limitations. *Journal of Public Health Policy,* **23** (4), 411–37.

Reuter, P. and Burnam, A. (1997). Drug warriors and policy reformers: the debate over medical marijuana. *RAND Drug Policy Newsletter,* **6** (1), 1–6.

Tashkin, D. P. (2001). Airway effects of marijuana, cocaine, and other inhaled illicit agents. *Current Opinion in Pulmonary Medicine,* 7, 43–61.

Appendix 2: Cannabis use and crime

Baker, J. (1998). *Juveniles in Crime – Part 1: Participation Rates and Risk Factors,* Sydney: New South Wales Bureau of Crime Statistics and Research and New South Wales Crime Prevention Division.

Bushman, B. J. (1997). Effects of alcohol on human aggression: validity of proposed explanations. In *Recent Developments in Alcoholism,* Vol. 13, ed. M. Galanter, pp. 227–43. New York: Plenum Press.

Chaloupka, F. J. and Saffer, H. (1992). Alcohol, Illegal Drugs, Public Policy and Crime. Presented at the annual meeting of the Western Economic Association, San Francisco, CA, July 1992.

Cohen, P. D. A. and Kaal, H. L. (2001). *The Irrelevance of Drug Policy: Patterns and Careers of Experienced Cannabis Use in the Populations of Amsterdam, San Francisco and Bremen,* Amsterdam: Centrum voor Drugsonderzoek, University of Amsterdam.

Dembo, R., Williams, L., Schmeidler, J., Wish, E. D., Getreu, A. and Berry, E. (1991). Juvenile crime and drug abuse: a prospective study of high risk youth. *Journal of Addictive Disorders,* 11 (2), 5–31.

Fagan, J. (1990). Intoxication and aggression. Drugs and crime. In *Crime and Justice, A Review of Research,* Vol. 13, ed. M. Tonry and J. Q. Wilson, pp. 241–320. Chicago: The University of Chicago Press.

Fagan, J. A. (1993). The political economy of drug dealing among urban gangs. In *Drugs and Community,* ed. R. Davis, A. Lurigio and D. P. Rosenbaum, pp. 19–54. Springfield, IL: Charles Thomas.

Fergusson, D. M. and Horwood, L. J. (2000). Does cannabis use encourage other forms of illicit drug use? *Addiction,* **95** (4), 505–20.

Goldstein, P. (1985). The drugs/violence nexus: a tripartite conceptual framework. *Journal of Drug Issues,* 15 (Fall), 493–506.

Goldstein, P. J., Brownstein, H. H., Ryan, P. J. and Bellucci, P. A. (1989). Crack and homicide in New York City, 1988: a conceptually based event analysis. *Contemporary Drug Problems,* 16, 651–87.

Gorman, D. M. and White, H. R. (1995). You can choose your friends, but do they choose your crime? Implications of differential association theories for crime prevention policy. In *Crime and Public Policy: Putting Theory to Work,* ed. H. D. Barlow, pp. 131–55. Boulder, CO: Westview.

Hirschi, T. and Gottfredson, M. (1988). Towards a general theory of crime. In *Explaining Criminal Behaviour: Interdisciplinary Approaches,* ed. W. Buikhuisen and S. A. Mednick, pp. 8–26. Leiden; New York: E. J. Brill.

Jessor, R. and Jessor, S. L. (1977). *Problem Behavior and Psychosocial Development: A Longitudinal Study of Youth,* New York: Academic Press.

Johnston, L. D., O'Malley, P. M. and Bachman, J. G. (2000). *National Survey Results on Drug Use from the Monitoring the Future Study, 1975–1999 Volume II: College Students and Young Adults,* Rockville, MD: National Institute on Drug Abuse.

Kleiman, M. A. R. (1992). *Against Excess: Drug Policy for Results,* New York: Basic Books.

MacCoun, R. and Reuter, P. (2001). *Drug War Heresies: Learning from Other Vices, Times and Places,* Cambridge: Cambridge University Press.

Makkai, T., Fitzgerald, J. and Doak, P. (2000). *Drug use among police detainees,* Contemporary Issues in Crime and Justice, Vol. 49, Sydney: NSW Bureau of Crime Statistics and Research.

Markowitz, S. (2000). *An Economic Analysis of Alcohol, Drugs and Crime in the National Criminal Victimization Survey,* National Bureau of Economic Research Working Paper 7982. Cambridge, MA: National Bureau of Economic Research.

Miczek, K. A., DeBold, J. F., Haney, M., Tidey, J., Vivan, J. and Weerts, E. M. (1994). Alcohol, drugs of abuse, aggression, and violence. In *Understanding and preventing violence,* Vol. 3, ed. A. J. Reiss and J. A. Roth, pp. 377–570. Washington, DC: National Academy Press.

National Research Council (1993). *Understanding and Preventing Violence,* Washington, DC: National Academy Press.

Reuter, P., Hirschfield, P. and Davies, C. (2000). *Assessing the crack-down on marijuana in Maryland,* Unpublished paper, University of Maryland.

Salmelainen, P. (1995). *The correlates of offending frequency: a study of juvenile theft offenders in detention,* Sydney: NSW Bureau of Crime Statistics and Research.

Skogan, W. (1990). *Disorder and Decline: Crime and the Spiral Decay in American Neighbourhoods,* New York: Free Press.

Stevenson, R. and Forsythe, L. (1998). *The Stolen Goods Market in New South Wales: An Interview Study with Imprisoned Burglars,* Sydney: NSW Bureau of Crime Statistics and Research.

Taylor, B. and Bennett, T. (1999). *Comparing Drug Use Rates of Detained Arrestees in the United States and England,* Washington, DC: US Department of Justice.

Taylor, B. G., Fitzgerald, N., Hunt, D., Reardon, J. A. and Brownstein, H. H. (2001). *ADAM Preliminary 2000 Findings on Drug Use and Drug Markets – Adult Male Arrestees*: National Institute of Justice.

United States Office of National Drug Control Policy (2001). *Pulse Check: Trends in Drug Abuse. November 2001,* Washington, DC: Office of National Drug Control Policy.

United States Office of National Drug Control Policy (2002). *Pulse Check: Trends in Drug Abuse. November 2002,* Washington, DC: Office of National Drug Control Policy.

White, H. R. (1990). The drug use–delinquency connection in adolescence. In *Drugs, Crime and the Criminal Justice System,* ed. R. A. Weisheit, pp. 215–56. Cincinnati, OH: Anderson Publishing.

White, H. R. and Gorman, D. M. (2000). Dynamics of the drug–crime relationship. In *The Nature of Crime: Continuity and Change,* ed. G. LaFree, pp. 151–218. Washington, DC: US Department of Justice.

Index